First published in Great Britain in 2023 by Spenwood Books Ltd

2 College Street, Higham Ferrers, NN10 8DZ

A CIP record for this book is available from the British Library

ISBN 978-1-9168896-8-2

Printing & binding: Sound Performance Ltd,
3 Greenwich Quay, Clarence Road, Greenwich,
London, SE8 3EY

Design: Bruce Graham, The Night Owl

Front cover image: Getty Images/Mick Hutson

Rear cover images: (clockwise from top left) Jessica McMillan,
Ian Duncan, Unknown, David Lewis Gedge, Peter Koudstaal

Photographs: P253 Terri Nelles & Tim Middlewick; P255 Catherine Wygal; P328-335 Jessica McMillan; P333 (top) Peter Koudstaal

spenwoodbooks.com

THE WEDDING PRESENT

ALL THE SONGS SOUND THE SAME

RICHARD HOUGHTON & DAVID LEWIS GEDGE

ABOUT THE AUTHORS

Richard Houghton lives in Manchester and is the author of 20 music books, including authorised titles on The Wedding Present, The Stranglers, Simple Minds, Orchestral Manoeuvres in the Dark, Jethro Tull and Fairport Convention. His *People's History* series of music books is published by Spenwood Books.

David Lewis Gedge lives in Brighton and is the founding member, lead singer and guitarist for the semi-legendary Indie band The Wedding Present and his 'other' band, Cinerama. He is also the author of several books, including two volumes (so far) of his illustrated autobiography, *Tales From The Wedding Present*.

Photo: Simon Cardwell

INTRODUCTION

'Hello! I've downloaded the attachment and opened it up on my laptop. I really like both of those guitar parts, actually. I got a shiver down my spine! The first one definitely sounds like a verse; I already have an idea for a vocal melody, in fact. The other one sounds more like an instrumental section. Hmmm. I could do a loud 'E-guitar' drone over that, maybe?'

And, with that, another song is conceived. Well, these days, anyway. The technology has changed beyond comprehension since four-track, cassette-tape recorders and a pen and paper, but the method is essentially the same. One of my talented band members will send me ideas – sometimes it'll be a couple of riffs, sometimes it'll be parts for an entire song – and it is from these building blocks that I will start my construction. If nothing arrives from one of said talented band members, I'll just fumble around on a guitar or keyboard until I come up with a starting point myself.

The aim, at this point, is to create a version of a song which a band will be able to play and arrange together. So, in advance of meeting up in a rehearsal room, I will have added singing and other instruments, and manipulated it into an arrangement that I feel 'works'. I say 'singing' but there are no lyrics, yet, just me warbling 'noises' that *almost* sound like words. I know what you're going to say here. *'Oh, David, we'd quite enjoy hearing that!'* Trust me, you wouldn't. And I say 'other instruments' but what I really mean is my guitar part, since I'm not a gifted multi-instrumentalist like so many of my colleagues have been. Okay, maybe in Cinerama songs and some Wedding Present songs I will have added keyboards and strings, but that's more me clicking a mouse while running some kind of music-sequencing software than tickling any actual ivories. Once those parts are programmed, I get *proper* musicians to play them.

We're now in the rehearsal room. With a *real* drummer. And *real* amplifiers. Our two-dimensional ideas are bursting into life. It's big and loud – or tiny and quiet – and here come more spine shivers. And then the interminable discussions begin. *'It's too fast.' 'If anything, I think it's too slow!' 'Shall we double the length of the chorus?' 'I was going to suggest that the chorus should be an outro. Or an intro.' 'I don't like my bit. I might not play in the verse.' 'But that's the best bit!'* And so on, and so on. I won't bore you with the details but, obviously, there are literally thousands of ways a song can be arranged. We'll end up trying most of them… just in case putting on that guitar pedal in the second verse takes us somewhere else. Somewhere we have never been before.

And then… I'm at home again – back in front of my trusty, but unhelpful, laptop – endeavouring to write a lyric. The camaraderie and team spirit of the rehearsal room is but a distant happy memory. It's now just lonely old me leafing through a notebook of ideas that I've been amassing since the mid-1980s. Lines about how I felt so euphoric after first meeting someone who, even then, I knew I wanted to be with forever. Lines about how I felt so heartbroken after that someone just told me that they no longer wanted to be with me. I know that if I transform these memories into lyrics, I'll be reliving those feelings every time I sing the song. I think that's a price worth paying, though. Especially when you play in front of thousands of people and they sing those exact same words right back to you.

Writing the actual words for a song takes me a while because I want it to be good. OK, that's a complete lie; it takes me an unreasonably long amount of time because I'm obsessed! I want it to be amazing! And believable and moving… and euphoric or melancholy. And I want to do it without repeating myself! Oh, and it has to rhyme! My wife will come in and ask, *'What have you been up to, today?'* and my weary reply will be, *'I wrote the first half of a verse but I'm not sure I'm happy with it.'*

Despite possible appearances, when the song is 'finished' and we are playing it live, the story's far from over. With every performance, something will be tweaked. It's inevitable because there's really nothing like playing a song in front of an audience to reveal its shortcomings. Some songs will have been quite radically transformed by the live process by the time we enter the recording studio.

Ah, the recording studio. Now we're disagreeing about tempos again because we played them faster live and a couple of us will have preferred those versions. Everything is now truly under the microscope. *'Are you really playing a D when I'm playing a C? Does that work? I suppose it sounds okay.' 'Now I'm hearing it properly… does that lyric make sense?' 'The guitar part you just overdubbed is amazing. We should make that the main riff!'* So, songs change again during recording sessions… but they can also change *after* recording sessions! Paul Valéry, the French poet, once wrote something in an essay about works of art never being finished, just abandoned, and I only abandon my songs because they have to be released at some point. But even after they're released, I know there's still a chance that we'll change something further down the line. It's more like they're never-ending works-in-progress, I suppose.

So, here's a book full of generous people discussing what a hundred or so of those works-in-progress mean to them. It's obviously very gratifying and flattering to hear how much those intermingled words, melodies and rhythms mean to people. And it's extraordinary how something as frivolous as a pop song can bring about such a physiological change in people.

If you were ever asked for an example of something where the whole is far greater than the sum of the parts, I think you might be safe to answer 'a song'. Or, by extension… *this book!*

DAVID LEWIS GEDGE, BRIGHTON, FEBRUARY 2023

MY FAVOURITE DRESS

NOLAN BENNETT

I felt like I was made out of air. Walking hand in hand in the summer sun – smiles, soft skin, sweet smells I'd never smelt before.

Sat on my teenage bed at home in Grimsby, one Sunday evening John Peel introduced me to The Wedding Present on his Radio 1 show. I can't remember his introduction, but I do remember the song was 'Kennedy' and I recorded it there and then onto a C90. Instantly beguiled by the frenetic funky drummer, head-nodding bass line, whirling guitars and initially senseless raw emotion, I found myself in a record shop in Hull with a few of my friends a couple of months later. It was a rainy day during the school holidays. I must have been 14 or 15. I'd not been able to find out much about The Wedding Present in those paper and magazine days, my friends liking varying doses of The Cure, Duran Duran and the Inspiral Carpets, and me being too young to know the live music scene. And 'she' liked Madonna, in whom we shared a mutual interest.

The four of us were all in different parts of the record shop and I picked up a cassette with a striking blue inlay – *Tommy*. Not recognising any of the songs listed, I decided that was to be my purchase of the day. And *Tommy* has given something to me ever since, some 30 years down the line.

Following this, I listened to *Tommy* frequently and loud. Its initial edge (The Jesus and Mary Chain's sonic haze of 'You Trip Me Up' being as serrated as I'd got before) soon developed into a deep, heart-splitting, comforting, rocking bucket full of every male angst emotion I'd ever feel.

Meanwhile, our young love had grown and we were seeing more of each other, in all senses of the expression. Getting on with the brown-haired 14-year-old lady I'd met at school was easy. We were finding ourselves and each other, growing quickly, twisting and turning, yearning. Playing off each other. Living, learning and laughing. I can see now the late evening sun going down, burning dusty orange through the tall leylandii that separated the wheat fields from the school field. I can see the shine of the sun on her sun-kissed shoulders, the outline of her thighs backlit through the cotton of her white, grey and yellow summer dress. I'm sure you understand.

Those days, they went on forever. We lay in fields of wheat, feeling release and only knowing what I was feeling years later. There were parties, times when there were people everywhere and more times when there was only us. In the middle of this, my mum and dad took me to France on holiday for a fortnight. I send a postcard, I miss her. I get sunstroke and I shower in the campsite communal shower block. I get back home and arrange to see her as soon as I can. It's at her house in the evening and there are a few friends there too by the time I arrive, including this lad that we both liked and who always seemed to be there. We knew him through a mutual friend. This time, though, his presence didn't feel heaven-sent. The evening moves on and I'm wanting that easy, frictionless loving but all I get is an uneasy sense of him being there; a knowing glance between them, shared exclusively but for all to see. Stripped bare, later I go home wondering what just happened, feeling lost.

A few days later, we meet again, this time alone. It's hot, humid heat all around us. It's the summer holidays and we're in the lower school grounds in a place both of us know we won't be found. It starts to rain, heavy with thunder and blue purple sky. She moves out into the rain and dances, but it feels like she is dancing away from me. Self-centred, I expect too much, absolute attention, with no effort. In turn I get the opportunity to take part in some ritual that thousands of generations must have taken part in, but not me. She dances in the rain, she should be drawing me in, but all I am seeing is him and her, exchanging glances. What happened when I wasn't there?

My refusal to take part, my fear-stopped objection, leads to her feeling like there's something missing, like I'm seeking something else. But all I want is her and she's getting further and further away. I blame what happened between her and him. She feels rejection. I can't see beyond his hand, what feels like a stranger's hand, on her sun soaked white, grey and yellow dress. And that's when I feel every emotion of 'My Favourite Dress'.

YOU SHOULD ALWAYS KEEP IN TOUCH WITH YOUR FRIENDS

JAY HOY, DAVID'S FIRST GIRLFRIEND

This song is very, very special to me. David and I were truly, madly in love. We always thought we'd be together forever, as you do at that age. I hadn't had a serious relationship before and neither had he. David was a year older than me. We were very young, perhaps 17 and 18, and he was getting ready to go to uni.

That summer, he and I went on holiday to the east coast. We were driving around in his dad's car. It was very sweet that his dad had loaned him the car, and we spent two or three days cruising around and staying in bed and breakfasts. This one particular day we were standing on a bridge in Scarborough and we made a pledge that day that, whatever happened, we would

Jaz Hoy was David's first girlfriend and inspired the lyrics of several early songs

always come back to that bridge every so often to reunite and remember the good times and the fun we'd had. Because we did have a lot of fun.

One line is, 'We walked to a bridge down by the sea, the day that we met there was ours eternally', meaning that we always would remember each other whilst standing on that bridge.

I know there were a number of songs that David put together after we split up, but not for one moment did I ever think that he'd taken inspiration directly from our relationship and our separation. It was only later on when I started to really listen to the lyrics a bit more that I thought, 'Oh my god, I remember that happening.' And then there was all the stuff being written about The Wedding Present and our breakup in the Nineties, when the first books started to come out.

It was a very, very special time in our lives, and still is. It was a very special relationship that we had, and we are still very much friends. Obviously, we've both moved on in our lives. I've been married twice and David is in a very serious relationship, and was in another serious relationship before this one, but we still have a very, very, very special friendship that will always be there.

When The Wedding Present performed in Brisbane in 2017, David dedicated 'You Should Always Keep In Touch With Your Friends' to me. We don't see each other very often any more, because he lives in England and I live in Australia, but when we do, we're right back on that bridge in Scarborough.

MY FAVOURITE DRESS

SIR KEIR STARMER KCB KC MP, LEADER OF THE LABOUR PARTY

Photo: Chris McAndrew

Sir Keir Starmer's favourite is 'My Favourite Dress'

I was at Leeds University in the early '80s and met Keith Gregory and David Gedge through my friend John before the band started, so I was aware of The Wedding Present from the very start of their career. My favourite song has to be 'My Favourite Dress'. David has managed to perfectly distil the tortuous agonising feelings of jealousy into three minutes of angst. The guitar hook is pretty great too...

A MILLION MILES

IAIN KEY

I moved from the West Midlands to Manchester in early 1985 and started high school with one term to go ahead of my exam year. The school had only recently merged with the girls' school across the road and most lessons were still all-male or all-female. I went from having a fairly large social circle where I'd grown up to knowing very few people. Being a bit shy with a Brummie lilt to my accent didn't help.

Iain Key (left) with his friend Danny, who introduced him to The Wedding Present

After leaving school I began to find my feet. I got on a YTS (youth training) scheme and started to make friends where I was placed, while in my spare time I got involved with a Manchester-based branch of a charity called Toc H. The volunteers for this were mainly in their late teens and early 20s and based around South Manchester, many of them students.

One of my fellow volunteers was Tina Connor. She'd been British Junior Women's Fencing Champion a couple of years earlier and was the daughter of former Manchester City defender Dave Connor. I had the biggest crush on her, but never said anything, although in hindsight she must have known – everyone else seemed to! Although Tina had been in the same year as me at school our paths had never crossed. If this was America she'd have been hanging with the cool kids where I would have been mixing with the geeks.

Throughout 1988 and 1989 we'd see each other regularly while doing charity stuff and nod at each other, occasionally saying hello if we saw each other socially, often at the Station Pub in Cheadle.

The reason 'A Million Miles' has always been a special one for me is that opening verse:

I must have walked past this doorway thirty times, just trying to catch your eye
You made it all worthwhile when you returned my smile
It all became worthwhile

My friend James lived a few houses down from the Connors' family home. This meant that when calling on him I'd have to walk past. More often than not she wouldn't be there, and I'm sure her parents wondered 'who is that and why does he keep looking in?' when I was walking past, but on the occasions that she was...

The last time I saw Tina was at a house party she held on 31st December, 1989. I spent most of the evening in the living room watching a four hour BBC2 special celebrating the music of the 1980s rather than enjoying the teenage hijinks and shenanigans going on around the house.

We never fell out. I guess our social circles just changed as the new decade began, but 'A Million Miles' will always remind me of Tina and that time of my life.

AIRBORNE
TONY FROST

You know how certain songs can make the hair stand up on the back of your neck? Well Cinerama's 'Airborne' does it for me every time. Latterly, I expect most fans will associate it with the instrumental entrance music sometimes played before The Wedding Present take to the stage, which should be enough alone to make it both nostalgic and exciting.

However, for me it evokes such strong feelings. For starters, the arrangement is just brilliant; melancholic, sweeping, soulful strings first draw you in and surround you. And the songwriting is just so perfectly framed – using the plane's physical departure as an allegory to a failed relationship which starts to unfold through the song. The lyrics feel so apt, without ever being *too* clever:

Cinerama's 'Airborne' is the song that Tony Frost plumps for

The vapour trail's dissipating fast;
I guess some things aren't made to last

and just feel heartfelt and so poignant. You can almost imagine yourself standing, watching and wanting to understand how it all went wrong!

Personally, I don't associate the song with a failed romantic relationship. I have just one brother who lives five thousand miles away who I rarely see, and somehow this song manages to evoke the finality of saying goodbye and knowing (for a short time at least) you will miss them more than anything else.

Your plane keeps shrinking, I stand here thinking...

I'll never understand why Cinerama weren't huge commercially, and also why so many hardcore Wedding Present fans still have no time for them. I think this was David's most creative musical period. And if you are reading this and still wondering what the Cinerama fuss was all about, perhaps start with this track? Hopefully, at the very least, it will invoke the excitement of a much-anticipated concert actually starting – which (writing) in these COVID-cursed, live music-starved times is probably more than enough to make the hair stand up on the back of all our necks!

I think they could come up with something better with a bit more thought.
The power of their simple songs live surprised me. It was the second time I'd seen them live within a few days - in fact it was only their second gig. The improvement over their first gig was quite noticeable. If they continue to improve at this rate they're going to make a name for themselves. Thoroughly recommended!

BIG TWANG

TUES. DEC. 10TH £2.50/2.00 CONCS

At the Royal Escape club
Marine Parade :- THE

LOVELY : Leeds lads

WEDDING PRESENT

FOR PEOPLE WITH GET UP AND GO

BOUNCING : Brighton babies

14 ICED BEARS

DANCING to every record at the big twang is applaudable but unlikely to write your name in the history books. So these chaps have picked up their instruments and are going to unveil their creation before an eager public on 10th December 1985. Their manager, himself a pop singer, Julian Cope has said in a press statement, "I was a bouncing baby, now I'm a bouncing(cont.P.9)

RECENTLY at the Big Twang club in Brighton normally sane youths have been taking part in the sort of activities that can only be described as enjoyable. These so called "TWANGERS" like to watch pop bands perform on stage and to dance wildly about to the crazed beat of records by groups with weird names like "June Brides", "Buzzcocks" and "Primal Scream". When asked about these events by us, community policeman P.C Bastard said, "Well cock you wouldn't catch me letting my kids go" Despite this sort of local protest the club is this week host to a group who thrash away at their guitars and drums with the sort of abandon that would make Elton John spin in his gravy. A banana(cont.P6)

Debut gig

NEW Leeds band The Wedding Present makes its live debut at the Astoria on October 19.

□□□

The band was formed when two members of Leeds band The Lost Pandas went to live in America leaving guitarist - vocalist David Gedge and bassist Keith Gregory out on a limb. Now they have recruited drummer Mike Bedford through a Pop Post plea and have guitarist Pete Solowka on loan from The Chorus.

□□□

"As a result the music, although retaining a strong emphasis on melodies has become more powerful than the old Pandas songs," said David.

IMPS PRESENT ......

tv personalities

&

the wedding prese

WED 30th OCTOBER

TOWERS REFECTORY,
LOUGHBOROUGH UNIVERSITY

JOHN PEEL'S FESTIVE 50

1985

1	NEVER UNDERSTAND	THE JESUS AND MARY CHAIN
2	JUST LIKE HONEY	THE JESUS AND MARY CHAIN
3	CRUISER'S CREEK	THE FALL
4	SHE SELLS SANCTUARY	THE CULT
5	AIKEA-GUINEA	COCTEAU TWINS
6	REVOLUTION	CHUMBA WUMBA
7	PRIMITIVE PAINTERS	FELT
8	THE BOY WITH THE THORN IN HIS SIDE	THE SMITHS
9	THE PERFECT KISS	NEW ORDER
10	FLAG DAY	THE HOUSEMARTINS
11	IRONMASTERS	THE MEN THEY COULDN'T HANG
12	YOU TRIP ME UP	THE JESUS AND MARY CHAIN
13	SALLY MacLENNANE	THE POGUES
14	DEATH OF THE EUROPEAN	THE THREE JOHNS
15	GO OUT AND GET 'EM BOY	THE WEDDING PRESENT
16	LOVE VIGILANTES	NEW ORDER
17	ALL THAT EVER MATTERED	THE SHOP ASSISTANTS
18	SUB-CULTURE	NEW ORDER
19	MOVE ME	THE WOODENTOPS
20	A PAIR OF BROWN EYES	THE POGUES

NEW MUSICAL EXPRESS

Six of the best

BOGSHED
TRACIE YOUNG
SLY AND ROBBIE
THE WEDDING PRESENT

(since Shaun joined)

1st March: Allerton Bywater "Shires"
supp.Dik Dik Dimorphic *encore*(v.good)(R)
18th March: Leeds University Union "R.H.Evans lounge"
supp.Bop Product (O.K.-empty!)(R)
24th March: Leeds "Adelphi"
supp.The Clues (O.K.-unmemorable)
3rd May: Leeds "Royal Park"
supp.The Vox (O.K.-unmemorable)
5th May: Leeds "Adelphi"
supp.The Clues (unmemorable again)
8th May: Derby "Old Bell"
supp.by The Chorus (11 people paid!encore-so good but lost l
* * * * "Go Out And Get 'Em Boy! released * * * * * * *
22nd June: Leeds "Haddon Hall"
supp.by Soldiers and Friends (O.K.)(R)
30th June: Leeds "Adelphi"
supp.The Clues (why did we play this place so much?)
19th July: York "The Windmill"
No other band (sloppy but good)*encore*Played GOAGEB! twice!
* * * *NME and SOUNDS interviews* * * * * * * * * * * *
16th August: Leeds "Central Station"
supp.by First International and The Clues (O.K.)Pete missing
20th September: Leeds "Royal Park"
supp.Bright Carvers (O.K. unadvertised sort of joke)
3rd October: Manchester "Wilde! Club"at"The Man Alive"
No other band (polite applause-boring)
11th October: Nottingham "Garage"
No other band (excellent)*encore*(R)
17th October: Leeds "Royal Park"
with Ritzun Patzun Rotzer and Charlotte (quite good)*encore*
22nd October: Manchester "Gallery"
No other band (Keith broke 2 bass strings)*encore*funny & goo
23rd October: Bradford "1 in 12 club"at"Queens Hall"
supp.The Inca Babies (O.K.)
26th October: Perth "The Plough"
supp.by This Poison (excellent)2 encores (R)
28th October: Leeds "Warehouse"
supp Age Of Chance supp.by Flowers For Agatha (terrible)(R)
30th October: Loughborough University "Refectory"
supp.T.V.Personalities (excellent)*encore*
2nd November: London "Ambulance Station"(Old Kent Road)
supp.June Brides supp.by Wolfhounds (played badly)*encore*(R)
13th November: Manchester "What We All Want club"at"Cloud 9"
No other band (quite good)(R)sold 5 T-shirts!
16th November: Leeds University Union "Doubles Bar"
supp.by ??? (unmemorable but...)Mike played bass.Labour bene
22nd November: Bedford "George and Dragon"
supp.Big Flame (unmemorable)(R)
7th December: London "Room At The Top"at"The Enterprise"(Chalk Farm)
with The Wolfhounds (excellent)*encore*(R)Mike played bass
10th December: Brighton "Big Twang club" at "The Escape Club"
supp.by Line and 14 Iced Bears (excellent)*encore*(R)(videod)

"Faster, faster, faster and faster!" David Gedge is explaining to me his current policy for writing songs, but he's lying of course, and anybody who has seen the band live or heard their tapes will know that melody is as important to The Wedding Present as sheer power. What they have in the can in the way of it is better than what they have on vinyl. Sometimes it's fast, sometimes it's slow, but always it's melodic.

"It's for that reason that we keep sets short," says David. "Any band in the world is boring after 20 minutes. It's better to have a short set with lots of punch than a long, dull wade through a mass of boring material."

They look terrible, they sound perfect, and in the near future their second single, a 12" 5-track EP provisionally entitled 'Once More', is going to blast its way into the heart of the nation.

In the meantime, the repressing of 'Go Out And Get 'em Boy!' is only days away. Go out and buy it and kill ugly pop!

RED RHINO DISTRIBUTION LIMITED
The Coach House · Fetter Lane · York · YO1 1EH · UK
Tel: 0904-2782

Received from 'The Wedding Present' 297 copies of 7" single on S.O.R, of which 20 are promotional copies. All copies sold will be paid for at 66p each.

with compliments

11th April 1985 No. JB 385
Received from P. J. SOLOWKA
The sum of Three hundred and forty three pounds and seventy five
Cheque 343.75
Cash
Discount
£118.7
WITH THANKS
M.I.S.L.

... except that I always like to begin with the local heroes. Top of the pile then are **The Wedding Present** whose latest waxing *Once More* is almost worth getting married for. Snappier than an alligator sandwich it does bear a passing resemblance to the Jam and the Redskins, vibrant yet fluid, though the similarity is born of a shared commitment to, well, commitment I guess, rather than stale imitation. An essential addition to the collection.

Gift of the year

GUARDIAN POP

1985 was a pretty nondescript year for most of our local bands.

However, one group with strong Middleton connections, had a remarkable year. That group was The Wedding Present.

Although based over the Pennines in Leeds, the group's nucleus comprises David Gedge (vocals/guitar) and Peter Salowka (guitar) both Middletonians.

Last year saw them make a storming vinyl debut with Go Out and Get 'em Boy. They have had interviews with most of the major music papers and the single was voted at number 15 in John Peel's Festive Fifty.

They have played concerts throughout the country and recorded a session for Radio One's Andy Kershaw.

As David says: "All in all, 1985 wasn't a bad year for us."

Their next single, Once More, will be ou on Reception Record on 31 January. It is bein distributed by The Car tel and will come i seven inch form.

Keep a look out for i because The Weddin Present make a very a ^able noise.

ONCE MORE
THE WEDDING PRESENT

The Wedding Present, on tneir 'Don't try & stop us, mother' :our as I write, are looking 'or a recording contract - :he kind where you get lots of ɪoney without having to be 'wacky' idiots.

They were formed on New Year's Day, 1985, since then they've recorded two singles on their own label (Reception), done 2 Radio 1 sessions, and fallen out with each other about a dozen times; Gargrave left the band and rejoined in Frowell Service Station once!

Wedding Present are:
David (vocals/guitar); he has a yearning for POWER and helicopters but he's very partial to silly shirts and Coronation Street.
Pete (guitar), nickname Grapper.
Keith (bass), nickname Reg.
Shaun (drums), nickname Gargrave.

> We won't be selling socialism to people who'd rather give £2 to our record company than to the SWF.
>
> There are quite enough professional moaners in pop music.

INTERVIEW BY LIGGER PIG

L: Tell us more about the band.
David: Are you sure you want to get to know us better?
L: Go on.
D: Well Reg wears Madonna T-shirts and likes to spend huge amounts of (borrowed) money on those penguins-on-wheels that you push aroud with a stick.
Shaun is the favourite to win the WP Subbuteo League and he's got tapes of all our jigs.
Grapper's hobby is pigeon racing and he's the band s socialist conscience and football brainbox.
Me, I'm just a nice bloke.. ..David (Nice Bloke) Gedge, in fact, is what they tend to call me around here...

Their favourite bands include the Fall, Velvet Underground, Postcard, Gun Club, Jesus & Marychain, SWANS and the exciting AGE OF CHANCE.

David: Singing & Guitar
Pete: Guitar
Keith: Bass
Shaun: Drums

> MATCH OF THE DAY
> Reg: Last week, Pat Jennings admitted that in 20 years in the rat-race of professional football he hadn't enjoyed it apart from looking back at good results. This is exactly how I feel about my BRILLIANT career in pop music actually; anything I've contributed to this group has been dreamt up while idly watching Match Of The Day.
> David: We're nothing special. We're not in a band to change the world, we're just pop-music lovers. I think we want to be involved and that's our motivation.

The Wedding Present
14, Churchill Gardens
Leeds 2

L: What do you think is your best track to date?
David: I know this sounds dea obvious, but my favourite W.P track is our next single, "This Boy Can Wait", because I don't think there's any other band in Britain right now who could come up with something as,...well, 'STRIKING'. I hope this doesn't sound arrogant, I don't mean it to, I'm just feeling proud, I guess.

Well, after hearing "This Boy Can Wait" in a Peel Sesh I'm tempted to agree.
David: When we recorded the Peel Session version, I was still recovering from a stomach bug and I almost fainted when we were thrashing out the ending...straight up, I could feel myself blacking out but I managed to keep on going to the end...heroic, eh'

GO OUT AND GET 'EM BOY!

Musically, Wedding Present ar a cross between the Woodentop and Age Of Chance: a huge reservoir of nervous, twitching energy, I said ENERGY...can't keep still..uncontrolable fits of exciting LOUD guitars EXPLODING into a furious barrage of sheer delight.
Just when you think it's safe to take another breath, they return faster and louder, even more intoxicating and totally O.T.T. sending ecstatic tremors through an already racing pulse.

THE WEDDING PRESENT

17

THE WEDDING PRESENT
'Don't Try And Stop Me, Mother' EP (Reception)

Oh, so glorious! A beacon of brilliance in a swamp of a thousand disposable singles. Charming, vivacious guitars blitzing through all those old glories of Buzzcocks.

Back by popular demand comes 'Once More' – perfect pop of simple grandeur and nobility; 'At The Edge Of The Sea' – an uplifting experience; and 'Go Out And Get 'Em Boy' – a splendid rush of demonic guitars, seasoned sourness, misty-eyed fever and golden lyrical ambiguity.

The soul of this record burns, burns, burns! 'Everything's Spoiled Again' deals with zeal, restrained moods, awkward moments and embarrassing feelings. Love, Power and Affection – The Wedding Present at work! This is how it should always be but never is. Ran close for SOTW.

NME C86

THIS YEAR'S MODELS

Yowsa! Yowsa! Yowsa! Five years on from our lavishly-lauded C81 cassette debut, *NME* is once again making a declaration of independents.

With the independent scene now in its finest fettle for ages, we have assembled a punchy parade of primetime pop starring 22 of this year's most crucial contenders. With almost all the tracks exclusive to *NME*, the C86 is a cool spool of stunning sonic spendour that already looks certain to go down as one of the compilations of the year. Just check the teamsheet below and post your order form pronto.

NME C86 – We've got a tapedeck and, boy, are we gonna use it!

LEMONADE

ISSUE ONE INCLUDES
THE WEDDING PRESENT
T.V. PERSONALITIES
MEMBRANES
JUNE BRIDES
AGE OF CHANCE
SOUP DRAGONS
SEE EMILY PLAY
PASTELS
SHOP ASSISTANTS
JESUS AND MARY CHAIN GIG REVIEW
FAB ARTICLES AND LOADS OF THINGS TO MAKE THE SUN COME OUT

BUY THIS SCUMBAG AND DO SOMETHING RIGHT FOR ONCE IN YOUR LIFE

The Wedding Present
LUU

The Wedding Present play guitar like Billy Whizz on amphetamines, and break strings more often than Phil Collins wins awards.

This set was smart, eight or so tunes owing a lot to the Velvet's 'What Goes On'. Rhythmic noise with an insistent drum beat, rapid strumming and impelling vocals. The songs may not be too distinctive yet, but then this was only the first time I have heard most of them.

LEATHER for BRAINS?!

The Wedding Present hail from Leeds.Individually the band comprises:

Singing + Guitar	David Lewis Gedge
Guitar	Pete (the odd) Grasper
Drums	Shaun Big Boy Charman
Bass	Sex Rash

They have released two singles on Reception records:'Go out and get 'em boys' and,more recently,'Once More'-both being particularly stirring,strident pop songs.The group will be performing live in York at the Winning Post pub on March 14th."

Q.Why should peole put down a good book to listen to The Wedding Present?

David: Have you got TIME to read a good book in 1986? Our songs ... for 3 minutes, not 3 days, but they still leave a nice taste in your mouth...
Go on, Sex Rash, argue....

Sex Rash:....No, I will not be baited on this. We are not a "We are the greatest band in the world" type group, but this week we've had Simple Minds, Age Of Chance, and fuckin' Raymonde, of all people, proclaiming themselves as such, and we're a good deal better than all three. Whether 'Go Out And Get 'Em Boy!' is more important than'Tess d'Ubervilles', however, is open to question.

Big Boy:I'm not sure people SHOULD put down a ...

POP BRAINS WITH PUNK HEARTS!

THE WEDDING PRESENT

GO OUT AND GET EM BOY - RELEASED SUMMER 85 QUICKLY SOLD OUT AND REACHED NO 15 IN PEELSFESTIVE SO THE FOLLOW UP "ONCE MORE" IS FAB - GO OUT + BUY IT KIDDIES -

I PUT THE FOLLOWING QUESTIONS TO THE BAND (CLICHE) PAH

DAVID:guitar, vocals, spots,girlfriend trouble, always keeps in touch with his friends.
PETE:guitar, leeds utd, pigeon fancier, militant, buys halves, sits at the edge of his seat.
KEITH:bass, handsome, winsome, 1 egg sandwich per day only, desparately seeking susan, very talkative, every mother's son.
SHAUN:drum, fat lad (4 cow-pies)?,leather jacket, sincere, entertaining, this boy can't wait.

Q-WHY SHOULD THE WEDDING PRESENT EXIST?
DAVID-We want to make Radio I listenable again...I love th
records they play inbetween the chit chat.When was the las
for the first time...probaly about 6 months ago.The more q
tter...then were gonna make a movie.
KEITH-Come to think of it,the disadvantages really outweig
aud being accomodating to these 24 carat olympic champion
Like those sarcastic types y'know the ones,who plunge you
"Oh popstars...Can I have your autograph?" I mean what did
ough is having student minions carting crates of free lage
r know.

Q-POP BRAINS WITH PUNK HEARTS?.
KEITH-Actually the original slogan was "Pop brains with p
per misprint.With popularity in mind we traded in our NHS
"Andsome"new barnets down at snipperfields.
SHAUN-I think small brains would be more appropriate...I
on the pavement outside a recent gig in Brighton and we j
kit's getting smaller every gig we go to as we leave anot
DAVID-Last night we turned up for a practise with two dru

Q-WHAT WOULD YOU DO IF YOU FOUND SNAKES UNDER YOUR BED?
DAVID-Actually once a weedy little grass snake stuck it's
back of our house and I ran blindly in a state of panic fo
SHAUN-If this question's trying to find out whether we're
or pete..who's not the sort of bloke who you spill beer ov

Q-HOW WOULD YOU SPEND YOUR IDEAL NIGHT?
DAVID-Round at me girlfriend's.She lives with a couple of
time they fall out with their lovers they attempt to comit
They head straight for the kitchen where they rattle the c
hand,waiting for someone to come and save them.Great fun,b

Q-Favourite Food/Drink/Pastime?
KEITH-Cakes/I'am a tetley bitterman yeah/Spend Spend Spend
DAVID-Indian/Pints and Pints of tea/Winding Shaun up.
Shaun-Chocolate,golden syrup + peanut butter sandwiches/Be
waiting while he sulks.
PETE-Chips/Beer/Football-(PETE COULD'NT MAKE IT TO THE INT

THE WEDDING PRESENT

The LEADMILL GIG GUIDE

Tel. 754500

JUNE	
SAT. 14	FROM DOWN-UNDER IN AUSTRALIA, THE VERY WONDERFUL The Church + JUNK 8.30>2AM ONLY £3
SUN. 15	JAZZ for LUNCH SCRUMMY 12>2AM 50p
MON. 16	ALTERNATIVE FEMINIST CABARET! ★★★ Lip Service £2/1.50 7.30 PM Don't be late!
TUES. 17	RADIO SHEFFIELD'S R.O.T.T. NIGHT WITH..... WEDDING PRESENT + THE PIG BROTHERS + TWO OTHER BANDS! 8.30>2AM. £2.50/£2.00
WED. 18	★ A BEAT CLUB SPECIAL! ★ GINO WASHINGTON +60'S DISCO ... £2.50

Q. What's your favourite TV children's program, past or present?

David: NOW you're talking. Oh the hours I could go on reminiscing about Lady Penelope and Mike Mercury. I bet kids tv has a greater influence on society than bunches of overgrown wallies dancing about with guitars on, it certainly did on me anyway. I used to like Watch With Mother, especially 'Tales of The Riverbank' when you had scenes of petrified young rodents trying to escape from being suspended in mid-air while the narrator would be saying 'Hammy is really enjoying his afternoon baloon ride...'Nowadays my favourite show is 'Thomas The Tank Engine'. Did you see the episode when they bricked a train up inside a tunnel for good? It was all just because he was too vain to come out when it was raining. That Fat Controller's a real tyrant. I'm also glad that somebody's twigred on the cultural masterpieces of Trumpton and Camberwick Green, even if it's only the over-rated 'Man 'Biscuit.

Sex Rash: I'd like to reccommend Moschops mainly for its 'In My Area' theme tune, but, more interestingly, there's this program called 'Splash' Which is the first post-DuranDuran tv show for kids, in that the producers have realised that our pop kids don't want majorettes and labradors, they want SEX, and so to this end they've got these three astonishingly good-looking presenters who jump into scanty swim-wear at every opportunity. It's breathtaking stuff, I'm telling you.

FINALLY CAN YOU SUM UP WHAT THE WEDDING PRESENT ARE ABOUT AND WHY YOU SEE THE NEED TO STARVE SO THAT YOU CAN RELEASE A RECORD?

DAVID: Entertainment! We'll leave "art" to those who are better at being artists. The Wedding Present aren't out to change the world or restructure the shape of popular music, although we can help with the odd repair here and there. Youth culture is so manufactured these days that it's constantly losing relevance and its dubious appeal. And even your most ideologically sound groups and labels are usually little more than Be-Your-Own-BusinessMEN. Andso we're under no illusions. I've written songs all me life - it's a hobby - and The Wedding Present will perform and record them as long as we enjoy doing it. It was our ambition to release a crackin' record (an obvious one, I think) and so it was easily worth suffering a few hardships for... something to show the grandkids. NOW, ask yourself, "are we worth getting married for"?

Almost worth

getting married for!

CONTACT: The Wedding Present
14 Churchill Gardens
Leeds 2

fab. exciting pop group!

THE WEDDING PRESENT

THE WEDDING PRESENT are the sound of happiness ... pop with power, pop with punch, and always pop with pleasure. This Leeds band are shooting stars with fast guitars - they mean energy, they mean excitement, they mean broken strings. Their songs soar from the stereo - bursts of speedy classics - oh, play it again, just once more! A passionate, cutting music topped with a dessert of dark, unmoved vocals. The current line-up - with appropiate nicknames - is Reg (bass) Grapper (guitar) Gargrave (drums) and David 'Good Bloke' Gedge (vocals and guitar).

YOU ONCE SAID YOU WOULD RETIRE AFTER MAKING FOUR GREAT RECORDS. HAVING RECORDED HALF THAT TOTAL SO SOON, ARE YOU GOING TO CHANGE YOUR MIND?

DAVID: So soon?! It seems like ages. But you're right, I will have to start looking for an alternative career very shortly. At the moment I'm considering cricket commentating.

REG: Er maybe that was a bit of a fib - I'd rather hoped that everyone had forgotten we said that! But don't worry, there is a new lie coming up on the horizon, it is 'We haven't made the perfect Wedding Present single yet and that is what we are all about, striving.'

PEOPLE HAVE COMMENTED ON THE WAY YOU DRESS & A CERTAIN COLOUR YOU PREFER. WHAT'S SO SPECIAL ABOUT BLACK? DOES THIS MEAN YOU ARE A BUNCH OF MISERABLE BASTARDS?

GARGRAVE: Black's not deliberate, it just happened to be what we were wearing on the day.

DAVID: But you wear black EVERY day! What annoys me right now are those people, you know the ones, who dress up to stand out - four foot mohicans and fishnet underpants - and then when you stare at them in the supermarket they sneer at you as if you are being objectionable to them!

(continued)

WEDDING RECEPTION?

l - r) Gargrave, Reg, David, Grapper

Contemporary Archives Present

THE AGE OF CHANCE

THE WEDDING PRESENT

George and Dragon, Mill St, Bedford
Thursday July 17, 8.30pm
£2.50 (£2 with UB40)

THE WEDDING PRESENT
'This Boy Can Wait'
(Reception Records) The Weddos try to sing while they're running and it doesn't sound as bad as what, say, Cyril Smith would sound like doing the same thing. They're in a hurry, for some reason. The seats of their pants are on fire and they're furiously trying to extinguish the flames. They end up setting light to their feet as well.

THE WEDDING PRESENT
This Boy Can Wait (Reception)
A FRENZIED guitar ushers in a breathless vocal and neither goes away throughout this prime slice of Leeds indie pop, free at last from the Gang Of Four hangover that has dogged so many of that city's favourite sons, and now veering more towards a deranged folkies-on-speed extravaganza that overstays its welcome by just about the right amount. The B-side is called "You Should Always Keep In Touch With Your Friends" which is sound advice and again it's like some sort of folk music gone mad with lots of room for the omnipresent guitar to clang about in. If I had enough to drink I think I would probably die watching this band play live.

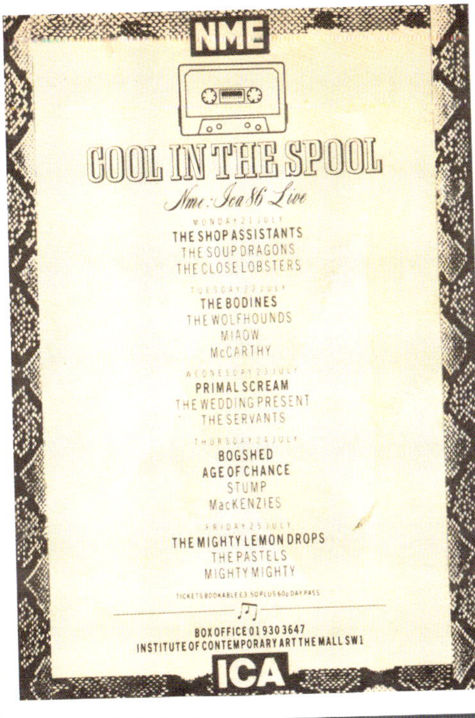

OCTOPUSSY
ANDREW WOOD

I was 16 when *Seamonsters* was released. It was quite a different beast from the previous Wedding Present albums I'd fallen in love with. But from the opening bars of 'Dalliance' I knew we'd get along beautifully. It was darker, more brooding, more broken; songs that swung from a whisper to a scream in a heartbeat. You didn't just listen to this record, you lived it. Everything about it seemed perfect – the rawness of the guitars, the relentless thud of the drums and bass; goosebump-inducing lyrics that hit the heart hard. Single word song titles that merely hinted at the tales of yearning and betrayal that lay ahead. Hitch's abstract artwork. *Seamonsters* had it all.

Yet while I could wax lyrical about each and every one of the album's ten songs, it's the closer, 'Octopussy', that really seals the deal for me. By the time we reach it, we've been on quite a journey – a 40-minute whirlwind that's left us battered, bruised, hurt and confused. Emotionally, we're on the ropes. Running on vapours as the guitars pick out those first faltering notes.

Next come the drums: four simple beats, like staggering footsteps at first, then suddenly, confidently picking up the pace. We're up, we can do this, there's enough in the tank.

Fifty seconds in, Gedge's voice sets the scene:

Some bits of snow still hanging in the air but that's outside
Take off your clothes and lie down over there
Oh, that's just right

A picture painted in 25 words. Here it is, our hard-fought happy ending. Gedge has got the girl and all's well with the world at last. Or has he? Because by the time the chorus lands, the doubt sets in:

You don't take away my hand like you ought to, you've become my family
I don't want to understand why I need you, you've just become my family

Is she really his? Does she belong to another? Is this another betrayal? So many questions, yet no time for answers as we hurtle into the second verse.

I lay down there and watched you getting dressed
It's still so clear
You laughed and curled you knees up to your chest if I came near

Past tense, reflection; a fond remembrance.

God knows, I've always had to fear the worst but not that time

You brought me home and then you kissed me first and you were all mine

There it is – proof of happier times. But where did it go wrong? As we wonder, the chorus comes around again, repeating this time as if to amplify the frustration. What's the score? Is this on or off? Confused, unsure, the music takes over. Temporarily lost in a wash of chords and drum fills, the opening riff soon brings us back – restoring order before the vocals return:

We don't have to do anything
We don't have to do anything except watch the leaves turning in the wind
Say what you want to say

We don't have to go anywhere
We don't have to go anywhere
Let's just sit and talk about the usual things
I couldn't move anyway!

So where do these closing lines leave us? For me they signify not an indifference but an acceptance. Forget what's been and what could be and just focus on where we are. Don't do anything or go anywhere, simply enjoy the moment, what's here and now.

I was 16 when *Seamonsters* came out. Now, almost 30 years on, the final fading note of 'Octopussy' still feels like the happy ending we all deserve.

(THE MOMENT BEFORE) EVERYTHING'S SPOILED AGAIN

RICHARD CULVER

There's probably something very twatty about suggesting that your favourite song from a band with a 35-plus year legacy is the B-side of their first single. But it is, and has been for all of those 35-plus years. The Jesus and Mary Chain had already provided the attitude and the aesthetics, but The Wedding Present seeped into my conscience in late '85. In '86 I was failing 'O-levels' thanks to too many late nights listening to John Peel and the ever-growing collection of singles I'd accumulated, an increasing love of cheap speed and weed, and a steady run of screwed up teenage flings which allowed me to play the role of spurned lover and misunderstood loner.

Those first three Wedding Present singles provided the soundtrack, with high volume assaults played on a crappy portable record player. The call to arms of 'Go Out And Get 'Em, Boy!' and 'Once More', the pent-up tension in 'This Boy Can Wait' – I couldn't, often – and then the crushing heartbreak and romance of my favourite:

Have I said something wrong? I always did...
Oh, don't leave me alone again. They always did...

It seemed to hold up a mirror to my world, the pain and suffering inflicted by each failed crush/dalliance/encounter and relationship, flying too high and always getting hurt in the end. But finding solace in that song.

Now, happily married for over 20 years, this is still my TARDIS. For a few fleeting moments I'm transported back to being 15 and 16 again – that gut-churning ache, the lust and the longing. It's still cathartic, still liberating, and still gets the hairs on the back of my neck tingling like no other piece of music.

Oh, and no one's supposed to know how I feel

NO

MICHAEL GILHAM

My favourite song is 'No'. I first heard it sometime in the winter of 1991 by virtue of DJing at my university radio station, WGMU, in Fairfax, Virginia. I'd gotten involved in such a capacity through my mandatory Communications Course project and was filling the airwaves as a volunteer in a very early morning time slot on Sundays. While I was already very enthusiastic about the band after being introduced to them through the 'Kennedy' video via MTV's *120 Minutes*, it was 'No' that really set the wheels in motion for The Wedding Present to become my favourites.

Michael Gilham's favourite Wedding Present song is 'No'

Conveniently, WGMU had made a cart of the song – carts were high quality large format cassette tapes which were played on special playback machines that were exclusive to broadcast operations. I'll never forget the pleasure of hearing 'No' for the first time whilst listening to the playback of it going out over the air.

The song has all of the elements that make the band – and that classic lineup in particular

– so special; one of DLG's most poignant kitchen sink narratives and the wonderful melodic interplay of Grapper and David's guitars which, buoyed by Keith's pulsing bass and Simon's backbeat, weave together until they escape natural orbit to produce the triumphantly exultant ending passage. One never wants it to end but, naturally, it must.

Flash forward several months and the band were playing a few gigs in the States whilst working their way back to the east coast from Pachyderm Studios in Minnesota. Thankfully, one of these dates was at the old 9:30 Club in Washington, DC. On an unseasonably cold March day, in which the Metro region had received a good bit of snow, I made my way down to the club for my first Weddoes gig. Although in advance of the show I'd made a point to pick up the American cassette version of *Bizarro*, around half of the set consisted of songs I'd never heard as they played several selections from *Seamonsters*, including 'Heather', which was dedicated to Keith's mum, and who David noted from the stage was in attendance that evening. It was one of the best gigs I've ever witnessed, and cemented The Wedding Present's status as my favourite band.

As an aside, from '91 on, I encouraged David to put 'No' in the setlist for a gig I was going to attend, or would simply shout it out as a request from the audience on the night. These entreaties were all in vain and I would have to wait over 19 years – for the US *Bizarro* tour in April 2010 – to hear it performed live for the first time.

GIVE MY LOVE TO KEVIN
WENDY RICHARDSON

'Give My Love To Kevin' sums up everything about breaking up for me. It's my 'go to' song and one I love hearing David sing live.

NIAGARA
MARTIN CARRITT

Martin Carritt thought *Seamonsters* was a leap forward sonically

I got into The Wedding Present in early 1987, and whilst I liked the jangly earlier stuff, it was with *Seamonsters*, when the band took such a leap forward sonically, that things started to get interesting. The guitars were heavier and crunchier, the arrangements sparser, allowing the songs to breathe. And it was this period that brought about the song 'Niagara', which brings a lump to my throat to this day. How this was left as a mere B-side still amazes me. It starts off as quite a jaunty, mid-paced track and then the chorus kicks in, and the guitars get really heavy, and it's then that you realise this is a breathtaking piece of music. There is that small break, and you hear David counting in and the song surges to another level. Whenever this is played live it remains a true highlight for me in the Wedding Present canon.

There's one other little titbit I'd like to share because it involves a song that I love which also has a backstory to it. In the summer of 1996, we were looking at houses in Otley and my wife had arranged a booking. I knew nothing about the vendor's name and when we arrived about 3pm on the Sunday afternoon we knocked on the door and I was greeted by Sally Murrell and the sight of David in the background vacuuming furiously. My exact words embarrass me to this day. 'You look strangely familiar.'

My wife thought I was quite mad, and I had to explain to her who it was. Even though she knew the band, she'd never seen them live (since rectified, I'm happy to say). We were shown round the house, which was gorgeous, and I remember one room in particular was essentially a music room filled floor to ceiling with tapes, guitars and ephemera of all kinds which I tried to take a sneaky peek at.

Naturally, I couldn't leave without talking shop, so we discussed *Mini* and the forthcoming *Saturnalia*, and I cheekily asked him if I could buy a seven-inch of 'Sucker' and he gave it to me, signed, for nothing. Top bloke. Sadly, there was no happy ending as our buyer, a recalcitrant Belgian chef, bailed on us. So 'Sucker', a brilliant track, also holds a special place in my heart for me in terms of my favourite songs.

BRASSNECK

DERMOT GREENE

'Brassneck' reminds me of a period of intense change in my life. In September 1989 I started my first full time job as an engineer in High Wycombe. Although I had spent a couple of summers as a student working in and around London, this was the big move – first job, new career and a world of opportunity and responsibility. Reflecting back now it was pretty lonely, initially as the enormity of the move and emigration sank in, leaving friends and family behind. I wasn't full of confidence in my abilities either, and so was a nervous starter in a first job.

Dermot Greene (left), here with Dale Farrington in Bangkok in 2019, favours 'Brassneck'

David and Jessica (right) in Bangkok in 2019 when The Wedding Present played there

But I was finally going to get some money in my pocket after a fairly broke summer. I had my weekends in London and I had (some of) my music with me and had made a mental note to check out a new band that I had only heard a few tunes of called The Wedding Present. So luckily my first salary pay cheque coincided almost exactly with the release of *Bizarro* on 23 October 1989. Our Price in High Wycombe stocked it, along with *Tommy*, and I bought both.

I was in a shared flat and luckily my flatmate Sean had a turntable. I can still remember the way the venom of 'Brassneck' just hit me in the guts – the blast of the guitars, drums and bass and that line: 'I just decided I don't trust you anymore.' I remember feeling and thinking that this was a lot heavier than I expected The Wedding Present to be, but it quickly grew on me.

The lyrics of 'Brassneck' are brilliant and timeless, and the song means more to me about that time and place in my life than any of its associations with broken relationships and lost trust. (Mind you it took on more meaning during those phases in my life as well!)

The album came out the week before they were playing in London so I can remember cramming in as many listens as possible to *Bizarro* before heading down to the National in Kilburn on a Thursday night in November 1989. I was blown away when the first song they played was 'Brassneck'. All hell broke loose and I'm pretty sure the moshpit collapsed. I barely made it back to Marylebone station in time to catch the last train back to Wycombe after an exhilarating gig.

The Wedding Present have always held a special place in my heart because of this. The job I got turned out to be a good one with a great company who gave me excellent training and opportunities to work with some excellent people all over the world. 30 years later, I'm still working for the same company and still listening avidly to my favourite band. That original album, played to death but still intact and playable, and still with the original price tag, is one of the few that have made it down to the southern hemisphere with me. It was also so amazing to catch the *Bizarro* gig in Bangkok in July 2019 and I feel privileged to have been there.

I'M NOT ALWAYS SO STUPID

GRAHAM FAIRS

Graham Fairs is a fan of 'I'm Not Always So Stupid'

This song tugs at my heart every time I hear the opening chords, although I've heard them a thousand and more times. There are, of course, many Wedding Present songs about love, loss and break-up but 'I'm Not Always So Stupid' seems to replace anger, angst and resentment with deep regret and a longing for what might, and perhaps should, have been. There's a case for it to be included under poignancy in every encyclopaedia of synonyms.

I'm not sure how often it's played live, but not enough that's for sure, and in my (humble) opinion it deserves the same live exposure as 'My Favourite Dress'. One memorable outing was at the *Indietracks Festival* in July 2008.

The Wedding Present's stage of choice (well, it probably wasn't) was in what can best be described as a small warehouse/greenhouse. The heat was intense, resulting in the inevitable 'perspiration' from DLG and, it has to be said, much of the audience. I'm not a dancer, more of a shuffler, but that song got the feet moving. Oh, those opening chords...

And it was a B-side. How did that happen?

NOBODY'S TWISTING YOUR ARM

JON FARLEY

I wasn't an early fan of The Wedding Present. At the time I was listening to the likes of Rick Astley, Madonna and all the mundane chart pop music. Back in 1988, I met up with an old school friend who was into the likes of Bauhaus, The Sisters of Mercy, The Smiths and of course The Wedding Present. He lived next door to a pub at the top of Penny Meadow, in my home town of Ashton-under-Lyne. We popped into the pub for a pint, a game of pool and a good catch-up. He was telling me about all the latest music he was into and in the background the TV was playing *The Chart Show*. It was the Indie countdown week and he stopped playing pool and told me, 'Listen to this band. They are brilliant.'

The track was 'Nobody's Twisting Your Arm'. Later that year I went to my first concert, to watch The Wedding Present at the Ritz in Manchester, and from that day onwards I have been a big fan. I owe a big 'thanks' to my old school friend, Cliff, for the introduction. Sadly, we lost touch – he got married whilst I was off out enjoying my new found love of all types of Indie music. We met up again in 2009 at a school reunion. He wasn't into music that much anymore and had lost touch with The Wedding Present. I'm still hooked!

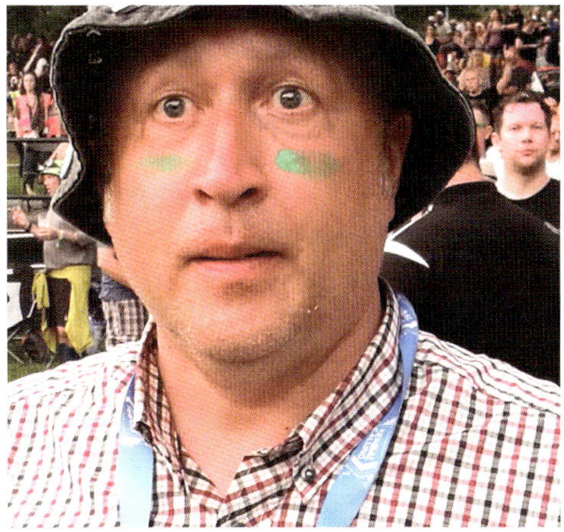

Nobody was twisting Jon Farley's arm

BRASSNECK

NIGEL PIERCE

I was at Liverpool Poly, a bedsit Morrissey clone who listened to everything John Peel played. I rented a room in a house owned by a cheeky Scouse taxi driver who would bring back his female passengers if they didn't have the money to cover the fare. I bought the hand-painted 'Brassneck' and marvelled at its beautiful cover. I played it lots but was always careful with the sleeve. One Friday, after listening to it, I put the record back in my record box and went home to Shropshire for the weekend to get my clothes cleaned and my belly fed.

Upon my return to my Scouse house, George the randy taxi driver apologised for the mess in my room. I bolted upstairs to find all my seven-inch records spread out over the carpet and all the sleeves of all the records drying out on a makeshift clothes horse. All the sleeves were a sludge colour. Turns out there had been a water leak in the attic and the water had dripped only into my record box. The 'Brassneck' single had ruined all the sleeves of the other records. I still love the record, but whenever I hear it, I'm reminded of those soggy, ruined record sleeves.

David Gedge with Nigel Pierce and Nigel's daughter Elodie

CAROLYN

TIMOTHY EYRE

Timothy Eyre got into trouble when he quoted the lyrics of 'Carolyn' to a girl named Carolyn

In the late 1990s, my girlfriend had a colleague by the name of Carolyn. Despite having German as her first language, she was able to engage in pub banter as well as any native English speaker. One evening we were chatting in a Bloomsbury pub. Here our friend Carolyn claimed that the name Carolyn was frequently used by songwriters and, extrapolating from this, claimed further that the name Carolyn was an especially good one. Regardless of their veracity, I was impressed by the sheer preposterousness of her claims.

Having been a fan of The Wedding Present since the late 1980s, I was reminded of the song *Carolyn* from *Seamonsters*. I mainly listen to Death Metal, with The Wedding Present being something of a deviation from my usual extreme tastes. The dark themes, heavy sound and distorted guitars of *Seamonsters* chime in well with my primary musical proclivities. As such, it is my favourite album from the Gedge œuvre, and one of my favourite albums of all time.

The relatively placid nature of *Carolyn* means that were I to rank the songs on *Seamonsters* in order of preference, *Carolyn* would likely come last. Nevertheless, it is a song that I like; *The Wedding Present* eschew filler tracks just as they eschew encores.

With Carolyn having made her claim, the next day I sent her an email containing the lyrics from the song of the same name. That evening my girlfriend reported that, on reading the lyrics in their shared office, Carolyn had anxiously asked my girlfriend, 'Have you told him? Have you told him?' Here Carolyn was referring to her recent affairs of the heart, which had involved a fairly inattentive stoner boyfriend. Carolyn was concerned that my girlfriend had blabbed her confidences to me, and off the back of this, I had found a song that not only bore her name but also closely resembled her own situation.

This was emphatically not the case; I was simply matching a song title to Carolyn's name and claim. What Carolyn was really experiencing was the genius of David Gedge's lyric writing. Gedge crafts his words in such a way that almost anyone can pour their own experiences of heartbreak into the outline provided by his songs. Like a skilled artist who paints an expressive face with just a few strokes, Gedge uses a few lines of natural speech to delineate an immediately recognisable complex of emotions that defy direct description. The brief use of mundane details ('Just before you go today') provide a sense of immediacy that serves to further heighten a song's impact.

So it was that when my girlfriend's colleague read the words:

You believed me when I said I tried but oh, Carolyn, I lied

She heard the voice of her stoner sweetheart awkwardly confessing his faithlessness at her front door, rather than the voice of a songwriter reciting his composition. David Gedge is on record as saying that he finds writing lyrics difficult. The results of his creative efforts are songs that frequently bear an eerie personal poignancy, despite being written for a general audience. As for me, in Gedge's lyrics, I find an intensity that I more usually seek in the blast beats, chromatic chord progressions and guttural vocals of extreme metal.

CRAWL

STELLA CREASY MP

Ever since I've been a little girl, I've been an unashamed music snob. I used to create gangs at school where you had to have a middle name that was the name of a bassist to be able to join. I like what I like. I know what I like is really good music and I don't care if anybody else doesn't like it. In that sense, The Wedding Present always spoke to me because they seemed almost indifferent to the era. I was a '90s Indie kid and everyone was obsessed with Blur and Oasis. We were living in Colchester and Blur were quite a big local phenomenon. But I was resolutely The Wedding Present and I feel that I have been proved right through the years.

I was introduced to them by my older brother. He went to see them and I wasn't able to go with him because I was only 13 or 14. He was 17 and you can understand a 17-year-old boy not wanting his younger sister interfering with his enjoyment of music. But he and his friends came back and they were raving about the gig and I wanted to see what all the fuss was about. The first Wedding Present song I ever heard was their cover of 'Make Me Smile (Come Up And See Me)' and I just thought it was the most amazing thing. I remember stealing my brother's CD and playing it at full pelt in my parents' front room. I thought it was this angry, slightly vitriolic, slightly sarcastic song David had

Stella Creasy (left) with (left to right) her brother Matthew, David Gedge and Jessica McMillan

written. I didn't know the original song. I don't know many other singers who can get sarcasm into their tone. I remember, very clearly, thinking, 'Wow, who are they?' and then being very jealous of the fact that my brother had been able to see them play live.

I listened obsessively to all their albums and there was that point with the *Hit Parade* where suddenly they became quite popular. I remember being quite resentful of it because I thought 'no, no, they're my band'. Various random people at school and in my social circle were discovering them and I felt they were Johnny Come Latelys.

My brother and I obsessively collected all of their albums and singles and then argued about whose copy was whose and who was listening to what. I should defend my brother's honour. He has grown up and become much more reflective about music, whereas I'm still stuck in that same '90s Indie kid grump. I took my brother to a Wedding Present gig to meet David and he was very awkward about it. Because it was 'here's my over-excited sister. I'm so sorry. This is all my fault.' I still feel like that when I go.

George Best is 'jump up and down in the moshpit' music. It's just joyful guitar. The riff of 'Kennedy' is extraordinary. You only have to hear the first three seconds of it and you are jumping up and down in your seat. That riff! Straight away you're up and you're dancing around the room.

Seamonsters has always been my favourite album, because it coincided with a period in my life where every single song seemed to speak to something that was happening to me at that point in time. When David asked me to write the sleeve notes for a *Seamonsters* re-issue I was completely blown away. Because I was worried about not being able to do justice to the sense of disappointment that I think is such an integral part of falling in love and falling out of it, and being somebody that people fall out of love with as well. I've always felt that album captured, in a way that other people don't, that sense of self loathing that comes when that happens.

There's the lyric in 'Blonde':

I'm just some name in your book
That's why you gave up writing weeks ago

Countless young men made me feel like that. I don't know what that says about my ability to fall in love with unsuitable young men. It's always an exquisite pain when you fall in love and then realise that you're the one doing the chasing and it's never going to last. And yet the point at which they do speak to you…

We didn't have mobile phones back in the 1990s. You had to wait tentatively to see them at the local Indie disco and hope they were going to show up. And then, God, you'd have to actually speak to them and you didn't know whether they would speak to you. 'You won't be getting in touch, oh, do you ever?' was what I would then listen to for the rest of the week. Because that would be the time in between going out on a Thursday or a Friday night as a teenager and waiting and hoping against hope that you were wrong and that, this time, this one was 'a keeper'. They never were. And thank God they never were, thinking about them now. I was probably unusual in that sense in having David's voice reverberating around my head as I tried to make nonchalant conversation with disappointing teenage boys. The thing about *Seamonsters* is that sense of awkwardness in a lot of the lyrics and a lot of the songs. There was just a sense of melancholy from knowing that you were on a hiding to nothing but wishing you were wrong.

There was always that presumption that girls would be heartbreakers but it was always the other way round for me. I was incredibly awkward. There was a terrible party I organised when my parents had gone away for the weekend. I spent much of the evening trying to play Wedding Present songs on a guitar to a young man who, unfortunately for him, was on the other side of the room from the door so he couldn't escape. It didn't work!

What *Seamonsters* does so well is speak to that sense of, 'This isn't going to end well but I'm going to give it a chance anyway.' 'Octopussy' is the one about 'I'm glad you came back'. You know from the tone that it's a surprise. Most other songs at that time were not about that awkwardness. They were not about what I think is the reality for most people falling in love, where you're awkward and uncertain and then it goes horribly wrong. The other big bands of the time were much more confident in their musical output and The Wedding Present spoke to me in a way that felt more real.

When I hear those songs, I can still see those boys, which is helpful because one day I will track them all down and now, as a middle-aged confident woman, I will say to them, 'Don't do that. Don't not call.' They're probably not Wedding Present fans and that's probably where I went wrong. I should have had it as a test.

One of the things that I'm gutted about is that lockdown cancelled all gigs. My happy place is in the moshpit, about a third of the way from the front. When I'm in that moshpit, I'm back to being 15 and angry with unsuitable young men who I summon up the courage to say what I ought to say to them. David does it for me, in my head.

I never got to see them live as a teenager. I put it off for so long because I thought, 'God, what if they're not what I hope?' I eventually went to see them live at the Kentish Town Forum in 2005 on the *Take Fountain* tour and it was extraordinary. Words that always strike terror into your heart from a band that you've loved for some time are 'and now we're going to play some of our new stuff', but actually I thought *Take Fountain* was brilliant, and more in line with *Seamonsters* in that sense of 'I should just get out of here… Will you even recognise my face this time next year?' It was almost like a return to the miserable form as opposed to the pogoing form of 'Kennedy'. And the conversations that you have between lovers, as in the song 'I'm From Further North Than You'. It just seems so real. The Wedding Present have always spoken the truth about what it's like to like somebody else and never be sure they'll like you back quite as much, and how that can eat away at you.

I regularly play The Wedding Present loudly in my office in Parliament when I'm working late at night. 'Crawl' is the song I played when I first walked into Parliament. That, and 'She Bangs the Drums' by The Stone Roses. 'Crawl' is another one where you only have to hear the first couple of seconds of the riff. And 'Everyone here could be a millionaire' seemed to be very apposite for walking into Parliament for the first time. I felt like a complete oddball teenager again. And that sense of nervousness and awkwardness? That's how I felt when I walked into Parliament for the first time. It felt very fitting to have the music of teenage uncertainty in my ear at that moment.

The first time I ever got off the whip as an MP was to go to a Wedding Present gig. That's what's weird about gigs now. I'll be jumping up and down and throwing myself around and someone will go 'ooh, you're my MP'. And I'm like, 'OK I'd better stop doing this, hadn't I? Because if you can see me mouthing along to all the words it's probably not what you want to see in your elected representative.' And at my age I can't really jump as much as I used to or get out of the way of an elbow. Having two small children is going to make going to gigs a bit difficult for a while.

I used to witter on for years about being miserable and sitting in my room listening to The Wedding Present. I still do it now. I just do it in Parliament.

The emotional connection is what's the truth about music. The songs that last and the songs that really touch you are the ones that you just hear the first couple of bars of and instantly you're in a different space.

My partner is a fan and that was probably a pre-requisite of us lasting. We have a shared musical canon, which means that our children have no chance at all of any independence of thought when it comes to this. I've already said that any kid of mine that comes back with a Katie Melua album is out the door. Or even worse, Travis or Coldplay. Although, for the avoidance of doubt, I'm sure Mr Chris Martin is a very nice man. I just wish he'd learn a third chord.

My staff are annoyingly indifferent to The Wedding Present. One of them suggested we play some Ed Sheeran. You can imagine what happened. And I'm completely comfortable with being a musical snob. I don't care if people don't like the same music as me. I care that it's good. I play what I like because at some point you've got to educate the masses.

If I was on *Desert Island Discs*, 'Crawl' is the song I would have to save but 'Blonde' would come a close second. And 'My Favourite Dress' as well. This is why I don't get to go on *Desert Island Discs*. 'You want me to choose?' When I DJ, I always say 'no requests and no repeats'. And people come up and they ask me and I say, 'What part of no requests do you not get?'

I warm to a band that goes against the grain, and is serious about it because that's real and authentic. David's not there to please you. He's there to play some good music and if you like it you like it, and if you don't that's your problem. The Wedding Present could have sold out a long time ago. They never did. David has remained a truth teller and that's something that we should cherish because there aren't that many of them about. When Bob Dylan is selling ladies' underwear, it does rather defeat the point.

I have a sneaking ambition to take David up on his pledge to play the Eurovision song contest because I think we'd win. Him being a Eurovision fan and being up for entering it is brilliant. Eurovision is very political and we often look like we don't respect the effort and professionalism that goes into it. I can think of nobody who would espouse more the quintessentially British view of life than David Gedge. Every year I start the draft of the 'Weddoes for Eurovision' hashtag. It's not quite got off the ground as yet, but it'll happen, when people realise it's our only chance of being taken seriously and rehabilitating our reputation in Europe.

I've done a lot of European politics. The Brits are often like the awful man your aunt married 20 years ago. You've had to put up with him at Christmas for 20 years and finally she's divorcing him. Sending in the Gedge to show that actually Britain has talent and also is European is the first step towards challenging Brexit. So no pressure on The Wedding Present, but there's a lot riding on it. Things have to change. He could do a very melancholy cover of 'Love Shine A Light'.

NOBODY'S TWISTING YOUR ARM

CARLOS CIURANA

The first song I heard from The Wedding Present was 'This Boy Can Wait', included in the *C86* LP from *NME* when it was released in Spain. I was shocked by the melody and the velocity of David Gedge's guitar. I had never heard anything like it. But my favourite song is 'Nobody's Twisting Your Arm'. It reminds me of when I first saw The Wedding Present in Valencia Arena in 1988. They played the song near the end of the show and I have it on the *Live 1988* CD. My devotion to 'Nobody's Twisting Your Arm' is such that I have the seven and twelve-inch versions of one of the best songs from The Wedding Present.

PERFECT BLUE

NIC

On 27th October 2013, following a Wedding Present gig in Aberdeen's Lemon Tree, I had a brief (but hugely important and genuinely amazing) conversation with David Gedge about the song 'Perfect Blue'. The gig marked the first day of a week-long adventure that would see my girlfriend and me travel from Aberdeen to Paris, via Broadstairs and London, and would – most importantly – include a proposal along the way.

At that point my girlfriend and I had been together for almost eight years; and, almost eight years previously, on the walk home from one of our very first dates, I was listening (for what could easily have been the thousandth time) to *Take Fountain*. Like most, if not all, Wedding Present fans, I strongly connect and relate to songs and albums and *Take Fountain* was no different… with the exception, at that time perhaps, to the last couple of tracks.

However, as I listened to 'Perfect Blue' on that walk home – a song I admittedly and ashamedly had probably skipped more than I had listened to – something changed. I realised I had fallen completely and utterly in love and genuinely felt like I was at the beginning of something very special. It was as though this was a scene in a movie and 'Perfect Blue' was the soundtrack. I connected and related to every word and every beat of the song, and it almost seemed like it had been written about us and about that very moment.

Almost eight years later, at the merch stand, following an outstanding performance at the Lemon Tree, and in a few brief moments while my girlfriend had nipped away, I was able to ask David about the song. He told me a little about what it meant to him and reassured me, to my relief, that I hadn't missed any alternative meaning behind it. As I told him of my intentions for the week ahead, my girlfriend returned and there was an awkward 30 seconds or so where we all just stood in silence and looked at each other before David, breaking the silence, very politely complimented my girlfriend's necklace and wished us luck as we said goodbye (much to my girlfriend's slight bemusement).

A few days later, on a beach in Broadstairs, I got down on one knee, opened a small wooden ring box and proposed. The inscription on the inside of the box read:

The more I have, the more I want you
The more you smile, the more I know I'll never let you down
But I should warn you that I just might never let you out of my sight

One year later we got married and, of course, had our first dance to 'Perfect Blue'.

The day after the wedding, we embarked on our honeymoon with no real itinerary other than an initial couple of nights in Edinburgh. Over the course of the next week or so, we journeyed as far as Wales, stopping at various locations along the way, returning to Edinburgh for one last night before heading home the following day to begin our new lives together as husband and wife.

That last night in Edinburgh was 11th November 2014. The Wedding Present were due to play at The Liquid Room and it seemed like a fitting end to an adventure that had begun at a Wedding Present gig a little over a year previous, if not on that initial walk home all those years ago.

It is difficult to describe the feeling and the enormity of being at that gig but, as my wife and I stood in the centre of a packed Liquid Room crowd as if we were the only two people there, at the very edge of the beginning of our new adventure together and with tears in both our eyes, it almost seemed, at that moment, The Wedding Present might be performing 'Perfect Blue' just for us.

SUCK or CRAWL

MELANIE HOWARD, BASSIST, THE WEDDING PRESENT & CINERAMA

It's hard to choose between these two as my favourite song. I absolutely love 'Suck' because it's the song that introduced me to the band before I ever met David. I actually heard The Twilight Sad's cover of it first and that's how I discovered David's work. But I also love 'Crawl' because it's just so much fun to play. That bassline is thick and lush and yet so simple at the same time, it's just perfect to me. The song feels like this wavering balance of happy-sad and it has such a nostalgia-inducing, climatic sound.

Photo: Richard Houghton

Melanie Howard can't choose between two favourites

DALLIANCE

KATE ARNOLD

I've been thinking hard about why The Wedding Present are my favourite band and how to pin down my favourite song of theirs, and I think I can tie the two together with 'Dalliance'. To me, it's just the sound of a heart breaking; the desolation, the fury, the bitterness, and finally the dignity – they are all there in the lyrics and the furious right hand. Ultimately, I think it's how everyone wants someone to feel about them, just once in their lifetime. It broke my musical heart the first time I heard it, and I've never managed to fix it, or wanted to.

My favourite gig memory is from The Joiners in Southampton in the mid-2000s. I was fairly near the back. I can't remember which song it was (probably 'Brassneck' or 'Kennedy', because everyone had gone mad) but in the stage lights I clearly saw a pair of glasses fly up into the air and, Wedding Present fans being the good eggs they generally are, the moshpit parted so that whoever they belonged to could pick them up. After the song, David said, 'Was that someone's glasses? Oh, thank God – I thought someone had had a heart attack!' That gig was the last time I let myself chat with David afterwards – I always manage to make a tit of myself so I decided to spare us both from then on. I like to think he appreciates the gesture...

Kate Arnold's musical heart was broken by 'Dalliance'

SNAPSHOTS

KARINA MALLEY

My favourite song, when I was a young girl, was always 'Kennedy'. I went to see The Wedding Present in a venue in Dundee (I forget the name of it). My now-husband's friends were one of the support bands (Skeezer) at the time. I was at the bar asking if they had a payphone (this gives an idea of just how long ago this was) and David turned and spoke to me. I was literally blown away with how down-to-earth and genuinely lovely he was. That was also the day I went from liking the band to loving them.

My favourite song now is 'Snapshots'. I lost a very special friend to cancer on Valentine's Day 2018 and every time I play it, it reminds me of how hard it was watching someone you care about suffering when there's absolutely nothing you can do but be there for them. It also encapsulates the beauty of the memories he left behind.

'Snapshots' has replaced 'Kennedy' as Karina Malley's favourite because of the memories associated with the song

TAKE ME!
DAVID BAMBER

David Bamber's favourite is 'Take Me!'

I have a few favourite Wedding Present songs, and which one it is generally depends on my mood at the time, but my all-time favourite has always been 'Take Me!' I've loved it since I first heard it 30 years ago – the lyrics and also the almost hypnotic guitar work. However, it has recently been taken to another level because it's almost as if it was written 30 years ago as some weird premonition! *time to reach for your sick-bag!* I say this because the lyrics perfectly describe how I feel about a girl that I've recently 're-met' (after about 20 years) and have fallen for in a very big way. So much so, that I hope we're still listening to this song together with such affection in another 20 years' time. The only lyric that I would change slightly to make them absolutely perfect for us would be to make it 'lemon slices' rather than orange. She knows!

I first heard about the band when I read a review of their debut album, *George Best*, in the *NME*. I was drawn to it by both the cover and the band's name. I bought it without listening to it. When I got home and played my new LP I was blown away by the frenetic pace of the guitars. In short, I loved it immediately. Some music grows on you but this just hit me square between the eyes and landed in my heart to remain forever.

My first gig was at Manchester International 2 on 14th November 1989 with my best mates Graham and Darren. Graham was studying at Manchester University, so we were staying over in his halls of residence. I'd driven down from Preston in my Mini and in the afternoon, as Smiths fans, we had a drive to find the iconic Salford Lads Club.

That evening the gig was every bit as good as we'd hoped for. We hung around afterwards and I managed to collar David and Keith for their autographs, the problem being that there was not a scrap of paper to be found anywhere – except for the £5 note I had in my pocket. After securing the highly-prized, and by 1989 standards, expensive signatures we decided on another drive – following the band in their minibus for as long as we could. I've no idea why – I suppose we just didn't want the night to end? The following day I headed off home up the motorway to Preston. However, all that driving had severely dwindled the contents of my Mini's fuel tank and I only had £5 to my name – yes, that £5. There was no way that I was spending it, so I just had to hope that I made it. The needle was on empty for what seemed like ages but my trusty Mini made it home on the fumes.

The next gig that I attended was on 24th May 1991 at Wolverhampton Civic Hall. My other mate, Darren, was studying there so it was free overnight lodgings again. My memory of that gig was that I didn't much care for the new material – *Seamonsters*. This album was obviously one of the 'growers' that I referred to earlier as I now love it for the masterpiece that it undoubtedly is.

I've seen The Wedding Present far more than any other band. Other stand-out gigs include *At The Edge Of The Peaks* on 26th August 2010. Graham and I went wearing my *Bizarro* and *Seamonsters* cycling jerseys armed with a fabric marker pen. We bumped into David outside the venue – the fantastic Holmfirth Picturedrome – where he obligingly signed our jerseys. The other bonus to this gig was seeing David's other band Cinerama perform – two for the price of one! We also got a few strange (or admiring?) looks on our choice of attire.

A friend of mine, Alan, was studying photography and managed to get special access to photograph the band at a local gig. Knowing that I was a big fan he kindly printed off some black and white copies for me. I'd always liked drawing and was OK at sketching as long as I had something to copy. I copied one of the photos – one of David playing his guitar in his semi-legendary shorts! The only problem being that his feet weren't in the photo (more practice required, Alan) so they didn't make it into my sketch either! I was, however, proud enough of my efforts to send it to David asking him to sign it. Which of course he did, along with the caption, 'Lovely Legs!' I'd also asked him for permission to paint the Reception rose on my Mini but had specified that it would only be six inches by four inches. I remember thinking that, if it was only small, permission might be granted? The reply from David, in a beautiful hand-written letter, was that I had permission on two conditions...

1) That it was bigger than six inches by four inches and
2) 'you send me a black and white photo showing the results!'

Sadly, I never did get round to doing it although I do remember receiving the offer of help from Graham to do it full-roof size.

Fast forward to July 2017. I was excited to hear that my favourite-ever band were playing at The Continental, a pub within easy walking distance of my house, so practically my 'local'. I never dreamed that would happen. Now – to get tickets. I immediately called at the pub only to learn that they'd already sold their allocation. But they did offer hope that the other stockist (Action Records) might have some left. As it was Sunday, I had an anxious wait until 9am the following morning when I phoned to be told that there were only two tickets left! I raced to town, endeavouring not to set off any speed cameras on the way. Car abandoned, I ran to the record shop and up to the counter where I breathlessly asked if I'd made it in time? Fortunately, I had.

Now to phone Graham and Darren to see who was going to claim the other prized ticket. Choosing who to ask was such a dilemma but easily solved because they are both notoriously hard to get hold of and slow to return calls. The winner was the first to return my call. On this occasion, Darren was the lucky one! On the night the band were on top form – as ever – in my favourite setting – a small venue with (I think) a 200 capacity. Beforehand, David could be found in his usual position at the merch stand. I got chatting to him and, among other things, asked him about a sketch I'd done of him 27 years previously – showing him a photo of it on my phone. Did he remember it? Sadly not. We had a good chat and then suddenly he asked me what time it was. When I told him he said, 'I'd better go, we're on in a couple of minutes!' That for me has to be my favourite ever Wedding Present gig. I really don't think you could beat seeing your favourite band play at your local!

LITTLE SILVER

MARK REED

Mark Reed opts for 'Little Silver'

'Little Silver' is perhaps an overlooked classic in the Wedding Present body of work. Unlike a great many bands, The Wedding Present have had a post-reunion, post-success career that is artistically as valid as their so-called glory years. By the time they got to 'Little Silver' they were 30 years in, and even though the band was always the same, and always different, there's something around this band that is always in essence, vital.

Also, if there is a bad Wedding Present song, you don't tend to get to hear them. Every song of theirs I have heard since they restarted in 2004 has been at least the equal of their 1984-1996 incarnation. Which is a nice way of saying that their reunion albums are the sign of an artist maturing and still producing work as good as ever.

One could be forgiven for thinking that *Going, Going...* would be the final Wedding Present album of original material. (And, at the time of writing, it is). The record is – and I dread to say it – a concept album that appears to cover the lifespan of a relationship, with each song sitting inside a certain part of that love. 'Little Silver' is easy to overlook amongst 20 other songs, but it sits near the start of the record, at a point where, in any relationship, two people are in the process of negotiating what life is and how it works. But the album isn't just about the relationship between people, but on a wider note, how people have a relationship with the reality around them and how they negotiate the basics of being alive and who and what to be. David Gedge was 56 when this album was released, and while it is easy to think that life should get easier with experience and the scars of the years, life doesn't get easier. It becomes a different kind of hard with the passing of time.

And 'Little Silver'? It's only 22 lines, and 181 words. But what words.

Why does this song mean so much to me? In a word: fear. 'Little Silver' is about overcoming and defeating fear. Even the first line – '*You looked so shocked when I said I'm leaving*' – is around how the narrator is confounding expectations, and taking the power back. About how they are overcoming the fear that kept them in place, and held them down in the place where the subject thought they would not have the courage to leave. Clearly, they didn't think that the writer would actually exercise the power of withdrawal from the situation, and remove themselves from it.

This song coincided with a period of personal revelation for me: I'd had a number of abusive corporate environments in the preceding years, to the point where my employers were surprised I wasn't prepared to put up with being treated a certain way any more in exchange for mere money. It took all my courage to walk into the unknown and risk financial ruin rather than continue to tolerate the intolerable. Maybe I'd been seen as someone who was not as strong as I actually was because I chose not to confront toxic and unhealthy situations, whereas I was using my strength to survive these situations. I was worth more than they thought, not worthless.

Fear had held me back. Wasted years of my life. Fear of what other people might think, or say. I was imprisoned by it. When the worst thing I could think of was happening – being threatened with everything I had spent my entire life working for and toward being destroyed – I realised living in that fear had actually not stopped my worst fears coming true. And that fear then, was useless. It achieved nothing.

I'm sure you're thinking I'll regret it but, in case you didn't notice, I'm a different person now
I became someone
And there's no point telling me to forget it; my life's no longer based on what you will allow
Those days have gone

In a battle of survival, I had to let go of fear. The worst thing I could have imagined – my ruin – was being threatened to me. My fear of this had prevented me acting before.

It did not stop me now. My regret was being afraid. But I evolved. 'I became someone' is a very important turn here. Before, when I was in fear, I wasn't the Me I needed to be, but someone I forced myself to be. I needed to believe in myself. When you don't stand for anything, you'll fall for anything. In the song, the singer became someone. Whereas before, by implication and by inaction, since they had no agency, they were no-one before they became someone.

'My life's no longer based on what you will allow.' At that point, this song became about empowerment. I didn't have to seek permission to be who I was. I only needed my permission and my authority to follow my own path. I had stepped out of my own shadow.

If anything, this song strengthened me in my most challenging moments. I felt braver, and my life is not based on what others allow, but on what I allow. I stand up for myself and what I believe in. I felt empowered by being myself. I long ago learnt that if I don't stand for something, I stand for nothing.

I became someone. And not the someone I once was, but someone I chose to be. It wasn't easy. In fact, it's terrifying to stand up for things you believe in, if you have not always done so in the past.

'Little Silver' for me, addressed the nature of identity and who we are, what we believe, what we do, and what is important. The release of the song occurred around the same time as I had a personal breakthrough and became a better, strong person. I learnt to let go of what other people think: I was stopping me being who I am. 'Little Silver' helped me change.

I became someone

I don't regret it. I am a different person now. My life is now based on what I allow. The old days are gone.

BLUE EYES
RICHARD POPPLETON

I have so many favourite Wedding Present songs and would find it impossible to select one as a favourite, but 'Blue Eyes' definitely means the most to me, and the older I get, the more it seems to mean every time I hear it. The first verse takes me back to 1992. I was in my early twenties and in love with my first girlfriend. I wanted it to last forever. We saw The Wedding Present a few times together. I was working in my first job at a greetings card warehouse, where I was surrounded every day with celebratory and sympathy cards and everything that can be sold to celebrate love – teddy bears,

Richard Poppleton is a big fan of 'Blue Eyes'

balloons, etc. She was meeting new people at Aberdeen University whilst studying biochemistry.

Christmas had arrived and she seemed overly excited about the four cans of Guinness she had been given by a student friend, James – who I'd kindly invited into her home – when he turned up uninvited to drop the present off. Being kind and friendly, I passed on to him a bright green hoodie I'd bought at a James gig that was far too big for me. In the next few weeks, I was not invited to various parties, student get-togethers, pubs and clubs, including her staying at his folks' home, and then jealousy took over me, as she told me they were 'just friends'. I made the odd phone call but the relationship ended. I was heartbroken. I only had the *Hit Parade* singles and the *Top Of The Pops* appearances to cling onto.

I took my mother to the theatre on a Thursday night to see *Arsenic and Old Lace*. I was upset and decided to go for a pint and then catch the bus home. But I also managed to catch him seeing her onto the bus home. To this day I'm not sure if they even noticed me, but I walked past them both with so much anger and hurt in my heart. I didn't say anything. I just walked onto the bus and watched her from a few seats behind her. I couldn't even manage to get off at the same bus stop, which was hers and mine, to walk home. But all I ever wanted was her home again.

I went home and watched the episode of *Top Of The Pops* that I'd recorded. 'Blue Eyes' came on. I was in tears at the lyrics:

I just want you home again
There's lots of things I used to say but that all changes from today

I was still hurting throughout all the *Hit Parade* singles and the many years that followed, but at least when David Lewis Gedge appeared in his James-mocking t-shirt for 'California' on *Top Of The Pops* in May, I realised that whatever happens in life, I will always have The Wedding Present to love and cherish, and I will always be thankful for such a wonderful band.

MANIAC
LEE HORREY

Lee Horrey (above), with his now-wife Anna, is a fan of 'Maniac' by Cinerama

I moved to Italy in 1998. My vinyl collection didn't make the journey, the hundreds of pounds invested in the preceding years was exchanged in Andy's Records, Cambridge, for about 35 pounds' worth of store credit. I used it on three CDs (Smashing Pumpkins' *Adore*; The Bluetones' *Return to The Last Chance Saloon* and *John Peel Sessions 1992-1995* by The Wedding Present) which accompanied me on my initial move along with my CD Walkman and about another seven discs. It took about a year to 'smuggle' the rest of my CD collection over. Each time I travelled a single suitcase was half clothes and half music.

In the beginning we were poor… or rather, we weren't sure… could we survive on one salary? It's tough to be certain or accurate, when a beer cost thousands of lire (the Euro coming in a year or so later). It was a lot of guesswork whether we could afford things or would be short at the end of the month. Changing job, country and living arrangements (from alone in the UK, seeing my Italian girlfriend for a long weekend every three months – this had been the setup for the last four years) was stressful and I needed music, a reminder of more settled times.

My parents kindly gifted us a proper home CD player as a flat-warming present. I listened to music a lot in those first weeks – partly because I didn't want to watch any Italian TV (more than 20 years later, and I am sticking to that original conclusion). I had watched a lot while in the UK, an outcome of having a girlfriend a two hour flight away. I wanted to reduce, and I was confident I could…

But it wasn't long before we were having a massive satellite dish installed. Taking up half the balcony, it was surely tracking deep space satellites, and not merely those in orbit. It felt like reconnecting. It had a number of channels like Sky One, with perfectly clear audio, but encrypted visuals. If I felt homesick, I could listen to new episodes of *Star Trek* and *The Simpsons*. And it had radio channels. One day it announced Cinerama featuring David Gedge from The Wedding Present would be doing a radio session. At this point, I had not heard any Cinerama. It was a stunning session – 'Comedienne', 'Honey Rider', 'You Turn Me On' and 'Maniac'. I may be the first person to record a Cinerama session off the radio using a VHS cassette.

On my next trip back to the UK, I bought the album *Va Va Voom*. To me, it's a wonderful unexpected change of direction, extremely consistent body of work, and I can never skip a track. Listening to it takes me back to 1998 instantly, and the challenges and excitement of such a life-changing event.

And when I made that stupid oath…

MY FAVOURITE DRESS

SHAUN CHARMAN, FORMER WEDDING PRESENT DRUMMER

My favourite Wedding Present song is quite an obvious one really, 'My Favourite Dress'. I remember when David first played it to us, it seemed like a real step up. It evolved quite a lot, originally having a different beginning, but it always stood out. We actually saved it as a single almost like a trump card, but played it on a couple of different radio sessions.

From the period after I left it's probably 'Kennedy'. Brilliantly simple, and in a way the culmination of the early sound we were heading towards. A proper Indie floor-filler as well, rather than the very early stuff which tended to empty it! Years later, people would do their 'too much apple pie' impersonations, the funniest being on one occasion in a Brighton pub, when I spun David round to introduce him to the person doing it. I'm not sure if David had heard, but the face on the bloke was brilliant! It's a great song.

SILVER SHORTS

GARY FUTCHER

1992 was a big year. Not only were Kate and I going to get married in May but The Wedding Present were going to release a single a month! Back then we both worked in Cheltenham and, because I had something of a vinyl habit, Kate was in charge of my cards. This was to ensure I couldn't just toddle off to Our Price and secretly add to the collection or, in this case, head to Badlands to pick up the new single each month and then drop in a heap of extra discs.

So it was, then, that on the first Monday of each month Kate would head to Badlands and pick up the next single, with each becoming a background to our wedding preparations. By rights, 'Come Play With Me' should be 'our' tune seeing as it was released in the month of our wedding but it's actually 'Silver Shorts' that has stayed with us. It was on the wedding day mixtape I prepared, has been a constant across 30 years of marriage (I can guarantee it's been played annually on 16 May), it's been bellowed along to by the kids as they've grown, and every time we hear it, it takes us right back to the big day.

'Silver Shorts' was on Gary Futcher's wedding day mixtape after being purchased by wife-to-be Kate

It's just a shame I forgot to take it with me to the reception. We wanted it to be our first dance but the DJ didn't have it and I don't think he had even heard of The Wedding Present. So we had 'Sit Down' by James instead.

FLYING SAUCER

IAN GRICE

The Wedding Present songs have always been about love. Unrequited love, yearning, heartbreak, betrayal. And I love them. Picking one is almost impossible. So I'm basing my choice on two things. The first is how seeing a song performed live elevates it even higher, making me fall in love with a song all over again, reignites my passion for it. And the second thing is friendship.

For these reasons, I'm choosing 'Flying Saucer'. Is it Gedge's finest moment? No. (Although both the *Top Of The Pops* appearance and single sleeve boost its status!) But live, it is simply awesome, right from those first two chords.

I'd always happily attended Wedding Present gigs on my own, but after a spell of attending Cinerama concerts with my mate Steve and a meeting with a large quantity of Scopitones online forum members in Wolverhampton's Wetherspoons before a Wedding Present gig in 2006, there has always been a number of friendly faces at any Wedding Present gig I attend. This song unites us all, makes us raise our arms and smile as we reach out and touch the stars above us.

Thanks to David for bringing us together, and to all the hilarious and kind people with equally wonderful taste in music.

For Ian Grice (left) 'Flying Saucer' has fans reaching out and touching the stars

MY FAVOURITE DRESS

SARAH YOUNG

Two words in this song take me back to being 18. The Wedding Present featured heavily in my student years. Experiencing the joy of live gigs, the new found independence of driving (borrowing Dad's car, driving too fast and playing cassettes very loud), dancing at Poly bops and large posters staring down from the walls of student digs. All of this was shared at the time with my first love.

We had gone away for the weekend camping on the Yorkshire Moors. It was my first trip away with a boyfriend. Over the course of the pub lunch we got into a very deep and emotive conversation. Who knows what it was about? Probably my

Sarah Young is transported back to a pub conversation when she hears the line about 'uneaten meals' in 'My Favourite Dress'

teenage insecurities and his frustration with them.

It doesn't matter where I am now – at a gig, driving the car or cleaning the kitchen. On hearing the line about 'uneaten meals' I am straight back 30 years to that pub with its dark wood furniture, tapestry seat covers, trying to hide my tears from the other diners, with a knot so tight in my stomach that I can't eat the Sunday lunch in front of me.

Oh the joys of first love… This wasn't the end. We had a few more years together before finally entering the working world and going our separate ways. But that was a whole new set of emotions and a Joy Division soundtrack.

NOT FROM WHERE I'M STANDING

RICHARD FARNELL

Richard Farnell thinks 'Not From Where I'm Standing' distils the essence of The Wedding Present into one song

Choosing just one favourite Wedding Present song is obviously a difficult task. I could have gone for 'At The Edge Of The Sea' with its superb melodic bass line or the brooding and atmospheric 'Crawl', or indeed any number of songs from *George Best*, *Bizarro* or *Seamonsters*, which are my favourite Wedding Present albums.

However I'm choosing 'Not From Where I'm Standing', the second song on the *Why Are You Being So Reasonable Now?* EP as I feel this song is a perfect distillation of all those signature Wedding Present elements – the fast, distorted guitar strumming, driving bass, pounding drums and of course those lyrics.

Gedge is on top form here and I think the lyrics here could well be his best, particularly the lines:

And when he tells her it's all lies she's making patterns with her spoon
And when he looks into her eyes she's staring round the room

The song is a perfect kitchen sink drama in miniature where Gedge plays the voyeur, watching a couple arguing in a cafe and remembering that he was in the same predicament 'just seven days ago'. It's a great example of economical story-telling – you can picture the whole scene and make assumptions about the characters' relationship, and also know that the same thing was happening to the narrator recently and will no doubt happen again to some other unlucky couple. In just a few verses a whole drama is played out.

Not only are the lyrics great but the band sound so together on this song – the guitars mesh wonderfully on the bridge at 1:37 with Gedge and Grapper doing that duelling guitars thing they used to excel at. Then it's all over in just two-and-a-half minutes of sheer perfection.

If I could live one day again, that day would be the one

LOVENEST

GAVIN MORGAN

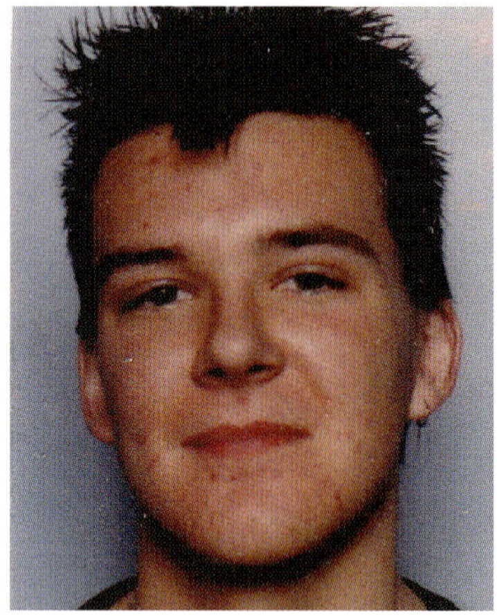

Gavin Morgan was listening to The Wedding Present in the sixth form

My girlfriend when I was in the sixth form… We would often listen to The Wedding Present and would go to gigs together, including the famous gig at the Roadmender in Northampton on the *Bizarro* tour in 1989. Going out in pubs in town over time, I was at a bar one night when I befriended this guy who wanted to talk to me as I looked like I was 'into cool music', or so he said. Anyway, eventually he ingratiated himself into our small social group and all seemed fine.

The relationship with my girlfriend ended when I went to university in the autumn of 1990, although nothing was ever said that it was actually over – it was just a tacit assumption. So we kept in touch and would meet up whenever I went back home.

Over Christmas, when I went home everything was different. Yes, I found out that she had been seeing that guy ('You wouldn't even know him if it hadn't been for me…'). *Seamonsters* hadn't been released yet though. It all came together a few months later, when it was. Alone in my university room, earnestly listening to the album, the lyrics of 'Lovenest' totally resonated with what I was going through. By this time, I was half-heartedly seeing someone else myself but, to be honest, I wasn't really feeling it, and – well, it just wasn't the same.

Then I heard David's vitriol – 'you wouldn't even know him if it hadn't been for me…' I just kept thinking of those words, and playing the track over and over – and yes, it gets worse:

I can't help thinking back to, well, the way we were
And then I start feeling guilty lying next to her
I know and it can't be right
Pretending that it's you
You still won't go away

Devastating. It still destroys me now, 30 years on.

NO NOMINATION
TOMMY DOCHERTY

Glasgow in early 1991. I was working on the night shift and living with Margaret, who didn't really listen to music. One morning she borrowed my Walkman as she went out for a walk along the waterfront to let me go to sleep. When I woke up later, she asked me what she had been listening to. I said, 'The Wedding Present.' She said 'oh' and that was it.

I spent ten days in early February telling her that we were going to spend Valentine's Night at the new Burger King in town, where one of my friends had just started working as the manager.

On the Sunday night we were getting ready to go out and she was not happy. I asked her what was wrong. She said, 'Bloody St Valentine's Day and you're taking me to Burger King. You didn't even get me a card, or flowers or anything.' I said, 'I'm really sorry honey, but I'm on night shift and I don't even know what month it is, never mind what day.' I said 'Look, we'll go into that exclusive new restaurant that's just opened and have a couple of glasses of champagne before we go to the Burger King.' She said, 'OK that's fine, that'll be a wee bit better.'

We went into the exclusive new restaurant and the waitress came over. I said, 'The name's Docherty. We have reserved a table for two.' Margaret was overwhelmed, and we went on to have a great night.

About a week later, she produced two tickets for The Wedding Present at Barrowlands in May that year. She said, 'This is a thank you for St Valentine's Day.' I said, 'So you did like The Wedding Present after all? We'll have a great night.' She said, 'No, I'm not going. You can take your friend. I don't want to listen to that shite.'

KENNEDY
KORDA MARSHALL, A&R, RCA RECORDS

Gedge was fantastic. An amazing artist. We had a lot of fun working together. My favourite song would have to be 'Kennedy' ('too much apple pie') because that was the first single off of *Bizarro*. I remember standing in the marketing meeting and playing the song to a roomful of record executives two weeks before it was coming out so that the whole company could hear it, explaining to everybody how this was a homage to American imperialism and capitalism and being stared at by 30-odd blank-looking RCA record execs who at the time were working with Dollar and Slade.

I fell in love with the sleeve of *George Best*. Their manager at the time was an old friend of mine. The photo of *George Best* was just amazing. It was quite a brave thing to do to put a footballer on the cover of an alternative record, because alternative music at that time was not a place that football fans engaged with, because they were quite different culturally. But I got the album and I thought 'this is really good'. I remember turning up at RCA and saying, 'We've got to sign The Wedding Present.'

I loved Gedge's independence. I loved that he had a female roadie. At the time I wanted to be able to put the needle at any point on a record, listen to eight bars and know within those eight bars exactly who I was listening to. And David's vocal and guitar had an intrinsic sound that was very much them.

I took Steve Albini to Manchester to see them and to get him to produce *Seamonsters*. This was before he'd produced Nirvana. I knew about his recording techniques because of his work with Black Flag, and how he got into real detail about measuring microphone distances from snare drums. He focused on capturing the energy of a performance rather than on the dry recording process. The first time I met him was on the train up to Manchester as he had just flown in from America. We arrived in Manchester and before the gig I took him to where we were staying that night and left him in his hotel room for an hour while I was on the phone. Then I couldn't get him out of his room. He'd discovered that there was a telephone in the bathroom and he'd never seen this before. He sat on the toilet and phoned all his friends to tell them, and I got handed a very large international telephone bill! But I took him to the show and he met the band and he loved them and he ended up doing the record.

David was really ambitious in a very clever way. I first met them when I went to see them somewhere and said, 'Are you going to do a fucking encore?' They said, 'No, they've paid £4, we've worked it out at 80p a song and so they've got their money's worth. We don't like doing encores anyway.' Having been a punk rocker I quite liked that approach, although as an A&R man at a major record label, I should've been sitting there saying, 'You need to do two encores and thank the audience.' I loved their nonchalant 'fuck you' spirit, done in a very pleasant Yorkshire way. And I really loved Pete, the guitarist.

We signed them and it was all hot and buzzy and we got all over the papers. Everyone was really excited that RCA had managed to secure a hot new band which they hadn't been doing for many, many years. And when we signed them, they turned around and said, 'It's all very good, but the first record we want to put out is a Ukrainian folk record.' How do I explain that back to RCA?

Another great story is when I told RCA we were going to release a single every month for twelve months, with an original on the A-side and a cover on the B-side. I remember the chairman of RCA just looking at me, shaking his head and saying, 'Marshall, what the fuck are you doing? You're breaking every rule in the book.' I said, 'I'm just following the band. It's the band's rules and this is exactly what they want to do and that's why we're a great record label.'

It taught me an awful lot about how to work with difficult artists, who are by definition nebulous and circular and have bumps and lumps that you have to fit into the square of a rigid corporate scheduling environment. It was always a balance. David was intelligent, so you could always have a proper conversation with him. In all the years I worked with him, I don't think we ever fell out. It was all very positive.

I don't think there was ever a time when I said 'no' to him, although there were one or two occasions when perhaps I should have. The artwork for *Bizarro* was awful. I couldn't put that on the poster or a billboard or on the back of the bus because it was just a squiggle pencil drawing. Commercially it would have been more sensible to persuade them to have a more brand value, more iconic sleeve. *George Best* was such a bold statement for an album sleeve, with no writing on it. And then they gave me a little orange squiggle for their first album with us. But I chose to back the act, not argue with them.

I took great care to avoid getting into a situation where it was a 'yes or no' conversation. I wanted to act on what we said when we signed them, which is that they would be free to pursue their creativity and their art in any way they wanted to - provided it didn't have a nine-inch erect penis on it or be morally or socially corruptible! As long as it wasn't illegal, I put out anything they wanted to put out. And that's what they did.

The *Seamonsters* album was huge. The *Hit Parade* albums were huge. It was just a huge result to get them on *Top Of The Pops*. And then when they did it, they didn't move. They stood there as if they were mannequins which they thought was a joke. But it wasn't really very funny. With hindsight, I probably regret the things I allowed them to do because they could've been a much, much bigger band had they played the game a little bit. But we loved them for the fact that they didn't want to play the game. They didn't want to do those things marketing-wise or image-wise or brand-wise.

They toured incessantly. And David is just a lovely man. Keith was 'Mister No'. He was the one who didn't want to do things. He didn't really want to sign the record deal.

I'M FROM FURTHER NORTH THAN YOU

SHAUN KEAVENY, BROADCASTER & RADIO PRESENTER

And then you said, 'No, I'm not from the south, I am from further north than you!'

What an audacious and inventive opening line to a song that is! Come to think of it, I can't think of a song that drops you into the middle of what feels like a conversation between lovers picking over the bones of their failed union like that. Well, since the last time David did it, I suppose. It's quintessential Gedge, of course. The monumental and the minutiae cheek-by-jowl.

This is a gorgeous little Fabergé egg of a tune that documents another doomed-yet-delightful dalliance (good name for a song) between fictional Dave and an ultimately unobtainable object of desire. And there's desire in spades. It's a lyric brimming with simmering lust and longing. And again, David shows his universality here, cos we've all yearned after someone totally unsuitable whose very unsuitability is the engine for deep attraction.

You were either drunk or you wanted me
And, you know, either way I wasn't going to disagree

This guy is powerless in the tractor-beam of this temptress! It's a true Feeding of the Five Thousand feat of ingenuity how the author manages to revisit his store of personal romantic experiences, mine them for lyrical inspiration and make it seem fresh every time! Many of us are now years – or decades – past such filthy chapters, but the wonderful thing about this song, and many in the WP canon, is how it takes you right back there, back in time to a moment of uncomplicated horny infatuation.

And when we bought that weird pornography
Yeah, that was a good day

The honesty is really quite a shock in this song! The band are musically on fire here as well. This song is taken off one of the mid-period meisterwerks, *Take Fountain*, and was recorded and mostly conceived in America. There are some real widescreen / Route 66 (well, Interstate 5 actually…) moments on there, but this returns to a form Gedge and Co seem to do almost better than anyone. Succinct romantic reportage set to driving indie guitars.

For fact fans, it turns out Gedge IS from further north than me, by about 30 miles.

KENNEDY
JO PHILLIPS

I once put my kneecap out dancing to this in Bradford.

A MILLION MILES
NICK GOLLEDGE

For me, like every Wedding Present fan, *George Best* was the perfect album at the time and I could relate to this song so clearly. But that's the beauty of that album. We could all relate to it.

HULA DOLL

AMANDA ARUNDEL

David Gedge's music has been the soundtrack of my life since 1988 when I first bought a *Tommy* cassette to impress the cool boys at school. The heady combination of intense guitars and heartfelt lyrics quickly had me way more hooked than the boys I was trying to impress, and the songs' strong female heroines taught me at a nice impressionable age that men are drawn to powerful women.

Bizarro and *Seamonsters* were the albums of my first big love affair, which peaked around the time of the Gorseinon concert in June '91. Then in '96 I discovered that a cute guy at work was a Weddoes fan, which of course made him irresistible. I warned Will that I was going through a wild phase and might be trouble, but he made me a compilation tape with 'Silver Shorts' on. 'I don't care what lies ahead, I just can't get out of your bed' (those words still do it for me...) We listened to *Saturnalia* together, but I resonated with the 'Hula Doll' lyrics: 'You said there's nothing that turns you on more than waking up with someone you've not woken up with before.' Of course, it was only a matter of time before I was telling Will I'd met someone else. He told me he went home and played 'Big Boots' and my inner sociopath was thrilled at the thought of scaring a boy to death.

The story ended exquisitely when Will introduced me to his best friend, Ian, at a Weddoes gig at the Powerhaus in Camden, following which Ian and I secretly went back to his place together. He had a girlfriend, I had a boyfriend, and we both knew Will wouldn't like it – an overwhelming aphrodisiac for us both. Ian played Wedding Present songs as he drove me to the Tube station the next morning and we promised never to say a word to Will.

A few years later I met my husband – sadly not a Wedding Present fan – but I did have a final fleeting indiscretion with a handsome stranger during 'Don't Talk, Just Kiss' at the Shepherds Bush Empire in 2005. I was relieved – and a tiny bit disappointed – that our kiss wasn't caught on film.

I'm now a 46-year-old mum but I only have to play a Wedding Present song and I'm transported back to my twenties and giddy on fun memories. I feel so fortunate that my favourite artist turned out to be one of the most prolific writers and performers of our generation. I've even taken my daughter to a couple of gigs. Thank you, David – my life would have been much poorer without The Wedding Present and Cinerama.

BAY 63
12 Acklam Road, Ladbroke Grove,
London W10. Tel 960 4590
Thursday September 11
THE WEDDING PRESENT
+ CLOSE LOBSTERS
8.00–12.00
£3.00/£2.50
All profits go to
AMNESTY INTERNATIONAL

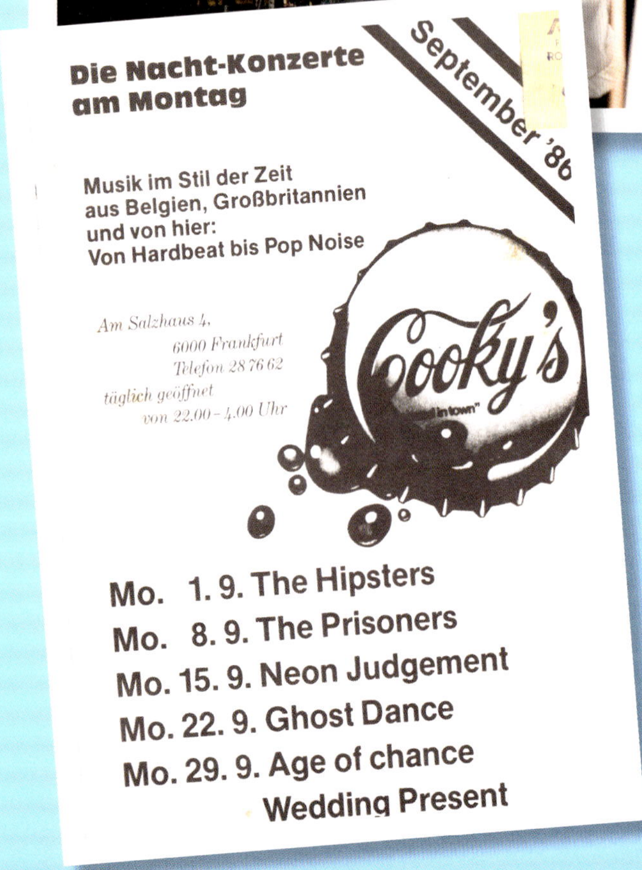
Die Nacht-Konzerte
am Montag
September '86
Musik im Stil der Zeit
aus Belgien, Großbritannien
und von hier:
Von Hardbeat bis Pop Noise
Am Salzhaus 4,
6000 Frankfurt
Telefon 28 76 62
täglich geöffnet
von 22.00 – 4.00 Uhr
Cooky's
Mo. 1. 9. The Hipsters
Mo. 8. 9. The Prisoners
Mo. 15. 9. Neon Judgement
Mo. 22. 9. Ghost Dance
Mo. 29. 9. Age of chance
Wedding Present

THE RETURN OF CAPTAIN AHAB
FORUM ENGER
SAMSTAG 20. SEPT.
The sound of young Leeds
THE WEDDING PRESENT & AGE OF CHANCE
Einlaß 20.30 Uhr
Konzertbeginn 21.30 U
The sound of young Leeds
THE WEDDING PRESENT & AGE OF CHANCE
Forum · 4904 Enger · Spenger Straße 13 · ☎ 45 45

The Wedding Present keep their pop-pretensions hidden under their jumpers and concentrate instead on porn. Every song is a ballerina in a Leeds Utd away strip stood rigid on one toe screaming about "love". Imagine a Brillo-padded Shop Assistants LP played rather loud. The Wedding Present justify their existence by the fact that they are truly "independent" of pop, that they are not just a pop band who are too plain *bad* to get a record contract with an efficient capitalist.

The C86 was neatly divided: pseudo-pop divs and the radical bands. The former are to be treasured, the latter should have their guitars stolen and redistributed.

TENTION!
ATENCIÓN
CHTUNG!
TENZIONE!

B for the / para el / pour le / bis zum

rotta segnalato B

BOARDING CARD
NORTH SEA FERRIES:
HULL — ROTTERDAM

EVENING CHRONICLE, OLDHAM, TUESDAY, AUGUST 12, 1986

Success for Wedding Present

The Wedding Present (left to right): Pete, Keith, Shaun and David.

FAST guitars are very much the order of the day on the independent scene. Gothic synth bands have been replaced by young men splicing plectrums frantically across hard-wearing guitar strings.

Age of Chance, The Close Lobsters, The Soup Dragons, Bogshed — the list is endless.

One band of this new breed with strong local connections is The Wedding Present (left). Although formed in Leeds, two of its members, David Gedge and Pete Solowka, hail from Middleton.

Outing

They put out their first single, "Go Out and Get 'em Boy" on their own Reception Records label a year ago. Success was immediate with plenty of airings on night-time Radio One and interviews in the music weeklies.

The follow-up "Once More", also climbed high in

TWO LOCAL BOYS IN GROUP

the indie chart and now their third vinyl outing, "You Should Always Keep In Touch With Your Friends" looks like doing the same.

The group have several refreshing ideals. Their songs are rarely more than three minutes long, sets are kept as short as possible and they have no plans to record an album.

Says singer Dave: "I am a great believer in the strength of songs. I have always said I would like us to do four great singles and then pack in. You do not need to make a boxed set of records to make a point."

Standard

Their latest offering is up to the previous high standard. The guitars chop in all the right places and Dave makes his plea for eternal comradeship earnestly and tunefully.

Reference points like Orange Juice, The Jam and even fellow-Middletonians The Chameleons are often quoted. But The Wedding Present's affable mixture of noise, energy and melody should be allowed to stand alone.

You seem to have more than a passing interest in Science Fiction eg. Thunderbirds T-shirts, low budget SF films,and an almost indecent obsession with William Shatner.Are you simply frustated astronauts forced to be popstars to make a living,or is Science Fiction important to you?

DAVID :"It's my life!"

THE WEDDING PRESENT, who have a Peel Session coming out on Strange Fruit, are touring at Liverpool Polytechnic November 1, City Of London Polytechnic 4, Mile End Queen Mary College 5, Middlesex Polytechnic 6, Newcastle Riverside 10, Nottingham Garage 13, Birmingham Polytechnic 14, Sheffield Polytechnic 19, Manchester International 20, Dudley JB's 21, Hampstead Westfield College 26, North Kensington Bay 63 27, Woolwich Thames Polytechnic 28, Brighton Escape Club 30.

Far be it for us to promote a slanging match between these two major forces in the pop world!So how important is it that the new single - "This Boy Can Wait" - is successful,and how do you judge success in terms ofthe single?

SHAUN :"As important as the others,that's all.I think singles should always be approached as though they are the first one (something I'm not sure we've done this time though but you've got to try.)"

KEITH :"I presume we all have different ideas of the meaning of success.Our record is a success in my view because I like it."

DAVID :"It's irrelevant.If the single flops a lot of things would become more clear cut."

GRAPPER:"A successful single is as imprtant as a successful season for Leeds United."

mann die Früchte der zweiten Hälfte seiner Noisepop-Tournee durch Nordengland. Eine Fülle von Fakten und Facetten erwartet den interessierten Leser.

NORDENGLAND 2

14 Songs und ein Tip-Kick-Se

In ds schmoren die legitimen Nachfahren einer immer noch unvergessenen Band. Einer Freude für alle, die gerne zusehen, wie einer Gitarre vor Freude alle Seiten reißen.

WEDDING PRESENT

And The Wedding Present? The new kings of speed (janglipop outboard-motored to illogical, breathless conclusions) or gormless black puddings, flat caps hiding flatter heads? I've always gone for the former and this quartet – the holy war fanaticism of 'What Becomes Of The Brokenhearted', 'You Should Always Keep In Touch With Your Friends' and 'This Boy Can Wait', plus the steely *never* of 'Felicity' (Orange Juice slopped through a blender) – stiffens that faith.

' DANNY KELLY

– When you play a song and you're singing words that you've written, is it kind of like an exorcism of the feelings expressed in the song? Does it help?

D: No, it doesn't help me. Quite the opposite in fact, I'm quite embarrassed. Everyone says, I don't know if you know, but we've got a song called 'My Favourite Dress' which people say is the best lyrics I've written, and all this, but for ages I was actually quite embarrassed, it is quite a personal song.

Not so lucky with their latest single were Leeds popsters **The Wedding Present** – dab hands at dealing with ICA hecklers on Wednesday night. All the initial seven-inch copies of their latest single 'You Always Keep In Touch' have been pressed with the same song on both sides! Those miffed at missing out on the C86 gem 'This Boy Can Wait' can either get an exchange at their local shop or contact Red Rhino at Fetter Lane in York.

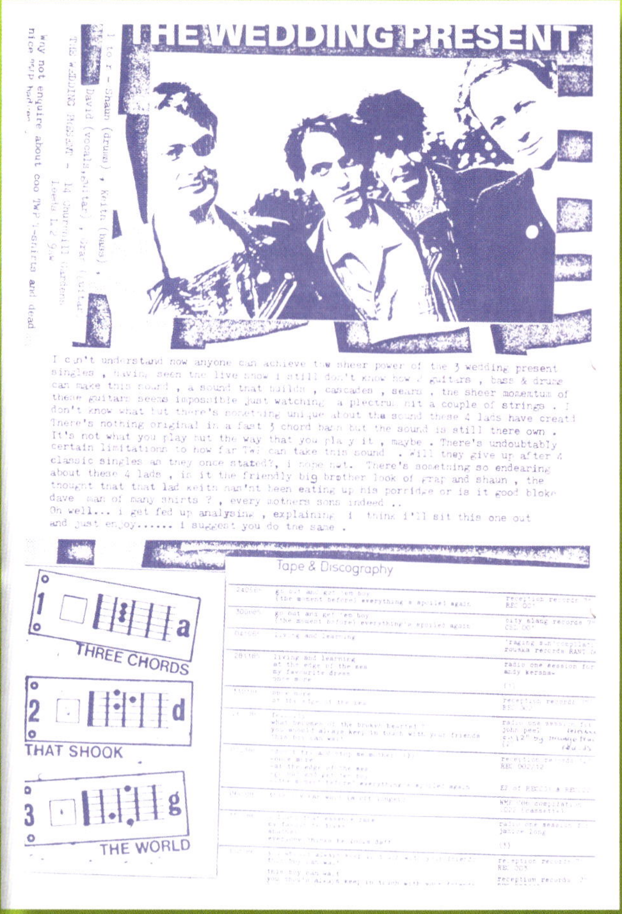

Now, with the spanner removed and the proper B-side, This Boy Can Wait, in place, the single has sold more than 6,000 and been at number three in the NME independent chart for over a month, behind The Mission and The Smiths.

- - - - "Once More" released - - - - - - - - - -

29th January:Preston "Twang Clubbe"
no other band -2 encores- (good though snowing before journey!)(R)
4th February:Leeds "University Riley Smith Hall"
supp. Alan Vega (surprise gig-last minute replacement for Win-boring)(R)
6th February:Bristol "Tropic Club"
supp. by The Flatmates (very good-punk rock!)-2 encores- (R)
7th February:London "Queen Mary College"
supp. The Mighty Lemon Drops (R) (O.K.-nothing special)
8th February:London Chalk Farm "Enterprise"
supp.by Mc.Carthy -encore- (packed but didn't play well)
25th February:Leeds "University Tartan Bar"
supp.by The First International and The Enormous Room (R)(awful)
2nd March:Lancaster "Gregson Centre"
only band -2 encores- (excellent)
13th March:Nottingham "Garage"
supp.by Legendary Dolphins and The Fairground (terrible)
14th March:York "Winning Post"
only band - 2 encores - (very good and sold out)
23rd March:Manchester "Boardwalk"
supp.by The Monkey Run -2 encores-(R)(got going)
24th March:Leeds "Ritzy"
supp.The Shop Assistants.supp.by The Passmore Sisters (R)-encore-(great)
26th March:London "Timebox"("Bull and Gate" Kentish Town)
supp.Big Flame.s.b.Pig Bros.,Noseflutes,The Legend!(O.K.)Mike-gtr.(R)
28th March:London Fulham "Greyhound"
supp.by The Clinch (R)-encore-(OK-home of pub rock!)
29th March:London Chalk Farm "Enterprise"
supp.by The Close Lobsters (R)(encore)(half empty-mix up about advertising)
1st April:Dundee "Tindalls"
supp.by This Poison -2 encores-(free gig-but still not many there)Mike-bass
2nd April:Edinburgh "Rumours"
supp.by This Poison -encore-(R)(strange ½ trendy ½ regulars audience)(M.-b
3rd April:Glasgow "Rooftops"
supp.by BMX Bandits (not very good-disinterested audience)-encore-(shouldn't have don
(Mike-bass)
4th April:Perth "The Plough"
supp.by This Poison -3 encores-(R)(brilliant)Mike-bass
10th April:Bradford "1 in 12 club"(Queens Hall)
supp.by Third Circle (boring-people at the back asked those at front to sit down!)
16th April:London "Walthamstow Town Hall"
supp.Half Man Half Biscuit.s.b.A Witness,Gone To Earth(big place,no time for encore)
24th April:Manchester Middleton "Litchfields"
supp.by ?? (strange-off usual circuit for David and Pete's home town gig)
25th April:Leeds "Royal Park"
supp.by The Right Stuff -encore-good(R)
1st May:Leeds squat gig Cookridge Street
Lots of other bands(R)(Dancing but not clapping!)
7th May:Huddersfield "Polytechnic"
supp.That Petrol Emotion -encore-(good)Mike-bass
10th June:London "Dingwalls"
supp.by ?? (V)Mike-gt
12th June:Bristol "Tropic Club"
supp.by The Elephant
17th June:Sheffield "Leadmill"
with Age Of Chance,Pi
18th June:London "Timebox"(Bull and C
supp.by Mighty Mighty
19th June:London "The Cricketers"
only band-encore-(goc
24th June:Leeds "Ritzy"
supp.James,The Bodine
25th June:Hull "University"
supp.Amazulu.s.b.Vict

28th June:Manchester "The Boardwalk"
supp.by Food Scientists,That Ted -2 encores- good and venue full
17th July:Bedford "George And Dragon" (N.B. 11th July - "This Boy Can Wait" released RECOO2)
co-headline with Age Of Chance(we played first)-encore-very good
18th July:Lowestoft "Kellys"
co-headline with Age Of Chance(we played second)-encore-good but large empty venue
22nd July:Brighton "Escape Club"
co-headline with Age Of Chance(we played second)-2 encores-excellent and full
23rd July:London "I.C.A."(N.M.E.C86 Rock Week)
supp.Primal Scream,s.b.The Servants-2 encores-(R)-brilliant big gig
24th July:London "Fulham Greyhound"
s.b.Chris Ford & The Conversation-2 encores-found out about gig the day before
played badly-agency mistake
26th July:Stockton-on-Tees "Dovecote Arts Centre"
supp.by Icy Eye-2 encores-(R) very good-hotel included!
29th July:Lichfield "Enots Social Club"
only band-2 encores-not many there but good
1st August:Edinburgh "Hootchie Cootchie Club"
supp.by B.M.X.Bastards-encore-we were noticably bored(R)
2nd August:Aberdeen "Venue"
co-headline with 23 Flight Rockers(we played first)-encore-OK,bad P.A.(R)
3rd August:Glasgow "Daddy Warbucks"
supp.by ?? -O.K.(R)
27th August:Halifax "Piece Hall"open air festival
supp.Shop Assistants,Ghost Dance.s.b.Excalibur,Pop Will Eat Itself,Psycho-Surgeons,Rose Of Avalanche.Mike-gtr.time meant we could play only 5 songs
11th September:London "Bay 63"
supp.by Close Lobsters-2 encores-(R)very good
17th September:Amsterdam,HOLLAND "Melkweg"
only band-Mike-bass.(R)-encore-not particularily good
18th September:Breda,HOLLAND "Para"
supp.by.Automatic Replay(R)Mike-bass-terrible-complaints about shortness of set
19th September:Oberhausen,WEST GERMANY "Old Daddy"
co-H.with Age Of Chance(we played 2nd)-2 encores-Mike-bass-(V)-good
20th September:Enger,WEST GERMANY "Forum Enger"
co-H.w.Age Of Chance(we played 2nd)-2 encores-Mike-bass-(V)-very good(& fast
22nd September:Hamburg,WEST GERMANY "Logo"
co.H.w.Age Of Chance(we played 2nd)-3 encores-Mike-bass-very strange
24th September:West-Berlin,WEST GERMANY "Loft"
co-H.w.Age Of Chance(we played 1st)-encore-Mike-bass(R)champagne but gig only O.K.
25th September:[illegible]-Hofstetten,WEST GERMANY "Treffpunkt E"
co-H.w.Age Of Chance(we played 2nd)-4 encores-bad PA,good gig.Mike-bass
26th September:Fribourg,SWITZERLAND "Fri-Son"
supp.Ghost Dance,s.b.Age Of Chance-Mike-bass-terrible
27th September:Schwindkirschen,WEST GERMANY "Rockhouse"
co-H.w.Age Of Chance(we played 2nd)-encore-Mike-bass-punk rock!
29th September:Frankfurt am Main,WEST GERMANY "Cookys"
co-H.w.Age Of Chance(we played 1st)-encore-Mike-bass-quite good
10th October:Exeter "Exeter and Devon Arts Centre"
only band-Mike-bass-encore(R)few people there,OK.(s.b.Porky The Poet)
11th October:Ilfracombe "Carousel Bar"
supp.by ?? and Porky The Poet..Mike-gtr,Sara-bass.partly 3 piece-encore-stran
13th October:Leeds "Trades Club"
supp.by Johnny Jumps The Bandwagon,Agit Rosta.badly advertised and attended
17th October:Rijswijk,HOLLAND "Het Festival"(venue unknown)
supp.Three Johns,I've Got The Bullets.s.b.Koolskool.very strange!
24th October:London "I.C.A."
supp.The Mighty Lemon Drops,[illegible]-encore-good
[illegible] "[illegible]"
supp.by Dr.Poodle,Dr.??.(R)-encore-O.K.

130

6th November:London "Middlesex Poly All Saints"
only band-2 encores-(better than previous two but still not many there)
8th November:Bangor "North Wales University"
supp.by The Wild Swans(not known band of that name)(lots there but not for us!)
10th November:Newcastle "Riverside"
supp.by The Rubber Men-2 encores-O.K.
11th November:Middlesborough "The Outlook"
only band-a disaster,hardly anyone there.
13th November:Nottingham "The Garage"
supp.by Pop Will Eat Itself,Danny's Boys-2 encores-(good)
14th November:Birmingham "Polytechnic"
supp.by The Dubious Brothers-encore-(R)-good,lots there,some for us!
19th November:Sheffield "City Poly Totley Hall"
only band-encore-(big place,empty even with reasonable turnout)
20th November:Manchester "The International"
supp.by Blyth Power-2 encores-(people only woke up at the end!)
21st November:Dudley "J.B's"
only band-(O.K.-nothing special,disintegrating drum-kit)
25th November:Reading "University"
supp.by The Bridge and others??-encore-quite good
26th November:London "Westfield College"
supp.by Blyth Power,The Bridge-(awful,few there)
27th November:London "Bay 63"
supp.by Tallulah Gosh,The Shamen,The Waltones-3 encores-(excellent)
28th November:London "Thames Polytechnic"
supp.by Long Lost Sons,??-GIG NO.100-(encore given but thrown glass stopped us playing it)
30th November:Brighton "Escape Club"
supp.by 15 Looks,Dragnet-(R)-(awful,apathetic atmosphere)
4th December:Paris,FRANCE "Rex Club" (V)
supp.Mome Rath(French band)(R)-Mike-bass-encore-(Played badly,technically unlucky)
5th December:Tours,FRANCE "Forum 18"
only band-Mike-bass-2 encores-(R)excellent
6th December:Groningen,HOLLAND "Simplon"
only band-Mike-bass-absolutely crap,complaints about length of our set
7th December:Horst,nr.Venlo,HOLLAND "Zoko"
only band-Mike-bass-4 encores-(R)-excellent,played for 1 hour 5 mins!

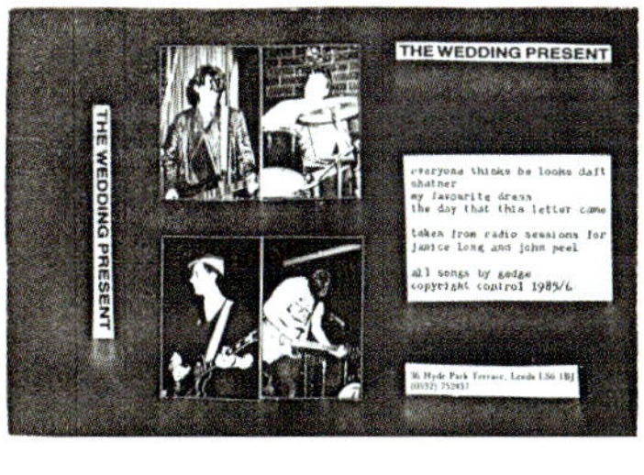

ECEMBRE

APRES LA SEBALE, L'IGUANE, LE MIC MAC MOCHE:

LES NUITS SANS GEORGES

en concert a 23h30

THE WEDDING PRESENT

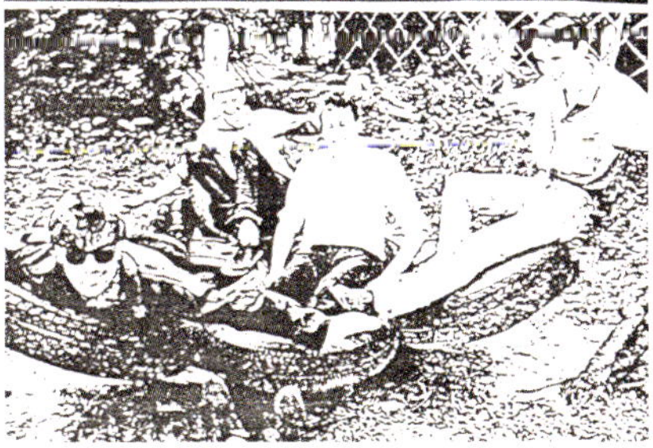

JUST a word to those Wedding Present chappies. Thanks for the lift following the Canterbury gig. We had to walk 15 miles from Chatham but it was a darn sight nearer than the 40 from Canterbury. *(And even nearer than if they'd dropped you off in Spain – Backlash Ed.)* Hope the conversation wasn't too objectionable. Sometimes I say the most stupid things, but I usually have a point. Anyway, fine gig and thoroughly appreciated hospitality. Perhaps I'll see you back in Manchester; sometimes I think I'd like to live back there too.

THE LEGEND!

AVOID THOSE PARTY PIT FALLS!

THE WEDDING PRESENT

THE WEDDING PRESENT are dull, drab. YAY! in the LAW!

... is gradually ... - there are ... records you simply CAN'T play below FULL volume; Husker Du, Laughing Clowns, RAMONES!!!, Saints, Membranes, Ut, WEDDING PRESENT! .... a select few, to be sure, and a power not to be abused lightly (for example, only in cases of extreme emergency do Nina Simone, Otis Redding, Tom Waits (never!), Soup Dragons get the full treatment - the aim is to distort, to blank the rest of the world out - as if, by turning up the sound as much as you can (not that loud!), you could. Some hope!) ... I mean, look at the Wedding Present, puritans all - a maximum distortion unit. Imagine.

That glorious instant when all the guitars come rushing in on 'Once More' (or even 'Favourite Dress' - but that is besides the point; it's the tremulous tentative nervous vocalising I love that song for, the guitars, the melody, the LOUDNESS) and the whole noise is one feverish distortion pitch, feeding back out of your mono, a continuous epileptic whine of abrasive trebled guitar sounds, screaming striving vocals ... the key word, as they say, for today is FRUSTRATION!!!

Frustration at not being heard, frustration at nothing going the way you want it to ("I want everything and I want it now"), frustration at the way nobody seems to care, frustration at not being able to articulate as well as you'd like to be able to, frustration at the way everything that is extreme is passed over for anything that is safe, bland and boring (Compromise - it's the only way to get on) (SHIT HERE'S THE FUCKING RAMONES AGAIN - EXCUSE ME A MOMENT, I REALLY CAN'T TYPE WHILST THEY'RE ON), frustration at your own inability, frustration at what you don't know, just EVERYTHING!

Adrenalin pumping through your veins (god, how macho - sorry, Legend! hasn't really gotten into bombing innocent Libyans recently, honest!), feet that refuse to keep from moving; this is the Wedding Present I'm telling ya!

The nearest thing to the mighty Mem's in years (lest that be the geniously ironic over-the-top Janitors (fuck tunes, let's dance!) at the Bull and Gate), anger FRUSTRATION yearning SPEED KILLS BUT SLOWDOM'S BOREDOM joy hope desire need - TUNES TUNES TUNES.

A scream of anger's fine by me, but if you can sing along to it it's even better! Whistle, you basterds, whistle! If you've no one to care for, why not care for INTELLIGENCE! PASSION! HONESTY! INSPIRATION! ???? YEAH! YEAH! Ye-hah!

SINGLE OF THE WEEK

THE WEDDING Present touch wood

THE WEDDING PRESENT 'My Favourite Dress' (Reception) It doesn't take a genius to work out that 1987 is going to be a year when Leeds scoops up all the awards for furthering mankind through the development of impulsive, brilliant records.

Age Of Chance's close proximity to Manchester moguls The Smiths at the top of Peel's Festive 50 was the most obvious sign, but whittling away at the nether regions of the chart were The Wedding Present. Their four songs – 'Once More' (number 16), 'This Boy Can Wait' (18), 'You Should Always Keep In Touch' (28), and a cover of Orange Juice's 'Felicity' (36) – made them the third most popular group in the chart, only beaten by The Fall and The Smiths.

'My Favourite Dress' provides little ammunition for the weapons of criticism. Although producer Chris Allison could be accused of scraping a little from the edges, the three songs (on the 12-inch) still carve a straight line between commerciality and credibility. 'My Favourite Dress' itself is a song that captures all the emotions and images that crush your lungs when you see someone a month after they've chucked you. (I imagine that if played near a poster of George Michael, it would cause the corners to curl as the paper spontaneously combusted.)

On the flipside, 'Every Mother's Son' tries to make amends for man's reluctance to see woman as anything other than the weaker vessel (I'll have W please, Bob), and 'Never Said' takes another ride along the road of the wrecked relationship. *"Sometimes these words just don't have to be said."* Time for another shot of this melancholy on the rocks.

15th May Friday

Doors 7·30pm.

NEAREST TUBES: GOODGE STREET. TOTTENHAM COURT ROAD RUSSELL SQUARE & EUSTON SQUARE

MALET STREET WC1

TELEPHONE: 580 9551

ULU: 580 9551 · PREMIER: 240 0771 LTB: 439 3371 · RHYTHM RECORDS · ROUGH TRADE RECORDS · ROCK ON RECORDS

UNIVERSITY OF LONDON UNION

THE

WEDDING PRESENT

TALULAH GOSH **THE WIGS**

NORTH OF CORNWALLIS

Tickets: £4 in adv £4.50 on the doors.

ULU ENTERTAINMENTS

SPONSORED BY NATIONAL WESTMINSTER BANK

DNA ENTERTAINMENTS PRESENTS:-

THE

Wedding Present

PLUS SPECIAL GUESTS
APPEARING ON SATURDAY 2nd MAY '87
AT TRENT POLY STUDENTS UNION

Tickets £3.00 adv

Doors 8.00pm

No cameras, tape recorders, bottles

№ 0564

■ **THE SMITHS, The Fall, Billy Bragg** and **The Wedding Present** have all donated memorabilia for an auction to be held at Lancaster University on May 8. The event is being held to raise money so the university can fund a black South African student to follow a degree course at Lancaster, something they maintain could not happen in South Africa under apartheid

---

SUN SPOT

OLD soldier David Gedge, 64, of Buckenham, Norfolk, is still using his army razor issued on call-up in June, 1942.

RAZOR CUTS

At last! The real reason for Peelie's recent absence from wonderful Radio One! But from whence the Knighthood, John? And is it the first for undying regal service to indie-pop?

And another stubbly veteran of the hip-hop and indie wars is the old soldier David Gedge of The Wedding Pressies, judging from *The Sun* cutting (far left). June 1942 also happens to be the date of the first ever John Peel Session featuring Vera Lynn's little-heard version of The Tiddley Widdley's classic 'I Lost My Pastels Badge In The Blitz'.

■ DAVID GEDGE, lead vocalist with The Wedding Present, was recently reduced to tears as his brand new £150 leather jacket – "it cost more than the rest of my clothes put together" – was burnt to snivelling cinder whilst watching glorious fatsos Three Johns. Gedge had smelt the offensive stench of burning leather but failed to n[illegible] the billowing pillars of black sm[illegible] churning from the sleeve of his jacket. That will teach these Indie gods not to get ideas above their station by purchasing parts of the hard rock uniform.

THE WEDDING PRESENT, whose single 'My Favourite Dress' has just finished a stint in the indie charts, have announced a British tour later this month. The band play Stirling University April 23, Strathclyde University 24, Northampton Five Bells 30, Trent Polytechnic May 2, Leicester Polytechnic 5, Lancaster University 7, Liverpool University 9, Sheffield University 11, Port Talbot Raffles 14, University of London Student Union 15, Canterbury Kent University 16.

WHAT HAVE I SAID NOW?
GORDON REEDER

I've been a fan since 1990. A friend brought *Bizarro* home from boarding school in the UK. And I loved 'What Have I Said Now?' The Wedding Present are big here – the guy at the grocery store told me how much he liked them. But I've never seen them. Fucking Iowa.

KENNEDY
JASON BLAKE

Jason Blake designed the original 'Ding Ding Dink' t-shirt

I got into The Wedding Present in late '89, early '90 with 'Kennedy' and 'Brassneck'. Those tracks drew me to the album *Bizarro* and beyond with 'Nobody's Twisting Your Arm' and of course *George Best*. There were so many songs that resonated with me; I'd just turned 19, left home for college, and unfortunately had a terrible car accident where I suffered a head injury – far worse than was known at the time, followed by an inevitable and tough break up. David Gedge's music, his lyrics really grounded me and carried me through.

During a Wedding Present gig in late '90, I started talking to someone on the t-shirt stand and simply said, 'I'm a graphic designer and would love to create a t-shirt.' I gave them my number and soon after Keith Gregory got in touch with me. I had a chat with him on the phone and told him one of my ideas, which was the 'ding, ding, dink' t-shirt. It was a fun phrase I would use when regularly going to a club in Leicester called Sector 5. I'd call the DJ 'Deej' and rather than say, 'Can you play 'Kennedy'?', I would drunkenly, and somewhat over-enthusiastically ask him to play 'ding, ding, dink', he'd always happily nod.

Keith had said 'let's meet', so in a pub in Leeds I was so pleased when he said, 'I really love this.' I'd created the lettering by hand carving into linoleum blocks. Using black gouache paint, I individually impressed the blocks onto white paper, including the 'rose', and 'The Wedding Present' as an option for the front, then mounted them all onto foam board. By the time the t-shirt came out, it was late '91. I went along to the gig at Derby in February '92 with friends that Keith was kind enough to send me free tickets and backstage passes for. I met David at that point – it was a brilliant night.

Over the years I've seen The Wedding Present in concert many times. At Northampton Roadmender in December 2019 I saw David was on the merch stand and started talking to him. I think he thought I was just asking for the t-shirt to be reprinted. It didn't quite register that I was the person who had designed it. I went on to send an email to the band and received one back from Jessica saying 'yes we'd love to do them again'. They've had a number of classic t-shirts reprinted so there's every chance, and it would be great to use the original artwork rather than a recreation. So I've transferred the design from the traditional prints to digital format and sent over a visual… fingers crossed!

Whilst they were doing *At The Edge Of The Sofa* in 2020, David and Melanie were having a conversation when a bell went off in the background and Melanie said 'ding, ding, dink'. That made me laugh. I thought it was brilliant that, 30 years later, they still reference it. If I look back on my career as a graphic designer, that's one of the things I'm most proud of. In fact, it's the only piece I have framed on the wall.

DALLIANCE
RICHARD MORRIS

I remember where I was on 9/11, when John Lennon was shot and when Lady Di died. And when I heard 'Dalliance'!

BLUE EYES
DAVID PASCOE

On my first couple of listens to 'Blue Eyes', I had the song going on to the mixtape for only one reason, namely David Gedge's Kermit the Frog impression on the third line of each verse, 'Oh it's been agesssss!' Almost uncanny really. But then one line pierced through and made me regard the track and The Wedding Present with a lot more admiration. The line in question comes in the second half of the song:

I just want you near
I don't have to own you...

Why so important to me? Well, I'm involved in amateur dramatics. Every time I've done a show, the realisation usually escapes me at the time, but is nevertheless true, that I am becoming part of a collective. I will be seeing fellow cast members, director, tech crew for anywhere between four to six hours a week. I will laugh with them, support them, pretend to be something I'm not (within the play), drink with them. They will essentially become my social life and when a play is really going well, and the atmosphere within it is sparkling, they can become like another mini-family. And then, after what seems like ages (or even 'agesssss') but is usually a blink of the eye, it's the last night and everyone is talking about what they're going to do next – either within the context of the drama world or in their life. Each show is unique and the chance of that exact group of people working together and sharing an experience together exclusively again is non-existent. Someone will be going travelling, someone else has work piling up ahead of them, someone has done their one show for the year and needs to get back to helping their spouse with the child minding, the young talented one is off up country to study drama at university and someone else is just passing through – 'I've enjoyed it, maybe I'll come back but I've got a few things to sort out in my life first.'

This is part of the amateur dramatics world and most of the time it's fine – I'm looking forward to moving on to the next play or putting my feet up for a couple of months (delete as applicable), but every so often, I'll do a show and someone – well not someone, but a woman – will be in it whose presence, energy and company will shine on me so brightly, that the thought of not being able to see them when the show has finished, if they have indicated that they're not going to be around for a while at least, fills me with gloom, melancholy and a tremendous bout of coughing – which has always been the poker like tell with me that shows something has worried or unnerved me.

Suddenly, the Sunday night that follows the last night of a play doesn't seem like a welcome chance to relax and unwind after the rigours of eight weeks (or longer) of rehearsals, but rather the gateway to a bleak and barren wilderness. The wilderness of one's own life which has been illuminated and made anew by the presence of whichever woman happens to have sparkled enough to catch my attention. In the days before I got married, I would try to allay this by approaching the girl in question and asking them out. Surprisingly, this worked each time I actually did it, except for those occasions when the girl got a whiff of the fact I might be interested in them and responded with a froideur that crushed all the feelings I may have had. Invariably, it didn't work out long term with the ones I did go out with off the back of a show but it meant that I at least got the feelings out of my system, and that was crucial because the thing I feared most was having to carry the maelstrom of emotion around with me in case equilibrium was never restored.

These days when I become beguiled, I go through all the angst of my youth, but at least experience has taught me that things will right themselves in the end. Social media helps obviously when it comes to maintaining contact but the perspective that comes with age does too. Nevertheless, the journey to get back to that level of inner peace remains just as cough-filled as ever.

In each case, my thought process is always the same: 'If I can't have you in my life, then at least be around my life, at least until I get my sense of balance back after you knocked me off my axis.' In pithier terms 'Let me be near you, if I can't be with you.' David Gedge and The Wedding Present understood that emotion better than anyone outside of Edwyn Collins. In 'Blue Eyes', Gedge captured the exquisite awfulness of emotional desire. Note the word 'emotional' before desire, because that is a defining characteristic of these show-related beguilements. It's never about lust or sexual desire in these situations. The women in question may look beautiful, but it's not the looks that draw you in, it's everything else: the intelligence, the ease of conversation, the shared sense of humour, the energy which recharges you just by being around it – all these things and more. If it slips out of your orbit, everything will go grey and lifeless again, especially my soul and the joie de vivre you've inspired. Ninety-nine per cent of the time these fears turn out to be groundless, but Gedge wrote about the one per cent, albeit from the perspective of someone who had genuinely loved and shared times with those he addressed the songs to.

Gedge is the only one I could trust to interpret those emotions. Morrissey may have felt them but would be too wrapped up in himself to suggest that they were anything you might be feeling. Mark E Smith would tell you not to be so bloody stupid and get a drink inside you. Gedge was Everyman and, regardless of how silly his voice sounded, he knew what we wanted of those we were powerless to influence, because he was as powerless as us. And yet, by writing songs like 'Blue Eyes', he empowered our ability to make sense of our feelings and begin the journey back to equilibrium.

KENNEDY
SIMON BAILEY

Sorry to be obvious but 'Kennedy' would have to be my pick. Not only was it the song that projected itself from the *John Peel Show* straight into my ears and taught

Simon Bailey made an 'obvious' choice with 'Kennedy'

me the ways of the Gedge, but I also had the pleasure of using it in a school musical a few years later. I wrote and directed an '80s jukebox musical and – whilst most parents were fine nodding their heads appreciatively to 'Temptation', 'You Spin Me Round' and 'Me And The Farmer' – most were somewhat baffled to hear the thrashing guitars of The Wedding Present. Particularly as the scene involved their beloved offspring charging from pub to pub in a determined effort to get as drunk as possible. A perfect soundtrack to the scene. Good times.

ONCE MORE
MARK CARROLL

I first remember hearing The Wedding Present on a compilation LP, *A Different Kind Of Tension*, in 1986 or '87. The featured track was 'Once More', which has always been a favourite ever since. And if I ever want to trump anyone with 'favourite Wedding Present track', I will always bring this one up. I took a tape copy of this compilation and The Smiths' *The Queen Is Dead* on a trip to Settle in Cumbria around that time. My then wife and I were on a trial separation sort of thing, separate holidays. I took the train to do some reading, listening and thinking. She went to Scotland with her new boyfriend. Ha! It was a rather desultory holiday, and listening to The Smiths probably didn't help, but the *Different Kind Of Tension* LP I really did find upbeat, and gave me back an interest in music.

MY FAVOURITE DRESS
MARK CHARLTON

Cassettes – remember them? We can talk about the romance of vinyl, the LP buying experience, the artwork on the sleeve and the beautiful crackle as the needle hit the record, but in reality a C90 filled with a mix of Indie sounds was simply, for a time, the best thing in the world. The age of Spotify, Apple Music and YouTube, where you can find a so-called musical rarity in seconds or pre-order a download before the band has even written the song, makes me very glad I grew up in a different time.

When I discovered music, the only technology involved was a tape recorder and my finger as I tried to stop recording before a Radio 1 DJ interrupted the song at the end with a nasally glib comment. Some people reading this might not be old enough to understand what I'm talking about. Many others will. Those who do grew up at a time where obtaining music was something of a challenge. You could blow all your pocket money on an LP that turned out to be utter rubbish, accidentally fall in with a boy band fad at school that was, looking back, a dreadful idea, or hear a song by chance that would change everything.

In the summer of 1987, hanging around with a gang of lads I'd just met, lounging around in someone's parents' house I didn't know, someone pulled out a C90 mixtape. The last track was 'My Favourite Dress' by The Wedding Present. Without wanting to sound like those cliched talking heads on a BBC4 rockumentary, I can't find anything better to chronicle the moment than saying: it blew me away. If the guitar riff at the start wasn't enough, the following four minutes of angst, pain and expressed disappointment delivered by David Gedge's broken-hearted angry voice lit a beacon to guide me in my confused adolescent years.

I was nearly 15-years-old and almost six feet tall with NHS glasses. My acne made my face so red I could stop traffic, and when it came to dates, I'd been stood up more times than a three-legged chair. The sentiment of 'My Favourite Dress' struck a massive chord with me. You have to put this in the context of its, and of course my, time. I grew up in the East Midlands in the 1980s. Life was largely disappointment. We had Thatcher in Westminster dictating our lives; in fact, police officers would catch buses from outside my house to travel to Yorkshire during the miners' strike. It felt like there were bad times and less bad times.

Don't get me wrong – my mum and dad were great, no complaints there. Yet everyone around me, or their parents at least, seemed to be reaching upwards. Better car, bigger house, exotic holiday, a grander salary to brag about. Everyone was so aspirational yet the reality, I felt, was actually very different. Looking back, the mainstream media and music were selling escapism. Our clothes needed big labels, anyone could be a millionaire so we all had to try, and the music on the radio was, from where I was listening, pampered men wooing supermodels or women giving men the reasons why they couldn't be their lover, or imposing a set of conditions that would, if achieved, make you that appropriate lover.

'My Favourite Dress' spoke to me on many levels. I had not sustained a meaningful relationship beyond a few weeks. When I saw a photo of The Wedding Present in the *NME* or *Melody Maker*, they dressed like me – t-shirt, jumper, jeans and boots. I bought the album *George Best*. It had a photo of George Best on the front in his Manchester United pomp. I don't know why. I've never questioned it. It just looked great, different to other records. The album was raw, edgy and had lots more heartache, pain and jangling guitars. Most people I knew didn't like it – and that was another plus. By pure fluke, I'd found something different. By the time I'd made it to university (I was the first in my family to go, I'm not sure if music played a role in this but I like to think so) I was regularly going to Wedding Present gigs. A friend on my course refused to go to a gig in Leeds with me because 'they are just too damn loud'. We are not friends anymore.

By the time I left university, Indie music, the genre which The Wedding Present and so many other great bands had helped to build track by track, was now something accepted by the masses – big news and big money. In the summer of 1995, Oasis and Blur went head-to-head to release 'Roll With It' and 'Country House' respectively. It was national news. I thought both bands were quite good, but it wasn't the Indie scene I knew. I was hoping 'Spangle' might cause a chart upset. It didn't, but this is the lot of a Wedding Present fan.

Everything was becoming very glossy. The bands wore expensive anoraks and trainers. Records were costing millions to produce. Oasis were selling out stadiums and putting Rolls Royces on their album sleeves. The Indie scene didn't seem that Indie anymore. I was also growing older, and my taste and priorities were changing.

I moved to Leicester in 2003. The Wedding Present were, and remain, regular visitors. However, there was one gig – December 2008 at the Charlotte. Midway through the gig – a combination of beer, intense heat (the Charlotte was a sweaty place all year round) and the emotion of the songs that made a setlist now spanning 20 years – when I realised we'd been on some kind of journey together. Every song felt like a greatest hit, everyone at the gig felt unified. Gedge's pain was our pain. Sure, we were all married now. Our acne had gone and the songs meant different things to different people. But we were now Team Wedding Present. We'd earned our place in the side. Over 20 years, we'd seen off all-comers trying to disrupt our musical adventure: soft metal revival, the second summer of love, rave, grunge, emo, the new corporate Indie or whatever. It all came and offered its own fashion, drug or fad. The Wedding Present never changed direction. It feels like they've grown up with me. Or I've grown up with them.

'My Favourite Dress' isn't even my favourite Weddoes song, not even close. 'Dalliance' probably is, since you ask, although it changes. Maybe it's 'Suck'. I don't know. Some music is about escaping reality and aspiring to something better. The Wedding Present's music, for me at least, is about understanding reality and realising that, deep down, we all feel the same way.

KENNEDY

CLAIRE MELVILLE & ANNE-MARIE

'Kennedy' was the first song we ever heard in Llanelli in 1990 thanks to friends from London who gave us a cassette of their favourite songs. It became an instant favourite of ours too. We finally saw them in March 2016 after 25 years.

SUCK
COLE JOHNSTON

I've seen them every time they've come to Vancouver. Years ago, I lived in a town called Kelowna and we had to drive four hours to see the *Watusi* and *Mini* tours. Mostly the memories are of screaming along to 'Suck' every time and of David graciously dealing with a fairly drunk me and signing whatever record I bring. For my 40th birthday, my wife somehow got hold of David and got him to send me a copy of *Valentina* with a birthday wish written on it. Quite possibly one of the best gifts ever!

EVERYONE THINKS HE LOOKS DAFT
PHILIP LEIGHTON

It was the pre-Internet age and so the 18-year-old me took the time to decipher David Gedge's words and handwrite the lyrics to *George Best*.

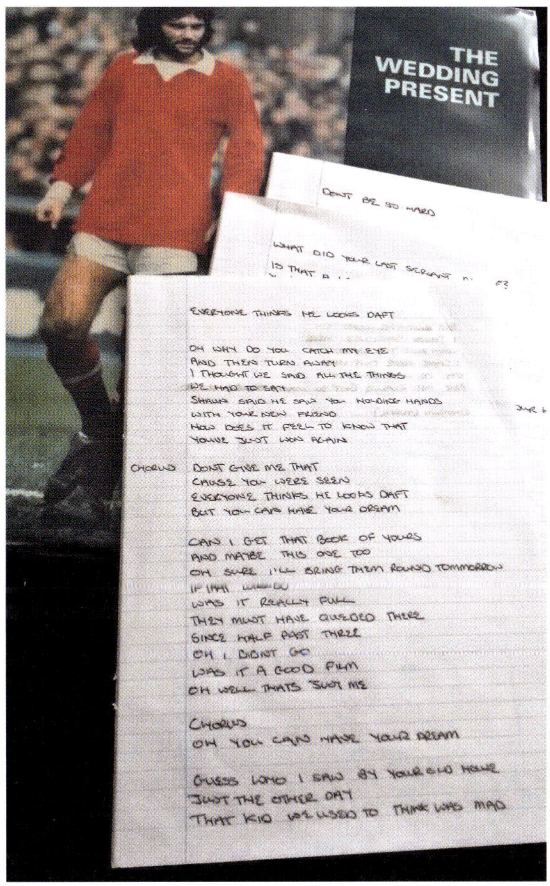

Philip Leighton's pre-Google deciphering of the lyrics to *George Best*

BEWITCHED
STUART HANCOCKS

It was June 2011 and Wakefield was hosting its first *Long Division* festival, an all-day event with over 40 bands performing in six venues across the city, with The Wedding Present headlining. The band were performing a late evening set at a venue called Mustangs, which was (badly) designed to resemble a wild west saloon! In fact, David announced at the start of the set that the band had played at the same venue many years before when it was known as The Rooftop Gardens.

The show progressed peacefully enough until it started to become apparent that the venue's security staff were not taking kindly to the dancing antics of those nearest the stage. A few scuffles broke out as the security team started to unnecessarily evict members of the audience from the venue – but the band played on.

That was until, rather bizarrely, an individual – who bore a passing resemblance to *Coronation Street*'s Roy Cropper – appeared on the stage carrying a shopping bag, and proceeded to attempt to engage in conversation with a somewhat startled looking Pepe le Moko, who was the bass guitarist at the time. Pepe said something to David and the band then left the stage.

There was then a period of impasse with everyone wondering whether or not the band would return, which eventually they did and continued with the show. Apparently, what had happened was that the gentleman who had got up on the stage had been expressing his concern at the treatment of the fans by the security staff. The band had left the stage in support of the fans and had refused to return until the security staff had been relieved of their duties. It was quite amusing to see security leaving the venue to shouts and jeers from the audience.

The band then completed their set without further incident. Edited footage of the gig is available on YouTube and the disappearance of the security staff during the course of the recording is noticeable. I spoke to David after the show, who said that such things were almost inevitable when a venue decided to use security staff familiar with monitoring club nights and not with gigs.

My favourite Wedding Present song is

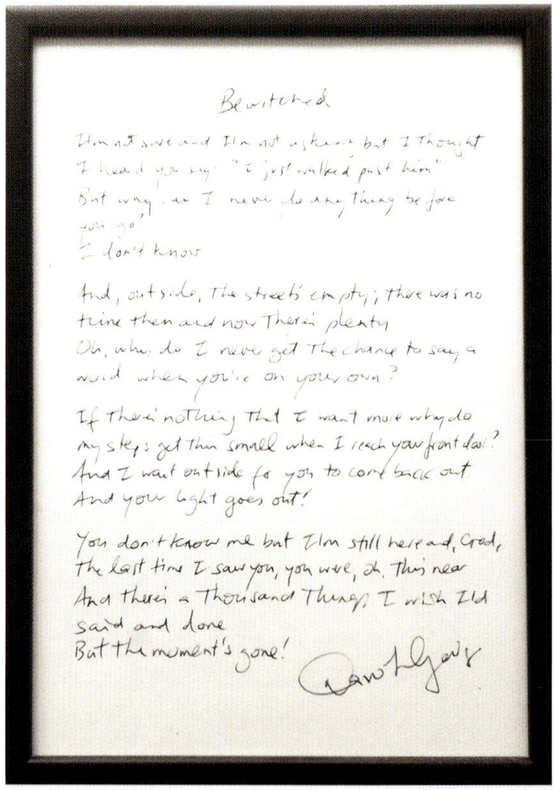

Stuart Hancocks' copy of the handwritten lyrics to 'Bewitched'

Stuart Hancocks' favourite Weddoes song is 'Bewitched'

'Bewitched'. It encapsulates everything about David's unique writing talents in one track, complete with superb guitars and backing harmonies. As John Peel famously quoted, 'The boy Gedge has written some of the best love songs of the rock 'n' roll era – you may dispute this, but I'm right and you're wrong.' And this song certainly backs him up.

I would also like to back my choice up by referencing a section of the sleeve notes from the *Bizarro* remastered release where Mark Beaumount sums it up just perfectly:

'And then there was 'Bewitched', possibly The Wedding Present's greatest moment and a high point in music's mission to map the mountains of human yearning. With Gedge gasping like a tortured teen throughout it was, arguably, the most direct and affecting snapshot of unrequited love ever put to record. That sound – that unbearable, all-consuming, jagged guitar clamour that follows Gedge's breathless cry of:

The last time I saw you, you were, oh, this near
And there's a thousand things I wish I'd said and done but the moment's gone

'That, friends, is the sound of a heart snapping.' Brilliant.

BIZARRO
GRAHAM FAIRS

I was a latecomer, in relative terms, to The Wedding Present. My time in the '70s and '80s had primarily been occupied by heavy rock and metal, with an occasional bit of punk thrown in. Indie was merely a word. That changed when a new colleague arrived at work in 1989 and my education began on the alternative music out there. Numerous tapes were put my way but nothing captured the musical passion as much as The Wedding Present – *George Best*, *Tommy* and *Bizarro*.

There have been many memorable gigs over the years, the majority in the company of said work colleague, friend and musical educator. However, there's nothing quite like the first time. Mine was at Loughborough University in 1990. There was a large audience, many probably Loughborough students, hot and tightly packed in a relatively small venue. Many of the songs were inevitably from *Bizarro* (although all the songs sounded the same) and the audience bounced as one, not necessarily voluntarily. One participant appeared to have passed out but was kept vertical, and reasonably in time, by those around him.

Great gigs between then and now, but the sheer energy, volume and passion of that first live Wedding Present experience, showcasing one of my all-time favourite albums, has stayed long in the memory.

A MILLION MILES
ANDREW HURLEY

'A Million Miles' always got me. That was me 30-plus years ago! It is my go-to Weddoes tune.

KENNEDY
MORAG GRAY

'Kennedy' just kept ringing in my head after the Bradford Festival in 1988. That was a bit life-changing!

INTERSTATE 5
DANNY HUNTLEY

Danny Huntley (right) with David Gedge

It was February 2005 when my love affair with The Wedding Present began. It was a good time to be in your early twenties. The Indie scene was booming and you could go to a gig or Indie club almost every night. This was a point in my life that, without any irony, I thought I was cool, even though I left the house every day wearing a cardigan. In my mind, I was a legend.

One day I was reading (most likely my flatmate's copy of) the *NME* when they ran a review of a new album from a veteran Indie band called The Wedding Present, comparing them to The Smiths. I loved The Smiths, so I went out and bought the album, *Take Fountain*. The Wedding Present were not like The Smiths at all. Although the Weddoes had songs about love gone wrong, they were not morbid or full of self pity. They were angry and bitter, asking questions like, 'Why does she still speak to her ex? Why is she not speaking to me? What have I done now?' These were songs I could relate to. Well, I could have done if I'd had a girlfriend.

'Interstate 5' was the first song from the band I ever heard. The song is pretty simple, a couple of chords played over and over again, but the lyrics were different to anything I had heard from a male lyricist. The song is about a man who was upset because a woman he spent the night with didn't return his calls. I had been raised through lad culture, so hearing the front man of a successful band admitting to being upset by such circumstances was really different:

You can surely sympathise; I just wanted more than one night

The Wedding Present are a successful band, even though my mates hadn't heard of them. The first time I saw them play, they packed out Shepherds Bush Empire. The last time in 2017, they packed out the O2 Academy in Leeds. It might not be Wembley Stadium, but it's still thousands of people in a room screaming for their songs. David Gedge has been doing this for over 30 years and his fans never leave him. I have been a fan for over 15 years now, and for me they are the greatest band in my world. I even called the top table at my own wedding 'The Wedding Present'.

Some blokes like football, some like fishing. I like The Wedding Present... and *Eastenders*.

FELICITY
DARREN PRICE

A cover, granted but my favourite Weddoes track is a 'William Shatner number', 'Felicity' on *Peel Sessions*. Right from the feedback in the intro… 'You Should Always Keep In Touch With Your Friends' and 'My Favourite Dress' came soon after. I've not liked any since quite as much, if I'm honest.

BRASSNECK
JULIE DUNK

During 'Brassneck' at the Arts Centre in York, somebody punched me in the head and knocked me out. I had a concussion for a week afterwards. I still love the song though!

ALWAYS THE QUIET ONE
DAVE BUTTERFIELD

Friday 10th February 2005, I was in a shop in Wakefield, West Yorkshire. It was lunchtime. I wasn't paying attention and someone sort of pushed past me. It was a nurse so I didn't really say anything but looked at her. I knew her. But from where? I watched her go out into the busy street, ignoring the request to pay for my purchase. I quickly did, and dashed outside to catch her up but she was gone. Instantly I knew who it was. My schooldays' girlfriend. At work that afternoon she was all I could think of. I thought she had moved away, so where did she live? Did she work at our local hospital? Would she recognise me? Was she married? How would it go?

On the Monday, I went back into Wakefield to buy the new Wedding Present album. Through circumstance I didn't get to hear it until the end of the week, and by then it's fair to say I hung around that shop at roughly the same time, most days. I did see her a few days later, but just watched from a distance and saw what bus she caught. I decided next time, I will speak to her. The next time, she was arm-in-arm with a man. I never did.

And then I heard track three off *Take Fountain*. David Lewis Gedge has read my diary. The absolute rotter...

For Dave Butterfield, it's as though David had read his diary

And so I'll watch you walk away and then waste my whole day, imagining the things you do
Like how you're bound to love quiet men and, if we meet again, how I'd actually speak to you

Here's the funny part; I wouldn't know where to start
That's because I'm always the quiet one
You've already gone

EVERYONE THINKS HE LOOKS DAFT

ADRIAN WEBB

When I first heard the opening to 'Everyone Thinks He Looks Daft' at an Indie night in '88, it had me hooked from the intake of breath to 'Oh, why do you catch my eye, then turn away?' And I remember seeing them in Bristol in 1992 and making my way to the front, only to be crushed like a hieroglyph for nine minutes whilst 'Take Me!' was performed. Utter joy.

CLICK CLICK
PAULO DI BRUCIO

'Click Click', 'Spangle' and 'Mars Sparkles Down On Me' fit in the diary of my life. 'Superman' or 'Hate' by Cinerama are the same. Any of David's songs can have this same meaning to me.

KENNEDY
RALPH WHITE

My favourite Wedding Present songs are 'Give My Love To Kevin', 'My Favourite Dress' and 'Lovenest' but that's not important right now. I was wearing my 'Kennedy' t-shirt at the Reading Festival in 1989 or '90 and it attracted the attention of none other than Genesis P-Orridge, who wandered over to me and, referring to me as 'Kennedy', sat down for a chat. We talked about his involvement in getting Brighton Dolphinarium closed down which, in case you're wondering, is a brilliant thing. So, yeah, 'Kennedy'. It's a fucking great tune 'n' all.

A MILLION MILES
RICKY FOULKES

'Nobody's Twisting Your Arm' was the first Wedding Present song I heard, on John Peel, but 'A Million Miles' spoke to my heart then and still does now.

SEAMONSTERS
CHRIS FERRIS

In a span of five days:

Girlfriend broke up with me
Lost my job for missing work trying to get her back
Got girlfriend back
Lost girlfriend (via phone call) the next morning

Seamonsters saved Chris Ferris's life

Lost my apartment because of no job
Was given a copy of *Seamonsters*

That album literally saved me. It brought me down to my lowest lows and at the same time gave me a sense of hope like I have never experienced before or since. And if you have to ask how, you need to listen to it again.

TAKE ME! & KENNEDY
TONY HEWIS

I went to see The Wedding Present at Nottingham Rock City just to see how anyone could play that fast. Turns out they couldn't, judging by the amount of broken strings!

CARELESS
MARK MORRIS

'Careless' by Cinerama is an absolute belter of a song, although the entire *Torino* album is class.

FLYING SAUCER
TIM JACKSON

I heard it in a cool bar in Knoxville, Tennessee, when it was released and this girl sitting next to me was singing along. She already knew the lyrics somehow. We talked about it and ended up dating for a few years.

VERKHOVYNO
ANDY MASON

'Verkhovyno' is my favourite of the Ukrainian songs. My love of this CD and the spin-off band meant that in 2002 I accepted a random chat request from a Ukrainian girl on ICQ. Eight years and numerous trips to Ukraine later, we got married. Now we have an eight-year-old boy who wouldn't exist without that song and CD.

The first Wedding Present CD I bought was *Bizarro*, based purely on the *NME* review, which I'm sure mentioned crazy cover versions and Ukrainian folk songs. I spent the

'Verkhovyno' has a family connection for Andy Mason

next few months tracking down all of their CD releases, but the one I didn't get was *Ukrainski Vistupi V Johna Peela*, as my friend had warned me off it because it wasn't like their other music. I was intrigued by the cover art and Cyrillic writing, though, and I finally bought it around the time of *Seamonsters*. I loved it all, but the song that really got me was the epic final track, 'Верховино'/'Verkhovyno'.

I'm a sucker for songs that go slow/fast and this is the perfect execution of it. I didn't care that I didn't understand a word of what was being sung. 'Verkhovyno' started to appear on my mixtapes right away and to this day I have it on my Spotify list of favourite songs of all-time and I regularly listen to it. I've also kept up with new releases by The Ukrainians since then and have seen them play many times.

In early 2002 I was chatting to a friend on ICQ, which was 'the' way to text communicate with friends over the Internet before the days of WhatsApp or limitless SMS. A feature of ICQ was that you could flag yourself to be available for random chats to anyone else in the world. I usually switched this off when chatting, but this day I had left it on and suddenly a window popped up saying, 'Hi, care for a chat?' I was making my excuses, saying I was already talking to someone, when I spotted this person was from Ukraine. I couldn't turn down this opportunity to converse with someone from the land of 'Verkhovyno', so I carried on both chats and stayed on talking long after my friend logged off. This Ukrainian was called Iryna and we stayed in touch over the following weeks and months. Then somehow in 2004 I found myself on a plane to Kyiv to meet her. Over the next five years I travelled there numerous times, visiting her family and friends in Kyiv, Lviv, Mykolaiv, Crimea, Odessa and her hometown of Izmail, along the way hearing some of the songs I knew so well being played by various musicians – including 'Verkhovyno' in a subway in Kyiv by a young guy on a violin.

In 2009, Iryna moved to the UK and we got married. Our son Alexander Yevgeniy was born in 2012. I think Iryna finds my love of English guys playing Ukrainian music a bit odd, but I know for sure that without the release of the Ukrainian Peel sessions, and 'Verkhovyno' in particular, I wouldn't have carried on with that chat in 2002, we wouldn't be married and Alexander wouldn't exist.

As I finish writing this in my car, waiting for Iryna outside Aldi, 'Hopak' has just randomly come on my Spotify mix. Is that serendipity? I don't know, but it's the perfect place to end.

BRASSNECK
PETER WINFIELD

'Brassneck' on a Peel Session about '89? A breath of fresh air. One of only a few bands I really make the effort to listen to and take in the lyrics.

WHAT HAVE I SAID NOW?
NICK TURNER

Although I loved and bought the singles and albums, the overriding feeling that the songs all reinforced was more important as a teenage male back then, and still is today. They taught me that it was OK to feel pain and OK to hurt. Not in a Smiths' 'let's hang around graveyards' type way but just in a very ordinary 'we all get dumped and it feels shit, but it's part of life' kind of way. Back in the day that wasn't easy, although maybe I was an early snowflake. However, I did hear a rumour recently that apparently nostalgia ain't what it used to be! Oh dear, what have I said now?

DALLIANCE
ABE VON STISASS

The noise part of 'Dalliance' blew my brain away in 1991 on MTV's 120 minutes. And that was absolutely essential because that time was full of adolescent doubt and pain.

KENNEDY
MART LAYTON

'Kennedy' was the song that started it all for me. It's not my favourite but I'm still very, very fond of it.

SILVER SHORTS (WELL, THE FOURTH T-SHIRT)

MARK O'DOHERTY

Obsessed with The Wedding Present as a teenager, I did a terrible thing after a gig in Brighton around 1992, and stole my mate's fantastic number four *Hit Parade* t-shirt. Although I knew it was so wrong, I had to have it and so secretly swapped my unwearable small sized shirt for his medium. 20 years later, and still feeling awful about it, I tracked him down via social media through a mutual friend. Having had no contact in two decades, he opened his post to a surprise – my apology, the t-shirt (I had kept it the whole time) and the cost of the t-shirt increased for inflation. He replied and was very happy, wore the t-shirt the next night out and gave the cash to charity. I made mistakes as a teenager but glad I have now put things right!

SEAMONSTERS

MURRELL, DAVID'S EX GIRLFRIEND & WEDDING PRESENT ROADIE

I arrived in Leeds in 1986 and quickly got down to seeing as many bands as possible. I went to every possible gig as it was such a great time for Indie music: the C86 'movement' was at its peak and I went to everything the *NME* listed. I was usually alone because my housemates didn't share my taste, but because the venues were small, I began to notice the same faces and after a TWP gig at the Royal Oak, met the band for the first time and found common ground with Shaun, who was also from Sussex.

From that point on, my life became entwined with TWP and the next two decades were filled with experiences I could never have imagined when I was filling out my university application form.

Some of David's songs are deeply personal and I'm not going to name them here. Sometimes there is an odd line in a song that alludes to an event, a remark, or a shared experience, and it's like meeting up with an old friend when I hear them. But with a few others, hearing them unexpectedly has in the past delivered a sideswipe, a raw punch of un-closured emotion. Mainly because David says things in songs that he can't articulate in real life, I suppose. Git.

He still remains one of my closest, dearest friends, even though our meetings are mostly limited to his concert schedule. When the band recently came to Leeds on the *Seamonsters* anniversary tour I took two of my teenage sons; I wanted them to understand what had dominated so much of my life. I bought them some expensive cheap beer and then left them at the back so that I could head to the front and dance, bumping into old faces and shouting along to some of my favourite songs. When I emerged from the throng, ears buzzing and throat sore, I was half expecting a bit of a moan and a 'let's get going' but instead they were grinning from ear to ear saying 'we get it now!'

I can't possibly pick a favourite song, although I will say that *Seamonsters* is my favourite album. I like the thumping, melodious cacophony of many of those songs, and no one ever believes how many guitar strings and snare skins we got through each night when they were played live. I love 'Heather', 'Dalliance', 'Niagara' and 'Octopussy'. But then there's 'Skin Diving', 'Health And Efficiency', 'Take Me!', 'Bewitched', 'Suck', 'The Queen Of Outer Space'… I just can't choose. I still listen to TWP and don't like the newer songs any less than the old ones, but those were such a huge part of my everyday life back then and are etched right through me.

There is one song, however, that takes me back to one moment, every single time I hear it. It's not because it's about me (it isn't) but because I remember so clearly when David came through from his song-writing room to tell me about the new song he was writing which he wasn't sure about, because the chorus was just his voice and the drums, and he was worried it might be too weird and did I think it would work? And I'm always so glad he held his nerve because, over 30 years later, when 6 Music blasts 'Kennedy' into my kitchen, I'm reminded just how absolutely brilliantly it did just work.

EVERYONE THINKS HE LOOKS DAFT

PAUL MCGOWAN

This song described a relationship of mine almost word for word from way back then. It transports me back every time. But things turned out like 'Flying Saucer' with someone else in the end!

MY FAVOURITE DRESS

JANE BETHEA

There are so many songs that have meaning for me. I just love 'My Favourite Dress'.

The tender caresses that bring out the man
I can't still be drunk at five
Oh, I guess I surely can

At nearly 50, this is still one of my all-time favourite lines.

CRAWL
CRAIG MILNE

I loved 'Crawl' from when I was a lad in Leeds ('I stole and of course I lied'). Then when I emigrated, and you can't take Leeds out of the lad, 'I'm From Further North Than You', which has the perfect put-down: 'Just not very many!'

CATWOMAN
KURT MERRIFIELD DAHLKE

You really can't beat seeing 'Catwoman' performed live. It still raises gooseflesh just thinking about it!

HEATHER
MARC SETTLE

It's not even my absolute favourite Wedding Present song.

OK, it's definitely in the top ten and on a good day it would certainly get into the top five, but it's not quite 'My Favourite Dress' or 'Don't Touch That Dial' or 'Take Me!' But nevertheless, 'Heather' holds a unique place in my heart and can cause shivers to run down my spine in a way that is matched by no other Wedding Present track. It helped me overcome my fear of flying.

To be more accurate, it helped me overcome my fear of taking off and landing because once you're up in the air, most plane flights can be quite enjoyable, being as they are a great chance to read a book, watch a film, sleep, eat or drink – once you've managed to dismiss from your mind the fact you're in a giant metal tube 38,000 feet above the ground.

But it's the start and to a lesser degree the end of a flight I've always struggled with, which has always been something of an inconvenience given that you can't get to the fun part in the middle without the bit at the start, and if you don't actually get to have the bit at the end, that's a sign that you've had something of a bad flight.

I needed something to calm myself down. And that became 'Heather'. Quite how it became 'Heather' is lost in the mists of nearly 30 years of time but for many years and many flights, I couldn't take off or land without listening to it. On some occasions that proved hard to achieve: an eagle-eyed member of the cabin crew once spotted me with headphones on when we'd been told not to, scolded me accordingly and I had no choice but to endure the take-off without 'Heather'. I often had to resort to creative and sometimes destructive ways to be able to listen to the track without it being anywhere near obvious. If I had a window seat, I'd arrange myself such that it looked like I was asleep against the window with just one ear of my headphones on, placed such that it couldn't be seen between my head and the window.

If I had an aisle or the dreaded middle seat, I remember deliberately breaking a pair of headphones such that I could thread the cable up through my sleeve and out into my palm. I'd then spend a curiously long time resting my head on my palm, earpiece against my ear, with my elbow on the arm rest. It may have annoyed whoever I was sitting next to, but if it meant I could listen to 'Heather', that was far more important than their comfort.

It wasn't even just any section of the song either. I had to time things such that a certain part of 'Heather' was playing as the thrust of the engines moved the plane down the runway and – most importantly – so the best and most reassuring bit happened just as the wheels left the ground and I felt the push as the plane became airborne. With take-offs and landings being the most dangerous part of any plane journey, my reasoning was that if I was going to die in a flaming fireball, I at least wanted to go out while listening to The Wedding Present rather than whatever was playing over the in-flight music system. I would have probably been using a cassette player (I don't recall ever owning a portable CD player) and this was well before the mini-disc era, let alone MP3 players and iPods, so I had to cue it up to juuuuuuust the right place of the song and press play at the right moment. If the plane was delayed getting to the runway, I'd have to rewind and try again.

Grab your copy of *Seamonsters* and start playing 'Heather'. The first 90 seconds are clearly an important part of the song as we can't get to the good bit without them, but it's from one minute 37 or so when the magic starts to happen. DLG's voice vanishes, leaving just Keith Gregory's bass and the odd bit of Simon Smith's drums. It's at this point I would press play, to coincide with the plane leaving the stand and taxiing to the runway. If you've ever flown from Heathrow, you'll know that the queue to actually take off can take a fair old time and I often had to rewind the cassette regularly to ensure I had the perfect bit playing just as the engines roared and we rumbled along the runway. The real cue I had to hit was DLG's anguished cry of 'oh' at two minutes 33 and it's NOW that the cushion in the small of my back is pushing into me as we speed down the runway and the world is rushing past and the wheels are beginning to leave the ground and we're starting to rise up through the clouds and I'm gripping the seat rests either side of me for dear life reminding myself that mankind was really not meant to fly. Oh my god oh my god oh my god what was that noise oh my god we're going to crash oh my god oh actually this seems to be OK what was I worried about after all... Yes, I'd love an over-priced whisky, thanks.

Getting the timing right was a lot harder for landing. There was one time coming into Berlin where we were descending through clouds and I hadn't even had the chance to cue things up properly before we'd landed; the cloud had become fog and we'd landed before the visibility cleared, which was usually my visual clue.

There will be many tales of rejection, lost love and the like (my own includes writing the lyrics to 'Take Me!' to a girl I liked on a postcard, which her parents saw and which she later told me ruined my chances), 'Heather' will always hold a unique and special place in my heart.

Not that I can listen to it now when I take planes: with two young kids, my attention sadly needs to be elsewhere these days.

I'M NOT ALWAYS SO STUPID

YURI GONZALEZ

'Every time somebody laughs I think it's you.' Great lyrics to a great song.

BIG BOOTS

MARK POTTER

The Wedding Present being one of my favourite bands, the whole of *Saturnalia* truly defined their sound as being loud, soft, sad, pop and dreamy all at the same time. I love 'Kansas' with that crazy guitar sound that sounds like an Australian horn, and the ending solo on 'Big Boots' gives me goosebumps every time.

GEORGE BEST

ROMAN HEEREN

The album *George Best* changed my mind and blew me away… and until that time I thought only trash metal like Slayer was the fastest 'sportsguitars' I have ever heard… but David changed my mind when I saw The Wedding Present live and I fell in love immediately.

EVERYONE THINKS HE LOOKS DAFT

DARREN BANKS

One day in 1990, my cousin showed me a cassette with George Best on the front. I thought, 'Why are you showing me this?' He played it and as soon as I heard 'Oh, why do you…' I was convinced my cousin was singing on a demo tape he'd made and not this David Gedge guy. (My cousin was good at voices). As a City fan, I'm quite certain I would have bypassed an album with a former (great) United player on the cover. But therein began my love for the band.

MY FAVOURITE DRESS
JULIAN JOHNSON

'My Favourite Dress' just hooked me from the first. Beautiful song.

KENNEDY
ИЛИЈА ЂОРЂЕВИЋ

Guitar kick to the head.

BE HONEST (ELECTRIC VERSION – PREVIOUSLY UNRELEASED DEMO)
EDWARD KOMOCKI

I always struggle with 'greatest hits' and 'best of' compilations. The songs of an album are meant to stay together. They're usually conceived during a specific period of inspiration, are arranged in a chosen sequence for maximum emotional effect and constitute a cohesive statement of intent. Pulling that apart disembodies a perfectly crafted musical experience. No one would consider taking favourite scenes from the movies of the Coen Brothers, stringing them together and expecting the result to be the greatest film they'd ever made. Although saying that, I probably would pay good money to see *Raising Serious Lebowski After Reading Inside Old Men (Where Art Thou)*.

Edward Komocki has chosen a demo version of 'Be Honest'

And it was this belief which almost denied me the chance to experience one of The Wedding Present's most glorious moments! I'd seen *Yé Yé: The Best Of The RCA Years* tucked away on the fifth or sixth page of online music store listings and occasionally come across a physical copy in the CD racks of HMV, but always dismissed it as some sort of contractual obligation collection of songs that, as a Wedding

Present obsessive I undoubtedly already possessed, probably several times over in multiple formats. In fact, its apparent rarity only confirmed to me that it obviously wasn't for the truly discerning Wedding Present fan. But one day, I did just happen to turn the CD case over and after snorting at the predictability of the selected choices, was suddenly presented with a moment of eyebrow-raising surprise for there, at the end of the listing, nestled 'Be Honest (Electric Version – Previously Unreleased Demo)'. A completely unexpected discovery and one that held too many enticing possibilities to let my preconceived ideas about compilation albums dissuade me from parting with my money.

And what a discovery. This 'Be Honest' was nothing like the gentle, soothing version I was accustomed to at the end of *Bizarro* with its relaxed tranquility and woozy shuffle. This 'Be Honest' was a whole new and startling beast. A version of urgency, insistence and excitement that kicked off at pace, gained velocity and then just kept accelerating. A 'Be Honest' that ticked every bullet point on a Wedding Present wish-list, from the characteristically dead-pan Gedge vocal to the final onslaught of what might well be the career pinnacle of their unfeasibly rapid hyper-strumming. It was the perfect synthesis of all the elements that make *George Best* and *Bizarro* so distinctive and thrilling. So, if I'm going to be honest (sic), this revelation taught me pretty quickly the folly of my musical prejudices!

But this 'Be Honest' offers more than just visceral thrills. It fills me with hope. A hope that, just maybe, there are even more unheard wonders languishing in the Gedge musical vaults. What if there are, like this 'Be Honest', completely unexpected versions of our favourites with horns or accordions or ocarinas? Might there even be unreleased new songs by both The Wedding Present and Cinerama of which we are completely unaware? Or, and this is may be where hope becomes pure fantasy, could DLG be a closet Neil Young, amassing a trove of temporarily-rejected whole albums in preparation for a future series of deluxe archival box sets? Nurse! I think I need to lie down in that darkened room now.

The original 'Be Honest' in its *Bizarro* setting is undeniably an interesting and quite lovely departure from our Wedding Present expectations, but this alternative version strengthens all we hold dear about The Wedding Present. Had it been the actual choice to bring the album to a close, it would have joyously reinforced that statement of single-minded purpose we all wore with pride on our t-shirts in that era – that all the songs really did sound the same!

CATWOMAN
VINCENT PONTIUS

Gedge can put that geetar of his into overdrive and then some! I once saw David rip into and ultimately lean into his geetar for 'Catwoman'.

KENNEDY
SARA KENNEDY

So many memories of so many Saturday nights out at MMU student union's 'The Stomp'.

TAKE ME!
GRAEME RAMSAY, FORMER WEDDING PRESENT DRUMMER & GUITARIST

As an Edinburgh student I'd be walking from Marchmont to King's Buildings for a lecture – a half-hour walk, which should be enough to listen to 'Take Me!' three times and allow for rewinding in-between. I wouldn't get around to that though, because one more bounce through the first eight invigorating bars was never satisfactory. With a fixed hold on my old Walkman, I'd be winding back to the beginning again and again as I imagined how it must feel to be the guy joining in on that second guitar. That climbing, energising, life-affirming riff: how could he do it without raising two fists in the air and grinning?

Listeners that let the song run, like a normal person, are pulled into a soundworld that's the essence of the band for me: drums that don't let up with a bass drum pedalled by a Terminator, guitars that are unmistakable yet weave together, battered strings somehow chiming instead of snapping, a bass tone like a best man and, just poking through and no more, there's some kind of northern love story through clenched teeth.

After a couple of minutes, a conventional (though fantastic) song has come and gone, but a further seven-minute sojourn in that jubilant soundworld carries on. Incessant drumming, every hit at full force, while two guitars and that bass meld riffs that seem to celebrate like best friends. There's also the 'Status Quo' bit, which I neither understand nor question.

If I could go back and tell my 19-year-old self that one day I would be the guy – well I wouldn't, because I'd only have spent years worrying that I was going to mess it up.

On *Bizarro*, and in the Wedding Present catalogue generally, 'Take Me!' is an unusually optimistic song, with an imperfect protagonist who's nonetheless sounding wholly positive about his offering. We can have it, we can make it, I can be it. I'll bet I'm not the only Wedding Present listener for whom that kind of thinking is generally out of character. Most people have songs that make us feel like we're winning, and this is one of mine.

When drumming, the final chord was the finish line in a gruelling test of stamina and consistency; playing guitar, it meant you'd reached the end of the tightrope of concentration and counting bars: the temptation to step off into whatever transcendent daydream or trance has to be resisted as you stay present enough to remember each precise variation on the riff, under unchanging chords, as the interplay of guitars and bass develops. As an immersed listener though, to The Wedding Present's longest and most euphoric song, that concluding D major is oddly bittersweet as you have a sense that the daydream is over: you're going back to normal now.

CALIFORNIA
JODIE CURTIS

Anything you want to do
I just know that I'll want to do it too
But we must go

These are words that inspired us to see this 'great big world somehow'!

KENNEDY
LEE DRUMMOND

I can't remember the venue but it was a London one with a balcony and red globe lights. I was on a second or third date with a girl and I was trying to impress. We got the train from deepest darkest Kent and headed to the venue. I had seen the boys five or six times already by then and was addicted. We sat up on the balcony and had a few drinks and watched the support. Now I had every intention of keeping my word and promised faithfully that I would sit upstairs with her and watch the band from there as I had seen them before. Easy, no problem.

The lights dimmed, the crowd cheered and the boys trooped on stage. A young Mr Gedge hit the first chord of 'Kennedy' and I turned to my date, shrugged my apologies and was down the front before the chorus. Not surprisingly, no more dates with her but thankfully plenty more with the Weddoes.

Many moons ago, in 1989, I saw the mighty four at a small venue in Folkestone, Kent, and had to hitch-hike the 20 or so miles there and back. All went well and the gig was stunning, but hitching home I was picked up by a bloke in the biggest lorry I had ever seen. He blasted out Pavarotti at full blast and showed me his photographs of him driving through The Alps, driving this very same truck with one hand whilst hanging out of the window taking snaps. My evening had gone from sublime to weird to bloody terrifying, all in the name of the Weddoes!

CRAWL
STUART ROFFEY

'Crawl' is my all-time favourite, but the best line for me is from 'No'. The words shelf, razor, myself spring to mind.

VALENTINA
TREVOR FONG

There are too many great songs by both The Wedding Present and Cinerama, but I love how Cinerama did a cover of the whole of The Wedding Present's album, *Valentina*. It's great listening to them back to back!

MY FAVOURITE DRESS
STEVE CHAPPELL

Steve Chappell remembers the first time

It was a Saturday and I set out on the bus to Rotherham, with some spare cash in my pocket and the intent to spend it. There were a couple of decent record shops in the town but I ended up in the one near the market. I think it was called The Sound Of Music. Whatever I had it in mind to buy is long since forgotten but they didn't have it in stock. I was sifting through the racks, because having invested in the effort and bus fare, I wasn't going home empty-handed. I was at some kind of metaphorical musical crossroads at the time or, less pretentiously put, bored. My early musical tastes were influenced by an older sibling and I was just generally looking for something new, something different.

I picked up a single with The Wedding Present on the front. I wasn't sure if that was the band or the song title. I had never heard of The Wedding Present let alone anything by them. Flipping it over I saw 'My Favourite Dress', and I am embarrassed to admit now that it made me think twice about buying it. What would I, a teenage lad from small-town South Yorkshire in the late 1980s, be doing buying something about a favourite dress? But it was purchased and stashed in the brown paper bag and not even looked at again until on the bus ride home, which is when I discovered it was also a beautiful white vinyl. I was starting to feel good about this.

I went straight into the bedroom once home and onto the red Technics automatic record player, pressed 'start' and hoped I hadn't just bought some terrible '80s pap. The opening guitar, then the cymbals followed by bass guitar, the jangling guitars, the tempo and – is that a northern accent? It was unlike anything I had heard before but strangely instantly familiar. I got it right from the off. This was the start of our lifelong relationship; OK, we had a bit of a break in the middle years but here we are still together over 30 years later. You never forget your first time and it still means the most to me, possibly not my favourite ever, but it is 'My Favourite Dress'.

SWIMMING POOLS, MOVIE STARS

ROBERT NEGRI

For Robert Negri it's 'Swimming Pools, Movie Stars'

'Someone rang for you.' The voice from behind the (closed) living room door called out as I got home from work. 'Who was it?' I asked my dad. 'David, from The Wedding Present.'

'Fuck off!'

After a bite to eat I went to see my dad who was watching TV. 'So who rang me then?'

'David from The Wedding Present. He'll ring back.'

'Right, OK.' I went to the phone and dialled 1471 to find out which one of my mates had tried to wind me up. Nothing. This was the days before (everybody had) mobile phones. I thought little more of it and went to my room.

A while later the phone rang. I answered, fully expecting one of my 'friends' to be laughing, or imitating (badly) a northern accent. 'Hello, this is David from The Wedding Present.'

'Er... hello' was all I could manage.

I'd gotten into The Wedding Present initially after hearing 'Why Are You Being So Reasonable Now?' and 'Nobody's Twisting Your Arm' along with the odd *George Best* track played at an Indie-ish disco during a drunken week in Torquay.

Back home, I was walking past the old Riverside Studios near home and heard 'Nobody's Twisting Your Arm' blaring out of the PA inside. It was a sign. A colleague at work gave me a copy of *Tommy* and we saw them together in London in '89. From that point on, I was hooked. I sought out every possible release they had, er, released, every compilation they appeared on – you know, as you do. I had taken to writing to the band

(David) whenever I couldn't get hold of something, always getting a reply and often getting a nugget of an import thrown in. After spotting some gaps in the discography in *Orange Slices*, he asked me to help fill them in. So that's how he had my name and address, and how he got my number.

The band had been invited to appear on the *Esther* show, alongside The Troggs, in a debate on old and new music. David realised I lived not a million miles (ding!) from the studios in Wembley, and thought he'd ring and offer me tickets. I can't imagine too many of today's pop stars doing the same, or at least not without sticking it all over their social media or having TV cameras there. It was a bizarre experience, with a pretty partisan crowd in favour of The Troggs. I thanked David briefly after and got out.

The song they performed was 'Swimming Pools, Movie Stars', and this will forever have a special place in my heart. It's either this or 'Crawl', during which I lost my monkey boot at Aylesbury in 1990, but that's all there is about that.

BRASSNECK
STEVEN STEWART

My dad offered to arrange for a colleague's CD player to be fixed as he knew someone who could repair electronic equipment. The colleague left a few CDs in the box with the CD player for 17-year-old me; The Shamen, The Stone Roses, Happy Mondays, Inspiral Carpets – and *Bizarro*. I can clearly remember playing *Bizarro* for the first time and being completely blown away. Hearing 'Brassneck' for the very first time will never leave me. This was a complete fluke that totally changed my musical taste instantly. The power of The Wedding Present.

Steven Stewart was gifted a copy of *Bizarro*

WHY ARE YOU BEING SO REASONABLE NOW?
GILES SKIPPER

I fell for them with 'Why Are You Being So Reasonable Now?'

TAKE ME!

BRIAN REYNOLDS

Brian Reynolds' mum was not as big a fan of 'Take Me!' as he was

I had the seven feet by seven feet box room in my parents' house as a kid. In my last year there I taped 'Take Me!' off Peel's *Festive 50*. I'd been aware of the band before but all the songs sounded the same (sic) so I never paid any real attention. Nothing sounded like this song, nearly ten minutes of pure guitar bliss buzzing across the airwaves. It completely blew my mind.

Just around then I bought my first CD player so rushed out to buy *Bizarro* on a shiny silver disc. I played it daily, full blast. It's amazing how loud it sounded in a room that small. It directly led to my mother cutting my speaker wires with scissors so I had to listen on headphones. Shortly after that incident, I realised it was time to leave the nest and find my own place. 30 odd years later, it's still the ultimate Wedding Present track for me.

(I have a number of other favourites, but they have soundtracked embarrassing occasions in my life which I wouldn't want published in a book!)

WHAT BECOMES OF THE BROKEN HEARTED?

ALEX MURRAY

George Best made me believe in music again, especially 'My Favourite Dress' and 'What Becomes Of The Broken Hearted?'

YEAH YEAH YEAH YEAH YEAH

BRIAN BREHMER

'Yeah Yeah Yeah Yeah Yeah' is my favourite song by The Wedding Present. I had mentioned that I chose it because of the type of relationship that I had when I was dating my now wife of 14 years, mentioning that a friend of mine, who happened to be a DJ on a local college radio station here, played it for her as a long distance dedication. After 14 years, this song is still our song, because the lyrics fit us so well:

Because you know that I'll come running to you, when you call
You know I'll come, whatever you've got planned
You know you mix me up; I can't think straight at all
My head tells me I shouldn't be here and my heart says: 'Yeah!'

Recently, my wife has had some medical issues, and I have found myself taking on more of her roles and doing things that she used to gladly do for the both of us. At times it is tough, but then I remember the song and how much I love her and how the words fit us so well, and things are a little bit easier to handle.

And how on earth did I get myself into this?
And how much stranger is it going to get?
And how do you hold me prisoner with just a kiss?
My head tells me I shouldn't be here yet my heart says: 'Yeah!'

How can you not love a song which tells the world and yourself as well, just how much you love the woman who said yes?

WHY ARE YOU BEING SO REASONABLE NOW? / POURQUOI ES-TU DEVENUE SI RAISONNABLE?

JOHN FLEMING

John Fleming (left) with David Gedge bought the English and French language versions of 'Why Are You Being So Reasonable Now?'

It's 1988 and I'm an American grad student studying in Belgium. I'm renting a small room in a student house in Leuven while attending an MBA programme at the local university. It took a while but I finally found the 'cool' record shop in Leuven (I knew there had to be one). That fall, I was excited to see the shop had the new single, 'Why Are You Being So Reasonable Now?'. I didn't have a record player back in my room but I bought it anyway. Now here's the best part: a week later this same shop actually had the French version of the single too, so I bought 'Pourquoi Es-Tu Devenue Si Raisonnable?' as well. Eventually, I bought a turntable, listened to the singles (no surprise – they were excellent!), graduated, left Leuven and went on with my life.

Fast forward 30 years. It's 2018 and I'm an American diplomat posted to Myanmar and visiting Japan. The Wedding Present are playing back-to-back gigs in Tokyo where they promised a 'different set each night.' On the first night, to my delight, they played 'Why Are You Being So Reasonable Now?'. That was a rare treat. After the show, I had a chance to speak with David and after mentioning the song, I said, 'I guess this means you'll play the French version tomorrow?' He laughed. *Hélas*, they didn't play it, but it was still a great set as well as great fun to show off my knowledge of the early discography and, of course, share a chuckle with David.

LET'S PRETEND

ANDREW DAVIE

For Andrew Davie, Cinerama's 'Let's Pretend' is the song that resonates

While 'My Favourite Dress' is without a doubt my absolute favourite song of all time, never failing to get me on the dancefloor despite my protestations that I cannot dance to save my life, it is a Cinerama track which resonates strongly with me.

I'd been with Alexis since the turn of the millennium, and having successfully introduced her to The Wedding Present and Cinerama I was, at least in my own mind, happy. Having been in a long-term relationship for nearly seven years, albeit with the occasional doubts, nothing really prepares you for that kick in the stomach when your girlfriend dumps you, seemingly without warning.

But I was yours for seven years
Is that what you call a dalliance?

When she stated that we needed to talk, alarm bells began to ring. Long story short, she was moving out and had already found somewhere (and someone) else, the only problem being she couldn't take the dog. So, two weeks later after some acrimonious words:

About what I said just before, you know, your clothes on the floor
I never meant to hurt you

We parted company. Alexis to her new life, and me left rattling around an empty house. Except it wasn't empty. It was chock full of her belongings. I assumed that eventually she would arrange to collect her things, but obviously that was never going to happen. After several frustrating weeks I resolved to remove all traces of her personality. Boxes were filled with all manner of things.

And now that I've begun I'm finding things everywhere
When I think that I am done, I'll find some underwear

Books, clothing, diaries, CDs, although no coaster set, or even a Corrs cassette mind you, resulting in a mountain of boxes full of things I just wanted shot of. Simple. I'd done the hard work, all she needed to do was collect them. No. I ended up dropping off box after box at her mother's, because at that time I didn't know where she stayed. I got lots of sympathetic looks and platitudes from her mother and sisters, but this couldn't last forever and I was in due course told 'no more'.

One evening I surprised her by piling the remaining boxes up at her front door and bluntly telling her that if she didn't pick up the final few boxes, they would be getting chucked out. End of story. Well, yet again, no. Needless to say, the charity stores welcomed the remaining books, and my bin was fuller than normal for a couple of weeks. And throughout this time, 'Let's Pretend' received a lot of play.

I'd like to think that I got closure at the time, but the real heartbreak was losing the dog. We'd only had him a couple of months but due to work commitments, it wasn't feasible to keep him and the day I rehomed him hurt much more than being dumped.

Happily however, I'm now with the gorgeous Yvonne who is a massive fan of The Wedding Present, although not as yet a huge fan of Cinerama! But there's still time.

BLONDE

ADAM CARTER

I love *Seamonsters* and this track epitomises it.

ROTTERDAM

ALAN GOLDBERG

1992 to 1996 were The College Years. I went in as a metalhead that became more grunge, and left as someone who was listening to Indie rock, ska and reggae. A broad palette.

I was working at the college radio station, and in my sophomore year, I met Pablo. His real name was Jon, but everyone called him Pablo and I didn't find out his real name until months after becoming friends! He became my Indie rock mentor. We were both music loving and collecting nerds, and he was the only one I had met to that point who, like me, had an extensive cassette and CD collection in his residence hall room. We bonded.

He turned me onto a lot of bands, one being The Wedding Present. He introduced me to *Bizarro* and told me this story of how the people at RCA who signed and released their record had left the company, so that when The Wedding Present went to RCA and said, 'Hey, we're on your label!', the response was, 'You are?'

I don't know if that's true, but I am a sucker for a good story and the impression that I got was, this band was so under the radar that their own label didn't know who they were. It was super-appealing!

'Rotterdam' is Alan Goldberg's favourite Wedding Present song, although he was totally dressed in corduroy when he saw the band perform *Seamonsters*

Pablo may have also introduced me to *Seamonsters* or maybe I found that at the college radio station. That record became my favourite. While I had shed my metalhead past, I do enjoy an aggressive sound, and I loved the 'Steve Albini drums' because you can hear it on subsequent productions of his. They sound clear and full. Every song on that record is great, and it's 'come for the drums, stay for everything else'.

This record spoke to my awkwardness of trying to figure out who I was. Conversations I wanted to have and didn't know how. My Indie friends were mostly straight, and I was coming to terms [with knowing / learning] that I wasn't. I didn't meet a lot of gay men at that time, and the ones I did, I didn't relate to and they didn't like my music. It was a frustrating time and I responded to the introspection, the sensitivity, and the 'things aren't going the way I would want them to' in some of Gedge's lyrics. There were the regrets and heartache in songs that I could empathise with even though I wasn't having those forlorn conversations with anyone in particular. With 'Rotterdam', I feel it. It's angsty, yet clean. 'I wanted you but not the way you think' resonated as I was trying to find my way. I love the sound of the guitars, Gedge's soft voice that in parts gets louder. The last minute of the song being all guitars and drums which sound like you're right there in the studio, feeling alive. The pounding of the drums in the last 20 seconds is a build up and release that I find perfect.

It was a highlight to see The Wedding Present play *Seamonsters* in full. I was totally dressed in corduroy for the show; sneakers, pants, shirt and hat!

I've lost touch with Jon (Pablo) but I am forever grateful that he introduced me to this band.

BE HONEST
CATHY LOUISE

'Be Honest' is a brilliant breakup song.

HEATHER
ALAN MCADAM

It used to be 'Dalliance', and has been quite a few others; *The Home Internationals* EP is worth a mention. But 'Heather' has usurped them all. There's something incredibly moving about those lyrics, and singing along loudly to it at a Wedding Present gig:

And I know I said I wouldn't be the one
But an empty bed, your clothes all gone
I didn't know how much I'd miss you until now
I didn't know how much you mean to me somehow

Quite a few Wedding Present songs are about romance dying on the vine, or troubled relationships, but this one resonates the most. I get goosebumps when I hear the opening chords. My favourite version, or the one I always return to playing is the *Marc Riley Sessions Volume 2* version from 2012. A wonderful song.

Special mention has to be given to *The Home Internationals* EP though, and 'Scotland'. That piano opening, and then the track including the Scottish voices, which is kind of similar to the inclusion of dialogue in Erland Cooper's music, except his are usually nice Orkney voices, not Glaswegian ones! I'm from Glasgow so I do like the accents, but Orcadians do have a lovely singsong, lilting accent. Also, the strings on the track. Quite exceptional, as are the other tracks on the EP.

TAKE ME!
PATRICK SUNDERLAND

Mine is not your regular 'me and my mates in the moshpit' memory…

In the early 2000s, when my daughter was about four or five, the two of us spent a lot of time in the car doing errands, making trips to the tip or going to the park, just getting out of the house. Obviously, The Wedding Present would be being played a fair amount. She would always ask for 'track nine – the long one'. She just loved the fact that it seemed to go on forever. It was just known as 'Track Nine' in our house, not 'Take Me!'. Now, whenever I hear the song at some random venue with middle-aged men and women going mad, and the band working through the guitar bits (especially the 'Quo' section), I think back to me and my little girl out on some trip. With her in her car seat, grinning and nodding her head to 'Track Nine'…

Patrick and Ellie Sunderland are partial to track nine off *Bizarro*

BRASSNECK

ROBERT HALLAM

Like David I am a hopeless romantic. Every song is a love song and that's why I connected with The Wedding Present so much. My all-time favourite line is:

But it was different then
And that's all in the past; there, I've said it now at last

YOU SHOULD ALWAYS KEEP IN TOUCH WITH YOUR FRIENDS

JOHN RAFFERTY

'You Should Always Keep In Touch With Your Friends' is still a favourite today.

OCTOPUSSY

NIK SANDS

We don't have to do anything
We don't have to do anything except watch the leaves turning in the wind
Say what you want to say

This song reminded me of one of my many doomed relationships when I first heard it. So sad… it taught me to listen more to what she had to say.

KENNEDY

CLAIRE GILDERSLEVE

For Claire Gildersleve, 'Kennedy' brings back memories of the late Sean Hughes

I first encountered The Wedding Present through Sean Hughes's GLR radio show in the late '90s, which I stumbled upon one day scrolling through the airwaves in search of a music education, as a teen with no older siblings to show me the way. At this point I had spent a few years fairly exclusively listening to Take That, so I very much needed guidance…

The Wedding Present (and Cinerama) became firm life-long favourites.

A few years later, in 2005, I happened to meet Sean and we bonded over music, spending hours upon hours with him playing me his old favourites and new discoveries, sometimes even venturing away from the comfort of his sofa to enjoy the odd gig. I went with Sean to his final three Wedding Present outings – Kentish Town Forum, the O2 Academy Islington, and The Roundhouse.

In a taxi to the Kentish Town gig in March 2016, he was incredulous that the driver didn't know of the band, asking, 'What? You don't know "too much apple pie"?!' The driver appeased him, put 'Kennedy' on and we sang along (possibly contributing to a reduced Uber rating for me…), Sean adding a pretty bad generic northern accent, exaggerated every time the 'too much apple pie' line came up. When the opening bars to that song struck up later that evening, he grabbed my arm excitedly, bouncing up and down! He was uncharacteristically un-laid-back at Wedding Present gigs. It was a joy to see, he just lit up.

He, of course, loved the whole back catalogue, but there was something in that song that captured him around those last gigs. Each time, on the way there, he'd put on the same bad accent, lean into me with a smile and repeat 'too much apple piieee'.

When Sean died, I was asked by his brothers to pick the music for his funeral. With the recent memory of those gigs, the introduction I'd had through him two decades prior, and all the hours we had spent listening to them, I knew the first song to be played during the service had to be a Wedding Present one. I'd been in touch with David to let him know the funeral details, but they were on tour in Germany so he was sorry he couldn't make it.

He told me that the last song they'd played live in the days before Sean died was 'Bewitched' at Cadogan Hall, complete with strings and a choir. He wished Sean had been there because he knew he would have loved it. He very kindly tried to get the version with strings they'd just recorded for Marc Riley's 6Music show to me in time for the funeral, but it didn't quite make it. He said Sean had expressed that 'Bewitched' was his favourite song.

If 'Bewitched' was his favourite, I'd say for those last few gigs at least 'Kennedy' was a very close second. So it felt absolutely right to have that playing at the funeral. For me, personally, it evoked lovely memories on a sad day, for others it brought a wry smile that a very solemn occasion was punctuated by loud guitars and a chorus of 'Lost your love of life? Too much apple pie!' At the wake more stories were shared of friends' experiences of Sean, and his love of The Wedding Present was a recurrent theme. I arrived home that night to find the CD from Marc Riley, with a lovely note. I took it round to Sean's house the next day and played it loudly through his speakers.

I was delighted when David agreed to perform an acoustic set at a charity show I organised, celebrating Sean's poetry and written word, and his love of music, on what would have been his 54th birthday in November 2019. David commented between songs that the lyrics seemed to take on a new meaning in that context. And indeed they did.

I am forever grateful to have stumbled upon that radio frequency one Saturday afternoon, to have had that time with Sean, and to have had him share his beloved favourite music with me.

There's always something left behind...

DALLIANCE

ANDREW WILSON

For me, it's got to be 'Dalliance'. The opening track of their greatest album. It's all sad and reflective and the chorus comes and the eyes start to prickle. It builds up until the sadness turns to a full on 'fuck you' rage of thrashing guitars that is wonderfully cathartic. While it's a very different song, it's up there with The Who's 'My Generation' as a song I never get sick of hearing. I commented on the recent release of an acoustic version of it that it's such a good song, I'd probably buy a sign language version.

'Dalliance' is such a favourite that Andrew Wilson would buy a sign language version of it

REEL 2, DIALOGUE 2

ANDY SHEARER

When I got engaged in 2002, the plans for our wedding took over the lives of my fiancée and myself, as they do for so many couples. There are so many important decisions – the venue, the dress, the cake, the stag and hen dos – to name just a few. One is of course the music and I figured it was an area where I might be able to have a little more influence. I lost my battle to have 'Dalliance' as my first dance but was told I could choose the music that played whilst we were waiting for the bride to arrive. I didn't twig at the time that the reason my fiancée agreed to this is that she would never have to hear it.

It was 2002 and The Wedding Present were on hiatus. It was all about Cinerama and one of my favourite tracks at the time was 'Reel 2, Dialogue 2'. I thought the music would be perfect but unfortunately the lyrics aren't entirely conducive to a wedding. In particular the line 'remember you're the one who slept with someone else' was troublesome. I didn't think my mum or my fiancée's dad would appreciate that one on their children's big day.

However, the band had always been very approachable and so I contacted them through their website to see if an instrumental version was available. Sally Murrell responded and said she was pretty sure there was a version that would work and she'd dig around to find it. She was good to her word and it arrived well before the wedding with a handwritten note. When I offered to pay for the track, she couldn't resist saying it was a wedding present.

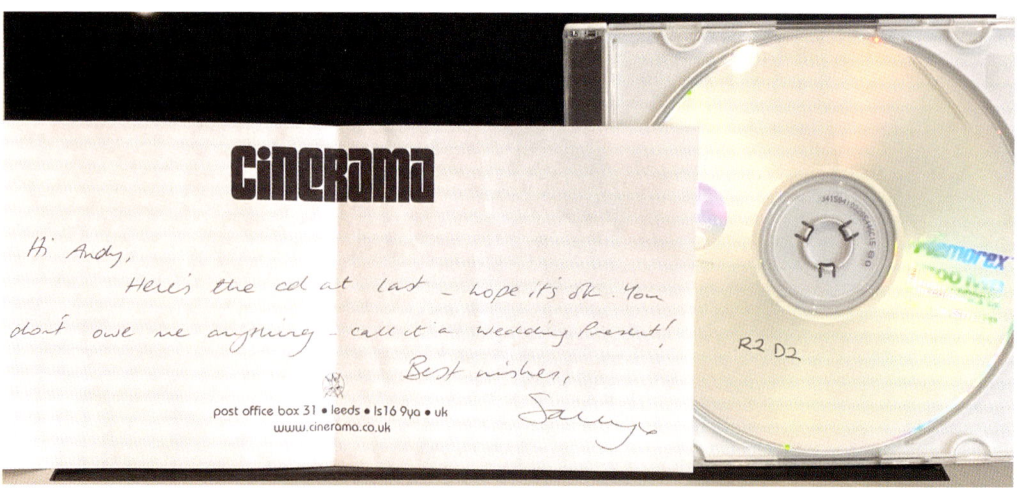

Andy Shearer got a copy of 'Reel 2, Dialogue 2' from Scopitones

The wedding occurred on a perfect August day in 2003 and the track was a fitting accompaniment as the guests took their seats in the hotel where we were to be married. It was a perfect day, but the story does have a very David Gedge-like ending as we ended up getting divorced because I slept with someone else.

SEAMONSTERS

BRYAN NEWRUCK

I've so many 'first time I heard...' memories with The Wedding Present and most, if not all, skated around romantic and epicurean highlights. However, to be concise, *Seamonsters* was the soundtrack to my boarding an intimate yet hedonistic cruise ship. Daniela was a Brazilian girl I'd met years before. We dated briefly. I was her first. Out of the blue, she called my parents whilst I was away at university. I phoned her back. Rather quickly, I learnt she was now in New York City, studying, had her own flat, and desired to see me. In a matter of two weeks, I found myself on a bus packed with some clothes and the *Seamonsters* compact disc. I recall we drank wine while the candles and incense burned away, listening to *Seamonsters*; giving in to the unrelenting waves of desire, lust and hunger. I needn't expand more as the rest can be read in an Anaïs Nin book. Dani promptly went out and bought *Seamonsters*. Our dalliance would continue monthly over the course of a year and a half and *Seamonsters* was always the soundtrack.

YOU SHOULD ALWAYS KEEP IN TOUCH WITH YOUR FRIENDS

CHRIS BOUNDS

Sheffield, February 2017. It's the *Tommy* 30th anniversary tour. I'm there with my oldest friends Mike, Rich and Simon, and David Gedge has just dedicated a song to the four of us. As another David once sang, 'And you may ask yourself, 'Well how did I get here?'.'

West Sussex, 30 years earlier:

If you know anything about Sussex, it won't be anything to do with the unexciting top left corner of it where I grew up. All the best-known places like Brighton, Eastbourne and Hastings are in East Sussex. The only famous location in West Sussex is Gatwick and that is right in the opposite corner! The Cure's hometown of Crawley is over that way too, which made them our not-that-local heroes.

The repetitive strain of our uneventful teenage lives was thankfully enlivened when

Photo: Tom Williams

Chris Bounds & friends - (left to right) Simon, Chris, Richard, Mike

we started going to watch gigs. The London to Portsmouth train line ran nearby which meant we could get to gigs in both, but only if we could persuade someone to take and collect us from the train station. Once we were old enough to learn to drive ourselves, a whole new set of possibilities opened up before us like a vast New Jersey freeway. Access to cars meant freedom; we were inside a Bruce Springsteen song. What else can we do now except roll down the window and let the wind blow back our hair because the night's busting open and this dual carriageway can take us anywhere? Well, maybe not anywhere but Aldershot, Brighton and Reading.

We were disciples of the gospel according to *NME* and *Melody Maker* and Janice Long's weekday evenings show on Radio 1 was our holy communion. (I didn't discover John Peel until a couple of years later). So it came to pass that in 1987, I sent off for a compilation tape advertised in *Melody Maker* called *Indie Top 20*. It's not overstating it to say that tape changed my life. It was a gateway into so much more music and I subsequently bought records or tapes by 16 of the 20 bands on it.

It was the first time I ever heard Half Man Half Biscuit (still one of my favourite bands to this day), Joy Division (not counting Paul Young's cover of 'Love Will Tear Us Apart' on *No Parlez*, which you definitely shouldn't), The Blue Aeroplanes (within six months, I was singing and playing guitar in a band named after a Blue Aeroplanes lyric and ending gigs with a very loud and sped-up Joy Division cover – have that, Paul Young!) and, most significantly, it was the first time I ever heard The Wedding Present and the song 'You Should Always Keep In Touch With Your Friends'. The frantically strummed noisy guitars grabbed my attention but the lyrics seemed to be telling an altogether more melancholy tale. A lost, or more probably unrequited, love with a friend from school.

When you're 16, clumsy and shy with hormones running riot and heightening every emotion to what often seems like unbearable levels, it feels like every short-term crush is actually *Love Story* and you can hear references to the sad little non-event that you laughingly call a lovelife in all manner of unlikely places. So those lyrics really said something to me about my life in 1987.

A school trip to the unlikely destination of Ostend had provided me with a precious opportunity to spend a few hours talking to someone else's girlfriend. That afternoon was the inspiration behind several of my own most cringeworthy attempts at lyric writing but I never came up with anything remotely as good as 'a bridge that stood close by the sea, the day that we spent there is ours eternally'.

I bought Volume 2 of the *Indie Top 20* tape when that came out. That had 'My Favourite Dress' on it and I loved that just as much. The next few Wedding Present singles bedazzled us further. 'Nobody's Twisting Your Arm' was a dance floor staple at our favourite Indie disco (Sister Ray in Brighton) as were the next singles, 'Why Are You Being So Reasonable Now?' and especially 'Kennedy'. Just after that came out, we saw them live for the first time at Kilburn National Ballroom, and a couple of months later we were back for more at Brighton Top Rank.

Bizarro… *Seamonsters*… *Hit Parade*… the noisy guitars got noisier, the records got even better, the gigs got wilder. Over the next few years, we saw them many more times in Portsmouth, Reading, Brighton and London.

But as people do when they get older, gradually we all dispersed. By the end of 1992, when we saw them play in Brighton, none of us were living in Sussex. The venue itself had been renamed from Top Rank to The Event. The times they were a-changing. Over the next few years, various circumstances caused us to make our homes in all manner of glamorous locations… Tokyo. London. Sydney. Istanbul. Auckland. Sheffield. Liverpool. Swindon. Portsmouth. Chippenham. Cheam.

Jobs, partners, children and the kind of responsibilities that go with being an actual grown-up followed and by 2010, the four of us somehow ended up living almost at opposite corners of England, with me in the North West. We were all 40 in 2010 and I noticed that a few days before my birthday, The Wedding Present were playing in Holmfirth, about an hour's drive from my front door. What's more they were celebrating the 21st anniversary of *Bizarro* by playing the album in full.

A couple of years before, we had been to see the reformed Pogues at Brixton Academy and had spent most of the gig watching from near the back, drinking our pints and discussing whether it was sensible to go down the front and get in amongst it. Were we too old to mosh? It's a young man's game, isn't it? Eventually we'd had enough beer to give it a try anyway and those sweaty last 20 minutes were the best bit of the gig by a mile!

Having survived that, we knew how we wanted to celebrate the big four-zero. So it was that we decided to go to Holmfirth and laugh heartily in the face of the ageing process by jumping around like lunatics down the front and pretending we were 19 again!

That Holmfirth gig was a bit of a Damascene moment for all of us. We realised that we needed to treasure every opportunity we got to see this band that meant so much to us. We went back to Holmfirth again in 2011, and since then The Wedding Present have become the catalyst for us to get together regularly for the best possible reason. Any tour announcements are followed by a flurry of excited WhatsApp messages as we work out which gigs we're going to and start researching nearby Travelodges and pubs.

In the last decade, we have met up to see The Wedding Present in Bristol, Chester, Wolverhampton, Blackpool, Wakefield, Liverpool and multiple times in London and Manchester. And Sheffield, which is where this tale began.

When Mike was getting married, he said he didn't want any kind of big stag weekend. He just wanted to meet up somewhere, have a few beers and go to see The Wedding Present. It was great fortune for us that there was a Saturday night gig coming up in February 2018 in Sheffield, a city we all have great affection for. Simon used to live there and we all have treasured (albeit hazy) memories of visiting him up there to explore the city's pubs, parties, curry houses and chip shops.

Shortly before the gig, I interviewed superhero drummer Charlie Layton for my website trustthewizards.com. I told him that the four of us were celebrating Mike's stag weekend at the Sheffield gig. Being the lovely chap that he is, Charlie must've asked David to give us a shoutout. We appreciated it all the more because we all know that's not the kind of thing David is comfortable doing. A bit too naff, fake and showbizzy. Like doing encores. One of many things that makes them the semi-legendary band they are.

Neither Charlie nor David would've known that the song they dedicated to us was the first Wedding Present song I ever heard, the one on that tape from *Melody Maker*. But the title of the song couldn't have been more appropriate. No matter how it ends, you really should keep in touch with your friends.

If I'm honest, the rest of that song's lyrics have lost most of their impact. The girl in Ostend is long forgotten, to quote 'A Million Miles': 'I can't even remember the colour of her eyes.' I'm not that lovelorn teenager anymore. Nor indeed am I the overgrown lovelorn teenager that I remained for many years after that. So as good as they are, it's not the lyrics that get me these days. That's not what hits me hard. It's the noisy guitars. It's still the noisy guitars. It will always be the noisy guitars. Nobody does it better. Baby, you're the best.

BRASSNECK
CHRISTOPHER SPRIGGS

It's playing now. Seven inches of black wax dizzying on the turntable. The voice of the guitar seizes you by the collar. Then the drums arrive, insistent. Gedge stands his ground, there's no love lost on this one. Something about a letter, and being in a bad mood. 'I'm not being funny with you but it's hard to be engaging when the things you love keep changing.' Then the break down, acoustic strumming, a swoop of feedback. Something in me wants to cry. I've no idea why the lyrics evoke that because for a long while I thought the lyrics said 'I might have been a beetroot' ('I might have been a bit rude'), but the emotion feels like mine.

For Christopher Spriggs, it has to be 'Brassneck'

That's the hallmark of a Wedding Present song; it It feels like your own. How 'Brassneck' became associated with me surviving school I'm not sure. Maybe it was because none of my friends had a clue who The Wedding Present were. Whilst they were still tucked up in bed, I was getting up at 5am every morning to do a three hour newspaper round in a dull Hampshire village. The best thing about working at the newsagents was seeing the new edition of *Melody Maker* and *NME* on a Wednesday. Before starting the delivery, as the sun came up, I would rest my bike against Balfours front window and leaf through the music mags for the latest releases, print ink grubbing my fingers. I was a short kid, bad haircut, introvert. Perfect for finding a teenage home in Indie music. Perfect for getting bullied at school. Lunch stolen every day. Kicked in the head.

The bastards could say what they liked but they couldn't take away my love of the Weddoes. I wasn't sharing my secret power with them because when I got home, I played 'Brassneck' at full volume on my Amstrad hi-fi and all the thoughts of getting up early, of another miserable day at school ahead, were lost in the noise of driving guitars, the rough riff and rhythm, the grouch of Gedge telling someone how things really are.

I would flip the seven-inch and pogo around my bedroom to 'Don't Talk, Just Kiss' in a 'Brassneck' t-shirt, so many sizes too big the hem reached my knees. My mum called it a dress. It was my favourite. When I gave my whole vinyl collection away, about 500 records I guess, I kept just five seven-inch singles even though I never thought I'd get to play them again now CDs were becoming the thing. 'Brassneck' was one I saved, because it saved me. This afternoon, 30 years later, I ordered myself a new 'Brassneck' t-shirt, one which fits.

I've grown up, but not grown out of the song. It's nearly midnight. It's playing now. Full volume. 'Brassneck, Brassneck, I just decided I don't trust you anymore.' The past thaws. The grief of school days is behind me. 'Brassneck' helped me through. It's the friend that didn't leave. Here come the drums.

I just know you weren't listening, were you?
Oh, please go, whenever you prefer to

I won't forget. The song is in my blood.

NO NOMINATION

MALCOLM WYATT

One song by The Wedding Present above all others? You're having a laugh, surely (and that's laugh with a hard northern 'a', this Surrey-born and bred fan has to admit). Right, time to try and narrow it down.

Could it be 'Everyone Thinks He Looks Daft' (ditto with that 'a' in daft)? It opened one of the most important LPs of the Eighties (or any era, as far as I'm concerned), and I'm thinking of that giant bunny counting down before the band tackled *George Best* after a short warm-up at Manchester Academy in 2007, the day before my 40th birthday, possibly the first of around 1,000 TWP record anniversary dates I've contemplated catching down the years. Did they play it at Reading Majestic in 1987, my first Wedding Present sighting (after a false start or two)? I don't reckon so, but we knew it well enough by the time that sparkling debut landed, the tie-in tour's University of London Union date a celebration for sure.

From the same seminal platter, 'My Favourite Dress' jumps out, Amelia Fletcher also adding her vocal charm on the finale, 'You Can't Moan, Can You?', and combining so well with David. And while we're talking early days, I still get a warm fuzz with 'Nobody's Twisting Your Arm', another Amelia co-vocal. The same applied when they revisited that in recent times, adding much needed light in dark Covid lockdown days, putting a smile on this virus-jaded fan's face. I'm welling up just thinking of those harmonies and Peter Solowka's accordion. Take it away, Grapper.

What else is in the running? The band's 1994 take on Marc Riley and the Creepers' 'Jumper Clown' hurtled straight off the turntable at me, the barefaced cheek of the original duly nailed. It proved a perfect pre-night out vinyl spin, my pal and fellow TWP devotee Jon Mahoney feeling the same way about the following year's fellow leftfield contender 'Sucker'. And how about that take on Mud's 'Rocket'? That's how you interpret a classic single, the spirit of glam alive and well. And value for money too when you factor in that it's merely the flipside of 'Flying Saucer', a track I last thrilled to live in late 2019 at Guildford's Boileroom, the last show before Danielle Wadey and Charlie Layton headed off 'on leave', in what ultimately turned out to be an unwelcome period of forced absence for us all.

What else? Well, those shared harmonies with Heather Lewis on 'Click Click' grabbed me from day one, taking me higher, and were wonderfully reinterpreted by Danielle when I caught the band across the Pennines at Hebden Bridge's Trades Club after an interview with David at a *Watusi* 20th anniversary show in the summer of 2014.

I could pick another half dozen from more recent years, but I'll settle on 'Rachel', thinking back to footage out there from a Brighton record shop rendition that warmed the heart. It should have been a big hit of course, but that's an argument for another day. And while we're talking David Lewis Gedge crossover pop mastery, let's sail into Cinerama territory for 'Ears', picking up 'Crusoe' en route.

What's that? Nothing from *Seamonsters*? Criminal, but I'll play the popular card and put 'Kennedy' in the mix. That's how you write a hit. I recall the time I heard it on daytime radio while shipped out to a Post Office admin centre in Redhill. 'Isn't this one of the obscure bands you bang on about, Malc?' asked Ford Capri driving '80s soul boy Terry. 'It's quite good actually.' Quite good? How dare he? 'Anyway, your turn to make a cuppa.' Yep, just another day when you realise your workmates don't get that same sense of euphoria.

There are at least two more sublime *Bizarro* moments for me: 'No', with its difficult to resist chunky bass and jangly guitar, and the moment the guitars come back in on 'Bewitched'… mesmeric. And, finally, 1992 and that classic year of 45s, where the intro alone to 'Three' has me in a mess. How many on my shortlist now? I seem to be up to a sweet 16. Now to whittle them down. Oh, hang on, that's the send button…

BOO BOO

IAN CUSACK

The first time I heard 'Boo Boo', my immediate response was to jump up and down on the spot, punching the air and roaring my incoherent approval. I was in my living room one Friday teatime at the end of May 2008, having just purchased *El Rey*. Almost a decade and a half later, *El Rey* remains my favourite latter period Wedding Present album and 'Boo Boo' my all-time favourite Wedding Present song.

To these ears, 'Boo Boo' is a musical tour-de-force, combining a profound, dispassionate yet ominous, growling wall of slow noise with quieter passages of precise, intense solo guitar manipulation, displaying forensic control and creating an atmosphere combining hope, despair and ambivalence. The achingly brief lyrics create the two most visual and affecting images in all of David Gedge's writing. DLG himself has gone on record as saying he feels the opening line, 'Well yes, it's late; the waiter's stacking the chairs' has a highly cinematic quality. I disagree, as my mind visualises an oil painting, composed predominantly in matt black, nocturnal blues and turgid yellow, creating a scene that incorporates a window table for two in an otherwise deserted restaurant, on a quiet side street in a sleeping, obscure town on an unremarkable midweek night. The lateness of the hour suggests this assignation may have connotations of a clandestine meeting, rather than a friendly catch up over a bite of supper. However, there are hints that one of those has emotionally moved on. It isn't him though.

The fact the lyrics are in the present tense increases the sense of immediacy and unpredictability surrounding the situation we are drawn into. There's no scope for reflection or analysis of times gone by; we know the two diners have a shared romantic history and the aching sense of yearning from the spurned narrator is genuinely heart rending. Is his former lover now simply his friend or is there a chance that the passion could be rekindled? When the second verse begins by describing how 'your eyes are glistening as you fill my glass to the brim', even the most disaffected, pessimistic ex must tend towards believing she still carries a torch, only to be struck down by how she makes her new flame the main subject of the conversation. Those optical lagoons of perfect blue drain and desiccate; barren and loveless. Has the hope of a moment before really been extinguished?

The real lyrical genius of 'Boo Boo' is that the song leaves the future ambiguous. There are no more verses. We don't learn if the night ended with wild, unbridled passion, a rancorous outpouring of bad blood, or a chaste peck on the cheek. The music offers no clues either; a vast, anthemic, crescendo of pummelling volume builds and builds and… dissipates. Again, we are in the throes of ambiguity; there isn't a climax, only bathos. Interpret the complementary sounds and words how you wish; all that is certain is the lack of finality, which leaves us yearning for more, even as the quite baffling 'Swingers' is bringing *El Rey* to a gloriously confusing close.

YOU SHOULD ALWAYS KEEP IN TOUCH WITH YOUR FRIENDS

DAMON BROWN

I left school in 1984 and started work. The only thing I was any good at at school was technical drawing, so I was fortunate to get a job as a trainee draughtsman. The company had a training department and took on four school leavers each year. We were sent off to college for our HNC on day release, which involved a 15 mile drive. One of the other lads was into music that I liked too, and he would make tapes of John Peel sessions and records he'd bought which we would listen to in the car. One song that really struck a chord (!) with me was by a band from Leeds called The Wedding Present, 'You Should Always Keep In Touch With Your Friends'. That song ignited my passion for the band and reminds me of those car journeys every time I hear it. It was a pivotal time in my life and the lyrics of this and the band's other songs seemed to be written by someone in tune with the things I was experiencing – both good and bad!

Damon Brown believes you should always keep in touch with your friends

Over the following four years we continued the tradition of making tapes for those car journeys, eagerly awaiting the next release or session from The Wedding Present. I grew up in Kent so there were few opportunities to see live bands locally, but evening trips to London were a regular occurrence. If someone drove there, we would listen to whoever we were going to see on the way and a mix of stuff on the way back. Looking back, they were great times and the soundtrack was written by The Wedding Present and a few others. Then, in 1988, I went away to uni and lost touch with those friends. I wish I'd kept in touch with them…

DALLIANCE
DAN COWLING

My first Wedding Present concert was at Kilburn in London in 1990 which is immortalised on the *Live 1990* album. I had just turned 17 and they opened with 'Dalliance', which just blew my mind away as it was the first time that I had heard it. So that may be a strong contender for my favourite Wedding Present song, although hearing 'Silver Shorts' at Salisbury Arts Centre in 1992 was quite special. And then there is 'Crawl', or 'Give My Love To Kevin' or 'What Have I Said Now?'. There are too many to choose from. I also interviewed the band several times during my uni days and one of my special memories is David phoning my parents' house to arrange one of them.

I'm a headteacher of a large secondary school in West London now in my normal life, but have always kept The Wedding Present close to my heart and ideals. It's amazing how David's songs have always remained in the background as a soundtrack to my life.

I had the t-shirt and still have the ten inch limited edition EP of *All The Songs Sound The Same*. And you should hear the story of the fiasco I had with Our Price and the bloody scratch that I had on it!

A MILLION MILES

PAM MOORE

How fitting that we met when he was working in a record shop, in a small Northern town, as 1989 drew to a close; the end of a magical decade. I was still in a big REM phase, and he still managed to charm me by making fun of Michael Stipe. For me it was love at first sight, and it was heart-wrenching to know that in a few short months I was due to leave for Canada with my parents. Too much backstory there, but I was born in Nova Scotia, my parents were retiring, and my sisters were already over there. Mum and Dad felt it was time to go back, and I was sadly carried along by their enthusiasm. Not the best decision I ever made.

He and I had such a short, but very intense, time together and music was everything to both of us. We shared so much, and he credited me with opening his eyes to all things 'fringey Indie'. He often wore a purple floral shirt, which I loved and which I called his David Gedge shirt. 'What's bad about that?' he'd say, to which I replied, 'Nothing, he's good husband material.' I'm still not entirely sure what I meant by that, but it made him laugh all the same.

His favourite band was The Stranglers, we both loved The Stone Roses and I always had great fondness for *George Best*, 'My Favourite Dress' and 'A Million Miles' being my two

For Pam Moore it was 'A Million Miles' and 30 years

absolute favourites. The whole album takes me back to those last days of the decade. Hearing any music of that time takes me straight back to those months we spent – even playing briefly in a garage band together – wondering what might have been, and if he still had that mixtape I made for him just before I left.

We were in touch at other times during those 30 years, but our moment never came. But in 2018, through a minor miracle of good fortune and timing, we had the chance to find out exactly how things would work out together. I flew back to the UK in September of that year, and we were fittingly reunited on an overpass at Newark Station (that moment itself really should be a Weddoes song). Almost 30 years evaporated in an instant, and we've been maintaining our long distance relationship ever since.

Neither of us managed to see The Wedding Present back in the day, so it was fitting we went to see them, together, in 2019 at the Holmfirth Picturedrome. When I heard those opening notes of 'A Million Miles', I had tears in my eyes. We were back in my front room, listening to records, and I was 22 again.

And, yes, he still has the mixtape.

BEWITCHED

JARED DEAN BLANCHARD

Jared Blanchard is bewitched by 'Bewitched'

I DJ'd for ten years and a part of that was at a college station in Vegas. My favourite day of the week was mail day because we would all gather around the crates of music that had just come in and the music director would start tossing music to each of us. I'd walk away with four or five CDs and half a dozen cassettes which I'd grab to listen to whilst I drove around delivering pizzas. I would usually listen to a full album, and if it really stuck I'd place it in between the front seats for later listening. (If it wasn't something where I even lasted a few tracks, I would toss it in the back seat to give to friends).

I distinctly remember putting in *Seamonsters* and the exact place I was driving, the time of day, the weather, my window rolled half the way down. All of the feelings and emotions are burned in my mind because I was so taken by the music coming from my speakers that I even had to pull over for a bit to listen. Not a great idea for somebody that delivers pizza – customers aren't big fans of having their food delivered cold. But for a guy that over the years of DJing, and as someone obsessed with music who had thousands of records, cassettes and even a few 8-tracks at my fingertips, to say that that tape stayed either in the deck of the car, or my player at home – wherever I was at the time, for a couple weeks straight, auto reversing continuously, just seems natural to me because I couldn't get enough.

I was in the car with my brother a while after that, playing 'Bewitched'. We had it cranked and when the song entered the soft/breakdown part we were both just staring out of the window, sort of hypnotized while we were listening. When the song came back in hard, I punched at the air in front of me right at the same time. My brother hadn't heard the song as many times as I had, and wasn't fully prepared for it to come back yet because he didn't know the timing. He screamed and yelled, 'Dude, you freaked me out!' I freaked the shit out of him. Hahaha!

In 2016, my daughter Paris and I were travelling to Barcelona for the Primavera Sound Festival. We stopped in England for a few days. I saw that The Wedding Present were playing in Leeds and told her I wanted to go. She said, 'Duh, of course we are going. They are your favourite band!' So off we went, hopping a train to go to the show. When we got there, we were first in the bar and went over to the merch table. I realised we didn't have any money so we went to hit an ATM and, when we came back, David was behind the counter organising the merch. I was talking to my daughter, turned to notice it was him and completely froze. I was in awe that he was just hanging up t-shirts and laying out posters, etc. I turned to Paris after a minute and whispered, 'That's David Gedge!' and she laughed and said, 'Um, Dad, I know – it is pretty obvious because you are acting very weird right now. Just take a breath and treat him like a normal person.' I can't remember if I did that, but I did have a great laugh after the show with her on the way back to our hotel.

EVERYONE THINKS HE LOOKS DAFT

PHIL SMITH

My love of The Wedding Present began when I bought *George Best* and *Tommy* on cassette. In August 1989 I went to Reading Festival with one of my flatmates from Essex Uni and I saw The Wedding Present live for the first time. We decided to form a band with two other friends and The Geezers were born, the name coming from the drummer – a big Status Quo fan – calling everyone 'geezer'. We played a number of gigs at both the uni and a local pub during our second and third years.

We were a covers band. Aside from 'Everyone Thinks He Looks Daft', our eclectic setlist included 'Next To You' (The Police), 'Down Down' (Status Quo), 'Slide It In' (Whitesnake), 'Don't Let Me Down, Gently' (The Wonder Stuff), 'Should I Stay Or Should I Go?' (The Clash), 'New Rose' (The Damned) and 'Rain' (The Cult). One of my other friends from uni, Nige Tassell, went on to become a journalist and writer, and interviewed David Gedge for his book *Mr Gig*, in which there are a couple of references to a Wedding Present gig we went to in 1990 and to my student house, which bring back very fond memories.

Phil Smith's band The Geezers covered 'Everyone Thinks He Looks Daft' and, er, Status Quo

IT'S WHAT YOU WANT THAT MATTERS

PETERJON CRESSWELL

Every couple of blue moons, I fall in love. Bang. Oh Jesus, help me. Here we go. No sleep, nil by mouth, joy, joy, joy. Bring it on. These blue moons are bands. Side One, Side Two, Side One, Side Two, wish upon, day upon day, I believe, oh Lord, I believe all the way. The Marys, the Buzzcocks, the Bunnymen. And then there's The Wedding Present.

As summer dovetailed with Euro 88, dovetailing with memorising reams of Russian for my finals, dovetailing with – let's see now – falling in love with an actual person and not just vinyl, *George Best* jangled out its gorgeous chords and kitchen-sink lyrics. I was hooked.

Much as I thought green eyes with hazel flecks were simply unbeatable and unrepeatable, that nothing could ever match those first bars of 'Fast Cars' circa '78, along comes '88, Tanya (hazy hazel) and *George Best*. It starts with… well, you're reading this, you know what it starts with. The thing is, I don't, not really. 'Oh why do you…'.

To this day, 35 years to the day after its release, I still have to wiki the tracklisting to write this piece. I know every nano-nuance of lyric, every middle eight, every intonation in that Granadaland accent, every exquisite lancing of relationship pain, every bang-a-ganga-banga intro ('He became a man at 23…'), every fade out (rock and roll whistling to wrap up the first track of your debut LP – what BALLS!), every melodic-chaotic-melodic thrash ('I wonder what our kid has bought her…'). It's all part of it; like the intro to the original 45-inch 'Ceremony' or the fade out to 'All I Want' to fade out 'Heaven Up Here' and send me over the River Styx satisfied. It's that good.

The segueing is immaculate. What follows is what should follow. A YouTube version I'm using to transport myself back to the summer of '88 throws in that wonderful cover (they did such great covers, didn't they?) of 'Getting Nowhere Fast'. It's a song I worshipped by a band I saw in awe at their peak, but here it's like an elephant in the soup. It shouldn't be there. It doesn't follow. What comes next could be snatched studio dialogue, it could be Brill-Building-marries-shoegaze-jingle whoosh, but it fits hand in glove with what came before.

That's why I barely know the tracklisting. I've never had to look at it. I've simply never bothered. I just know.

Upset, regret, soon, wounds, there'll never be another time… it's the rainy domain of the late-night bus-stop pre-commitment domestic, it's waiting for the phone to ring, it's the break-up while the make-up runs. It's her handwriting. There'll never be another time.

Many's an aficionado whose favourite must be 'My Favourite Dress', the bar call of The Wedding Present tunes. Requests for it were barked the night I consummated my relationship with *George Best* – Brixton Fridge, June 9th 1988. The night before *Euro 88*. The night before Russian Literature. The night before my first night with Tanya. I requested nothing (how could I?) but I do know that I went doobastardlally down the front for 'It's What You Want That Matters'. I know this because I cracked at least one rib in all the thrash frenzy. Felt nowt. Yet felt it all. 'And this is for you, you must know it's for you…'.

YOUR CHARMS

JOHN WILBERFORCE

Although my love of all things Gedge started with The Wedding Present, as I grew older so my musical tastes shifted a little as well. Initially, I adored the mountainous guitars and yelled angst – in particular when I was a lovelorn teenager, getting over the latest Jenny or Rachel. I can remember the first time I saw The Wedding Present live – it was in Manchester, and they opened with 'Dalliance'. It was ferocious, and I was instantly and completely hooked. Over 30 years and around 80 concerts later they remain a huge part of my musical life. Hell, I even saw them in Mongolia!

I digress. As I aged, I started to pay more attention to Cinerama. There were pianos, string sections and even the voices of women. As I was in my thirties by this stage, The Fall had given way to The Carpenters on my turntable, and Cinerama represented a compromise that the 18-year-old John and the 35-year-old John could both listen to. Even now, my record collection is equal parts The Fall and The Carpenters.

I had a wedding to plan by this stage – and on a whim, I decided that the ultimate romantic gesture would be to sing a song at the reception to my wife. I sent a copy of the song to the wedding band, and we even met up a couple of times to give it a run through. The band liked it too.

And so, on a September evening in Grasmere my family and friends bore witness to me and a folk band rattling through 'Your Charms' to my bewildered wife. I loved doing it, and having watched it back subsequently it was rather good. It was also the start and end of my career as a rock and roll star.

There was no happy ending to the love story, sadly. We divorced a few years later in a blizzard of acrimony that was more Wedding Present than Cinerama. In fact, 'Dalliance' would have been a better fit, seeing as 'I was yours for seven years'.

Still, I will always have Grasmere.

I'M NOT ALWAYS SO STUPID

MARKUS LARS-ERIK

I remember it being broadcast on the famous *Bommen* show on Swedish Radio P3 on a Sunday evening. It was a real 'I hit gold' feeling...

SEAMONSTERS

ROB HANCOCK

I'd heard a couple of Wedding Present tracks on the *John Peel Show* but nothing really clicked until I heard The Wedding Present on John Peel's 50th birthday show on Radio 1, and was immediately impressed. Within a couple of days, I'd bought *George Best* and *Tommy*, but none of the songs sounded like the ones I heard on the radio; a grungy jangly one, one about Kennedy and apple pies, a slow one that got quiet then loud. It was probably a couple of months later that *Bizarro* came out and I heard those songs again. I saw them live for the first time that November (when they still did encores) and a couple of times a year every year, usually in Birmingham and Wolverhampton, until babies and young children got in the way. After a long break I finally saw them again in 2019 on – what else? – the *Bizarro* 30th anniversary tour at Birmingham Institute, where I'd seen them perform the whole of *Seamonsters* in 1991.

THE WEDDING PRESENT

Uit Leeds afkomstig en voor de tweede keer in Nederland is THE WEDDING PRESENT van zanger, songschrijver en gitarist David Gedge. Hij richtte de band ooit op als 'bruidsgeschenk' aan zijn broer, maar inmiddels heeft THE WEDDING PRESENT zich ontwikkeld tot een van de betere groepen uit het aanbod veelbelovende nieuwe gitaarbands die zich vooral via de onafhankelijke labels presenteren.

Ook staat de groep op de C '86 verzamelplaat, die aanvankelijk door de Engelse New Musical Express is uitgebracht in de vorm van een cassette.

Begon de groep, vooral geïnspireerd door de Velvet Underground, de 12" singles 'Don't try and stop me mother' en 'This boy can wait' die hoog in de Engelse Indie-charts stonden laten een eigenzinnige groep horen. John Peel was zo enthousiast, dat hij THE WEDDING PRESENT uitnodigde voor zijn befaamde Peel-sessions. De groep staat momenteel met haar derde single 'My favourite dress' wederom al wekenlang in de hoogste regionen van de indie-charts.

THE WEDDING PRESENT

Band line up is : David(Just like the four tops) Gedge,guitar and voice-over. Keith (Bony Hands) Gregory, bass. Shaun (Reasonable) Chairman, drums, and L.U.F.C. Grapper Esq. guitar.
Formed on New Years Day 1985
- no previous convictions -

DOC:Whatabout SOQ?Is it mebbe a lil too streetwise for 100 purcent limeys like you kids?

D: Don't understand that much of it. Sorry

K: The only thing I don't quite get is why the 'straight-edge' question is so central.

DOC:So why,I mean why friends did see fit ta start a band?

: We want to change the world

: The bands who make the best interviewees are the ones who can invent the best lie to answer this

DOC:The worruds in some a ya songs gimme the impressionation yaz got summit meaningful ta say.I'm not mistaken in this here insinuation wun' ya say?

K: Weve been called 'near feminist but its not a label we'd make a

DOC:This heres me fave question at the present-what kinda cock 'n bull d'ya git upta come the weekend?

D: I used to really look forward to Saturdays but it's annoying that nowadays weekends are exactly

A 'first' for the Wedding Present

HE Wedding Present have started vork on recording heir debut album, aving just returned rom a sojourn to the etherlands.

It will be released in ctober, and be preeded by a single in the hops in late September.

David Gedge, vocalist ith the Leeds-based and, said the album as likely to feature only wo songs that had previously been released.

He said: "The gigs in Holland were very useful for knocking some new stuff into shape. The idea is to feature as many recent songs as possible on the album."

David, from Middleton, said the trip to Holland was the most enjoy able tour yet — apa from when he attempte the popular Dutch spo of canal jumping an ended up sinking int the mud on the bank.

That is the sort o wacky things touring po groups get up to.

The Wedding Present have, as yet, failed to break into pops' mainstream. Yet their marriage of groomed lyrics and unbridled guitar have achieved unrivalled independent success. With their songs of hurt and happiness are these engaging Leeds lads manically strumming their way to the top? David Gedge and Pete Solowka hope so, but not too impatiently.

● It's Saturday aftie in Leeds and David Gedge of The Wedding Present and myself are trying out this conversational idea for WELL RED. Meanwhile, down in London, lead guitarist Peter Solowka is trying it out over a pint with Paul Moody. Novel idea, eh? To interview two different members of a band on the same day at opposite ends of the country. So while they pull the pints, we pour the tea.

Not since The Smiths' early days have a band so dominated the indie charts. Their album 'George Best' went straight in at number three and spent several months at the top, sales are now on the healthy side of 50,000. Their latest single 'Nobody's Twisting Your Arm' inevitably reached the number one position and just missed the top 40.

ARE THEY CONTENT in being in pole position as 'the next big thing' or are they hungry for fame? "We're not consciously 'going for' the top 20, we haven't changed the way we write or arrange songs", replies Pete pausing from his pint, but, in Leeds, singer and conversational songwriter David Gedge puts down his tea and admits, "It'd be nice to get into the top 40 mainly so I can phone my Mam up and say 'Mam, I'm on *Top Of The Pops* tonight'".

It's only a matter of time. The next single, due out in Septem-

WEDDOS on BBC Radio One

Als ich David frage, ob diese Session auch in Maida Vale aufgenommen wurde (dort stehen die BBC Studios, ich hatte Peel allerdings so verstanden, daß ihm die Ukranian Session von den Weddos zugeschickt wurde), kommen wir auf den Namen dieses Fanzines "MAIDA VALE" zu sprechen. David meint, es sei ein passender Name für ein Fanzine.

MAIDA VALE

Ich erkläre ihm, daß ich ein großer Fan der Peel Sessions bin, da sie meist etwas ganz Besonderes darstellen (die Songs werden fast live in einem sehr guten Studio aufgenommen).
Ich zeige David eine Liste, auf der ich versucht habe, alle WP-Sessions zusammenzustellen. David kramt in seinem Gedächtnis, um die fehlenden Stücke in der Liste zu finden und zusammen schaffen wir es dann, eine fast komplette Sessionliste aufzustellen.

Die Tatsache, daß eine Peel Session (die vom Feb 86) in der Strange Fruit Serie veröffentlicht wurde, schreibt David ganz dem Engagement Peels zu.
Ob noch weitere WP-Sessions auf Strange Fruit erscheinen, weiß David nicht genau, aber eine zweite Session mit ukrainischen Liedern wollen sie auf jeden Fall machen!

Mir gelingt es, David ein wenig zu überraschen, wenn ich nach der Band frage, in der er zuvor spielte, The Lost Pandas. (Es war wiedereinmal John Peel der mal etwas von einer solchen Demokassette der

THE WEDDING PRESENT
BBC Radio One Session

Dez 85 Andy Kershaw Session
*living and learning
*once more
*at the edge of the sea
*my favourite dress

Feb 86 John Peel Session
*felicity
*what becomes of the broken hearted
*you should always keep in touch with your friends
*this boy can wait

Jun 86 Janice Long Session
*my favourite dress
*Shatner
*(Gang Of Four) Cover
*everyone thinks he looks daft

? John Peel Session
*all about eve
*Cover Version
*never said
*don't be so hard

Jun 87 John Peel Session
*getting nowhere fast
*something and nothing
*a million miles
*give my love to Kevin

Nov 87 John Peel Session
"Ukranian Session"
*the freedom fighter
*you decived me
*the avaitening
*Katushia

"Look, the reason I write love songs is because sex is the most important thing in the world."

David Lewis Gedge, Wedding Present, 26.9.87

Gedge's lyrics are the confession of an "average" man, stripped of all defences and steeped in pain. Monosyllabic and often conversational, his words still transcend the ordinary, gaining all their eloquence in the act of expression. Simply put, he sings the words you've always wanted to say.

TOP TEN ALBUMS

1 STING — Nothing Like The Sun.
2 BRUCE SPRINGSTEIN — Tunnel Of Love.
3 PET SHOP BOYS — Actually . . .
4 SMITHS — Strangeways, Here We come.
5 MICHAEL JACKSON — Bad.
6 ERIC CLAPTON — The Cream Of . . .
7 CHRIS REA — Dancing With Strangers.
8 COMMUNARDS — Red.
9 BEE GEES — E.S.P.
10 WEDDING PRESENT — George Best.

● *Charts supplied by Andy's Records.*

IPSWICH EVENING STAR
OCTOBER 24th

THE WEDDING PRESENT
"George Best" (Reception)

SINGER David Lewis Gedge pops round for a cup of tea and chats incessantly about bus stops, discos and his new girl friend. Guitars chop furiously or steadily depending on the mood. It is a bit samey, but occasionally, on songs like "Everyone Thinks He Looks Daft" and "My Favourite Dress", choruses are thrown out of the riff machine. In George Best

THE IDEAL GIFT

THE WEDDING PRESENT: "George Best" (Reception)

I WILL never moan again.

I have just heard The Wedding Present's first LP for the eighth time this week and I will never moan again. Life's too short, it really is. I will also be nicer to my relatives, take in blind puppies left on m[y] doorstep and stop scabbing for cigarettes. *"Oh why do you catch my eye and turn away?"* ("Everyone Thinks He Looks Daft").

If I told you they were as melodic as Abba but faster than The Ramones, you'd probably raise an eyebrow. If I told you that the lyrics were worthy of Pete Shelley at his very best, you might scratch your chin doubtfully. If I told you that there is a great pictu[re] of George Best on the cover and inner sleeve, you might whip off your belt and strap yourself to the bedpost (getting carried away, Graham . . . relax, relax, talk about the lyrics . . .).

"And when they're out with all his friends, he does forget that she's even there." ("Don't Be So Hard").

Dave Gedge, lead singer and all-round good-guy, is a mighty impressive songwriter, using simple, conversational language in order to touch lightly on our basic experiences: those uneasy romances, the self-indulgent misery of unrequited love, and the wrong words blurted out in an unguarded moment. I say simple language, but there's nothing simplistic about the emotions conjured up in the songs. Many a happy hour to be spent unravelli[ng] the mysteries of everyday life, methinks . . .

THE WEDDING PRESENT

«GEORGE BEST»

Reception-Radical Import

La aparición de grupos como ést[e] en el panorama pop británico es con[-] secuencia lógica de la expansión ame[-] ricana en el imperio; secuelas de l[a] mejor nueva ola inglesa atentas [a] combatir de modo irritante al inva[-] sor. Gentes como Half Man Half Bis[-] cuit o estos Wedding Present (impre[-] sionante nombre, sí señor) retomar[on] el camino que años atrás dejara[n]

Not only is the music irresistible, these lads from Leeds are hysterical without being comical. Anyone with titles like "What Did Your Last Servant Die Of?" or "You Can't Moan Can You?" is all right by me. It's not just their humor that I find so compelling but rather their soul. The urgency with which these pop masterpieces are performed is uncanny. Emotion? This record could not hold another single drop. If you like any of the current crop of British guitar pop bands (Bodines, Primal Scream, Weather Prophets, etc.), then you'll love the Wedding Present; they're miles above the rest. Without a doubt, my choice for record of the year.

The Wedding Present 'George Best (Reception).

Rumour has it that this album could have been even better if i had been titled 'Don Masson' and had had a photo of the god-like genius on the front cover. That said, this is a trul great album encapsulating some of the best songs to come out c the new wave of British 'guitar' bands.

Bitter, twisted love songs backed up by an awesome wall of melodic sound pushes this up amongst the top albums of the championship season 87-88, an essential purchase for anyone wh prides themselves on having a discerning musical taste (i.e., not Phil Collins or Dire Straits). Lift up your bobble hats and get an earful of this, its lunderful (sic)

The Wedding Present — **George Best** (Reception)

It's rare that a band plays music as joyously as The Wedding Present. They are as enthusiastic as a child discovering two shiny quarters in an old coat. Their guitars careen across each other like those two coins jiggling in their pockets. The bass rumbles and roars, creating yet another layer of melody. Over it all, David Gedge sings in his deep, sonorous voice about boy/girl relationships. His lyrics have a naive quality to them, which makes them all the more endearing. In "A Million Miles" he sings "I must walk past this doorway thirty times/Just trying to catch your eye/You made it all worthwhile/When you returned my smile." These guys aren't wimpy though--their guitars bite as hard as the Buzzcocks, and "All This And More" has a frantically fast rhythm that leaves you breathless. There are no superior tracks here because The Wedding Present attacks each song with the same consistency. This unmitigated exultation in music is a Present anyone will cherish forever.

Megan McLaughlin

THE CHOCOLATE HOUSE PRESENTS:

THE WEDDING PRESENT

THE DENTISTS

THE BIG THREE

& K*SOL RADIO

VENUE Medway Arts Centre
Chatham
DATE 19-12-87
DOORS OPEN 8pm
TICKETS £3 in advance
£3·50 on the door

BEST LP

1. **STRANGEWAYS HERE WE COME** (The Smiths)
2. **THE JOSHUA TREE** (U2)
3. **SIGN O THE TIMES** (Prince)
4. **GEORGE BEST** (The Wedding Present)
5. **DARKLANDS** (The Jesus And Mary Chain)

BEST GROUP

1. THE SMITHS
2. U2
3. R.E.M.
4. HOUSEMARTINS
5. NEW ORDER
6. THE FALL
7. JESUS AND MARY CHAIN
8. THAT PETROL EMOTION
9. WEDDING PRESENT

ALBUM

1 THE JOSHUA TREE **U2**
2 FLOODLANDS **The Sisters Of Mercy**
3 HYSTERIA **Def Leppard**
4 STRANGEWAYS, HERE WE COME **The Smiths**
5 DAWNRAZOR **Fields Of The Nephilim**
6 APPETITE FOR DESTRUCTION **Guns N' Roses**
7 DRILL YOUR OWN HOLE **Gaye Bykers On Acid**
8 GEORGE BEST **The Wedding Present**
9 TUNNEL OF LOVE **Bruce Springsteen**
10 KISS ME KISS ME KISS ME **The Cure**

NEW ACT

1. THE PROCLAIMERS
2. TERENCE TRENT D'ARBY
3. THE SUGARCUBES
4. THE CHRISTIANS
5. T'PAU
6. THE WEDDING PRESENT

NEW BAND

1 CRAZYHEAD
2 ALL ABOUT EVE
3 FIELDS OF THE NEPHILIM
4 GUNS N' ROSES
5 T'PAU
6 THE PROCLAIMERS
7 THE CHRISTIANS
8 THE SUGARCUBES
9 VOICE OF THE BEEHIVE
10 DEAD FLOWERS
11 POP WILL EAT ITSELF
12 THE WEDDING PRESENT

STIRLING STUDENT ASSOC. ENTS Presents;—

THE

Wedding Present

("A THRASHY GUITAR BAND" —L. DOUGAN)

ON THURSDAY 8th OCTOBER

Tickets: £2.60 Doors 9.00pm

The Managenent reserve the right to refuse admission.
No glasses, cans or tape recorders.

Nº 0138

INDIE ACT

1 CRAZYHEAD
2 THE SMITHS
3 FIELDS OF THE NEPHILIM
4 NEW ORDER
5 THE WEDDING PRESENT

THE WEDDING PRESENT

FEB 22
7" and four track 12"
Limited Edition-
7" in Gatefold Sleeve
Now available as
Compact Disc single
RECEPTION RECORDS
in association with
Red Rhino Distribution.
DISTRIBUTED BY THE CARTEL
REC 009

NOBODY'S TWISTING YOUR ARM

THE WEDDING PRESENT

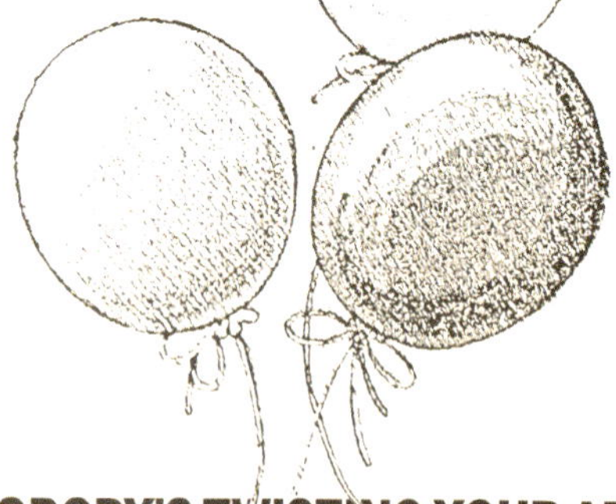

NOBODY'S TWISTING YOUR ARM.

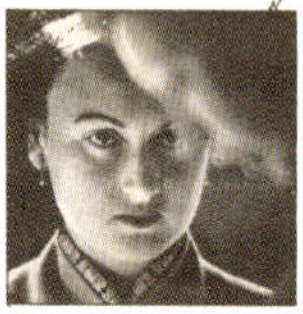

RECEPTION RECORDS
IN ASSOCIATION WITH RED RHINO DISTRIBUTION
PRESENTS
REC 009
7" / 4 TRACK 12" / CD
LIMITED EDITION 7" IN GATEFOLD SLEEVE
DISTRIBUTED BY THE CARTEL

FEBRUARY TOUR

Fisticuffs flew at **THE WEDDING PRESENT** gig at the Leeds Astoria after loca hooligans with good taste in pop but appaling manners (to be polite about it) attacked the support. **DAVID GEDGE** made an appeal for calm and ended up getting chinned himself.

HONEYMOON OVER?

Drummer quits and bassist "not keen on touring"

THE WEDDING PRESENT, who play a short tour in mid-February as a prelude to their new single, 'Nobody's Twisting Your Arm', on Reception, have lost the services of drummer Shaun after a series of "musical disagreements".

He'll be replaced by a new drummer whose identity hasn't yet been officially announced.

And there are reports that bassist Keith may also be leaving the band after the dates this month because he's not keen on touring.

The band's spokesperson could not confirm that Keith was leaving but said: "Since the success of their 'George Best' debut album last autumn the nature of the band has changed. From being a home-grown project it's had to gear itself up to a more professional level and establish itself as a touring outfit.

"Some members of the group may not wish to commit themselves to the extent that is now required but even if they don't remain full-time group members they'll still be involved with the band's activities because that's the sort of people they are. There's no fights or anything; it's just people adapting to changes in the group's status.

"And of course the essential character of the band won't change because David Gèdge is the writer and the singer in the group."

LOVE SONGS

"It's a very easy subject to write about. Every chart record is about love but it's done in such a banal way it makes it completely worthless. There's such a wealth of emotions to write about, but nobody tries. My favourite is Dionne Warwick's 'Walk On By': very poignant."

"It took us three years to make our first LP and I'm willing to wait as long again rather than just include fillers on it."

Sgt. Pepper Knew My Father

THE
ACCLAIMED
1988 RE-RECORDING
OF THE BEATLES'
CLASSIC ALBUM

ALL PROFITS ARE DIRECTLY DONATED TO
"CHILDLINE" FREEPOST 1111,
LONDON EC4 4BB.
TEL: 01-236 2380

ChildLine
0800 1111

NME PEP LP 100

NME

Sgt. Pepper Knew My Father

featuring

WET WET WET
BILLY BRAGG • THE CHRISTIANS
COURTNEY PINE • THE TRIFFIDS
HUE & CRY • THE FALL
THREE WIZE MEN
THE WEDDING PRESENT
SONIC YOUTH • MICHELLE – SHOCKED
FRANK SIDEBOTTOM

ISLAND

NME PEP MC 100

They're the fastest guitar-slingers in town. Premier exponents of the 2½ minute thrash, which they cleverly combine with kitchen-sink sagas of life in a Northern town. They're The Wedding Present.

"It's a good idea and it's a good cause. It was a rush decision to do it, we were phoned up and the next day we rehearsed it and the day after that we recorded it . . . I don't like the original LP, to tell you the truth, it's not the greatest Beatles LP, but that is one of the best songs. It's a pop song. I'd have been in two minds about doing one of those strange psychedelic ones. We did it in our style, sped it up, turned up the guitars and rattled it out."

David Gedge, The Wedding Present

Weddos Against Apartheid

THE WEDDING PRESENT play a one-off gig at the Brixton Academy on June 9 – likely to be their last live appearance until the Autumn.

It's an anti-apartheid benefit with all proceeds going to the City Of London AA Group, who've been manning a continuous picket outside South Africa House and suffered continual harrassment and arrests.

They'll be supported by The Gargoyles who have an album coming out on Reasonable called 'Steamflapper'. Tickets are £6 (concessions £4.50).

The Wedding Present also enliven the airwaves over the Bank Holiday by recording their sixth Peel session which will be broadcast on May 30. Peel's listeners put five of the band's songs into the Festive 50 last Christmas.

The band plan to record a new single next month, but they won't be releasing it until September. They've also been working on a compilation of early singles which should be out in July

GET YOURSELF ON THE WEDDING PRESENT GUEST LIST....... FOR LIFE!!!!

Yes, unbelievable though it might seem, we're offering you and a chum the chance of being at the VERY TOP of the guest list for <u>every single Wedding Present concert</u> from the 31st of November onwards! Just imagine... above all the journalists and A&R Men, the agents and the liggers, your name +1 will be left with the manager of each venue, with our compliments... and, if that wasn't enough, the lucky winner will als be sent assorted T-shirts, posters, and rare Wedding Present records and artefacts.

HOW TO ENTER: Have a crack at this spectacular prize by simply voting for your three favourite Wedding Present songs of all time, in order, and then guessing the combine WEIGHT IN LBS of David, Keith, Simon and Grapper!

The winner of the competition will be the sender of the first card out of the hat to correctly guess the weight of the band (or nearest to). All entries must be on POSTCARDS or the backs of sealed envelopes. The draw'll be made on thursday, the 31s of November. (The judges' decision is final).

Send your entry to "THE WEDDING PRESENT GUEST-LIST COMPETITION, PO BOX HP25, LEEDS LS6 1RU". One entry only will be accepted from each contestant!

The Wedding Present release their single 'Why Are You Being So Reasonable Now' on September 19. This classic tale of unrequited love features 'Not From Where I'm Standing' on the flip side, while the 12 inch also has 'Getting Better' from the 'Sgt Pepper Knew My Father' album and an acoustic version of 'Give My Regards To Kevin'. The Weddoes will also be playing a third date at the London Town And Country Club on October 13 and they might be making some more additions to their tour later on.

THE WEDDING PRESENT
FREE DRINKS AFTERWARDS
TOWN & COUNTRY CLUB
THURSDAY 20th APRIL
ADMITS ONE ONLY

RCA

DARE
CHRISTOPH MARK

The first time I heard them was after the first *Hit Parade* collection came out. The tone of the lead guitar on 'Blue Eyes' and on 'Falling' sparked an obsession with trying to achieve that sound on guitar for the next 30 years. Now when I write a new song, I often have to de-Wedding Present it at some point in the process. My favourite line is still:

I can't still be drunk at five
Oh, I guess I surely can

But my favourite song is still 'Dare'. When the distorted lead kicks in, it still gives me goosebumps and butterflies, like falling in love.

TAKE ME!
IVAN LUIZ DE ALMEIDA VIANNA

I love – really love – this song. I've spent so many hours in my life listening that I'm able to start listening to 'Take Me!' in the middle – the guitar section – or near to the last quarter and precisely point out how long it will take to get to the end!

GEORGE BEST or *TOMMY*
GARY ARMSTEAD

Anything from *George Best* and *Tommy*. They spoke volumes to me.

LOVENEST & CORDUROY
JOHN GASSEL

Two Wedding Present songs had a large impact in my life. Seeing them live on the *Seamonsters* tour in a small bar called The Hi-Pointe in St Louis, Missouri, they played 'Lovenest' and 'Corduroy' back-to-back. My ears rang for several days after and my hearing has never been the same. It was glorious and I wish I could go back in time and experience it all again.

John Gassel has had hearing problems since seeing The Wedding Present but wishes he could go back and experience it again

BRASSNECK
COLIN GRIFFITHS

'Brassneck' made me realise that bands didn't have to mime on *Top Of The Pops*.

BEAR
YOSHIAKI NONAKA

It was late August of 2016. I was hospitalised for a while to get surgery. Before I got to the hospital, I'd pre-ordered the *Going, Going..* download edition on iTunes (release date was September 2nd) via my iPad because I just wanted to listen to the long-awaited new album from my favourite band in the world while in the hospital. The date of operation was August 31st. The surgery was completed, but soon after I fell into a coma.

Two days passed. My wife noticed the iPad at my bedside and launched the iTunes app to play her husband's favourite band. She realised there was a notification that some download had completed so she just played it for no reason at low volume.

Yes, it was *Going, Going...*

When track seven started, she noticed my consciousness gradually return as the tune progressed. And, towards the end, that line... 'Now who'll be catching me when I fall?'

'You woke up right after the end of that song!' she said.

David, it was you. Your music and voice actually caught my soul from the bottom of the abyss. For that reason, I'm moved to tears when I listen to this song even now.

HEATHER
ANDREW YOUNG

It's Monday the 27th of May 1991. I'm a couple of months shy of my seventeenth birthday and I've just finished a horrendous shift at work. It had already been a difficult few days, my having been unceremoniously dumped the previous Friday by my first ever serious girlfriend. To compound matters, I'd spent the majority of my meagre YTS wages for the week drowning my sorrows over the weekend and knew I wouldn't be able to afford the new album – *Seamonsters* – by my recently found new 'favourite band' until the upcoming Friday at the very earliest.

I'd discovered The Wedding Present after the demise of my two previous 'favourite bands', The Housemartins and The Smiths. I loved the jangly guitars and the sheer relatability of the lyrics, despite still being very much a beginner when it came to relationships and everything that comes with them. It's admittedly a cliché, but in my teenage head it felt almost as if David Gedge was reading and then writing my thoughts and putting them into song.

I had a few minutes to spare before my bus home so popped into the local Woolworths in Aberdeen for a wee look. I was still kicking myself for spending all my money over the weekend and having to wait until Friday to hear it in full. I was about to put the cassette back down when something caught my eye. Side two. Track four.

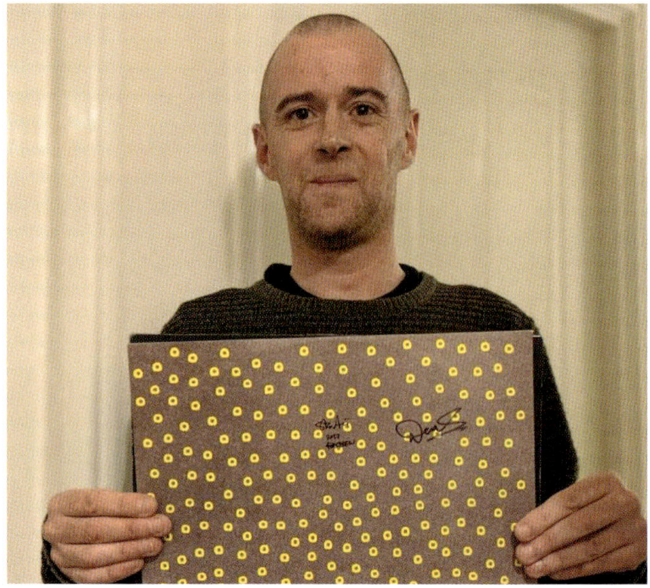

Andrew Young couldn't believe David Gedge had written a song named after the girl who'd just dumped him

'It can't be,' I thought to myself as I rubbed my eyes in disbelief. You're maybe ahead of me here, but the girl who'd ruined my weekend and administered my first dose of heartbreak was called Heather. Friday could not come quickly enough (although how I chuckled on the Friday, once I'd finally taken it home for its first listen, and found it was actually the plant David Gedge was referring to).

It's now 30 years later, *Seamonsters* is still my favourite album of all time, and DLG is still writing songs which strike a chord with me with every release, and long may that continue.

BRASSNECK

PETER PRITCHARD

I decided not to trust her anymore...

MY FAVOURITE DRESS

CHRIS BIRCH

'My Favourite Dress'. My ex-fiancée had one and I went through that exact situation with another hand on my favourite dress...

A MILLION MILES

ANDREW KING

Andrew King (right), and pictured here with his brother-in-law Mat, loves 'A Million Miles'

There is a single moment that changed my whole music love and knowledge at the age of 16. It's that deep inhalation at that start of 'Everyone Thinks He Looks Daft'. It made it seem raw and exciting after listening to commercially polished music. My mate had cut me a tape of various Indie music and this was the first song on the compilation. I was hooked!

Add to that the clearest memory of my first Wedding Present gig, on 30th January 1990 at The Studio in Bristol, and launching myself into the mosh on the first chord of 'Kennedy' with the biggest smile and feelings of euphoria with my fellow Indie music-loving friends. I can still smell the sweat, see the band, hear the chords and breakneck guitaring with Simon Smith's drums rolling through the song; I can vividly recall regrouping with my pals later in the set, sweating profusely and just grinning like a Cheshire cat after our first proper moshpit. I left the gig with a precious new t-shirt and a 30-plus-year love affair with the mighty Wedding Present.

The next memory is one that has defined not just friendship but some of my later life. In 1997, I went to pick up my new girlfriend for one of our first dates. She asked if I could give her sister and boyfriend a lift to the pub, which I duly did. He got in the car and asked what I had playing on the tape deck and I said, 'Oh you won't like it, it's Indie stuff'; a response I'd got used to giving after years of 'what's this racket? Why do all the songs sound the same?' etc., etc.

I popped the tape in and played it and within a chord he excitedly said, 'The Weddoes! Love them' and we sang along to 'A Million Miles' on the short journey to the pub. That boyfriend was Mat and nearly 25 years later he is my brother-in-law and my constant gig companion; I've lost count of the gigs we've been to and the number of times we've seen the boy Gedge. A friendship I treasure dearly, and quickly formed from our love of the same music and bands.

OCTOPUSSY
TERRY DE CASTRO, FORMER WEDDING PRESENT BASSIST

I'm sure lots of people are going to say this, but it's hard to pick a favourite song by The Wedding Present. It's not just the number of songs (pushing 300, I think), but there are so many of them that are my favourites for different reasons. Back in 2015, David asked me to stand in for a couple of gigs in California. It had been five years since I'd 'retired' from touring, and I was absolutely ready to play live again. Initially we were only meant to do one show, in San Francisco, but I talked David into booking one in Los Angeles as well. I lived there, and since we were rehearsing there as well, why not? Available venues were thin on the ground because it was a last-minute booking, and we ended up playing at a Mexican restaurant/dive bar in downtown LA called La Cita Bar. It may have been the smallest stage The Wedding Present have ever played, but David would have to verify that (we did play a pretty minuscule venue in Luxembourg in 2005).

The stage itself was a tiny raised balcony that we all had to cram onto, with a painted mural behind it. Our sound engineer, Pete Magdaleno, said we looked like we belonged in a natural history museum as a band diorama. I genuinely like divey venues though, and I was excited to be playing in my hometown. David wasn't so keen. While we were setting up our gear on the little balcony (a challenge) he kind of chuckled in mock outrage saying, 'How did I let you talk me into this?' Sure, it was a little ropey, and at the start of the gig, it took a while for the PA to switch on. We opened with 'Interstate 5', so when that big explosion kicked in after the droning guitars it was only through the monitors, which was a little anti-climactic. Regardless, I thought the gig was pretty good overall.

What does this have to do with my favourite Wedding Present song? 'Interstate 5' was always one of my favourites to open gigs with, and it would surely go into my top ten. But like I said, it's hard to pick just one. When we were rehearsing in Los Angeles, former guitarist Patrick Alexander had put the setlist together, a job that I used to do when I was an actual band member. Each time Patrick announced what song we were rehearsing next, I'd say, 'Oh, I LOVE this one!' He was amused by this and said, 'You can't love all of them!' But it was true – I did love them all, for different reasons. I WILL pick one though, and this brings me to another divey venue: Dingwalls in Camden.

I couldn't remember what year it was, but I was sure David would have it logged someplace on a spreadsheet. I was right – when I asked him, he told me it was October of 2002. This was in the Cinerama years, and we'd just started introducing Wedding Present songs into the Cinerama sets. I thought it was amazing – I loved playing these great songs that people knew really well, and it added a layer of excitement to the gigs for me. We were actually on a UK tour in 2002, and Dingwalls was the last venue. The gig was a bit of a disaster, though. There was no stage barrier, and there was a big crush of people at the front. Monitors and mic stands were getting shoved around, and beer was flying everywhere (I loved it). After the gig I was elated, but when I asked David afterward if he enjoyed it, he said, 'Look at me!' He pointed to a big gash on his forehead where he'd been smacked quite hard with the microphone.

This finally brings me to my favourite song, which I'll at last disclose: 'Octopussy'. We had been rehearsing it along with a few other Wedding Present songs for this particular tour. I can't remember how many we played, but I do remember that the very first one we tried out was 'Anyone Can Make A Mistake'. The first time we rehearsed it, Simon Cleave was playing so fast that Sally Murrell fell on the floor laughing. I also remember talking to Sally about what a great song 'Octopussy' was. 'It's beautiful, isn't it?' she said. I've always assumed it was about her, but that's another thing David would have to corroborate. I adore this song: the post-rock drum pattern, the minimal, plucky guitar part, the soaring bass line, the heartfelt strangle of David's vocal, and the matter-of-fact but tender lyrics that manage to be both stark and playful at the same time. David sets such a vivid scene you can see the snow still hanging in the air outside. I recently recorded a guitar part for a 'lockdown session' of 'Octopussy', and it prompted me to study the song all over again. It is a perfect love song.

Back to Dingwalls… That night, on that unprotected stage, I had a transcendent experience. From an early age, I thought I wanted to be a 'rock musician', but the idea that it might actually happen in any kind of substantial way never occurred to me – it seemed too rarified. But then it happened, and whilst (like everything else in life) it's not quite how you think it's going to be, and it's really not that rarified, it does come peppered with some extremely gratifying moments. I distinctly remember being onstage at Dingwalls, playing 'Octopussy', and I know it sounds corny, but I got lost in the music. I was listening to that magnificent wall of sound as much as I was contributing to it. I was more ecstatic than I had ever been onstage. It was as good as live performing ever gets: playing a cracking great song in front of a heaving crowd of people going nuts. I was even aware of it at the time, acknowledging that this was one of those moments, something that felt truly sublime... and then the contents of an entire beer hit me right in the face.

EVERYONE THINKS HE LOOKS DAFT

MICK SMITH

When I first heard that song circa 86/87 on John Peel, I was hooked.

GIVE MY LOVE TO KEVIN
SUZANNE CLARK

My favourite has to be 'Give My Love To Kevin' – the acoustic version, hands down. It spells out the anguish of a break up, unrequited love that the poor lad can't handle. The acoustic version is soft and the sadness in the lyrics is suited best to it. At the end of the song, you're never quite sure what his intentions are; where he's going or if he's ever going to contact her again.

HARD, FAST AND BEAUTIFUL
ROB MARSHALL

Biscuit tin of memories. Crumbs of comfort were unsent love letters and jars of hope in the larder. The trick of adolescence is to always keep dreaming. Wishes spoken at the greased water-well of the kitchen sink. Enter songs, stage left. This teenage Indie terrorist launched John Peel vinyl-bombs all over the school walls and furniture of diary houses. Revolution was the whimsical lyrics of The Shop Assistants to the sensitive thrum of The Pastels.

Slate grey Welsh skies were swapped with academic shores. Pluto, Keats and Shakespeare sailed by, but my harbour was the chance to watch live music. Like a drunk always finding their way home, I followed reels of cassette tape through life's maze, to gig havens. Adventures in the skin trade were just a stage away. And so it came to pass that The Wedding Present berthed at Birmingham Hummingbird. Gedge and the lads strummed until their fingers bled. It felt so real and visceral. Four days later at a ubiquitous party, Alison laughed at my *George Best* t-shirt and teased me, 'You must have walked past that doorway 30 times.' For historical accuracy, it was actually ten times to try and catch her eye. Or 30.

It was the summer of trains. As the UK sizzled and eggs could have been fried on pavements, we were tangled and boiled in the Euston to Holyhead tracks. The conductor clicked tickets to the pulse of my Walkman. Every platform sang a different song; each passing town shimmered the landslide of love. Lust wore the green fields of England.

It was meant to be Alison and me together, forever. Like diamonds. Forever. Endless days of delicious seclusion. Reality was a damp bedsit and a lonesome pillow nested on a wine-stained bed. She was to play Sylvia Plath to my Ted Hughes, Taylor to my Burton… Terry and June. The loneliness of a hungover Sunday morning. From the smallest window I watched falling leaves carpet London a certain shade of rust, whilst she munched croissants with her parents across the city. My coffee tasted bitter.

On the morning she danced away, rain sluiced through the darkness and the milk float rattled a mournful dirge. She had changed. Such are the (bi)cycles of life. If bestiality had ever come into vogue, she would have been seen at all the right parties with all the right animals. But I was her animal and this wounded dog tied himself to the life-support stereo in the corner of the room. For every memory of my favourite dress, there were the tastes of her different lipsticks; for every photograph of us, there were myriads of polaroids waiting to be shot. Who wants to grow up? Who wants to go back?

Amongst my blue box of memories, nests a cathedral of love lost and chapels of happiness. My Feng has never quite aligned with my Shui. Yin kidnapped Yang. I sometimes think of Alison. Wherever she is, I hope she occasionally dances to *George Best* on a dank winter day. Flailing limbs, sliding heels and back arched as a bow to fire so many suggestive arrows. 'How could I ever think it wasn't true..?'

EL REY

KARL KATHURIA

I've always liked it when The Wedding Present play 'the new one'. In *Sometimes These Words Just Don't Have To Be Said* I wrote about what an effect 'What Have I Said Now?' had on me when I first heard it at the 'Evening Of Ukrainian Folk Music' in early 1989. When Cinerama played what turned out to be one of their last concerts as David's main band, in the Cambridge Boat Race, he quipped (as he often does), 'This next one's a new song, so if you want to go to the toilet, now's the time.' I remember that particular one, because so many people actually did, and his 'I was only joking' comment was ignored by most. That night was the first time I heard the future classic, 'Mars Sparkles Down On Me'. As he said afterwards, 'You'll be shouting out for that one next year.'

So, for me, it's always 'the new one' that I look forward to the most, which made the call to action for this book somewhat difficult – I can't write about my favourite song, I quite possibly haven't heard it yet. In 2022, we're being treated to 24 new recordings in the *24 Songs* project. At the time of writing this, we're quickly getting through them, and every month at least one of the songs just so happens to be 'probably the best one so far', and worthy of a place in the list of 'Best Wedding Present Songs Ever'. How do they keep doing that? It keeps things fresh, and there's always an ever-increasing library of songs to make every setlist an absolute blinder.

And what about 'the old ones'? Well, there are so many that I love that I'm happy to hear pretty much any of them at any time. I say 'pretty much', because we all have our favourites and not-so-favourites, but really, let's face it, any of them will do when played live! I will admit that I had a bit of an aversion to *El Rey* for a while. It wasn't that I didn't like it, I just didn't really ever think to put it on, but a couple of things changed that. First was Gary, a friend of mine in Toronto, where I used to live. He and I had a long pub discussion about the album, and he made me listen to it with fresh ears.

The second one was also in Toronto, when The Wedding Present played in 2018, on the same day as the cinema premiere of the documentary *Something Left Behind*. On that tour, they were sometimes playing 'Don't Touch That Dial' and other times playing 'Boo Boo' as an epic mid-set moment. I expressed a preference for hearing 'Don't Touch That Dial', as I thought any rational person might. But in the sound check it turned out it wasn't going to work, and they tried 'Boo Boo' instead. It absolutely blew me away, it sounded so much more powerful than I had remembered, even without an audience in the room. When I heard it again at the concert, it became, for a few brief moments, my favourite song ever. It brought *El Rey* back into occasional rotation on my stereo, and helped me finally make sense of the album. Now, if only the BBC would release the version that was played at the 'Big Band Special' in their broadcast back in 2010; it was the only one that didn't make the cut.

Oh, and if you ever need proof of the reach of *El Rey*... When Come Play With Me Records put on the live web stream for the launch of *Not From Where I'm Standing*, the Bond themes compilation, it was presented by Abi Whistance, who was said to be a 'young, up-and-coming DJ from Leeds'... who just so happens to have *El Rey* tattoos to show her devotion to that album. Let me know when any other 60-something 'Indie' singer has *that* kind of effect.

THE MOMENT BEFORE (EVERYTHING'S SPOILED AGAIN)

NICK GOLLEDGE

I'll never forget when I discovered The Wedding Present. It was all down to Calvin Curtis, in his flat in Chippenham. I bought *Tommy* and the line 'no one's supposed to know how I feel' touched me then and touches me still. It's just raw energy and guitars played at a million miles an hour and was my first introduction to The Wedding Present.

Nick Golledge was introduced to The Wedding Present by his friend Calvin Curtis

GO OUT AND GET 'EM, BOY!
MIRO MOIR

I have many Wedding Present stories from the early period. I had heard the first single, 'Go Out And Get 'Em, Boy!', on Peel and it blew my mind. Peel as usual read out the address and I got the first single. I called the number on the back of the single and talked to Shaun, the drummer, for two hours. Then I put on my first gig in Perth and organised a Dundee gig. They were massive Postcard fans and super excited to play in Scotland. We had a blast and they asked our band, This Poison!, to support them and put out our first two singles, the second of which got single of the week in *Melody Maker*…

BEAR
PAUL WOOD

Paul Wood (left) nominates 'Bear' as his favourite song

I've had a long love affair with the Weddoes, from bouncing around to 'Lost your love of life? Too much apple pie' with my mates in a busted Allegro in the '80s through to 'And did you walk from the town into the heather to where we used to lie down when we were together?'' and bouncing back with 'Don't Talk, Just Kiss'. I lost touch with the guys when I emigrated to Australia in the 2000s and there aren't many Weddoes LPs in the W section of an Australian record shop, but a few years ago in 2017 I was amazed that they were doing a tour here with a gig 300 kilometres away in Sydney. It was amazing! I got a selfie and autographed t-shirt with DLG and they played new stuff from *Going, Going*…. I immediately ordered this online after the gig and it was like, 'OK, OK, OK, OK, WOAHHHH! It's the Weddoes!'

I loved 'Bear'. They've still got it. As the great man once said about another band, 'The Wedding Present – always different, always the same.'

MY FAVOURITE DRESS
PAUL BYRNE

There comes a moment in our lives when we discover live music. Then nearly kill three of our friends. Or maybe that was just me.

In 1989 I was 17, growing up in a non-essential town in the East Midlands of England. An only child, I'd found escape in music, drawing inspiration from the burgeoning Indie scene in the UK. The Madchester scene of The Stone Roses and Happy Mondays was warming up, the stalwarts of The Smiths and The Fall still splashed across the front pages of a thriving music press.

I grew my ginger hair long and bushy, and proudly sported flared jeans and Dr Martens footwear. A combination of styles that often led to rougher chaps chasing me through the town after a night of lagers and cigarettes in the rammed pubs of the day.

I also had a driving licence and access to my mother's yellow Ford Fiesta. My mother was a community midwife, who toured the local area assisting in the production of new lives. The boot of the car was stuffed with the necessary equipment, so bar the long years of training, I was fully equipped to turn my hand to a dab of midwifery in-between driving my friends around.

One day in October, we piled into the yellow motor to trundle to Northampton Roadmender to see one of the biggest Indie groups of the time – The Wedding Present.

Snappily known as the Weddoes to true fans, David Gedge's band produced blisteringly emotional walls of guitar-based genius. Their debut album, *George Best*, was released in October 1987 and became a classic of the Indie rock world. And there was a song about William Shatner, so what's not to like?

God, I loved that album! When the chance came to see the mighty Weddoes in real life I had no choice really. And nor did my three friends who joined me on that evening jaunt to nearby Northampton in my trusty borrowed yellow Ford Fiesta.

I hadn't been driving long and was little used to driving at night. The first time I'd driven alone after passing my test, a drunken Scotsman drove into the back of the car. He kindly handed me what was left of my bumper through the window before veering away.

I learned nothing from this experience.

I managed to park somewhere nearby, and carefully locked the car to deter local breast pump thieves. It was raining of course. It rained through most of the '80s in the UK. We arrived at the gig soaked to the skin. Luckily so was everyone else. Wearing a raincoat to a rock gig wasn't really acceptable.

Our tickets checked, we were propelled into the venue to join the hordes of young people dressed in black clothes with surly expressions. We wanted to sup on pints of watery lager, but our innate politeness offered us little chance of forcing our way to the front of the crowd building around the bar.

The options would have been lager or bitter. In plastic pint glasses that would sag in the middle without fail, making you frantically drink before spraying your drink over everyone within a six-foot radius. You could cause a silence to fall across the bar by requesting wine. Stumbling towards the ominous doors, pints lost down our jeans, we would find ourselves alone in a dark and cavernous space, shared only with roadies pulling wires across a vacant stage.

We were yet to learn that it really wasn't cool to be early. Much as any rock band worth its salt keeps their audience waiting until they're properly aroused, we learned that late '80s Indie audiences tried to turn the tables on their musical stars by hanging around the bar for as long as possible.

So we went back to the bar area, and stood around like a bunch of teenagers smoking cigarettes in soaking wet t-shirts until a wave of sweaty men carried us back into the main hall to welcome our heroes on stage.

The sound that was unleashed poured over and around us, the loudest thing I'd ever heard, the familiar songs raised to epic wonderment as we worshipped with all our hearts. The music those ordinary men produced raised them to the status of gods as all who looked upon them screamed and raved.

A man behind me got so excited he forgot to leave the floor and head to the toilets. Luckily, he was able to relieve himself all down the back of my jeans. Being far too scared to turn around, and not being overly clear whether this was traditional behaviour or not, I acted as though nothing was happening, and continued to enjoy 'My Favourite Dress' as warm urine soaked through my denims. We confirmed it was wee by the smell emanating from my legs after the gig.

So heady were the days, I forgot where I'd left the yellow Fiesta. Managing to get even wetter in the blistering rain, we trudged the back streets of Northampton trying to light cigarettes and display an aura of cool nonchalance.

And there it was. Where I'd left it, breast pumps safe. Desperate to be home in the warm and dry, I started to drive. My three friends offered little assistance, other than steaming the car up. Not really understanding the mechanics of steamy windows, I set the windscreen wipers swaying at full pelt. Which didn't work.

And so, driving along without being able to see through the windscreen, I managed to crash through some roadworks and then out the other side. Only when I stopped to check any damage to the car could be covered up did I realise I'd driven the car across a huge hole in the road, each wheel just about staying on the edge. The hole was around ten feet deep and full of water. Had I driven into it, we'd probably all have died. Which would have put a real dampener on my first ever gig with the mighty Wedding Present!

ON RAMP/INTERSTATE 5

PAUL JENIONS

I had a copy of *George Best* taped from a mate back in the day on a C90 – and the only true product I owned was the seven-inch of 'Nobody's Twisting Your Arm'. I never delved any further into The Wedding Present until… fast forward to July 2013 and they announced a gig at Bridport Electric Palace, just a 45-minute journey from me where they were playing *George Best* in full. Three of us went, only really knowing *George Best* and the *Bizarro* singles. We had a great night and my main memory (due to a few beers) other than *George Best* was the start of the gig and what I now know to be 'On Ramp' into 'Interstate 5'! How had I never heard these songs before? A flick through the CDs at a local HMV found me a copy of *Take Fountain* and then I was hooked. All the back catalogue was promptly purchased on CD, and more recently on vinyl, and many gigs have been attended since!

Paul Jenions was reacquainted with The Wedding Present via 'On Ramp' and 'Interstate 5'

Thank you, Bridport, Dorset and 'On Ramp'/'Interstate 5'!

PERFECT BLUE

PETER KENNEDY

I got married in 2014 to a girl I've fancied since 1987. When we first got together, I sent 'Perfect Blue' to her as it sums her up in so many ways and it blew her away. We got married in Vegas without telling anyone and 'Perfect Blue' is the song we listened to. It's a beautiful song that is especially mind-blowing live, and one I like playing on my piano for her.

KENNEDY

PHIL ANNETS

'Kennedy' ticks all the boxes for me as to what makes a fantastic song: an instant attention-grabbing and exciting opening guitar riff; a very guitar-centric tune throughout supported by a driving drum beat; loud, fairly aggressive singing; UK-based band (and sound), anthemic effect with a rumbling bass element (about half way through); and two minutes of instrumental outro containing a frenetic guitar-driven repeated rhythmical beat leading to a crescendo finish. Of course, I love other types of music too, but this is pure bliss, although practically no-one else from the singles-buying public thought so. (Only 'Come Play With Me' graced the Top Ten, for one week.) That's another contributing factor as to why the song is so fondly loved by me.

The Wedding Present is a classic Indie band, creating a sound that was never intended for the mainstream but which, if you gave it a chance, would have you hooked; a very British rock guitar sound with a growling vocalist and a strong melodic overtone. The band has its hardcore fan-base, but has failed to expand beyond it. I personally dipped in and dipped out of their music, but I was very much in the minority. Even a very exploitative commercial campaign of releasing one single for one week only each month during 1992 (providing them with a record of most new material to chart in any one calendar year) failed to capture the imagination of the record-buying public, and so an Indie cult band they remain.

In my opinion 'Kennedy' is the band's pinnacle and another of those songs that I instantly turn up to at least eleven when it is selected by my iPod shuffle mode. I practically always listen to it again immediately after it has concluded, and on one particular journey up the M6 I replayed the song 15 consecutive times, each time turning the volume up one more notch until it felt as if my ear drums were going to burst. During that hour or so I have no recollection of the landmarks on the motorway that I passed, lost as I was in the cacophony of their outstanding guitar-based sound.

GO OUT AND GET 'EM, BOY!

JOHN MURRAY

It's actually pretty difficult to choose just one from The Wedding Present's back catalogue, which is dense, varied (although obviously all the songs sound the same) and of very high quality. Whenever a random song comes up on shuffle from an album I'm less familiar with, I'm always left wanting to hear another track.

For reasons of personal history, shameless nostalgia, as well as the sheer vibrancy of the song, I would have to choose their first seven-inch single, 'Go Out And Get

John Murray has chosen 'Go Out And Get 'Em, Boy!'

'Em, Boy!'. It may not be their greatest song and it's not the most timeless, being firmly rooted in the unmistakably jangle pop days of the mid '80s but, with those teetering-on-the-edge, urgent, shimmering, duelling guitars played at breakneck speed, about to crash and burn at any moment, 'Go Out And Get 'Em, Boy!' still has an incredible energy to it, some 150 years or so since it burst onto the world stage (via Leeds 6).

John Murray lent Keith Gregory (above) his bass and never saw it again

That I got a credit on the back of the single 'Without whom' as 'Talkin' John' (distinguishing me from the other John, who presumably talked less) tips the balance for me. I got the name-check for lending Keith Gregory my bass guitar. I say 'lending'; I never did see it again and gather it fell apart. Hardly surprising when you hear how fast they were hitting their instruments. So whilst I love 'My Favourite Dress', 'Crawl', 'Corduroy', 'Interstate 5' and many more, I've got to pick the only seven-inch single I ever got a dedication on.

Now I think about it, my brother Pete got a mention on the back of *Modern Life Is Rubbish* as Blur drank in his Bloomsbury pub whilst recording it. Whilst that album undoubtedly sold more copies, that they misnamed him 'Dave from the Plough' means I still win.

ONCE MORE
JOHN OSBORN

Three may have a better time but John Osborn rates 'Once More' as the best

I love so many Wedding Present tracks – 'What Have I Said Now?', 'Blue Eyes', 'Dalliance', 'Sports Car'... but the one that really takes me back is 'Once More'. I was a student at Reading University and was really into the Indie music scene – going to gigs and being an alternative DJ at the Students' Union. My girlfriend at the time got elected as Entertainments Chairperson which meant that she got to book the gigs. She didn't take much persuading to book The Wedding Present as we had both become fans. They were duly booked for the compact Coffee Lounge in the Students' Union in November 1986. I had the privilege of doing the support DJ slot (under the name of The Burning Lampposts) and I couldn't resist playing my copy of 'Once More', which the band had signed earlier, and then later abandoning the decks for the energy of the gig. I keep coming back for more. Thankfully The Wedding Present lasted longer than The Burning Lampposts.

LEE THACKER, ILLUSTRATOR OF DAVID'S AUTOBIOGRAPHY

Lee Thacker couldn't choose just one

My favourite track by The Wedding Present? Impossible to single out just one, so here are my top three as of 20th February 2021.

THIS BOY CAN WAIT

Reasons?

1. The fastest guitars ever recorded! It's still an amazing thing to see that right hand become a complete blur when played live.
2. I was, being a proto-feminist virgin at the time, also in awe of the final lines: Tonight, when I hold you in my arms and I prove that I'm a man Oh, well, I hope you understand
3. It was a few months later when I first heard 'Go Out And Get 'Em, Boy!' and realised the line had been recycled for this single.

It also reminds me of my ultra-tolerant parents. I had a Saturday paper round at the time. My parents would go shopping in town every Saturday afternoon as I delivered free papers to the unappreciative people in the surrounding area, and they (my parents, not the unappreciative people in the surrounding area!) would always ask if I wanted anything. I would write down what I wanted from St Martin's Records – paid for with my paper round money – and they always dutifully brought it back for me. I was gutted when I played this single as both sides were the same ('You Should Always Keep In Touch With Your Friends'). The following week they exchanged it; still the

THE ORIGIN OF
TALES FROM THE
WEDDING PRESENT
#0
£3
I BID YOU... RISE!!
WHAT ARE WE SUPPOSED TO DO AFTER WE RISE?
MAYBE TRY TO GET JOHN PEEL TO PLAY ONE OF OUR SONGS ON THE RADIO?

TALES FROM THE
WEDDING PRESENT
NO. 1
£3
FEATURING...
DAVID GEDGE
TERRY DE CASTRO
JESSICA MCMILLAN
SALLY MURRELL
SIMON CLEAVE
Lee Thacker
IT'S NOT LIKE WORKING DOWN A MINE.

No. 6
TALES FROM THE
WEDDING PRESENT
£3
THIS IS JUST WHAT WE NEED TO PARK THE VAN IN MANHATTAN!
SUPERMAN!
SUPERMAN? HE LOOKS MORE LIKE CLARK KENT WITHOUT THE GLASSES.
X-PRESS PRINTERS
HIGH ENERGY
boutique
Pay half
NO PARKING
TOW AWAY ZONE
KEEP CLEAR
No Parking
EAT

£3
TALES FROM
THE WEDDING PRESENT
7"
THIS BABY HANDLES LIKE A DREAM.
YEAH, BUT I THINK A VAN WOULD HAVE BEEN MORE PRACTICAL.
NICE.
TRUE STORIES

Tales From The
WEDDING Present
The Official Biography of David Gedge
No. 10 £3
I THINK WE'RE GOING TO BE LATE!
ARE YOU SURE YOU KNOW HOW TO DRIVE APOLLO'S CHARIOT?
HOW HARD CAN IT BE? I'VE JUST GOT TO MAKE SURE I HAVE IT BACK BEFORE SUNRISE.

MAY 2018
Issue # 15
SCOPITONES / RAW SHARK
£3
TALES FROM
THE WEDDING PRESENT
I CAN'T BELIEVE WE FINALLY SOLVED IT!
I KNOW... THAT WAS A REAL MYSTERY.
IT WAS LIKE ALL OF THE BEER JUST SPONTANEOUSLY... VANISHED OUT OF OUR DRESSING ROOM!
AND ALL ALONG IT WAS THE PESKY SUPPORT BAND!

The Official Biography Of David Gedge
TALES FROM THE WEDDING PRESENT
#19
ENTRANCE FEE: £3
I WONDER WHICH EXHIBIT THIS IS?
MAYBE WE'RE THE EXHIBIT!
I KNOW I'VE BEEN AROUND FOR A LONG TIME BUT THAT'S TAKING IT A BIT FAR!
DINOSAURS

NUMBER 20
TALES FROM THE WEDDING PRESENT
Selected cartoons from THE OFFICIAL BIOGRAPHY
By DAVID L. GEDGE

same problem. After their third try to acquire it for me, I finally had the correct version. The guy who worked at St Martin's Records advised them to keep the single they'd brought back to exchange as it would 'probably be worth something some day.' I still have both versions of the same single.

4. I wrote out the lyrics and displayed them proudly on my dorm room wall the following year. However, I misheard the opening lyric as 'I can stay and talk with you I'm strong', something my dear friend Louise pointed out to me when she came over to visit me and saw it.

MY FAVOURITE DRESS

Reasons?

1. The bravery of releasing a single by an all-male band with 'that' title and my realising the context within the lyric. Genius!
2. I'd already bought the single, but there was a white vinyl version available for free with the initial copies of *George Best*. The first coloured vinyl single I ever owned, setting off a lifelong obsession with coloured vinyl singles and albums.

RACHEL

30 years after falling in love with 'This Boy Can Wait', I first heard this track a few months before the album was officially released. I was staying over at David Gedge's flat (THE David Gedge!) in Brighton to attend a comic book signing event at a Brighton comic book store. Hardly anyone turned up, but I remember sitting on his sofa (THE David Gedge's sofa!) the following day and listening to *Going, Going*.... After 'Rachel' ended I said, 'Well, that's as good as anything you've ever written.' It really is.

It was played live at a gig in Wolverhampton in the week of my 50th birthday. I rarely ask for more than me plus one (the 'plus one' always being Kirstie Wilson, my partner and soulmate for the past 27 years) to be put on the guest list but I cheekily asked for eight people to be put on the guest list for this gig and David kindly obliged. I was really chuffed to get a name check and a 'happy birthday' from David between songs.

GO, MAN, GO
LEIGH HOVEY

Leigh Hovey shared a love of The Wedding Present with his Uncle Mick

With such an extensive catalogue of incredible songs, and so many that I can attach to specific (sometimes defining) moments in my life, it's almost impossible to distil it down to a single song. However, I'm going to go with 'Go, Man, Go' for a long and convoluted reason.

My Uncle Mick sadly passed in May of 2020, although not from anything Covid-related as he had feared. Suffering from debilitating multiple sclerosis for more than 50 per cent of his life, he was rightly terrified of the pandemic and took every precaution to isolate and keep himself safe. So much so, that when we held a surprise 80th birthday party for my mother (his big sister) it was all done via Zoom. Towards the end, he suffered a massive heart attack that killed him instantly. As a large, close and very loving family, the only comfort we could take was that he spent his last moments surrounded by all of his family, albeit remotely.

It's an old cliché, but Mick was like a father to me, more so than my own. He shaped me, encouraged my love of music and film and defined my musical tastes. He had the most impressive collection of vinyl I've ever seen and often regaled stories about some of the fantastic concerts he'd attended in his younger and physically able days. He particularly enjoyed gloating that he saw The Who at Charlton in 1976.

His musical taste was wide and varied and he was always keen to 'discover' new bands. After first hearing *Bizarro* in the spring of 1990, I rushed round to his house to play it for him. We were both hooked and our shared love of The Wedding Present began on that day. I still remember as a small child having snowball fights with him, but by the time we'd discovered the music of David Gedge he was confined to a wheelchair and his days of attending concerts were well behind him.

Fast forward several years, many Wedding Present and Cinerama concerts behind me and countless hours sitting with Mick listening to all the wonderful David Gedge songs that came over the next decade, and of course many 'meetings' with David at the merchandising stands at various concerts.

In conversation with my cousin, it occurred to us that as David was such a down-to-earth, normal bloke, maybe it was worth a try reaching out. So we did just that. Contacting David through email we explained how much Mick loved his music, but would sadly never be able to see The Wedding Present (Cinerama at that time) live. The next few weeks were a blur, I can't remember the exact content of the various emails that went back and forth.

But on a bank holiday weekend in (if memory serves) August 2000, David and Sally Murrell arrived at my uncle's house and spent the afternoon having tea and cake with us. He brought his guitar and played a set of six songs, both Cinerama and The Wedding Present. Amongst them was 'Go, Man, Go'. It was magical, David and Sally were perfect guests, a lovely afternoon of conversation, cake and songs. To see the pure elation in Mick was wonderful.

For several years Mick had told me that he wanted 'Go, Man, Go' played at his funeral – listen to the lyrics with that in mind and they take on a totally different, beautiful meaning.

Fast forward again to just a few years ago and a new venue opened up in nearby Dover with superb accessibility provision. Mick was finally able to see The Wedding Present live, twice. His message to me was that it was everything he'd dreamed of and more.

When Mick did pass, it was just prior to one of David's lockdown gigs and a Facebook post was asking for requests. I duly requested 'Go, Man, Go' be played as part of the set, just for me really. I knew that Mick, as a staunch atheist, would not be listening in from anywhere. I received the following message from Jessica McMillan, and the rest is history: 'Hi Leigh, we're so sorry to hear about Mick. What if I were able to convince David to do a video of 'Go, Man, Go' to be played at the funeral?'

I will never share the video – it is personal to me, to our family and to Mick. Suffice to say, when it was played at his funeral there was not a dry eye in the house.

KENNEDY

CRISPIN ERRIDGE

After 'doing' a term at sixth form and despite my best efforts (burning the damn thing), my father got hold of my report. Suffice to say that for two subjects it just said, 'Who's Crispin?' I was offered a choice by my old man. Start studying or start working! I chose the latter and worked for a poxy insurance company who provided me with a salary but worked hard on destroying my soul.

I was into punk, loved the Buzzcocks and through a friend at work, met Tony

Suspect who took me to see Mega City 4 amongst others. It appeared music had not died with the Pistols, the Clash and Buzzcocks.

Resenting the fact that despite the company's best efforts, I appeared to be quite enjoying myself, I was transferred to a different department where amongst a cluster of feckwits – car, mortgage, kids and all at 19 – I met one or two who were alright. My attention was drawn by a quiet young bloke who, it turned out, had shared a house with mutual friends. After talking to him a bit and going out and getting hammered on a nightly basis, he introduced me to some new music I had never heard of.

'Kennedy' spoke to Crispin Erridge

I think 'Kennedy' was the first track he played to me and I was lost/found.

The song spoke to me – there's no other way to put it! My mate was suffering from depression, seriously, and I was angry. I had seen pathetic office romances, failing marriages and the 'me, me, me' culture with which Thatcher had replaced society.

In the end, I had to create a little space between my mate and I as my anger at the puffed up contentment of people who were kidding themselves that having a big TV, a new Ford Sierra and 2.4 kids was making them happy; they didn't seem happy. It started to draw me down the rabbit hole. They'd had too much of a good thing but real Conservatism began to bite as we moved into a mini economic crash.

This is what 'Kennedy' seemed to be talking about to me. OK, the names were different but I had seen 'Harry' walk away with 'Johnny's' wife. I'd picked some people up, I'd let some people go. I'd been amongst the tittle tattle of an office and I had lost my love of life. Gnawed by self doubt and witnessing terrible tragedy, I laughed at humanity, its stupidity, arrogance and shallowness. Humanity hasn't changed!

Back in Steve's flat on that first listen, guitars happened! One thousand people had picked up electric guitars and were playing a melody which was beautiful, intricate and POWERFUL! How was it possible to make that sound? Suddenly nothing else mattered. Nothing else mattered because some genius had created this sublime barrage of sound.

I think it was in about 1993 that Steve and I finally got to see The Wedding Present live at the Joiners Arms in Southampton. Drink and other things have robbed me of details. I don't think they were touring *Bizarro* but I do remember hearing that unmistakable guitar intro. A latter-day poet told us what was wrong again. Suddenly six years of troubles seemed to have been forgotten and 1,000 people were hammering guitars. My cynicism intact, this is the song that speaks for me and will declare my faith at my funeral as that perfect wall of guitar sound annoys the locals.

'Kennedy' will be cranked up to eleven when they bury me. Preferably after I die!

VERKHOVYNO

'THE LEGENDARY' LEN LIGGINS

This was one of the first Ukrainian folk songs that Peter Solowka and myself discovered. We loved it, and played it a lot round at Peter's house on Brudenell Road in Leeds. It didn't become a contender for recording though until The Wedding Present's second Ukrainian John Peel session, which we recorded in March 1988. We realised it was a great song, but it was ex-Mott the Hoople drummer Dale Griffin, who produced the session at the BBC's Maida Vale studios, who got us to extend the ending. The result was eight-and-a-half minutes of pure adrenaline-fuelled Cossack punk, so we've been playing it that way in The Ukrainians ever since.

Little did we know when we were casually unloading our gear outside Maida Vale Studios that we would still be in there after midnight and would record one of Peel's all-time favourite sessions. I remember feeling incredibly nervous when we started to set up. David, Peter, Keith and Simon had already recorded four sessions for the BBC but this was only my second. It also didn't help that Dale was quite terse with us. Listening back, I can still hear the trembling in my voice and fiddle playing, but now I like the delicate nature of it. It was when we were mixing 'Verkhovyno' though, late into the night, that I felt most proud. During one playback, about halfway through the song, David said, 'What's that twiddling sound? It's really exciting!' and Peter said with a grin, 'That's Len's fiddle'.

I always thought it was very generous of David to let Peter and myself temporarily 'hijack' the band, just when The Wedding Present had signed to RCA, a major label. At a really important point in their career, they experimented with a completely different kind of music with a different singer. It seemed like such a risk, but to David's credit he let it happen. The resulting *Ukrainski Vistupi V Johna Peela*, a mini-album, went on to sell 70,000 copies worldwide and got to number 22 in the UK album charts. Yet, in spite of this, the band knew that nothing could derail them from their continued English language Indie guitar success. Six months later *Bizarro* hit the charts, then came *Seamonsters*, and the band's place in music history was firmly cemented into place.

It was at that time, in 1991, that Peter and myself decided to develop our interest in Ukrainian music and formed The Ukrainians. It's hard to take in sometimes that we've since released eight studio albums, two live albums, numerous compilations, and toured extensively throughout Europe and North America. Yet all of this, to my mind, came from a spark that was generated when Dale Griffin mixed 'Verkhovyno' on that fateful evening of the 15th March 1988. We'd taken a traditional Ukrainian folk song, 'Verkhovyno, svitku ty nash' ('Verkhovyna, you are our world') which describes the peaceful, natural beauty of the Ukrainian highlands, and punked it up beyond recognition. What amazed us too, was that as well as Indie, punk, folk and world music fans – and John Peel of course – people in Ukraine really loved it.

DALLIANCE
PHILIP TAYLOR

The year was 1991 and I had been listening to my tape of *Seamonsters* for a couple of months. I was travelling from Manchester to Birmingham to see my team (and DLG's) Manchester United play Aston Villa. My mate Pete was driving but I took a couple of tapes with me. *Seamonsters* and *XL* by 808 State.

Phil Taylor (right) and his mate Pete in Rotterdam. But 'Dalliance' is his song

All was going fine until we broke down on a bridge just after Hilton Park Services. We were blocking everything and had to push the car into a lane that was coned off. We couldn't believe it – we were going to miss the match. Then a car pulled up alongside us. 'I can take two,' he shouted, and they were clearly fellow United fans. Me and another mate Daz quickly glanced at each other and both dived into the back of the car and left Pete with his stricken car.

I rang him the next day to check he got home OK. He said he did and then said, 'You don't think you are getting your tapes back, do you?' 'No, it's yours,' I conceded and every time I hear the opening notes of 'Dalliance' I am taken back to that balmy August night in the West Midlands.

NOTHING COMES EASY

ROB FLEAY

'Nothing Comes Easy' reminds Rob Fleay of his late friend John

The Wedding Present song that means the most to me is 'Nothing Comes Easy', one of the B-sides to 'Nobody's Twisting Your Arm'.

I bought the CD single when it was released in early 1988, as my parents had just got their first CD player and the only CDs we had in the house were Roy Orbison's *Greatest Hits* and some James Last *In Concert* monstrosity. I needed one of my own to listen to. It's hard to remember quite how incredibly clear CDs sounded back then, but it really did sound amazing compared to scratchy seven-inch vinyl singles on old second-hand record players. The only problem was that the CD player was in the front room, and so were my parents for 90 per cent of the time. It's fair to say that my mum, as an amateur opera singer, had very little time for the tones of Gedge. 'They'd be better if they got a singer who could actually sing' was her usual polite way of saying 'please turn this awful racket off'.

As I recall I ended up having to tape it so I could listen to it in my bedroom, but then a couple of months later they went on holiday for two weeks and left me to look after the house alone for the first time, aged 17.

My friend John would come round and we'd explore the drinks cabinet whilst listening to my one CD full blast in the front room. John became obsessed with 'Nothing Comes Easy' and once he realised that you could set the CD player to repeat the same song over and over, we must have listened to it hundreds of times. He was a bit of a contrarian and he loved the way it didn't sound like any other Wedding Present song, but still had some incredible energy. It never fails to 'Take Me!' back to that fortnight in 1988.

I'm sorry to say that John died in a car accident in 1996 (25 years to the day – which is what prompted me to write), but although there is sadness whenever I hear the song now, it also helps me to remember him and his crazy ways. Above is a photo that he took of me that week – note *George Best* in the foreground and the 'Nobody's Twisting Your Arm' video on the TV. CD player just out of shot!

ONCE MORE

SIMON STUART

Autumn 1991 in a northern English coastal town, and 16-year-old me is drifting on a shallow sea of disaffection. Yearning to be somewhere else, yet devoid of any idea where, I'm following the course set by legions of miserable young men before me and trying to piece together meaning through music. Savvier friends, and their older siblings' record collections, provide a dawning sense of direction, but I'm still not sure what I can call – what I want to call – mine.

Sitting in an A-level English class, wondering when or if it gets interesting, my eye is drawn to a classmate's folder. On it he's stuck a bewitching picture, snipped from an inky music magazine, of some guy with a red shirt and an uncertain smile that seems to say, 'I too find all of this bleakly absurd'. If I'm honest, though, at first it's all about the hair; a great thick mop of jet-black locks, unstyled to perfection. I could do that!

I dare to ask, 'Eh, mate. Who's that, then?'

Phil, my classmate, is significantly cooler than me – not, in fairness, desperately difficult – but he's decent with it. He hides any exasperation at my daft question. 'It's Gedge, innit?'

'Oh. Yeah! Right.' The pause is just long enough to be painful. 'Gedge.'

A brief tut, not unkind. 'David Gedge, mate. Out of The Wedding Present. You need to hear *Seamonsters*. You'll love it.'

That Saturday morning, I hop on the little black-and-yellow bus into town. My meagre finances preclude actually purchasing anything, but the big library has a little LP-lending operation. Whilst this is heavily stocked with some of metal and prog's least essential output, it harbours the odd gem, and I'm

Simon Stuart wanted *Seamonsters* but got *Tommy*

cautiously optimistic. I rifle through the dusty sleeves to W. WASP, Roger Waters… here we go! The Wedding Present. No *Seamonsters*: that's still far too new. But there's something called *Tommy*, which seems to be a compilation of early stuff, and that feels as good a place as any to begin.

Tommy tucked under my arm, I walk home to save the bus fare. Three-quarters of an hour later, feet smarting in my knock-off Chelsea boots, I'm home, and my folks aren't. This means I have a free run at the shared stereo – and, importantly, can crank it up. *Tommy*'s first two tracks are a pleasing racket of guitar and growl, but track three…

Track three! That first drum thwack, the siren soar, the speed and the clatter. I am spellbound. It ends. I hoick back the needle and play it again. And again. And again. It's like being machine-gunned by melody. And then there's that refrain:

It doesn't really matter at all
Just let me go out there once more

This is the song I have needed to hear. It feels like a validation. Like freedom. This band is mine.

And here, now, 30 years on, they still are.

MOTHERS
SKIZZ CYZYK

I first heard The Wedding Present in 1989, when the *Bizarro* album arrived at WCVT, the college radio station just North of Baltimore, Maryland, where I was the music director at the time. I loved it! *Bizarro* has been a favourite album of mine ever since. Over the years, I've picked up every Wedding Present and Cinerama release I've come across, amassing quite a large collection in the process. In 2009, I joined a local music club, where members would get together monthly to share and discuss music. At one point I realised there didn't seem to be many people in the club familiar with The Wedding Present, so the next time it was my turn to present music to the group, I knew what I needed to turn them on to. Which song, though? How could I pick a favourite when there are so many great songs to choose from? Certainly, it would have to be something from *Bizarro*, my go-to Wedding Present album. As I kept thinking about it, there was one particular song that kept popping into my head, and it didn't sound like anything on *Bizarro* (except 'What Have I Said Now?' has some similarities). I wasn't sure what it was called or which album it was on, so I had to go through my collection until I found it, which I did, on the double CD, *Singles 1989-1991*. The song was called 'Mothers', and now that I knew what it was called and where to find it, I couldn't stop listening to it. I don't know how successful that song was at creating new Wedding Present fans among my music club friends, but I now knew that my favourite Wedding Present song wasn't from my favourite Wedding Present album. Fast forward to 2017 when I saw the band perform at the Rock & Roll Hotel in Washington, DC. They included 'Mothers' in their set that night. David Gedge announced it was a cover. What? I never thought to check the songwriting credits on the CD, but sure enough, the original version is by the Jean-Paul Sartre Experience, a band I was familiar with from my college radio days, but apparently, I wasn't familiar with that particular song. It seems weird that my favourite song by The Wedding Present, a band whose original songs I love so much, would be a cover. Then again, I love The Pixies, and my favourite Pixies song is a Neil Young cover ('Winterlong'). Truthfully, though, 'Mothers' isn't my favourite Wedding Present song. It's just one I like as much as 'Brassneck', or Take Me!', or 'Everyone Thinks He Looks Daft', or 'Rachel', or…

SUCK & OCTOPUSSY
STEPHEN COWE

November 2012 at the Liquid Rooms in Edinburgh was the first gig I'd been to with my new girlfriend, Shelley from New Zealand. She knew all about my love of The Wedding Present dating back to 1988 and 'Nobody's Twisting Your Arm'. She was a fan, and although a few years younger than me, had *Bizarro* when growing up in Hastings, on the North Island of New Zealand.

Stephen Cowe and his wife Shelley, who walked down the aisle to 'Octopussy'

We'd been listening to *Seamonsters* a fair bit as our relationship developed, but to see The Wedding Present do *Seamonsters* again 20-odd years later for me, with Shelley, was special. When they played 'Suck', I can remember squeezing her hand, the noise, the lyrics, just amazing. She squeezed back and I knew this woman was special.

On 1st March 2014 in Dunfermline, Shelley walked down the aisle to marry me to the tune of 'Octopussy'. ('Suck' didn't feel right!). The intro before David begins to sing is just fantastic. If I wasn't emotional enough, once I heard that guitar and saw my wife to be, it was amazing.

MY FAVOURITE DRESS

STEPHEN REID

Stephen Reid has nominated 'My Favourite Dress'

I was 19 and my other favourite band had recently split up. The Wedding Present were loud, really loud. They were also less complex, more visceral and from Leeds. I lived on a farm in Wiltshire and Leeds brought back my childhood heroes – Allan Clarke & Co. This was a single but I played the *George Best* album a lot. I loved everything about that LP – the iconic artwork, of course, but the angry guitars and the (what I would now call) self-involved lyrics were right up my street. In fact, the last minute or so of guitars is every bit as important as the preceding lyrics. I was young and was having yet another unsuccessful fling with a former girlfriend who now had a new boyfriend (who also looked daft!). Sound familiar? She rarely wore dresses but that did not really matter. 'Jealousy is an essential part of love.' I really believed that then. I was a judgmental young man and am now a slightly less judgmental middle-aged one. But I still love this song.

KENNEDY

CHRIS WIDDOWSON

For me it had to be 'Kennedy' off *Bizarro*, with those crunching guitars and those starting chords which launched hundreds of drunken stampedes onto Nottingham's nightclub dance floors to thrash about uncontrollably. Growing up had never been so much fun. Any song with the lines 'Lost your love of life? Too much apple pie' said it all. The song is as fresh today as it was when I first heard it and resonates of a time of no inhibitions, clubbing in Nottingham and just going for it on the dance floor, week in, week out.

Following the release of *George Best*, a John Peel staple, *Bizarro* delivered a far more muscular, aggressive sound and even faster tunes. With the crunching opening chords of 'Kennedy', I was hooked. The Friday night ritual was beer, more beer and then clubbing with as much crazy dancing as you could muster. The sweaty nightclub beckoned, waiting to be served at the bar, with 'Kennedy' piercing the air.

Young and free, with no cares, the world at your feet, for five minutes nothing else mattered as Gedge & Co took you on a journey of discovery – great times, great song. The stampede followed onto the dance floor – pushing, barging, arms flailing, spilt beer, a mass of arms and legs, big grins, with a common love for this guitar drenched classic.

'Oh, have you lost your love of life? Too much apple pie' just must be one of the best lyrics ever. I was even challenged by my best mate – another Weddoes fan – to put it into my wedding speech to calm my nerves. I never did, but 'Kennedy' did get played at the reception.

Chris Widdowson is a fan of 'Kennedy'

MY FAVOURITE DRESS

STUART LANGSBURY

My favourite song is 'My Favourite Dress'. I was at *Festival No. 6* in 2015 and David Gedge was doing a semi-acoustic set at the 'Lost in the Woods' stage. It wasn't a full band but just three of them. It was very intimate in a magical setting and 'My Favourite Dress' was the last song and it was just brilliant. There were probably a hundred people watching and the song captured the mood perfectly. Whenever I see the band – which I've done several times since – they usually do this song and I always think of that night.

THE WEDDING PRESENT: Why Are You Being So Reasonable Now?

"Much of what I said above applies to this as well. It seems to me that The Wedding Present are ripe for some kind of backlash and that makes me sad even though I appreciate that it's an inevitable part of the pop process. The Wedding Present's virtues are that they make records which are direct and uncomplicated and it seems that these are now being regarded as vices in some quarters. It would be gratifying to see David Gedge become exceedingly famous if only because I still have several demos which he gave me in the days of The Lost Pandas and obviously these would then become extremely valuable."

THE WEDDING PRESENT 'Why Are You Being So Reasonable Now?'

RECEPTION

The french version — 'Pourquoi Es Tu Devenu Si Raisonnable?' — available in a separate format to the English 45, adds a whole new dimension to the Weddoes 'up and at 'em' indie beat. This is perhaps their finest moment to date — for once the girly backing vocals work and the song itself is a corker.

THE WEDDING PRESENT release their second single of '88 this week – a new David Gedge composition, 'Why Are You Being So Reasonable Now?'.

The single is backed with 'Not From Where I'm Standing'. The 12-inch has two extra tracks – 'Getting Better' and an acoustic version of 'Give My Regards To Kevin' – and the five-track CD and cassette has a French version of 'Reasonable' called 'Pourquoi Est Tu Devenu Si Raisonable'.

And there's more vinyl on the way. The band's LP of Ukranian and Russian folk songs is due for budget release in early November.

They've also added another night to their stint at London's Kentish Town Town And Country Club. The band play three nights finishing on October 13.

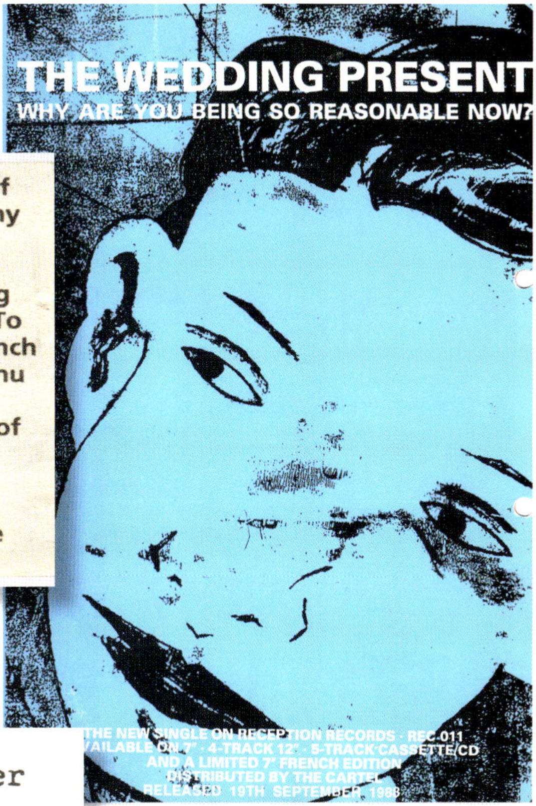

ence. However, the riproaring cover of the Beatles' "Getting Better" (also on the SGT PEPPER KNEW MY FATHER comp) is utterly euphoric.

THE WEDDING PRESENT
Why Are You being So reasonable Now?
Reception Records (dist: Red Rhino/Cartel)

The ravishing guitars of the unfeasibly magnificent Wedding Present return, triumphant, with yet another diamond of a single. All the customary ingredients we know and love are here, without compromise, still prosaically appealing and roguishly handsome. Why, there's even the added sophistication of a fluent French translation – a rare feat not so deftly attempted since the halcyon days of Teardrop Explodes. National stardom can only be a spit away. ****

* **Candy Patrick**

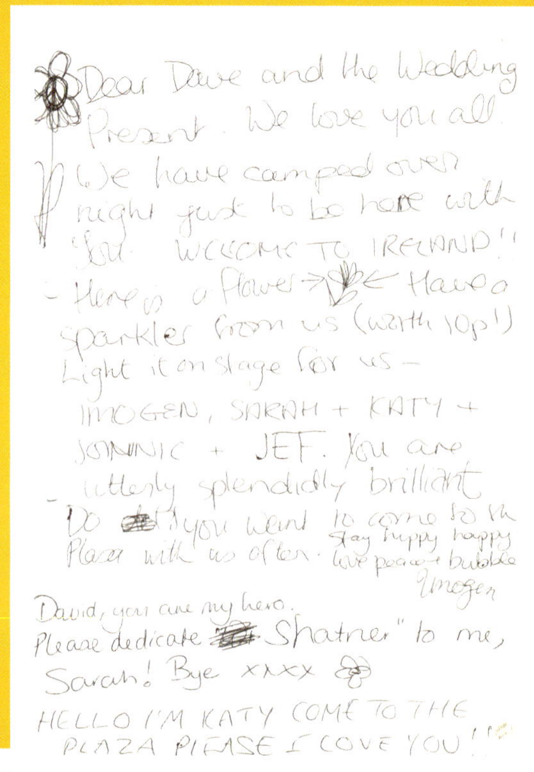

Dear Dave and the Wedding Present. We love you all.
We have camped over night just to be here with you. WELCOME TO IRELAND!!
- Here is a flower → ← Have a sparkler from us (worth 10p!)
Light it on stage for us -
IMOGEN, SARAH + KATY + DOMINIC + JEF. You are utterly splendidly brilliant
- Do you want to come to the Plaza with us after.
Stay happy happy love peace + bubble
Imogen

David, you are my hero.
Please dedicate "Shatner" to me,
Sarah! Bye xxxx

HELLO I'M KATY COME TO THE PLAZA PLEASE I LOVE YOU!!

THE WEDDING PRESENT: The Evening Show Sessions (*Nighttracks*)

David Gedge and friends have triggered off a frighteningly vociferous debate on your user-friendly newsdesk, resulting in two ardently divided schools of thought regarding the group's correct nickname. Supremo Staunton plumps for The Pressies every time, while The Boy Lamacq shouts the odds for The Weddoes with a knowing sneer. In the interests of goodwill and the smooth-running of the tea-making rota, the debate will be suspended for the time being while I review this four-track sesh from the spring of '86.

Having never been the biggest fan of The WPs, it's nice to discover that my personal fave 'Everyone Thinks He Looks Daft' starts the ball rolling on this EP, and it finishes with a rather pleasing reading of the Gang Of Four's 'I Found That Essence Rare'. With the exception of the Gene Vincent recordings from 1971, this is the best of the series so far.

THE WEDDING PRESENT

live at THE OUTLOOK

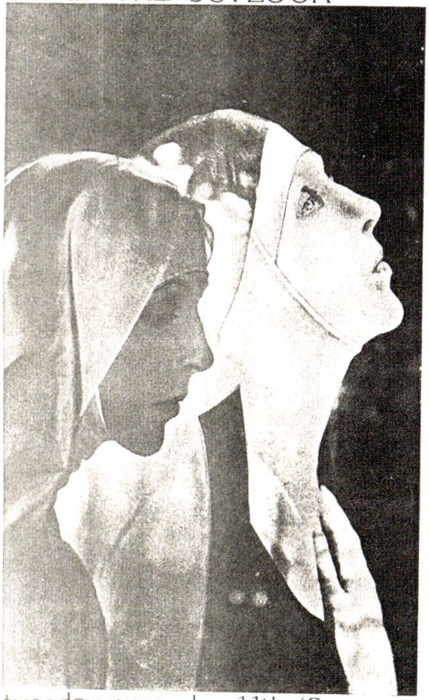

tuesday, november 11th. (8p.m.-12p.m.)
£2.50 or £2 with u.b.40.

* GROOVY MUSIC ALNIGHT..........

THE WEDDING PRESENT
The Hummingbird

The Wedding Present have been accused of having a formula: thrash out a catchy three chord riff, stick some "I met her at the chippie" type lyrics on top and hey presto! there's your cult classic. If, indeed, they have a formula, it is an original and appealing one.

The Weddies' songs are potted yarns of homely life (tongues securely housed in cheeks as they declare "Everyone thinks he looks daft") which work successfully live partly because of the ferocious quality of the music and partly due to the comforting but sharp lyrics. The act owed much to David Gedge's charisma as a performer; either exchanging pleas-

THE WEDDING PRESENT/THE HEART THROBS
Hull University, October 17th 1988

Well, once again, I managed to miss the support band at a concert. However, from the comments I heard during the wait for The Wedding Present suggested a mixed reaction to The Heart Throbs. It wasn't until I heard their new single "Here I Hide" on John Peel a few days later that I regretted my late arrival.

There was never any doubt what sort of reception Dave Gedge & Co would receive, whatever the quality of performance. From the opening bars of "Everyone Thinks He Looks Daft" to the closing encore of "This Boy Can Wait" every song was met with a large barrage of cheers. It was the sort of sweaty, non-stop gig that is all too rare in Hull nowadays. As it was the band put on the blistering set of Indie thrash that has seen them elevated to the ranks of "Smiths Successors". The chart near miss "Why Are You Being So Resonable Now?" appeared early on, but the biggest cheer of the night was reserved for "Nobody's Twisting Your Arm" which Mr Gedge dedicated to all people from Hull: "You're from Yorkshire and don't let anyone tell you different!" (Instantly elevating him to hero status).

Most of the "George Best" LP was featured and therefore kept the massed ranks moving in a sea of sweat and beer. The only tint on the whole evening was the large dickhead in front who attempted to beat everyone into oblivion in his frenzy of slam-dancing.....see him at Donnington next year !

"GRIP 66"

"I think festivals are rubbish," muses Pete. "Stood in a field for three days watching 15 million bands in the rain, having to queue up for the bars and the toilet and that . . . it's not my idea of fun. I suppose it's somebody's idea of fun, but . . ."

"I'm a born entertainer, me," retorts David. "I can cope with it."

The Fred Astaire of the whizzy guitar, David readily acknowledges the essential dichotomy concomitant with outdoor rocking.

"It's quite nice to go out there on stage and see a lot of people smiling," he ponders, "but there's nothing that puts you off more than seeing people smiling and throwing bottles at you."

And then **THE WEDDING PRESENT** rocked on. Their appeal is a strange one. David Gedge's peculiar voice is directly descended from that used by Edwyn Collins on the first Orange Juice singles, his guitar playing is a mad dervish thing quite unrelated to the lumpiness of the songs and only the splendour of the song titles – 'Granadaland', 'Brassneck', 'Everyone Thinks He Looks Daft' – is really enticing, but the nation holds the Weddoes in high esteem. Gedge's shorts were rather good, however. No amusing Ukrainian songs were performed, but 'Granadaland' appeared to turn into 'Silver Machine' at one point, which was alarming.

NME

Aquatic adventures for **THE WEDDING PRESENT**, who played some gig in Bradford in the middle of a lake. Many sex-crazed fans zipped up their anoraks and started flipping around in the water, trying to get closer to their loved ones. But the whole affair became alarming when this shambling flotilla neared the island and officials feared that the electricity supply would frazzle the little blighters. Unfortunately, the supply was cut off.

Indie traitors – we love 'em! Top 40 band **THE WEDDING BLOODY PRESENT** have requested that their agency make the band's upcoming tour itineraries *filofax-compatible!* Not for **GEDGE AND THE LADS** themselves, you understand – just for the benefit of their girlfriends and RCA execs. The band's will be etched on beermats in cheap biro as always. Phew!

The day's dose of major-indie was provided by everyone's darlings, The Wedding Present. David Gedge stunned the audience with his style: shorts, shoes and socks and so proving once again that it's hip to be square! Their rapid jangle powered set was entertaining, with The Gedge rolling across the stage with his guitar, and strong. I'm no expert, but there was definitely some new material in their set; it had a far more rocky feel to it, but still very 'them'. A friendly band playing to an obviously friendly audience (they were at this point anyway), I was impressed!

SOME BIZARRO WEDDING MARCH

THE WEDDING PRESENT have confirmed the dates for their British tour which starts in late October to coincide with the long-awaited release of their second album, 'Bizarro'.

'Kennedy', their first single since signing to RCA last year, comes out on September 25. Full details were exclusively revealed in *Sounds* three weeks ago. The 12-inch and CD feature two additional tracks – 'One Day All This Will Be Yours' and a cover of the Tom Jones classic 'It's Not Unusual' – and a limited number of the 12-inch also comes with a free poster.

The Weddoes have been warming up for their autumn dates with occasional prestigious gigs at the Reading Festival and John Peel's 50th Birthday Party (as well as a live slot on *Club X*).

Weddoes announce British dates to promote second LP

Their tour starts at Liverpool Royal Court on October 25, continuing at Bradford St George's Hall 26, Sheffield Polytechnic 27, Northampton Roadmenders 28, Portsmouth Guildhall 30, Folkestone Leas Cliffe Hall 31, London Kilburn National November 1-2, Coventry Polytechnic 4, Cardiff University 5, Birmingham Hummingbird 6, Nottingham Rock City 7, Blackburn King George's Hall 8, Aberdeen Ritzy's 10, Glasgow Barrowlands 11, Newcastle Mayfair 12, Leeds Polytechnic 13 and Manchester International 14-15.

Tickets are £5 everywhere except London which is £6.

7. THE WEDDING PRESENT
'Bizarro' ***(RCA)***
FAST, FRANTIC and frenetic, the Present have cornered the f-word market. 'Bizarro' sees them grow up in public, avoiding the softening out routine and guitar riffin' into a zillion bedsits. The finger grazing six-string chafing combined with Gedge's luvvy duvvy guff are still heartwinners. The unlikely lads are flying a supreme high. **JR**

26 THE WEDDING PRESENT: "Bizarro" (RCA) More or less what we expected, more tales of love-gone-astray. "Bizarro" shattered no one's preconceptions but made a lot more disenchanted Smiths fans very happy. "Bizzaro" was as sensible and straightforward as it was sparkling and sentimental.

THE FINE ART OF SHOPLIFTING

THE BEST of 89

FANZINE

we asked people to fill in forms (at various gigs around the country, during october & november) Out of the 700 retuned forms this is the result.....

GROUPS

I. The Wedding present
2. The Stone Roses
3. Inspiral Carpets
4. Cud
5. the Groove Farm
   The Field Mice
7. Pale Saints
8. Mega City Four
9. Brilliant Corners
IO. Jesse Garon & The Desperadoes

FANZINES

I. Waterbomb
2. Woosh
3. The Cymbaline Music

T.V.

I. Brookside
2. The Wonder Years
3. Home and Away
4. Blackadder Goes Forth
5. Transmission

the WEDDING PRESENT

kennedy

Lost your look of life
Too much apple pie
Oh have you lost your look of life
Too much apple pie
And now Harry's walked away with Johnny's wife

You've gotta pick some people up
You've gotta let some people go
But if the least thing does come up
Oh well I really want to know
Because everybody loves a TV show

Repeat verses once

Repeat first verse

Ahh

Words and music by D. Gedge
Reproduced by permission Hallin Music Ltd/EMI Music Ltd
On RCA Records ← incorrectly!

BAND OF THE YEAR

NME Readers' Poll

1. **THE STONE ROSES**
2. Happy Mondays
3. The Wedding Present
4. New Order
5. The Wonder Stuff
6. Pixies
7. REM
8. The Cure
9. Inspiral Carpets
10. James

LP OF THE YEAR

1. **THE STONE ROSES The Stone Roses (Silvertone)**
2. DOOLITTLE Pixies (4AD)
3. THREE FEET HIGH AND RISING De La Soul (Big Life)
4. TECHNIQUE New Order (Factory)
5. HUP The Wonder Stuff (Polydor)
6. BIZARRO The Wedding Present (RCA)
7. AUTOMATIC Jesus And Mary Chain (blanco y negro)
8. SENSUAL WORLD Kate Bush (EMI)
9. DISINTEGRATION The Cure (Fiction)
10. NEW YORK Lou Reed (WEA)

SINGLE OF THE YEAR

1. **FOOL'S GOLD The Stone Roses (Silvertone)**
2. WROTE FOR LUCK Happy Mondays (Factory)
3. SHE BANGS THE DRUMS The Stone Roses (Silvertone)
4. JOE Inspiral Carpets (Cow)
5. DON'T LET ME DOWN, GENTLY The Wonder Stuff (Far Out/Polydor)
6. KENNEDY The Wedding Present (RCA)
7. CAN'T BE SURE The Sundays (Rough Trade)
8. INTERESTING DRUG Morrissey (Parlophone)
9. MONKEY GONE TO HEAVEN Pixies (4AD)
10. INFO FREAKO Jesus Jones (Food)

THE WEDDING PRESENT
BIRMINGHAM INSTITUTE

15/7/91

FUMBLING THROUGH the pitch blackness of the Birmingham Institute – three tiers of sweating Gedge clones – is rather like waking up to find yourself trapped inside a Wedding Present song. There are no lights and you stumble in a haze of disorientation towards the glimmer of light falling on the stage.

Gedge's wrought vignettes of stressed and stripped hearts, songs of desolate grace that lure and confound, are delivered with equal parts piquant zeal and crushing despair.

Like a shot across the bows, 'Dalliance' is a warning, a chilling foresight of what's to follow. The Weddoes snap the song instantly into metal/melange overdrive that leaves you feeling like you've been kicked from Birmingham to Donington.

Paul Dorrington's guitar screams wildly as The Weddoes waste not one moment of time in ripping through 'Dare' then 'Suck'. Soon it becomes apparent that a wholesale re-interpretation of the 'Seamonsters' LP is, as they say, 'on the cards'.

Gedge, holding a tune with more ease than he's ever done before, hunches malevolently over his guitar with an expression of such distaste and Hannibal Lecter intensity, that his instrument virtually shakes with fear. It is quite aware that it is in for some treatment starting at 'severe' and escalating towards 'apocalyptic', stopping off to nail a cat to the floor *en route*.

With the LP tracks still ringing in their ears, The Weddoes give the crowd what they've been yelling for. A brilliant rendition of 'Brassneck', played at deathmetal speed, precedes the opening chords of 'Kennedy'. A fountain of beer spews up from the delirious mob at the front as the band ferment an audacious guitar thrash that just – and only just – manages to keep a grip on the tune and loose control at the same time.

True to form, they depart with no encore, leaving a gasping and speechless audience stunned by not so much a top pop performance, as by a glimpse into a man's tormented soul.

Jonny Thatcher

Only "Corduroy", the oldest song here, presents any kind of picture of contentment. That aside, "Sea Monsters" is all about passion turned mad, bad and sad; it dwells obsessively on the cruelest things lovers do to one another. Infidelity is a recurring theme; "Dalliance" has Gedge shopping for presents that his paramour will never dare take home because of the man who's waiting there for her, and both "Lovenest" and "Heather" are similarly haunted by the spectre of a third party who stands between DG and the fulfilment of his dreams. "Suck" is perhaps the bleakest thing the Weddoes have ever written, a singularly unhealthy stew of desire, guilt and despair, with Gedge fatally, irresistibly attracted to someone he knows will do him no good.

There are no more abstract word games along the lines of "Kennedy" here. To some extent, Gedge is going over old ground - literally so in "Heather", in which he takes a sentimental journey to the places he and his ex used to go to together. But he's never sounded so *intense* about these bruises and betrayals before. By the end of "Heather" he's screaming, out of control.

Afterwards, there's one last masterpiece left. "Octopussy" is the calmest thing here, with its sweet, circling melody, but it's still full of tension, like the smouldering silence that follows a blazing row. "I want to understand why I need you," croons Gedge, hurt and bewildered once more, trying to be detached and objective about things and, of course, failing miserably. Again. If you've never suffered from loneliness or rejection, then don't bother with "Sea Monsters" because you won't understand it, and long may your good luck continue. For the rest of us, this is a record to treasure, and to save for exceptionally dark hours.

The Wedding Present have never before sounded this raw, this powerful and this moving. One from the heart.

DAVE JENNINGS

("Sea Monsters" is released on May 28.)

This is the 'Seamonsters'

THE WEDDING PRESENT announce details of a long awaited new LP and single this week. The album, their first since 'Bizarro' over two years ago, was recorded as-live in just 11 days at Cannon Falls, Minnesota, with producer Steve Albini (who also worked on 'Bizarro').

Titled 'Seamonsters', and released May 28, the LP features a re-recording of 'Corduroy' (included on the last 'Three Songs' EP), and the new single, 'Dalliance' (out on Monday). All songs were written by Gedge and have one word titles. An insider close to the band told *NME* that the album is harder and more dramatic than any previous release.

The Weddoes have also added extra dates to their forthcoming tour, at Newcastle Mayfair (May 29), Leicester De Montford Hall (30), Swansea Penyrheol Theatre (31), Portsmouth Guildhall (June 1) and Cambridge Corn Exchange (2).

"Sea Monsters" is a dizzying sonic roller-coaster ride, a record that should be heard by anyone with an interest in the outer limits of guitar pop. "Dalliance", the first item here, sets the unsettling tone, building slowly from a choked whisper to a desperate plea, before that astonishing avalanche of gritty noise near the end sweeps away everything in its path. "Sea Monsters" has plenty of similar shocks in store; and if Peter Solowka really is considering changing his role in The Wedding Present, maybe it's because the dazzling display of guitar fireworks on this record would be damn near impossible to follow. Don't worry, we're not talking interminable solos here. It's the range of *textures* on this album that is so astonishing. Considerable credit is therefore due to leading American psycho Steve Albini, who in his role as producer displays an inspired sense of drama and dynamics throughout. The guitar tones have the touch of a feather one second and that of a power-drill the next. There are

---

By not hi-jacking the groovy train in order to revive a flagging career, The Wedding Present now stand virtually alone amongst their mid-'80s indie contemporaries.

But then, they've kept moving the goalposts ever since 1987's George Best debut established David Gedge & Co as post-Smiths champions of the bedsit. Their attitude has, paradoxically, become more independent since signing to a major two years ago. 1989's *Bizarro* maintained its predecessor's pop suss but brought darker forces into play, notably a flirtation with the dissonant power of American underground guitar heroes like Sonic Youth.

Now *Sea Monsters* sees this affair blossoming into a torrid marriage. Recorded in just eight days by that enfant terrible of the US noise scene, Steve Albini (nefarious force behind Big Black and Rapeman) it digs beneath the cuddly innocence of old, at last finding the appropriate musical match for Gedge's perennial themes of betrayal and rejection. The brutally simple Albini technique - bass and drums loud, guitars louder, let the vocals fend for themselves - has prompted the band to cast off their remaining inhibitions.

Witness the opening 'Dalliance'. Its slow, brooding pace drags us into a three-way love affair with Gedge, as ever, the losing partner: *"But I was yours for seven years/Guess that's what you call a dalliance"*. Likewise 'Suck' develops its account of insatiable desire by means of an expertly marshalled groove that recalls The Pixies' *Surfer Rosa* album - another genius Albini production - and eventually finds release via some seismic guitar riffing. Gedge now has so much more room in which to twist his emotional daggers; perhaps to most impressive effect on the epic closer, 'Octopussy'.

This is The Wedding Present's very difficult third album, alright, and it seems no one's told them you're supposed to mellow with age. But whatever their original fans make of its bleak songs and incendiary guitarplay, *Sea Monsters* is a triumph of art over artifice. And there ain't too much of that these days.

(9) Keith Cameron

Wedding rhythm

THE WEDDING PRESENT
Manchester Academy
23rd May 1991

"Don't stand at the front", they told me. "Not if you fancy staying alive". This was good advice.

The thing is, people can't help dancing violently to the Wedding Present. It's a sound, for the most part, which whisks you from one energetic plane to another, dropping you down exhausted for some fleeting moments before hurtling you back into frenzied rhythms.

The new material from the LP "Seamonsters", out this week, has the addition of smoother, gentler rhythms which crash into the vibrant abrasiveness of old. Gedge no longer throws flippant attacks at the microphone, he uses his voice more, and the result is, for me, the best music that the Wedding Present have ever done.

Despite all this and Gedge's own reticence to turn back to performing songs from "George Best", frequent demands from the audience of "Shatner!" and "Kevin!" (in vain), proved that their debut album is still much loved by fans.

It was hard to see much whilst being thrown around pin-ball style, but when I did see him, Gedge was either performing little balletic hand movements to add flavour to the well-known directness of his songs, or leaning over the guitar, his arm a blur with that pursed-lip concentration characteristic of him.

Having begun with an energetic "Crawl", they went on to perform their current single "Dalliance" before launching into some old favourites like "Don't Talk Just Kiss", "Bewitched" and "Take Me" which were all met with an uproar of approval. It was just as well that "Kennedy" was followed by the subdued "Carolyn", no-one could have stood that sort of pace for much longer.

Gedge laughed in his good-natured manner before taking a deep breath into the microphone for a song he knew would be enthusiastically greeted: "Everyone thinks he looks daft" was flung out into the hall with confidence, beautifully knit and wonderfully exuberant.

In no time at all, they had finished with "Brassneck" and another song from "Seamonsters", "Heather". It all spoke well for the future of the group. I'm sure many people were there who begrudged Peter Solowka's dismissal from the group, but the Weddoes' live sound did not seem to suffer as a result. The friends who I was with told me that this was the best live that they'd ever seen the group, and I can well believe it. If dripping, flushed faces and bruised limbs are any measure of a successful concert, then everyone else approved too.

DEBBY SALMONS

The Students' Association
proudly presents

THE WEDDING PRESENT

the union theatre,
st.andrews
tickets £6
from bess, rock city,
union general office
and groucho's, dundee

thursday 8th
november 1990
doors open 8pm

the students' association
it's getting better all the time

BAD THING
EDWARD KOMOCKI

This is something I need to get off my chest. 'Bad Thing' (off *Search For Paradise: Singles 2004-5)* is my Wedding Present guilty pleasure. A cacophony of squally noise that thunders and roars, a guitar sound that moans and screeches, a veritable dirge that offers brief moments of calm before exploding into an avalanche of churning thrash only to collapse into the spectral coda of a needle stuck in the groove of a 1930s phonograph. Which on paper all sounds like some form of aural nightmare, but this is The Wedding Present in overdrive and this is what they do so magnificently.

Then why the feelings of guilt at loving every second of this fabulously monstrous noise? Because, in my heart of hearts, I'm pretty certain I shouldn't. This track is not indicative of DLG's sublime and inspired musical evolution from purveyor of raucous blasts of whirlwind guitar to today's eloquently lyrical master of subtle melodies and unforgettable hooks. 'Bad Thing' is OLD Wedding Present, not NEW Wedding Present! In all honesty, 'Bad Thing' is… well… it's *Seamonsters* and it's *Seamonsters* through and through. It should be nestling between 'Corduroy' and 'Carolyn', not rising Kraken-like from the calm resplendent musical waters typified by *Take Fountain* and *Valentina*. Now that's not to say that the post-Cinerama Wedding Present don't know how to rock out with fire and passion, but 'Bad Thing' is in a whole different league of raucously explosivity.

And so, I shouldn't like it! I shouldn't be acting like some throwback, negating all the joyous sonic experimentation that's come during the days of Cinerama and The Wedding Present Mk 2. Surely I, too, should have moved on from the noise and the thrash to appreciating these more fertile musical pastures? But what intensifies my guilt further is the fact that everyone else seems to feel the same way. Each and every one of the multitude of online comparative Wedding Present polls in which we all diligently participate always end up ranking OLD Wedding Present ahead of NEW Wedding Present. It's always 'Kennedy' over 'Santa Ana Winds', 'Take Me!' over 'Queen Anne', and 'My Favourite Dress' over 'Panama'! And with no small amount of remorseful unease, I am forever left wondering how on earth DLG must feel when we all cast our votes with such unerring predictability? Crushed? Please no! Hopefully nothing more than a shrug, a wry smile and a reinforced creative determination to make us see the error of our ways.

Confessional catharsis over. I have publicly acknowledged my inappropriate love for 'Bad Thing'. I will learn from this. I will grow and I will move forward. And the next time Twitter offers me the democratic right to express my Wedding Present preferences, I will demonstrate my new-found self-awareness and I will do the RIGHT thing.

So, let the canvassing begin! Vote 'You Jane'! Vote 'Spiderman On Hollywood'! Vote NEW Wedding Present! You know it makes sense.

SUCK

COLE JOHNSTON

I came late to The Wedding Present in 1993 or so. I was 18 and had just moved out and was living with some friends. My friend Kevin asked if I had heard *George Best* and played me the first earth-shattering record by my new favourite band. I promptly declared this the greatest record ever made and it became the only thing I listened to for the next few weeks. One day, Kevin told me I should listen to this other record by them because it was even better. I remember actually refusing because how could *George Best* possibly be topped? Finally, he pinned me down and pressed play on *Seamonsters*. Hey, wow. This song 'Dalliance' is pretty good, especially when those guitars kick in. Then it bleeds right into 'Dare'. Hmmm, Kevin might be onto something.

Then something absolutely magical begins to play. 'We've talked so long…' and that bassline. It's quiet and lovely. 'Because I can't fall asleep…' A perfect love letter. At about the one minute mark, that first guitar kicks in, the build up begins and now you're really paying attention. Where did those guitars come from? After the chorus, things shift to that almost jarring buzzsaw guitar sound over the top of everything.

I didn't have to search for you

Everything gets a bit more immediate. That next little ramp up in the guitars – 'No, no, no… don't stop…' – and you're thinking, 'Jesus Christ! This song is in overdrive! We have hit the peak…!' and then it keeps going. By the time the final chorus crashes into that sliding guitar you are almost exhausted. Needless to say, I apologised to Kevin for ever doubting him and the next time I travelled to Vancouver (a four-hour drive and the nearest place that had any kind of decent record shop) I came home with my own copy of *Seamonsters* and 'Suck' is almost like a talisman.

When I met my now wife and introduced her to The Wedding Present, this became our song. It played at our wedding and we have waited eagerly for it to be played every time (which is far too infrequent) David would bring the band to town. One time, I may have drunkenly accosted David at the Town Pump and pleasantly requested/belligerently demanded he play 'Suck' as an encore especially for my girlfriend. I will maintain to this day that he did so graciously, playing the only encore ever just for us.

Others (like David) might say that it was going to be the last song anyway and he couldn't understand what that intoxicated young man was going on about, but I think we all know the truth.

RACHEL
COLIN CLARK

Glasgow ABC 2013 – (left to right) Yanhua, Rachel, Andy, Colin, Jenny & Steve

I have many, many memories having been to over 45 Wedding Present gigs over the years since the first one at Queens Hall in Edinburgh in 1998, and mostly accompanied by my best mate, Andy 'Nobby' Brown. The Wedding Present have been the soundtrack to my life but the song that stands out for me is 'Rachel'.

My fiancée, Rachel, had attended a few Wedding Present gigs over the last ten years due to my love of the band and all things (Mr) Gedge. In mid-2016, I heard an inkling through the Scopitones fansite that The Wedding Present were releasing a song called 'Rachel', and when I first heard it in late August 2016, I immediately loved it. The guitar, the vibe – and the lyrics, which were just our relationship in a perfect bubble.

We live in Balfarg, north Glenrothes, Fife and were absolutely overjoyed when Graeme Ramsay joined The Wedding Present. Little did we know that after travelling to gigs and festivals all around the UK to see my favourite band, they would then play The Greenside in Leslie (just one and a half miles from our doorstep) for several consecutive years whilst Graeme was in the band and afterwards. It's such a great small venue, low ceilinged and produces a great sound. As David can probably attest, there's a great Indian restaurant in the village too! When 'Rachel' was played there in 2017, it was very special and turned my fiancée from a partnering concert goer into a Wedding Present acolyte. It's the song that now keeps my Rachel coming back to see them.

I've found that, UK-wide, Wedding Present fans and family are the most friendly bunch and it genuinely feels like a community at gigs. Thank you, David and the band (throughout the years and decades), for doing what you do and for bringing us as a couple closer together through a shared love of The Wedding Present.

WHAT HAVE I SAID NOW?
DAVID DUFFY

David Duffy was obsessed with *Bizarro*

I've had the opportunity to talk to DLG at his concerts over the years. One time we discussed favourite albums. I expressed some surprise that *Watusi* was his partner Jessica's favourite Wedding Present album. David pointed out that people's favourite album is usually the one most strongly associated with the time when they fell in love with the band. That's definitely the case for me: *Bizarro* is my favourite album and 'What Have I Said Now?' my favourite song. At some point in the sixth form, Simon (to whom I owe an eternal debt: thank you, wherever you are) gave me a tape with *George Best* on one side and *Tommy* on the other. As someone whose musical taste was maturing from the white funk of Level 42 to embrace what is now called Indie rock, I was immediately hooked and have been ever since.

Bizarro was released soon afterwards and by the time I saw them live on that tour I was obsessed. 'What Have I said Now?' is the quintessential Gedge epic, with relentless soaring guitars and heart-rending, conversational lyrics. 'Why can't I ever say what I mean?' spoke loudly to a typically tongue-tied 18-year-old. The wall of sound guitars in the last 30 seconds of the song seem to distort into the sound of bagpipes to these ears. 'What Have I Said Now?' seems to presage the sound of The Wedding Present that Albini helped create in *Seamonsters*.

To this day, when the song comes on, I stop what I'm doing and get goosebumps. The version that the band played at *Keep It Peel* to celebrate the life of John Peel shortly after his death carries great emotional intensity.

DAVID LEWIS GEDGE'S FIRST GIRLFRIEND WAS CALLED JANET

Is it any wonder that there have been so few classic pop songs called 'Janet' when the only words that rhyme with it are 'planet' and 'granite'? The Wedding Present, however, have three songs about this particular Jan — but they won't reveal which!

"I met her in the sixth form at school," David tells me in his best Simon Bates voice. "She was having an argument with her boyfriend in the common-room and he said, 'I know why you don't want to go out with me anymore. It's because of him innit?' And he started pointing at me. I asked her out and she said, 'no'."

BRIXTON
ACADEMY
211 STOCKWELL ROAD, LONDON
SW9 9SL Box Office: 071-326 1022
METROPOLIS MUSIC presents
WEDDING PRESENT
with Special Guests
buffalo tom
BRIXTON
SATURDAY
25th MAY
1991
Doors: 7.30pm
Admission £7.50p Advance
ACADEMY
STALLS
No 3398

PRESENT PRESEN
seamonsters seamonsters
DIAVORTRAG DIAVORTRAG DIAVORTRAG DIAVORTRA
ARVED FUCHS
Die russische Arktis
Mi 23.10.
CCH Saal II
THE WEDDI PRESE seamons
THE WEDDING PRESENT
amonsters

MY
FAVOURIT
DRES
MY
AVOURITE
RESS

13 12 '92

EXIT
EXIT

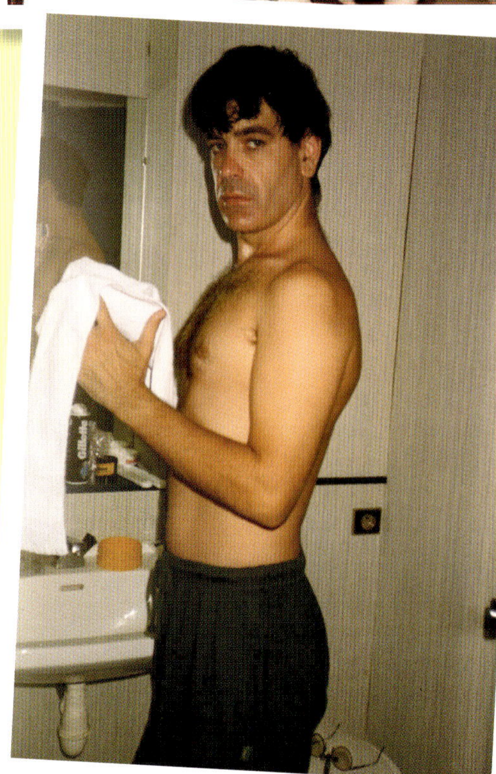

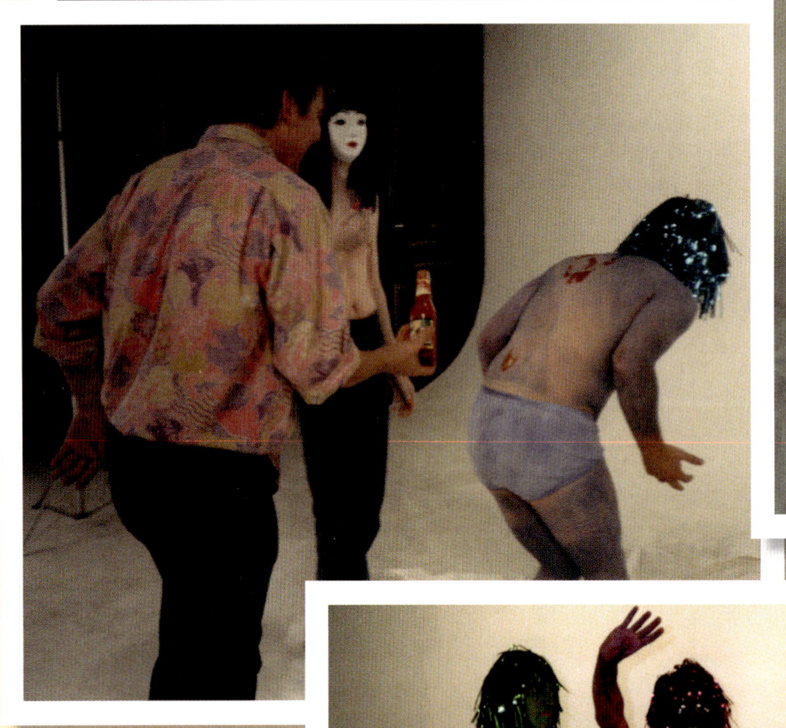

4

FLOWER
PLOWER

Newbury Comics

Universal Post - 12th October 1994

Gedge your rocks off!

The Wedding Present
Newcastle University

There's something about Dave Gedge, lead singer of the Wedding Present. Even by looking irritated and bored he still manages to incite near riots from his legion of fans. I suppose that's the result of nine years of solid touring, recording, and playing.

Yet all the same their fans can't be knocked for lack of enthusiasm when they played Newcastle Poly last year they virtually demolished the stage. Anyway, when the Wedding Present play it's worth going just to see the fans.

"Dave is God" I hear someone shout as they come on stage, instantly confirming the dedicated fan theory. Then as Dave strikes the first magical chords to new single *It's a gas* the crowd as one leaps to its feet and begins to jump up and down, something which doesn't stop for the full set.

By the time of *Flying Saucer* the third song, Dave seemed to have perked up considerably, and you could tell. During the long drawn out typical Weddoes end he really looked to be enjoying himself. As was the crowd, by now ecstatic.

They raced through their fourteen song set sealing several with their overlong trademark. The new album got a considerable airing, however the shouts for old stuff drastically outweighed the calls for latest material.

Not to be put off by this they played 8 songs from the new album and six of their greatest hits including *Dalliance*, *Blonde*, and of course *Kennedy* which inspired very nearly the same result as at the Poly last November.

Despite the blinding end to the set with *Click, click* Dave gave the impression he wasn't too happy by the end, however by then the audience had been treated to a dazzling set of pop songs, from a man who is basically a frustrated pop star. Who knows, maybe his day is coming. I hope so, let's face it he deserves it.

Mathew Pardo

THE WEDDING PRESENT
Watusi
Island

The Wedding Present won't take the easy way out. The Leeds, England, quartet could have contented itself with the kind of deliciously insubstantial pop tunes that slide in one ear and out the other, leaving just enough residue to hum by. The elements are in all place: Paul Dorrington's cozy guitar peals and Darren Belk's low-profile bass ambles amiably through quirky melodies and twitchy rhythms, while Simon Smith's slap-happy drums keep perfect pop time. But singer David Gedge is like a kid who can't leave his scabby knees alone. He picks and picks at love's painful minutiae, making the Wedding Present's fifth album, *Watusi*, a dream-pop album that obsesses instead of dreams.

Gedge's scenarios take place on the intimate level of conversation, and they ring as squeamishly true as an

THE WEDDING PRESENT

IT'S 10 years or so since David Gedge first aired his romantic torments in song, and in that time his band, The Wedding Present, have done much to help define the term "indie rock". They've never been predictable. Their first album for a major label consisted of rocked-up Ukrainian folk songs. During 1992, they released a single a month, all of which reached the Top 30. Now they're back with a new album, "Watusi", which displays all the raw emotion and drastic dynamics of their very best work. No doubt it will be previewed here at Reading. You really shouldn't refuse the gift.

Watusi continues Gedge's trademark lyrics about failed or confusing love, Gedge's trademark northern accent and, well, all the other Gedge trademarks those wooed by the Weddoes have come to expect. Gedge and the lads have produced another classic Weddoes lp to stand astride *George Best*, *Bizarro* and the Steve Albini-produced *Seamonsters*. ***Barney***

Indie/Lo-Fi by Jono Scott

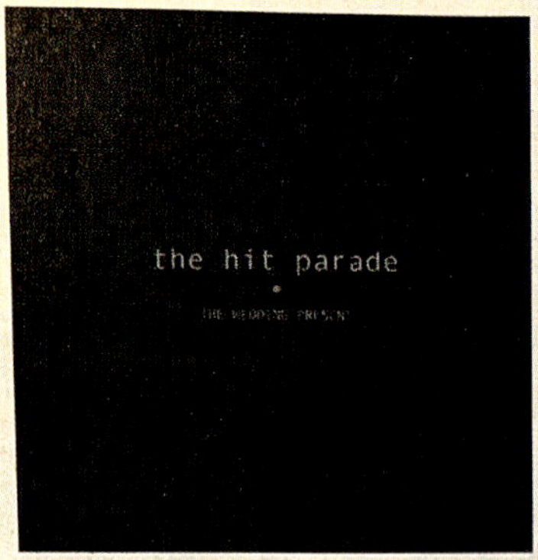

THE WEDDING PRESENT
Hit Parade
Camden Deluxe 82876 50395 2
(2-CD) (42:01) (40:15)

Hit Parade, which follows Camden's attractive repackaging of *Bizarro* and *Seamonsters*, documents a successful year-long hijacking of the pop charts by a bunch of rather scruffy-looking Northerners back in 1992. The plan was a simple one: release a new song (with B-side cover) once a month on limited-run 7"s. Between them, fans and collectors would rush out, snap up every copy and pole-vault the single high into the pop charts. The plan worked, and the Wedding Present still hold the world record for the most Top 30 singles in one year.

After six months, *Hit Parade 1* was released, and its sequel came out in early '93. Now, at last, we have all 12 A-sides on one disc, with the Bs on Disc Two. The most successful, in terms of chart position, was May's 'Come Play With Me' (No. 10). However, the WP ploy, branded by many as cynical, made the band as many enemies as friends.

January's 'Blue Eyes' was a perfect start, and, unusually for David Gedge et al., was based around quite a tricky riff. February's 'Go Go Dancer' was a disappointing follow-up, while 'Three' and 'Silver Shorts' (both produced by Ian Broudie) kept the ball in play. Overall, the leading lights were 'Boing!' and 'Flying Saucer', the latter a triumphant slab of extended indie 12-bar, while 'Boing!' captured everything that was great about the Wedding Present — lovelorn lyrics sung over a plucked, gently abrasive three-chord verse, before DG's monstrous one-finger guitar part heralds a noisy chorus.

Disc Two will be the one that gathers dust. A faithful version of the Go-Betweens' 'Cattle And Cane' is a tender take but, on the whole, the invention that made the band's mid-90s cover of the theme from *Cheers* so successful is missing. 'Pleasant Valley Sunday' is nothing special, while both 'Think That It Might' and the Close Lobsters' 'Let's Make Some Plans' miss the spot. Some tunes *are* fun: 'The Theme From *Shaft*', for example, while the cover of Elton John's 'Step Into Christmas' is excellent and makes up for December's disappointing A-side.

The benefit of *Hit Parade* is that it allows us to evaluate the project as an album. It lacks the power of the preceding *Seamonsters*, and the fun of 1994's *Watusi*, but a celebration of the throwaway pop single was always going to contain a couple of clunkers. In fact, the 12 singles haven't retained their value, although four associated promo CDs, each containing three singles, are still sought-after.

The original 7" version of 'Boing!' would have been nice and a limited-run vinyl version of *Hit Parade 2* featured a second record, with session takes of all 12 singles. So why not add these?

Still, this repackage makes an adequate document of a quirky piece of music history. Where next for the WP repackaging programme? As this is the last of the RCA era, can I make a humble plea to Island that they re-release *Watusi*, which has become, in DG's own words, "the lost Wedding Present album".

THE WEDDING PRESENT were superb. There, it's guaranteed that my colleagues here will think I'm deranged for another few months. But I swear that, if this was a new band, springing from nowhere with songs as diverse as the bitter, turbulent "Dalliance" and the joyous fizzy pop of "Flying Saucer", then critical praise would be heaped upon them.

They pushed things to the furthest possible extremes, David Gedge stretching his cramped voice to its limits and the guitars moving from sonic violence to spangled sweetness. There's fresh life in The Wedding Present yet. That's bad news for my friends here, but it should be good news for you.
DAVE JENNINGS

MELODY MAKER

Do you think you'd be the same band if you lived in London?
Simon: "No we'd all talk funny, wouldn't we?"
David: "We'd sound like Sham 69".

THE NEWS, Thursday, December 10, 1992

NEWS CRITICS

The best this year

The Wedding Present,
Pyramid Centre, Southsea

THE Wedding Present have often seemed dour and impenetrable in the past, their wall of guitar powerchords flatly unyielding.

But last night they proved that their pop sensibilities have made them a great band.

The novel idea of producing a single every month during this year seems to have paid off – not just in record sales, but in the transformation of the band.

The gloomy characters of a couple of years ago have been replaced by a group with real pop songs. But pop songs with the roughest edges imaginable.

The power that was always instinctive to The Wedding Present has been retained, the sound is still as abrasive as broken glass, but now it is uplifting rather than being an aural battering ram.

Combined with a deceptively simple light show, this set of just over an hour was quite simply one of the best – if not THE best – Portsmouth has seen this year.

It's just a shame there aren't another 12 Weddoes' singles in the pipeline for 1993.

BARRY RUTTER

Pub in the charts

A PUB which can hold no more than 150 people is to host current chart group The Wedding Present before it goes on a national tour.

The group, currently hovering in the mid-30s in the charts with its single called Three, will play The Ship Inn at Oundle on Monday, July 6.

A spokesman for the pub said: "We were very lucky to get the gig. We told punters about the gig earlier this week and tickets have almost sold out."

"I'm well aware that I don't have a particularly brilliant voice. I'm not one of those people who opens their mouth and flowers appear on trees."

● **THE WEDDING PRESENT** aim to match Elvis Presley's 1957 record of 12 consecutive Top 30 hits in one year with the release of their 'No Christmas' 45 next week, backed with a version of Elton John's 'Step Into Christmas'. Meanwhile, Gedge and co embark on their Yuletide tour this week, visiting Aberdeen Music Hall (Thursday), Glasgow Barrowlands (Friday), York Barbican (Saturday), Liverpool Royal Court (Sunday) and Manchester Academy (Monday).

The Mean Fiddler *presents*
THE PHOENIX 1993
AT LONG MARSTON AIRFIELD
STRATFORD-UPON-AVON, WARWICKSHIRE
(SUBJECT TO LICENCE)
FRI 16TH, SAT 17TH
SUN 18TH JULY 1993
GUEST TICKET

presents

THE PHOENIX 1993

AT
LONG MARSTON AIRFIELD
STRATFORD-UPON-AVON, WARWICKSHIRE

FRI 16TH | SAT 17TH | SUN 18TH | JULY 1993

GUEST TICKET

NAME WEDDING PRESENT COMPANY
NP/PAID
ENTER SHOW VIA GUEST/BACKSTAGE ENTRANCE

WEDDING
PRESENT

flüft,

5
SiX
TEN

COOLE

DAVID

BUMY

THE
WEDDING
PRESENT
edsel RECORDS
EDSJ 9010
CD 1 ℗ 1994 Cooking Vinyl Limited
except track 10 ℗ 1997 Scopitones.
© 2014 Demon Music Group Limited.
Marketed by Edsel, a division of
Demon Music Group Limited,
a BBC Worldwide company.
Manufactured in the EU.
LC 13222
MINI
CD1

621 AOK

The Wedding Present are old hands at this game. David Gedge takes the stage to a reception worthy of Damon Albarn - except tonight there's an over-18 (and thus over-11) policy. After 15(*?*) years they've developed a large back-catalogue of lovelorn classic pop songs. From C86 to the Guinness Book of Records they have come full circle to an indie label again. Tonight they demonstrate their talents fully with a superb set running from as far back as Favourite Dress, all the way through Corduroy and to their current Mini LP which has sparkling tunes and a great feel. The top pop that Britain has to offer. **SMcH**

THE WEDDING PRESENT
'MINI'

With the WEDDING PRESENT you're never quite sure what's going to happen next. "SUCKERS" their male order only 7 inch was No.3 in JOHN PEEL listeners poll THE FESTIVE FIFTY. MINI (SIXth mini album)

Released 22nd january
CD/Ltd 10inch vinyl.

The Wedding Present

Undeterred by trends, armed against fickle fashion and elegantly surfing through C86, Madchester, grunge and now Britpop, the iconoclastic David Gedge has ensured Fall-like status for The Wedding Present. Their vast canon of perfect pop-punk discord ('My Favourite Dress', 'Kennedy', 'Octopussy') reminds audiences of the unsteady walk into maturity from the bedroom idealism of listening to Peel. 10 years, umpteen singles and half a dozen albums on, 'Two, Three, Go!' (Cooking Vinyl) is a typically euphoric WP single with a difference. The Weddoes play the Powerhaus for three nights (Sep 12-14) in the sort of space they work best. Unmissable.

MINI
FRED THOMAS, ALLMUSIC.COM

By the time this brief collection of songs that seemed to be about cars arrived in 1996, The Wedding Present were more than a decade-old institution of indie pop, with several line-up changes, label changes, and amazing records under the collective belt of bandleader/vocalist/songwriter David Gedge and his many collaborators. Not quite a proper LP and too strong to simply be tucked into the "stopgap EP" category, *Mini* landed between the micro-grunge of 1994's *Watusi* and the comparatively toned-down *Saturnalia*, which appeared later that same year. More than a proper album-length statement, the shortened *Mini* shared the same lively highlights-reel approach as *The Hit Parade*, the band's 1992 collection of singles and cover songs. On these six tracks (later expanded to nine and re-released as *Mini Plus*), the band's C-86 jangle and early indie songwriting roots are in fine form from the grippingly fuzzy opening track, "Drive." A master of conveying urgency, humor, and regret at once, Gedge's vocals deliver with melody to spare on almost every track, from the age-old story of infidelity and sexual jealousy on "Love Machine" to the almost Beach Boys-esque verses and warm organ solo of "Convertible." Automobile metaphors and the band's special, sad pop magic abound, with "Sports Car" serving as a fitting closing track, bridging the high-octane fuzziness of *Mini* and the increasingly drained, depressive tones that would follow soon on *Saturnalia*.

MELODY MAKER, April 20 1996 17

THE WEDDING PRESENT

LEE'S PALACE, TORONTO

AFTER hearing "Mini", I have been pondering how a band could become the antithesis of themselves. Where there were once gleeful, hands-afire Albini-style guitar flailings, there are now widdly-widdly, jingly janglyisms which shout "Sign us to Creation – and pronto!"

And so it translates live. When I saw The Wedding Present at the Town & Country Club in 1987, it was a frenzied, out-of-hand audience who leapt up and down from the moment the first chord struck. But now, rather than bodies wigging, heads are wobbling.

Albeit wobbling with joy.

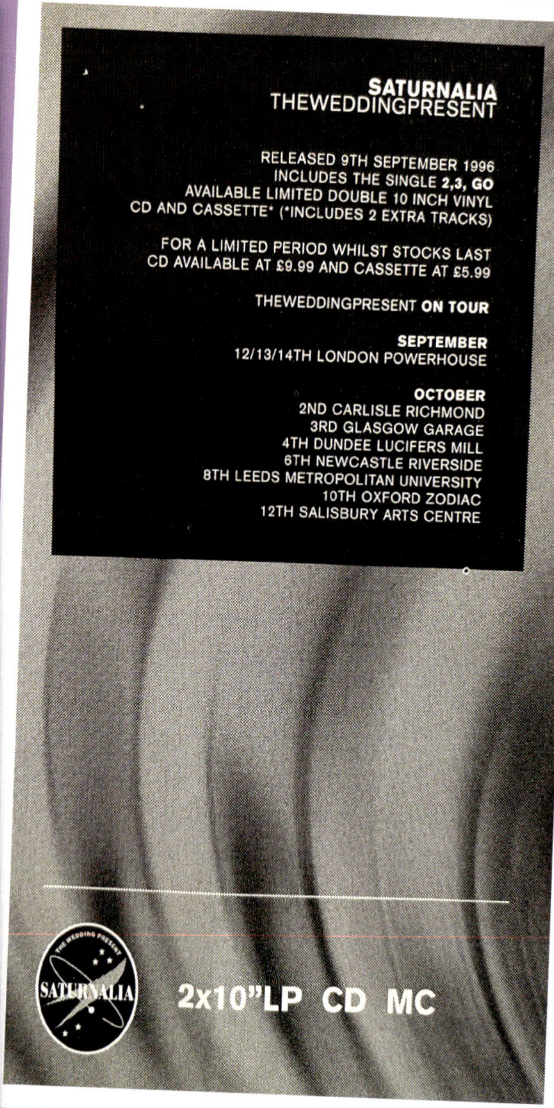

WEDDING PRESENT
Saturnalia
(Cooking Vinyl)

There are two schools of thought on the Wedding Present; one maintains they peaked with 'George Best', the other holds up the melancholic

Leeds' unknighted: The Wedding Present

resonance of 'Sea Monsters' as their finest moment.

The 'Best'-is-best faithful are most likely to gravitate to 'Saturnalia's restless strumming and chainsaw guitars – no moody grindalongs here – as Leeds' most enduring update the lovelorn lo-fi tantrums of their early days into a series of ever-unfolding epics.

measures his old self against his new public persona – surrounded by sycophants, feeding his paranoia. 'Sex Drive' is a litany of chat-up lines, grown cynical with use.

His voice is often just a synthetic growl, throwing Martina's high tones into relief. He has her singing repellent lines, like a witch's familiar, but on the

From the relentless surprise of opening shot 'Venus' through to the romantically frustrated '2, 3 Go' and nimble grooving of 'Sports Car', this is just what we wanted – a '90s take on classic Weddoes to remind us why we loved them so much in the first place. Heavenly. **8**

Ben Willmott

WEEZER
Pinkerton
(Geffen)

It comes as a great disappointment to find that travel, fame and relative wealth

Whatever happened to standing outside girls' houses stabbing pins into a wax effigy of HIM?

Ahh, seems Dave Gedge has grown up, lost his spots and gained a few lines of experience. He's no longer the angst-ridden teenage dump magnet that helped many through their Clearasil phases. Sure, he's still an emotional punchbag of the highest order, it's just that his inner turmoil has matured to the point where he can – gasp! – *cope with it*. The REM-ish twanger 'Montreal' finds him resigning himself to his loved-one's buggering off abroad with subdued grace, while 'Jet Girl''s tale of a relationship-hopping emotiopath is draped over a cheery romp of hula guitars and classic hooks. In fact, the only time Dave lets loose a guttural cry of primal angst occurs during closer '50s', and even that's offset by the melancholic dancehall-waltz verses.

The true position of Gedge's head, however, is contained in 'Kansas', a rampant pop beauty in which Dave packs his bags at a moment's notice and flies off to an unknown future – a spangly new beginning, who cares where. After all, while his guitars have stayed mammoth-proportioned and his vocals still gargle from a hard day's bricklaying, ten years on, pop music is slowly coming around to his way of thinking again. So, hook up the Valium drip NOW because The Wedding Present's time might just have come once more. Shocked? You will be, my dears, you will be… **(8)**

Mark Beaumont

MIDDLETON GUARDIAN 16-7-98

Top degree-to-pop star Dave opts to go solo

BRIAN and Marjorie Gedge weren't too delighted when their son announced he was joining a band after gaining a First Class Honours degree as a Leeds University science student.

But after two years on the dole he and the band he was with landed a record deal and went from strength to strength. That was the group Wedding Present which has enjoyed Top 40 hits in the UK and America.

Now his parents from Dixon Street, near Boarshaw's Clough Road recreation park off Rochdale Road, are seeing their son chime to a new career — as a solo artist backed by his girl friend, Sally.

And that for the time being means no more "heavy" guitars. It's violins and a string section instead.

Under the name, *Cinerama*, he and Sally have recorded 11 songs for an album to be released later this month while his new single, *'Kelly Kelly'*, is out this week.

"I told the rest of the band I wanted to take a year off to do a few other things and they were quite supportive. And when they heard a tape of the new stuff they understood - it's totally the opposite of the Wedding Present sound," said the 36 year old, a Middleton Moorclose High pupil before going on to university

"Stomp + Stammer" (USA) V.4. No.1

Wedding Present frontman **David Gedge** is putting that band on hold for the moment to pursue another musical project called **Cinerama**. A collaboration with longtime WP associate **Sally Murrell**, Cinerama has a debut album just out on spinArt called *Va Va Voom*. Much of it sounds like the Wedding Present with a breezier, lighter sheen; elsewhere it veers further from that band's signiture sound into Euro-pop territory.

If you ever dyed your hair black and hated your parents, the Wedding Present probably provided the soundtrack. But now the band's leader, David Gedge, has discovered light lyrics and happy tunes. Veena Virdi can't wait for the fans' verdict

Cinerama Va Va Voom CD (spinART) ... Ur – British duo composed of that chap from The Wedding Present and the fetching Sally Murrell, playing exceptionally baroque, orchestral, romantic, fucked-up pop songs that evoke obsessive relationships of the sort you've either had or snickered at from afar. Quite delicious, through the tears. SCRAM (USA) #9 USA

In the cold late night, scraping every last speck of ice off your passenger side mirror while snow rains down around you and you're thinking about her. Cinerama's 'Va Va Voom' is that moment. The answering machine message that starts off the first track sets a resonating tone for the entire album that seems to carry over from track to track, and that tone is heartache.Trust me, you'll catch yourself happily singing along with each of one of these lonely, lonely songs. Simply put- these are 13 less than action packed, well thought melodic sing along love songs courtesy of the Wedding Present's David Gedge.

THE WEDDING PRESENT AND CINERAMA
PPRECIATION SOCIETY (VALENCIA SINCE 1986)
SALUTES TO DAVID AND SALLY
D WE PICTURE WITH YOU AFTER THE GIG?

Breeze
99

CAT GIRL TIGHTS

MELANIE HOWARD, BASSIST, THE WEDDING PRESENT

My favourite Cinerama song is 'Cat Girl Tights'. It has that perfect blend of being dark and dramatic, but with a really understated pop vocal holding all this tension and vulnerability beneath it. I think it would also really work as a great Wedding Present song because it has this grit and these gnarly guitar parts slowly crawling their way out of the layers of strings and things. And it just becomes so explosive at the end.

Photo: Richard Houghton

Melanie Howard has a favourite Cinerama song too

SUPERMAN

DAVID WALKER

I remember one of Cinerama's first gigs in Manchester. I can't remember the venue but David was on the merch desk with (his now ex) Sally. I was with a new girlfriend and remember David selling me a signed copy of the 'Superman' single. It was in Spanish but I still bought it for £5 just to impress my new girl. I remember turning to David and saying, 'I can always put myself in certain situations that you sing about.' He looked me in the eyes and said, 'All my songs are universal.' I'll never forget that. The girlfriend was impressed too!

NO CHRISTMAS

ED SCHLEESSELMANN

How do you choose a favourite? I can, however, think of a 'highest climber' in my own personal Weddoes chart. 1992 saw The Wedding Present releasing one single each month. Having spent the previous eleven months rushing to get my other pre-ordered copies (from Covent Garden Our Price, a five-minute run from work), the anticipation of completing the set in December 1992 was in keeping with my Christmas party mood. I wondered, could it be a song for the ages, and join 'Step Into Christmas', 'Wombling Merry Christmas' and 'Another Rock 'N' Roll Christmas' on seasonal compilation albums for years to come? Would it get single of the week in *NME*? Would my flatmate let me play it without headphones? The answer? An emphatic 'No Christmas'. Although I appreciated the irony of an uncommercial climax to what was 'possibly the best marketing ploy ever devised by an Indie band' (copyright: everybody), my main thought was: I wanted others to love this band and they stuck out a wilfully obtuse ball of noise. At Christmas.

December 2018: Arts Club, Liverpool. 'No Christmas' is played live and revealed to be the juddering, cinematic, emotional snowflake of a song it always was. If only I'd listened properly at the time.

INTERSTATE 5

MIKE DE WIT

I have been an admirer of David Gedge since 1989, as a composer, but especially as a lyricist. When he put The Wedding Present on hold and continued as Cinerama in 1997, I continued to follow him. It took some time getting used to, because the music was really different. I bought tickets for The Beautiful South's *Quench* tour at the Paradiso in Amsterdam in January 1999. As the concert approached, I thought, 'Wouldn't Cinerama be a nice support act? Appropriate in music, appropriate in lyrics.' What a surprise it was when they became the support act! For a moment I felt clairvoyant. Few people were paying attention to Gedge and his band, on the stage of the fantastic large hall in the Paradiso. But I was down the front, thoroughly enjoying the gig.

In 2004, I bought a ticket for Cinerama at the Rotown in Rotterdam. *Torino* had been out for a while. The Wedding Present was more reflected in the music than on the first two albums. The concert was great. After 'It's A Gas', David said, 'This next song is new. And uh... it's so new, we've never played it before, anywhere in the world. So, if it's a bit rubbish, you'll know why. No, it'll be great – honest. Now, where to start…? Uh, it's all coming back to me now.'

The song was 'Interstate 5'. Right away I thought it was a great song. What an intro, with guitars until one minute 15 and then drums coming in until the two minute mark. Then the vocals. What a build up. Long intros – I like that. Not rubbish! I'm glad I found a bootleg recording of this memorable night.

The Wedding Present were definitely back. The day after the concert I decided to post a message on the Scopitones forum entitled 'The Wedding Present re-incarnated in Rotterdam yesterday' and said, 'The new song 'Interstate 5' is a gem! Haunting, raw guitarish stuff. I love it and hope they will release it soon! More Wedding Present than any Cinerama stuff.'

When The Wedding Present were back in September 2004 with their last Peel session before his death, it came full circle. For a moment, I felt clairvoyant again.

On April 2, 2005, with *Take Fountain* in my car CD player, I drove to Rotown again, a one-and-a-half hour drive, and 'Interstate 5' was blaring through the speakers. I was in no doubt that that night the song would be played again. With my recording equipment carefully placed on the stage the concert could not begin soon enough as far as I was concerned.

The concert started. No introduction. 'On Ramp'. Then straight into 'Interstate 5', played at a much faster pace than a year before. David sang as early as one minute and 15 seconds in. Too fast! I wanted a longer intro!

There was no announcement afterwards, just straight on with 'Crawl'. It didn't matter; 'Interstate 5' needed no introduction anymore, and it will forever be linked to the night I was one of the first to hear it live. It turns my steering wheel into a drum kit driving to any concert. I don't have to be clairvoyant to know that this song will always be a favourite.

Mike de Wit (aka Fonzie) has gone for 'Interstate 5'

WHY ARE YOU BEING SO REASONABLE NOW?

KAREY PARSONS

This isn't my favourite, but it was my introduction, so it's important to me – and I do love it.

I first heard/saw The Wedding Present playing this song on a music video show – I guess it was MTV. I was living in a shared house after uni, with a bunch of mates who are still some of my best friends. It just stopped me in my tracks. The incredible guitars, David Gedge's voice – that growl – the idiosyncratic lyrics, and the sheer joy of the video. I love those early videos! (And on that note, 'Loveslave' must get a mention. I love the song anyway, but the video still makes my day!)

I saw them at Wolverhampton Civic soon after and it was such a fantastic gig. I was hooked. I never imagined then that I'd still be seeing them in my fifties, but I've seen them and Cinerama many, many times since – and each gig brings back a bit of that youthful joy.

They're such an incredible live band and their gigs are a highlight of my year. I love that so many previous and connected band members play *At The Edge Of The Sea*, I love the very special fans, and I love the fact that David and the band are still creating brilliant new songs.

KENNEDY

JIM CLARK

I penned a blog in 2008, when I did a rundown of my 45 favourite 45s at 45 (the number 1 was published on 18th June 2008, my 45th birthday). The only proviso for any 45 to be included in the rundown was that I had to have bought the single at the time of its release. Oh, and you could only have one entry in the chart! 'Kennedy' came in at number 8.

I came late to The Wedding Present. I didn't listen to their early stuff simply because everyone in the press was touting them as the natural successors to the recently disbanded The Smiths, and I just didn't want to know. I was able to miss out on them, simply because the band got next to no radio play other than late at night, and this was a period of great change in my life when I was never listening to the likes of John Peel.

So, for the best part of four years, my knowledge of the band was restricted to what I read and not what I heard. I do remember being amused that a band from Leeds would release an LP named after the greatest footballer ever to wear the shirt of Manchester United, given the animosity between their fans and those of Leeds United. It still didn't make me buy it though.

One Sunday evening sometime in 1989, when the radio was on as the latest singles chart was being run down, I first heard a song by The Wedding Present. It was called 'Kennedy', and it was (I've since discovered) a new entry at number 33. It was loud, it was frantic, it was joyous and it was something I immediately fell in love with. And with that, I became a convert to the church of David Gedge of which I've been a faithful member ever since. I'm a regular attendee at the places of worship, ie. gigs, and I'll also contribute as and when required to the coffers (ie. records, t-shirts, videos, CDs, etc.).

There can't be all that many Indie bands still going strong 20-plus years after their initial formation. OK, so I know that The Wedding Present took a short break and turned into Cinerama, and also that for a substantial part of their career they were on major labels such as RCA and Island Records. But you can't really categorise them as anything other than Indie…

There must be something in the region of 300 songs, and very few of these, even the most obscure of B-sides, have ever been total duffers. They're also a band with a love for cover versions, with around 50 being widely available now thanks to the relatively recent release of all the *Peel Sessions* in a box set. And every one of those covers, whether a pop, soul, blues, rock, country or disco classic, sounds instinctively like a Wedding Present original.

But I still don't think they've ever bettered the song that first made my ears prick up and listen. Even now, almost 20 years on, it remains a live favourite, although David now tends to follow it up with a slow-tempo number so that the old folk jumping around down the front get their breath back and avoid the risk of a permanent injury. None of us are as young or fit as we once were, and pogo-ing up and down is, at best, achievable for a maximum of five minutes at one stretch.

Just in case you're wondering, the seven 45s listed ahead of 'Kennedy' back in 2008 were:

7 : The Smiths – Hand In Glove
6 : Joy Division – Transmission
5 : Bourgie Bourgie – Breaking Point
4 : The The – This Is The Day
3 : Orange Juice – Felicity
2 : The Clash – (White Man) In Hammersmith Palais
1 : New Order – Temptation (original 12' version)

SOMETHING AND NOTHING

JIM BASS

For Jim Bass it's 'Something And Nothing'

Without hesitation, my favourite song of The Wedding Present has always been 'Something And Nothing', the Allison-produced version on *George Best* naturally. I'm really old school when it comes to Gedge's music. Although I've absolutely loved pretty much everything he has ever produced, *George Best* just can't be beaten. The original line up. The gigs. Grapper in full flow. Magical. That album captured an essence that they've never repeated in my opinion. There's something incredibly endearing about a native Manc-come-Yorkshireman pouring his heart out whilst furiously scribbling strings. The signature and soul of the outfit has always been the blending of the twin guitar melodies. 'Something And Nothing' encapsulates this at its very best, then add the drums and bass, a quick snippet of an argument with a sound engineer to whet your appetite, and the result is glorious. The blistering middle eights, the alternating bass line from Keith near the end, the lyrics… it's just the best. It reminds me of '87 of course, the album that spent 18 months on my turntable, only lifted to be turned over, holding back over 50 other albums I owned. The gigs that year too. Balloons everywhere. I had to wait a long time to hear this track live again, the anniversary gigs! Such a poignant track, taking centre stage in a masterpiece album. I will never tire of it.

TAKE ME!

JON STEWART, THE WEDDING PRESENT & SLEEPER GUITARIST

Friday, April 15, 1994, in Rennes, France. The Rock'n Solex Festival: Sleeper, Blur, The Wedding Present. Sleeper's first main stage concert, in a huge tent, during a massive rainstorm.

We played in the late afternoon and then watched Blur while packing away our equipment. Everything was already pretty damp during our set but then the water began to penetrate the canvas, cascading in a sheet across the monitor speakers in front of the band. I remember thinking that it resembled the 'elephant's graveyard' scene in that old black-and-white Tarzan movie, the one where Johnny Weissmuller walks through a waterfall to find a cave behind. Every time Graham Coxon stamped on his effects pedals a knee-high splash of water flew into the air. That's not good for the onstage electrics, and I was amazed no-one got a shock. The Wedding Present famously dealt with the downpour by draping towels across their amplifiers, like that was going to make a difference, which showed you just how crazy the situation was. During the final changeover, as the headliners took to the stage, we piled our gear onto a handy tractor and ferried it across the liquid mud before loading it into the back of the van. Drunk and exhausted, I staggered to my room in the artists' accommodation – a spartan student hall/youth hostel type building that overlooked the festival site. The walls were paper thin and shook in time with the music which was, by now, incredibly loud. I drifted in and out of consciousness listening to the end of their set. It seemed to go on forever. The Wedding Present were playing 'Take Me!'

Bizarro, and particularly 'Take Me!', never left my CD player over the ensuing decades. It's still my 'most played' track on Spotify. The best song on a near-perfect album. Two-and-a-bit minutes of desperate vocals followed by screaming guitars that are somehow the same, somehow different, every eight bars for the next seven minutes. It sounds like no-one else. Pure genius. The greatest playout in Indie history.

25 years later I was asked to join the band for the final leg of the *Bizarro* anniversary tour. I've been lucky enough to experience a few wonderful and unexpected 'pinch yourself' moments, but never one that happens every night. Not, at least, until that *Bizarro* tour.

'Take Me!' is a total concentration job. It's like a mindfulness meditation. If you're on stage playing 'Take Me!' with The Wedding Present there's nothing going on in your life apart from the single undeniable fact that you're on stage playing 'Take Me!' with The Wedding Present. You give yourself to it and get lost in it. It's wonderful and engrossing, a song like no other. You start out thinking, 'OK, here we go, this is going to be fun,' and then, about six and a half minutes in, you just lose all sense of self and enter a totally different mental space – and there's still three minutes remaining. That's nearly as long as some other songs. It's a unique experience for a guitarist. A natural high. Then it ends, and everyone cheers. 'I have been to the mountaintop… and I have looked over.' That's how it felt for me, anyway.

CRAWL
JEFFREY DIAMOND

Jeffrey Diamond loves 'Crawl'

For me, talking about a favourite Wedding Present song is inextricably tied to their live performances. To quote David's lyrics from 'Emporia', they go 'hand in hand'.

I came late to The Wedding Present, in the summer of 1991 while working on Brighton Pier. It was the summer of Inspiral Carpets and EMF and Carter USM. For me, it was the year of listening to *George Best*, *Tommy*, and *Bizarro* on a boombox inside a creperie kiosk overlooking the English Channel. Perhaps inevitable in my introduction to The Wedding Present, I was going through a brutal far-from-home divorce as well. It was then, in 1991 and forever onwards, that I became hooked on The Wedding Present. I listened to their new album *Seamonsters* and especially 'Dalliance' over and over again until the cassette tape was almost transparent. You would think that is my favourite pick (it is one of my favourites) but not the one picked for this book...

A few months later I was home back in the States, living in Hoboken. For those who do not know, Hoboken is across the Hudson River from New York City so, while it's located in New Jersey, it's really a borough of Manhattan. I made up for lost time, seeing the band live anytime they came anywhere near NYC. There was a club in Hoboken called Maxwell's. Situated at the end of a hallway in a medium-sized pub, the back room held 150 people. While intimate, some of music's biggest names played there. When Talking Heads split up, Maxwell's was the venue David Byrne chose to launch his solo career. And it was the go-to spot for one of Gedge's all-time faves, The Fall. Mark E Smith and his band played Maxwell's whenever they toured the East Coast.

As a resident of Hoboken, and a frequent customer at Maxwell's, I knew when bands usually did their soundchecks for that night's gig. But only for The Wedding Present did I make the effort to catch the soundcheck. Mid-afternoon on one beautiful sunny day, I did just that, and was leaning against a column in the back room of Maxwell's as The Wedding Present went through their soundcheck. I had seen them enough and they had seen me around enough for them to take no mind to me, and I was happy to blend into the background. It was on this day they played a version of 'Crawl' that has stayed with me ever since. Just a beautiful, gut-wrenching version of the song. Hearing it that way, in an otherwise empty room, without anyone in the crowd shouting over the silent bits, or likewise talking over the perfect guitar strumming that propels the song, was magic. The mystery of the lyrics, the simple but easily brilliant turns of phrase, the building drama in the song that ends not in a crescendo of noise but in the confident, strong and strident guitar punctuated by David's final guttural plea.

There could easily be two dozen candidates for 'favourite Wedding Present song'. But for me, 'Crawl' holds a special place. Thirty years later, the emotional impact and slow build of that song can still move me to tears. It is a masterpiece track.

DALLIANCE
LEE MORGAN

My favourite Wedding Present song is still 'Dalliance'. I absolutely adore its brilliance in going from a tender semi-acoustic lament for lost love into a full-on cacophony of noise. A cod-James Blunt ballad bursting – no, exploding! – into a Pixies-meets-Phil Spector wall-of-sound. It's great with headphones on. Even greater with a hangover.

GAZEBO
LISA BARONE

'Gazebo' reminds me of someone I have been madly in love with since I was 12 years old. The acoustic version is my favourite. It just feels like a raw emotion that I think many people can relate to. We all have that 'one'. And this song just makes me feel it, as it's a feeling that I still like to visit after all these years.

MY FAVOURITE DRESS
SHELLEY GREATOREX

I started working in Nottingham city centre in 1987 and on payday would go straight to Selectadisc and spend a fair chunk of my wages. I used to read *NME* avidly in those days and one of their recommendations was *George Best*, which I promptly bought and would listen to in my bedroom, over and over again. It quickly became a firm favourite. In those days I would listen to LPs from end to end (which might seem quite alien to young people now!) and although I loved every single track on that album (and still do), my absolute favourite track was 'My Favourite Dress'. Not many of my friends liked the same music as me (they thought I was weird, and probably still do!) but later that year my cousin introduced me to his friend Mark as he knew we liked the same sort of music.

For Mark and Shelley Greatorex, 'My Favourite Dress' is their song

Although we were both shy, we soon overcame that and started chatting about our favourite bands. The Wedding Present cropped up in the conversation and we spent ages talking about *George Best* and Mark said that 'My Favourite Dress' was his favourite track too. We spent all that night chatting about music. Mark was in the same position as me; none of his mates liked the same music as him so we agreed to start going to gigs together, or at least the ones his girlfriend at the time didn't like. I was just happy to get to any gigs really!

When The Wedding Present played at Confetti's in Derby in October 1988, we each went with different people – Mark with his girlfriend and me with a friend who I'd roped into going with me. We stood relatively close to each other and when they played 'My Favourite Dress', we both looked over at each other, knowing it was our favourite track, and something just passed between us then that was really special.

We then just went to Wedding Present gigs (and lots of others) together – and stayed friends for another 18 months. Mark then split with his girlfriend and although it took quite a long time, we eventually got together (everyone else knew we were made for each other) and got married in 1992. Unfortunately, we couldn't take control of the playlist that night, otherwise it would've been The Wedding Present all the way!

We've travelled all over to see them, actually planning holidays around gigs (New York and Berlin were probably my favourites, although the Devil's Arse gig was quite unique) and it's not something we do for any other band. We can even remember when they did encores!

We've seen them over 50 times and we have just such a fondness for this band that mean so much to us both.

LOVENEST

MATTHIAS BOSENICK

Photo: Andrea Smolka

Matthias Bosenick fell for 'Lovenest'

My first encounter with The Wedding Present was in 1991 on the school bus. The daughter of my family doctor gave me the *Seamonsters* LP, which she had bought because of the cover and which she also recommended to me because of the music. Last row of seats, rocking vehicle, plastic bag, twelve inch vinyl with red tips on a deep blue background – my interest was piqued.

My young, chart-dominated mind had just recently opened up to alternative music and from then absorbed everything that deviated from those once so formative charts. And *Seamonsters* deviated. Dark music, heavy drums, very subdued vocals, unexpected structures, heavy outbursts, eternal feedback and yet engaging melodies: the album immediately cast a spell on me. In addition, the band remained a secret, because without the internet it was difficult to get any information or even photos. Also, unlike other bands, the singer seemed to hide behind the music like behind a massive column in an otherwise empty cathedral. That was unusual and aroused my curiosity.

And then, Side 2: 'Lovenest'. This piece of brutal violence that leads to an almost infinite squeaking, that merges into a nearly happy 'Corduroy' as if nothing had happened. That was how the album finally convinced me and formed the cornerstone of a comprehensive, but unfortunately never complete collection. Thank you for the recommendation, Ms Meyer!

DALLIANCE

NICK GOLLEDGE

Ten minutes before they were due to come on at Kilburn Ballroom in London, I bumped into DLG and asked what the first song was going to be. He said, 'A new song called 'Dalliance'.' I went back to my group and said, 'Bet you a pint they start with a new song' and promptly won four pints! But this a great song for many more reasons than that!

BLONDE

MATTHEW CHILDE

'Blonde' reminds Matthew Childe of a teenage heartbreak

In 1991 I was 18 and heartbroken. She was not like anyone I'd ever met… To see it all in a drunken kiss… Usual story. By August of that year A-levels were over and I was getting ready to head off to uni. The Wedding Present were playing at Wakefield Rooftop Gardens – my first chance to see them live – and she was going to be there. I harboured dreams of telling her how I felt and winning her back.

In the weeks leading up to the gig, I listened to *Seamonsters* pretty much non-stop. It was, and still is, my favourite Weddoes album (perhaps my favourite album full stop). Something about its rawness, its darkness, its simplicity suited my mood. 'Blonde' was the song that connected with me most. As soon as that drum beat starts to fade in and those first notes ring out, I'm transported back to the summer of 1991. It's also the song in which David gives one of his best demonstrations of what I call tuneful shouting – there's something so powerful about the way he sings, 'I still can't believe that's all you took me for', and it definitely served to fuel my teenage self-pity!

The gig was great – hot and sweaty in the slightly incongruous surroundings of a *Hitman And Her*-style nightclub. They played 'Blonde' and the sound desk recording was later released as one of the band's official bootleg tapes, so I have it for posterity.

I saw her as I was leaving. We had a brief chat about the gig and then said polite goodbyes. I never saw her again. There were a thousand things I wish I'd said and done, but the moment's gone.

MY FAVOURITE DRESS

JAMES LOWEN

It's so hard to choose a favourite Wedding Present song. 'Crawl' is bonsai perfection. 'Kennedy' evokes sweat and energy. 'Rachel' is a perfect love song. 'Perfect Blue' too. 'Interstate 5' hits the podium by dint of it being my personal Wedding Present comeback song, after a few years in the wilderness (immature to the end, I sulked through Cinerama).

But for the favourite song, it has to be 'My Favourite Dress'. It was the first Wedding Present song I ever heard, as a 14-year-old, when my best friend's sister came back from the record shop, put it on her bedroom turntable and we were invited in to listen. I had never heard anything like it and was immediately smitten. It's fair to say that record changed my life in as much as it set into train an acoustic love affair that has lasted 34 years and counting; I wouldn't be closing in on 100 Wedding Present gigs without it.

James Lowen loves 'My Favourite Dress'

BEWITCHED

IAN GELLING

I've tried to avoid this being an opinion piece, but I have failed. Here's why:

Trying to identify a favourite song penned by David Lewis Gedge is like the proverbial choice between various of your children or pets. It could be a tune that meant something at a certain time of life or a particular song that stands out when played live, or maybe just an earworm. So I became a bit analytical, not unlike DLG himself, and thought about what for me makes one of his songs great and then which song has all those elements. So what are they?

Firstly, a top-drawer Gedge song has great lyrics. If the delivery or the lyrical context is idiosyncratic then even better. A lot of early stuff falls into this category. Not only that but the songs need to be plausible. DLG has never committed to the authenticity of the stories he tells in the lyrics, but the best ones all ring true. You can visualise them.

Because they are plausible, they are emotional, and that is another key element. I reckon Wedding Present fans, mostly blokes of course, read themselves into the situations in those stories, and the response is an emotional one; think 'My Favourite Dress' or 'Perfect Blue'. To me, Cinerama songs are well crafted and sometimes very clever, but they don't have that character.

Next, they have to be his proper songs, those that are fully formed and extremely well put together. If they have the trademark changes of pace and dynamics, then even better. That's what makes them so good live, too.

Last, but by no means least, they have to have that extra ingredient that makes them special. It's difficult to define but it is what has made The Wedding Present in particular such an important band to me and why I have made the effort to go and see them so many times.

I thought long and hard, but after all this my choice was obvious. I actually have David's hand-written lyrics to this song on my wall and it's not hard to see how it fits the bill. It has the best of his story telling lyrics. It could be any one of us in that situation, and it really rings true. The lack of confidence, the awkwardness, and not being in control of a situation. It's a great tune; one of his best and it goes down a storm live every time.

The extra ingredient? I can't actually hear or read the last line without getting a catch in my throat, even after all these years and all that listening. It's amazing, and out of all the candidates it is this that tipped the balance. That song is 'Bewitched'.

READING FESTIVAL SETLIST 1989

IAN DAVIS

Having been a fan of The Wedding Present for such a long time, where does one begin? There are so many classic songs and most fans' favourites will remain with them from the time when you first got into the band, so I should really say something off *George Best*. However, my personal choice is going to be a little different, because it is not one song that sounds the same, but nine songs that sound the same!

Ian Davis (centre) with Charlie Layton and Danielle Wadey

It was my second full weekend camping at Reading Festival with my (now) wife. We were completely blown away with the choice of bands available including The Wedding Present, The Pogues, The Men They Couldn't Hang, New Model Army, The Wonder Stuff and New Order, all of whom we have seen countless times since.

On Saturday 26th August 1989, compere John Peel introduced the band and as they entered the stage, David Lewis Gedge dressed in a pair of shorts muttered the words, 'Hello… of course, as soon as we start to play, it's gonna pour down. You know that, don't you? A certain amount of inevitability about that,' before launching into a full-on 'My Favourite Dress' followed by a blistering 'Kennedy'. Then the immortal lines after 'Kennedy'. 'Thank you very much, like these shorts? No? What do you mean 'no'? First time wearing shorts, this, for a concert, in England, no underpants either. These photographers here will get some really good shots.'

The set continued to flow at 100mph with 'Brassneck', followed by 'Everyone Thinks He Looks Daft', then 'Take Me!' (which went on forever, with the crowd by now going completely berserk), 'What Have I Said Now?', 'Nobody's Twisting Your Arm' (why wasn't this on an album?), 'Bewitched' and 'Granadaland'. This was also interspersed throughout with DLG on fine form and, no, you don't look like Angus Young.

For me, this was 45 minutes of sheer perfection and is what made me love The Wedding Present so much. Going to watch them has since become a habit (an obsession, according to my wife!) that I don't want to break.

GO-GO DANCER

DARIN HALIFAX

I loved the concept of *Hit Parade* and 'Go-Go Dancer' is my favourite track of the twelve. It is the perfect Wedding Present song with a crescendo to melodic chaos. It is also amazing live.

YEAH YEAH YEAH YEAH YEAH

HELEN MCCOOKERYBOOK

What a great song! I have played this both times at The Wedding Present's *At The Edge Of The Sea* Festival in Brighton, once solo and the second time when I did an arrangement for my horn section, when we were playing as Helen and the Horns. It has such joie de vivre and perfectly describes the way love completely knocks you off your feet. The lyrics are cheeky and youthful and genuine and a parody all at once – and I love the Northern Soul drum sound mixed with the guitar sound that is very much of the time of release in the early 1990s. And I-spy a green Gretsch guitar in the video, although I didn't tell my own Green Goddess. When she looked in the mirror and asked, 'Am I the fairest of them all?' the mirror replied, 'Yeah, yeah, yeah, yeah, yeah!'

LOVENEST

GREG JARVIS, THE FLOWERS OF HELL

The song's sound is onomatopoeia for post-relationship angst! I was 20 and splitting up with my girlfriend of a couple years when I first heard the boy Gedge sing:

I heard another voice this morning on the 'phone
But just the other day I thought you said you slept alone

It killed me again and again as I'd visualise my girl waking up with someone else. He was cathartically echoing and giving voice to all the youthful insecurities and anguish I had about my breakup. And the pummelling blasts of noise around the line, 'Pretending that it's you; you still won't go away,' summed up all the feelings of my bursting heart.

Seamonsters has long been a regular fave in our tour van and 'Lovenest' still hits me where it hurts.

DON'T TOUCH THAT DIAL

MATT PARTRIDGE

When 'Don't Touch That Dial' was released by Cinerama, it perfectly encapsulated the break up of my marriage. It was as if David was a fly on the wall when she walked out of the door for the last time. Back then, I likened it to having toothache. You know it's going to hurt if you play with it but you just can't leave it alone. The Wedding Present's *Take Fountain* version took this song to another level, giving it a rawer edge, making it sound even more profound. It grew into my favourite ever song, by any band. It is, and always will be, the greatest Cinerama/Wedding Present song… ever!

Matt Partridge (centre) holds 'Don't Touch That Dial' close to his heart

HARD, FAST AND BEAUTIFUL

GREG MEAD

My wife and I are both huge Wedding Present and Cinerama fans. *Va Va Voom* was the only album that my wife wanted to hear during the labour and birth of our first daughter, Eleanor, and 'Hard, Fast And Beautiful' made a new Cinerama fan out of our midwife.

That whole album means an unimaginable amount to us, and our daughters love it now, too. 'Hard, Fast And Beautiful' will always remind us of how lucky we are to have two great children.

'Hard, Fast And Beautiful' reminds Greg Mead and wife Helen (third left) of the birth of daughter Eleanor (second left) and how lucky they are to have her and Suzannah

SEAMONSTERS

GAIL O'HARA

I was an editor at *SPIN* magazine in NYC in 1992 and I did an interview with David Gedge via phone in the summer of that year. My best friend Pam Berry (also the singer of Black Tambourine) helped me come up with the questions. When the story ran in *SPIN*, it only had a few small quotes in it so Pam and I decided to start a fanzine and publish the whole thing. Our zine was called *chickfactor* – it's still published from time to time, and Belle & Sebastian wrote a song about it.

Pam and I lived in different cities (she in DC) and the zine was a way for us to keep our friendship going after I moved away. We were massive Wedding Present fans. When we first started hanging out a lot, *Seamonsters* was just out. Our friend Mike Schulman worked at Vinyl Ink Records in Silver Spring, Maryland (he was also in Black Tambourine and runs Slumberland Records). I remember a road trip with him, Pam and Dan Searing (of various DC bands) when we listened to *Seamonsters* a ton. The guys from Velocity Girl were also huge fans, as were Brian Nelson and Archie Moore from

Black Tambourine.

Chickfactor had a cartoonist named Shawn Belschwender. I used to see Mark Ibold from Pavement around town all the time and he was always wearing a t-shirt from The Wedding Present monthly singles series (the 7-Up logo, the 8-ball, etc.). Because I saw him everywhere I went, I thought it would be funny to have a cartoon image on each page of *chickfactor* using him wearing the t-shirts as page numbers. Our cartoonist decided to make it his own and instead created the legendary Pavement Boy™ comics. We published it and stand by the hilarity of it but, by all accounts, Mark Ibold is a very nice person who didn't deserve that and I am sorry for the grief it may have caused him (I met him once years later and he was very kind about it). Pavement were a little bit too cool for school and we made fun of them, but I don't know that I imagined they'd ever even see our tiny zine!

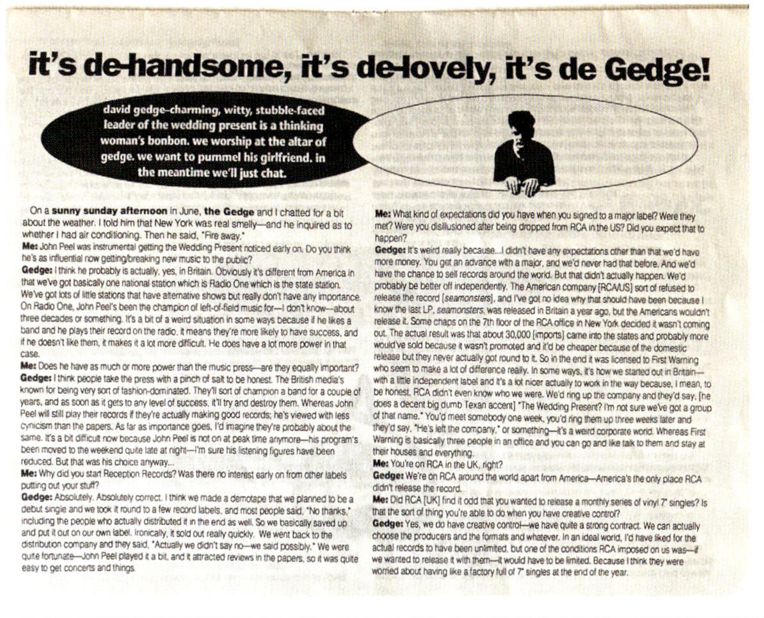

it's de-handsome, it's de-lovely, it's de Gedge!

david gedge–charming, witty, stubble-faced leader of the wedding present is a thinking woman's bonbon. we worship at the altar of gedge. we want to pummel his girlfriend. in the meantime we'll just chat.

On a **sunny sunday afternoon** in June, **the Gedge** and I chatted for a bit about the weather. I told him that New York was real smelly—and he inquired as to whether I had air conditioning. Then he said, "Fire away."

Me: John Peel was instrumental getting the Wedding Present noticed early on. Do you think he's as influential now getting/breaking new music to the public?

Gedge: I think he probably is actually, yes, in Britain. Obviously it's different from America in that we've got basically one national station which is Radio One which is the state station. We've got lots of little stations that have alternative shows but really don't have any importance. On Radio One, John Peel's been the champion of left-of-field music for—I don't know—about three decades or something. It's a bit of a weird situation in some ways because if he likes a band and he plays their record on the radio, it means they're more likely to have success, and if he doesn't like them, it makes it a lot more difficult. He does have a lot more power in that case.

Me: Does he have as much or more power than the music press—are they equally important?

Gedge: I think people take the press with a pinch of salt to be honest. The British media's known for being very sort of fashion-dominated. They'll sort of champion a band for a couple of years, and as soon as it gets to any level of success, it'll try and destroy them. Whereas John Peel will still play their records if they're actually making good records; he's viewed with less cynicism than the papers. As far as importance goes, I'd imagine they're probably about the same. It's a bit difficult now because John Peel is not on at peak time anymore—his program's been moved to the weekend quite late at night—I'm sure his listening figures have been reduced. But that was his choice anyway...

Me: Why did you start Reception Records? Was there no interest early on from other labels putting out your stuff?

Gedge: Absolutely. Absolutely correct. I think we made a demotape that we planned to be a debut single and we took it round to a few record labels, and most people said, "No thanks," including the people who actually distributed it in the end as well. So we basically saved up and put it out on our own label. Ironically, it sold out really quickly. We went back to the distribution company and they said, "Actually we didn't say no—we said possibly." We were quite fortunate—John Peel played it a bit, and it attracted reviews in the papers, so it was quite easy to get concerts and things.

Me: What kind of expectations did you have when you signed to a major label? Were they met? Were you disillusioned after being dropped from RCA in the US? Did you expect that to happen?

Gedge: It's weird really because...I didn't have any expectations other than that we'd have more money. You get an advance with a major, and we'd never had that before. And we'd have the chance to sell records around the world. But that didn't actually happen. We'd probably be better off independently. The American company [RCA/US] sort of refused to release the record [*seamonsters*], and I've got no idea why that should have been because I know the last LP, *seamonsters*, was released in Britain a year ago, but the Americans wouldn't release it. Some chaps on the 7th floor of the RCA office in New York decided it wasn't coming out. The actual result was that about 30,000 [imports] came into the states and probably more would've sold because it wasn't promoted and it'd be cheaper because of the domestic release but they never actually got round to it. So in the end it was licensed to First Warning who seem to make a lot of difference really. In some ways, it's how we started out in Britain—with a little independent label and it's a lot nicer actually to work in the way because, I mean, to be honest, RCA didn't even know who we were. We'd ring up the company and they'd say, [he does a decent big dumb Texan accent] "The Wedding Present? I'm not sure we've got a group of that name." You'd meet somebody one week, you'd ring them up three weeks later and they'd say, "He's left the company," or something—it's a weird corporate world. Whereas First Warning is basically three people in an office and you can go and like talk to them and stay at their houses and everything.

Me: You're on RCA in the UK, right?

Gedge: We're on RCA around the world apart from America—America's the only place RCA didn't release the record.

Me: Did RCA [UK] find it odd that you wanted to release a monthly series of vinyl 7" singles? Is that the sort of thing you're able to do when you have creative control?

Gedge: Yes, we do have creative control—we have quite a strong contract. We can actually choose the producers and the formats and whatever. In an ideal world, I'd have liked for the actual records to have been unlimited, but one of the conditions RCA imposed on us was—if we wanted to release it with them—it would have to be limited. Because I think they were worried about having like a factory full of 7" singles at the end of the year.

Gail O'Hara got to interview 'de Gedge' in 1992

FLYING SAUCER

GAVIN PAUL

Gavin Paul saw 'Flying Saucer' performed at Bestival

'Flying Saucer' stands out for me, not for sentimental reasons but simply because of the brilliance of the band at the time they played it. It was at Bestival on the Isle of Wight on 5th September 2008. Torrential overnight rain had turned the site into a mud bath and caused the opening of the main stage to be delayed until 3pm, with all bands due on before then cancelled. It meant The Wedding Present were the opening act on the main stage of the first day of the festival. I can't imagine this would be welcomed by many, but I have never forgotten how brilliantly they played despite the conditions. Of the songs played, it was the last song of the set, 'Flying Saucer', that was the most unforgettable. As I write this, I can still see (and hear) it being played with the three guitarists beautifully synchronised in their movement as the song reached its climax... which looked brilliant. I even took a photo of the band playing the song. It was probably the highest stage relative to where the audience was standing that I've ever seen.

KENNEDY
DAVID LINGERAK, PERSIL

As half of the band Persil, I would say my favourite Wedding Present song is 'Kennedy'.

Early in the life of the band we wanted to play some covers, and as The Wedding Present was one of our favourite bands, it made sense to select a song from their repertoire and twist it a bit! 'Kennedy', with the strong guitar energy, seemed perfect for a Persil makeover.

Except there is no way I could play guitar as speedy as that, so that had to be left out. Also, there was no way to play bass as pumping as that, and we didn't have a bass guitar, so that had to change too. But to make a cover song sound the same as the original makes little sense anyway, so we cherished the changes!

The bass was transformed to a basic synth line and the drums were replaced by some electronic noises. We aimed to keep but transform the energy, and obviously Persil vocals would become female.

To our delight, Gedge got to hear it through John Peel's show and we were asked to join as support on a tour. We thought it would be a nice service to fans (or a smart marketing move) to have some 'Kennedy' CD-Rs (yes, it's a while back) as a giveaway for fans buying our albums after the gigs. Buy an album, get a Weddoes cover CD-R for free! Sales skyrocketed way beyond expectations and we saw our big pile of home-burned discs shrink to zero around halfway through the nine-gig UK tour.

Either we played less good at the later gigs, or it was indeed the attraction of the 'Kennedy' freebie, but once this special offer came to the early end sales became, let's say, a bit tame. It seems Wedding Present fans saw a better investment in another Wedding Present t-shirt purchase than in a Persil album.

Still, despite the regrets of not making more CD-R copies, 'Kennedy' somehow made our tour, and there's a lot of great memories from it. We still hope Gedge doesn't send us an invoice for royalties.

MY FAVOURITE DRESS
IAN MOXON

I was first introduced to The Wedding Present by Mandy (soon to be my girlfriend) in my first year at Manchester Uni back in 1985. I remember the gig the Weddoes did at the Manchester Student Union (in February 1988) very clearly. I had no idea what to expect as I was an Indie band virgin, but I do remember I was blown away. I bought – and wore to death – the white t-shirt with balloons on. Sadly, I no longer have it.

There began a love affair with the Weddoes that has lasted to this day, much longer than the eight years with Mandy. Many evenings were spent together during uni days listening to the first, raw and arguably still their best album, *George Best*. My girl preferred DMs, jeans and t-shirt to a dress but she had one or two which I always admired when she wore them. When we split and she wore one to see someone else, all of a sudden I was singing the lyrics with tears in my eyes! Classic relationship heartache by Gedge.

My favourite band ever. My favourite song, 'My Favourite Dress'.

BIZARRO
SHELBY SMOAK

In 2010 The Wedding Present were touring the US. I was a huge, huge fan. But I lived in Chapel Hill, North Carolina and they were not coming there. They were playing DC and then skipping North Carolina for Atlanta. My friend was also a big fan and wanted to see them. It was the *Bizarro* tour too! We couldn't decide whether to go to DC or Atlanta, but with work we went to DC. It was an amazing show.

Shelby Smoak met the woman who would become his wife at a Wedding Present show in DC

I met a girl at that show. We hit it off. Then we began long distance dating. The next year, I moved to DC and we married. We have our ten year anniversary this year. The Wedding Present gave us the best wedding present! You can't write this and have it be believable!

For our one year anniversary we went to the *Seamonsters* tour. We tried to catch the band and tell them our story, but we couldn't find a way to connect. It's hard to claim a favourite song, but *Bizarro* was the tour that brought my wife and I together.

My wife, Vicky Hawk, has reminded me that the show where we met was at the Black Cat in Washington DC. In addition to meeting and later marrying from that show, we also now have three black cats – all rescue kitties!

SUDDENLY IT'S TUESDAY

STEVE PRINGLE

A few months ago, I wrote a blog evaluating all the Wedding Present songs called *Suddenly It's Tuesday*. Here's my top ten (in reverse order):

10 INTERSTATE 5

Although 'Interstate 5' (an almost-1,400 mile highway that runs from the Canadian border to Mexico) makes only a cursory appearance in the lyric, it's an appropriate title: the song has an epic, expansive quality that suggests hitting the highway, putting your foot down and escaping the mundanities of everyday life.

The single version opens with an abrasive, insistent single chord that feels like the song is revving up, uncoiling; the album version, following the chilling ambience of 'On Ramp', has a dark, ominous tone. In both cases, they unfurl into a snaking, malevolent groove that grips you and simply doesn't let go.

The lyric is a neat role-reversal from your traditional seduction song: it's 'her' that's just after casual sex; 'he' is reduced to withering barbs – 'will you even recognise my face this time next year?' There's an almost embarrassing pathos to 'I thought just boys were meant to behave in this way?'

Musically, it's a powerhouse; taut, and full of barely-restrained energy. Drummer Kari Paavola excels, driving the song with muscular flamboyance, especially during the 'there was one particular glance' passage. The double snare hit and guitar onslaught that follows 'I guess I've not succeeded' is another gut-wrenching moment. The song concludes with a two minute coda that throws in a twangy Western soundtrack, sweeping strings and Mariachi horns. It works; a different kind of epic, one that gives you a bit of a breather after the intensity of the previous few minutes.

9 DALLIANCE

The Wedding Present's partnership with Steve Albini led to a shift in the band's sound: less fizzing jangle; more gritty distortion. The tone of the lyrics also changed. Whether the fact that David turned 30 after the release of *Bizarro* and *George Best* had anything to do with it is just idle speculation on my part, but there was certainly a change in focus from youthful romance (as in 'Bewitched') to more mature relationships. This darker, more adult inflection was immediately apparent in *Seamonsters*' lead single and opening track.

Inspired by publisher Sarah Johnson's account of her affair with Leo Cooper, husband of writer Jilly Cooper, 'Dalliance' finds Gedge as vulnerable, shattered and embittered as he has ever sounded. The song opens with an understated yet menacing rumble; the drums shuffle tentatively; there's a ghostly arpeggio. There's a sense of barely restrained anger at the injustice – the other man has taken her back, despite the lies – and the callousness ('you don't care'). The anger is turned inwards too: frustrated at the fact that he still wants her after all she's done, the narrator can't even find the words ('That I'm so...'). David has a real knack for a simple turn of phrase that captures a distinct image or emotion. Here, he evokes the frustration and impermanence of the doomed, clandestine relationship with the lines,

And throwing presents straight away
Because you could never take them home

It could be argued that 'Dalliance' follows a predictable path, from quiet to louder to very loud. But that doesn't matter, not when the escalating tension is so deftly handled. The scratchy, insistent guitar introduced in the second verse drives the song towards its inevitable eruption, and when it arrives, it's perfect – a headstrong rush of incendiary noise and emotion.

We're not done, though. The explosive moment is followed by a 16-bar barrage of noise and then a final verse, a passage that, live, tends to lead to utter mayhem down at the front of the audience. But just when you think the band are at full throttle, they step it up yet another gear for the final, frantic chorus, Gedge battling successfully (just) to be heard above the glorious cacophony.

8 BEWITCHED

Despite a dip into slightly more abstract territory with 'Kennedy', *Bizarro* generally stuck with the same vignettes of romantic regret, frustration and loss that populated *George Best*. Despite the fact that Gedge was in his late twenties when these two albums were released, there's something very teenage about many of these stories. This is by no means a criticism. These lyrics weren't immature or childish; what they did – often incredibly vividly – was to capture that period of time bookended by holding-hands-in-the-park crushes and moving in together/'where is this relationship going?' uncertainties.

This era of sixth-form couples, house parties and first relationships to have anniversaries measured in years rather than weeks is where we find the protagonist of 'Bewitched'. Over a churning, circular riff punctuated by bursts of stomping distortion, he is the personification of clumsy timidity, never finding the courage or the opportunity to express his feelings: 'Why do my steps get this small when I reach your front door?'

The sweet charm of Doris Day's vocal (taken from 'Bewitched, Bothered And Bewildered') hovering in the background seems only to mock his romantic yearning. Gedge again demonstrates his ability to paint heartbreak and rejection in only a few words ('And I wait outside for you to come back out and your light goes out') and signs off with one his most memorable lines:

There's a thousand things I wished I'd said and done but the moment's gone

The instrumental second half of the song sees the stomping riff swirl away in ever-decreasing circles, echoing young love's fading hopes. The moments leading to the crashing dénouement, as the music fades into almost nothing are – especially live – one of those hair-on-the-back-of-the-neck moments. I saw The Wedding Present play this at Huddersfield Poly in January 1990. As the band gradually slowed and quieted the riff, everything else seemed to fade with it. The brutalist concrete architecture, the outrageously overpriced cans of Red Stripe, the six inches of snow outside and the thought of a perilous car journey home – all of these mundane things dissipated, and just for a few seconds nothing on earth mattered except the wait for that thunderous chord. And when it came, I swear I had to take a step backwards from the sheer force of it.

The LP version exits in a haze of feedback and a contrastingly melodic farewell from Miss Day. The version on the **PUNK* video, recorded in Leeds four months after my Huddersfield experience, captures it in all its live glory.

7 BLONDE

The first recorded appearance of 'Blonde' came courtesy of The Wedding Present's eighth Peel session, recorded in October 1990. Whilst the crunching chorus and wah-wah-infused closing cacophony were already in place, the intro was rather different from the LP version. The early incarnation opens with an understated shuffle from drummer Simon Smith and jangling chords that seem more *Bizarro* than *Seamonsters*, although the new, harder edge was embraced in the choruses and finale.

Come the album, Simon Smith in particular had transformed the intro, deploying a brutal, muscular beat that combines and contrasts beautifully with the delicate, hesitant guitar arpeggio. The song deals with rejection ('You won't be getting in touch – oh, do you ever?'), and although it's one of Gedge's more opaque and minimal lyrics, it contains both the witheringly snide ('Oh, you're clever') and the achingly forlorn ('I'm just some name in your book, that's why you gave up writing weeks ago'). Yet again, David gains the maximum emotional effect from the few words, especially in the desperate closing howl of, 'That's all you took me for.'

The Peel take is a fine one, but the LP version wins out due to its atmospheric, bleak intro. In addition, the slow fade out, combined with the equally gradual fade in, gives the song a circular quality, emphasising the endless cycle of rejection and heartbreak.

6 SUCK

I named my blog *Suddenly It's Tuesday* because it's a phrase that is one of the best examples of something David frequently does incredibly well: capturing the startling thrill of a connection with someone new; something electric, dangerous, undefinable; the all-consuming obliviousness to the passage of time where there's nothing in the world but the two of you.

The intensity of the music – the taut, clattering drum fills, the headily melodic bass line, the grainy drone of the guitar – is matched perfectly to the theme. The rest of the lyric is an edgy mix of romance ('I can't fall asleep even in my own bed until you're near'), sexuality ('There's nothing I won't do to feel your body sliding all around me') and darkness ('You thrill me with your screaming') that culminates in a series of impassioned, sustained notes and David's final guttural 'You suck it all'. 'Suck' is an intoxicating blend of precision and power; and of love, darkness and obsession.

5 FLYING SAUCER

After the previous five tracks' worth of brooding intensity, July's *Hit Parade* offering brings a bit of light relief. No dark obsessional angst here; instead, David indulges his love of all things comic-book and sci-fi in concocting a gleefully cartoonish lyric – 'My fireball is going to call' and, 'Oh I want her, she kind of launched a flying saucer right inside my head.'

It's a perfect combination; a cracking, hooky pop song with a heads-down three-chord thrash finale. If 'Flying Saucer' doesn't put a smile on your face and elicit at the very least some appreciative head-nodding, then there's no hope for you. The only thing wrong with it is that the closing passage always feels at least a couple, perhaps even five minutes too short.

4 ANYONE CAN MAKE A MISTAKE

It was the slashing, fuzzed-up guitar-only outros that first hooked me on *George Best*, but this is the song that has stayed closest to my heart over the last 30-odd years. The first verse is full of those kitchen sink drama rhyming couplets that define the era, such as, 'Do you have to ring her up so soon? That's rubbing salt into these wounds,' and was there ever a more Gedge-ish opening line than:

When I set foot upon the bus, you laughed and said: 'That's the end for us!'

Like 'You Should Always Keep In Touch With Your Friends', 'Anyone Can Make A Mistake' manages to be simultaneously joyful and melancholy, the exuberantly skittering guitar framing a disconsolate separation story:

What can I say to change your mind?
There'll never be another time

Gedge's muttered asides at the end of each chorus – 'Oh, I know that now' and, 'It's so clear to me now' – have a weary poignancy, but the latter is followed by an uplifting, frenetic finale. Objectively, it's no more than a breakneck sprint through a standard four-chord progression, but the energy and passion the band inject into it still takes my breath away three decades later.

Like 'Flying Saucer', the coda could go on forever for me, as it transports me back to lying on the narrow, uncomfortable bed in my first year student room, smoking a cigarette, daydreaming about what it would be like to thrash a guitar on stage and wondering vaguely about what the future might have in store. And sometimes that's all you want from a song.

3 TAKE ME!

You might think that the early singles and *George Best* songs could have exhausted Gedge's capacity to find different ways of expressing the rush of young love and the frustrations of miscommunication, but *Bizarro*'s penultimate track finds him still going strong. 'The things that you said last night', he ponders, 'did they mean nothing or were they filled with hidden clues?' before uttering one of his most iconic couplets:

Can you really have stayed till three?

Orange slices and that Fall LP

The mere mention of 'her' name is like, 'A panic and a rushing sound in my head... a huge weight pressing on my chest', but life is never easy for a young lover:

And now I spend hours trying to look my best
But I still meet you the day before I wash my hair

Two high-octane spins round verse-chorus plus a charming little middle eight ('Warm hands and the things you say...') and you have a perfectly formed if rather breathless pop song. Of course, it doesn't end there; what elevates 'Take Me!' to the heady heights of number three in this chart is its extravagantly lengthy end section. It's a thrilling ride, an exhausting exploration of the possibilities of thrashing the living daylights out of a simple D-A-G progression and seeing where it takes you. There's a clear influence of The Velvet Underground on The Wedding Present of this period (Gedge himself has alluded to it) and it's at its most noticeable here. 'X sounds like Y on acid' used to be a lazy music journo cliché, but it's hard to resist the temptation of describing 'Take Me!' as the Velvets' 1969 'What Goes On' on speed.

Watching it being performed live, it's almost impossible not to feel exhausted on the musicians' behalf, even if they do have the 'Status Quo' section around the five-minute mark to give them a little bit of a breather. I'm sure I can't be the only amateur guitarist to have tried (and failed) to play along with it in its entirety.

At the time, the song suggested some sort of logical conclusion to the Wedding Present sound; you wondered where on earth they could go next. Perhaps this was what the *NME* meant in their *Bizarro* review when they said that The Wedding Present were 'treading water rather than walking on it'. Of course, we didn't yet know about Mr Albini and *Seamonsters*. But before that paradigm shift, you could simply revel in nine minutes of truly glorious noise.

2 PERFECT BLUE

The final Cinerama album, *Torino*, has often been described as a Wedding Present album in all but name, but it's probably fairer to say that it saw a new sound emerge – one that saw Gedge start to wed successfully the lighter sound of Cinerama with a more traditional Wedding Present approach. The first signs of this hybridisation came with the 2000 single 'Wow', which – although it still included such distinctly Cinerama elements as flute and bongos – concluded with a four minute guitar-heavy workout that harked back, albeit tentatively, to the 'Take Me!' days.

Torino took this process a step further. Although songs like 'And When She Was Bad' and 'Health And Efficiency' were awash with strings, they also contained crunching guitar passages that were a long way from anything ('Wow' excepted) heard on *Va Va Voom* or *Disco Volante*. Changes were also afoot live. In the summer of 2002, just two days after *Torino*'s release, my good friend Gricey and I went to see Cinerama play at a small pub in North East Leeds called the New Roscoe. In the first few years of Cinerama, David had refused to play any Wedding Present songs (requests would be met with the response, 'You've got the wrong band') but we had heard vague rumours that a few might be about to appear in the set. Positioning ourselves down at the front of the tiny stage, we couldn't help but take a peek at the setlist, and were delighted to see that 'Bewitched' was the opener (they played 'Octopussy', too).

The Wedding Present finally re-emerged officially at the end of 2004, and released *Take Fountain* in February 2005. You might have expected them to treat Cinerama as something David had got out of his system and make some sort of effort to turn the clock back to The Wedding Present's glory days. The fact this didn't happen is because they didn't even decide it was going to be a Wedding Present album until they were mixing it. As David explained, 'When we started *Take Fountain* we all thought we were making the fourth Cinerama album and so that's how it was recorded.' The transformation was an evolution rather than any sort of nostalgic U-turn, resulting in a beautiful balanced marriage of the two approaches. 'Perfect Blue' (first played live as a Cinerama song in 2003) is the pinnacle of how successful that was.

It's unashamedly sentimental. David's 'I can't believe I deserve a woman as wonderful as you' schtick is well-worn by now, but there's a heartfelt sincerity about it that stops it from becoming at all, as David puts it, 'drippy'. Instead, lines like:

It wasn't rehearsed, there really was no warning
Now, you're the first thing in my head each morning

– crooned over a bed of tender guitar, swooning strings and Terry de Castro's dreamy backing vocals – feel like being bathed in warm sunshine.

The extended coda builds slowly and subtly, and for much of it, it's the strings rather than the guitar that construct the emotional heft, a swelling tide of anticipation. When the guitar finally enters (at four minutes 28 seconds) the whole thing is so impossibly stirring that you think that must be the peak, but then the French horn adds a final flourish that is just utterly transporting. During their extensive tour to promote *Take Fountain*, 'Perfect Blue' was regularly deployed as the set closer and often extended to eight or nine minutes in length, the final section a deliriously exciting swirl of epic guitar.

1 CRAWL

To all intents and purposes, 'Crawl' is a B-side: when *3 Songs* was released, most fans saw 'Corduroy' as the 'lead' track and it was 'Make Me Smile (Come Up And See Me)' that got most of the mainstream attention. 'Crawl' opens with an unassuming, almost shy acoustic strum (I don't know the name of the chord, but it's a C slid up two frets (I think the low E-string is played with an A, so this would not be strictly right!) should you be interested) before a deep, coiling bass line and taut, understated drums emerge.

Gedge's voice is deep and steady, almost tender but also strangely dispassionate, which stands in intriguing contrast to the optimistic tone of the opening words:

Everyone here can be a millionaire
Just take these wings and fly up into the air

As a jangling arpeggio emerges, Gedge seems to turn to the familiar subject of the 'other man' ('It's time for him to crawl back under his stone') although there's nothing that follows that really puts this into context. In fact, the lyric remains stubbornly enigmatic throughout; although there are lines that feel like they might be pieces of a familiar story ('You stopped me once and you could do it again'; 'Okay, you're right, I haven't changed from before'), there's no obvious thread that runs through it. This absorbingly cryptic ambiguity is emphasised by the repeated hook line, the unexplained, 'It wasn't really like that...'.

The Wedding Present are often at their most effective when they just do simple things exceptionally well. In addition, their best work is frequently characterised by their ability to build suspense and tension before releasing it in an emotionally stirring fashion, whether it be through sudden eruptions – 'Bewitched', 'Don't Touch That Dial' – or gradual building and layering – 'Perfect Blue', 'What Have I Said Now?' (in the case of 'Dalliance', both). 'Crawl' certainly ticks the first box. It contains moments of exquisite simplicity: the chord change at one minute 56 is nothing more than an obvious shift from G to A, but here's something unfathomably gorgeous about its timing that it melts my heart; Gedge's 'ah!' at two minutes six seconds is one in a long line of exclamations that transmit a wealth of feeling in a single syllable and tee up the finale perfectly. What's really impressive about 'Crawl', however, is the way that it meets that second criteria – not in the usual five or six minutes, but in a compact two minutes 44. The fact it takes you on such a thrilling, mysterious journey and rouses your soul to such great heights in under three minutes is a mark of genius.

I bought *3 Songs* in September 1990, three years after I first heard 'Anyone Can Make A Mistake'. I had graduated only a couple of months earlier, and was poised at the beginning of what was to be a rather aimless and wasted year. I had no idea what I wanted to do with my life, and whilst I'm not going to pretend that 'Crawl' provided me with any answers, it provided great comfort to me at the time, because it suggested that there was magic out there to be tapped into somehow. I don't really believe in magic, of course – not in the supernatural sense, anyway – but back then, 'Crawl' *was* my magic. And it always will be.

INTERSTATE 5

NICK GOLLEDGE

The song that announced that The Wedding Present were back. Such a brooding, building crescendo and one of my absolute favourite songs by any artist. Oh, and I have a sister-in-law in Bellingham, Washington and we have driven south on Interstate 5!

SEAMONSTERS

ANDREW WOOD

A venue more suited to *The Hitman & Her* than Gedge & Co, Wakefield's Rooftop Gardens seemed a strange place to go and watch The Wedding Present in August 1991. Yet go we did, myself and a group of mates from school. I can't remember just who was in attendance or how we got there, (train, bus, borrowed car) but I do remember how warm it was inside. Dressed in our usual Indie kid get-up of jeans, Docs and long-sleeved tops we were boiling long before the band took to the stage and blasted into 'Lovenest'. No doubt, we cooled ourselves on the cheapest, strongest beer the bar would sell us, which would account for why my memories of the night are a little hazy.

Thankfully, the entire set surfaced a few years ago as CD 1 of the *Live 1991* album. Listening now all these years on, it reveals that we were treated to more or less all the tunes from the recent *Seamonsters* release, with a couple of *Hit Parade* numbers thrown in for good measure, and 'Kennedy' making an appearance too.

A distinctly young-sounding and jocular DLG enjoys a bit of banter with the audience and yes, I've strained my ears to see if I can pick up my younger self shouting requests or heckling but, alas, to no avail. But there's one thing that's unmistakably clear. That's the raw energy, emotion and excitement that first drew me to the band and continues to do so today.

FLYING SAUCER

MARCUS KAIN, FORMER WEDDING PRESENT GUITARIST

Photo: Richard Houghton

Marcus Kain (right) has chosen 'Flying Saucer'

It's a tough choice to make, but I had so much fun playing this song that I can't go past it… 'Flying Saucer' is my favourite Wedding Present song. It was an awesome chance just to turn everything up loud, enjoy playing as a band, and have fun with the crowd. Some of the other songs with more complex arrangements and nuanced melodies were definitely cool, but for me it was all about enjoying the energy of loud live shows. There were some nights on tour in 2017 when my brain felt completely fried from learning lots of new (new for me at the time!) songs with slightly tweaked arrangements, so the appearance of 'Flying Saucer' at the end of a 90 minute set always felt like a gift from God. 'My Favourite Dress', 'Brassneck' and that one that goes for about 48 minutes are all brilliant, but 'Flying Saucer' was my jam. I think David stopped needing to ask my opinion during rehearsals on which songs to add to the live set since I'd always answer with a shopping list of the loudest, most guitar-heavy tunes.

WHAT HAVE I SAID NOW?

ALEX RUSSON

There's a line in my favourite Wedding Present song that's become a family treasure. When my kids first heard it, quite innocently as we travelled through Walsall in the family motor, they laughed out loud and demanded it be replayed. (They do the same with 'Bob Dylan's 115th Dream'; listen to the opening and you'll see why.)

The three of them were between five and ten years old at the time and in jolly mood having embarked on their latest confectionery sugar rush. I cranked up *Bizarro* as we tootled along and it reached 'What Have I Said Now?', and specifically the line, 'I'm not being unfair, OK, I am but who cares?' The three of them fell about laughing in the back seat – they couldn't stop giggling.

It wasn't so much the lyric as the spite with which Gedge delivered it. They could relate. It spoke to their experiences of sibling rivalry. Someone was permitting the frustration that they often harboured, a grown adult passionately spitting out an impatience which they too often experienced. They found it hilarious, and comforting. It was a beautiful moment, and one we recreate all these years later when in the car together. There's a myriad of Wedding Present lyrics that tickle the funny bone, but this one provides such a wonderful memory.

Alex Russon's children Emily, Ernie and Freddie thought the lyrics to 'What Have I Said Now?' were a giggle

YOU SHOULD ALWAYS KEEP IN TOUCH WITH YOUR FRIENDS

ROBERT CROWE

The track I've chosen is 'You Should Always Keep In Touch With Your Friends' which also happens to be the first Wedding Present track I ever heard. It was one of the tracks on a *Melody Maker* Indie Top 20 cassette from the summer of 1987 which came out just before I went to Durham University. It was from a time when, through John Peel and Annie Nightingale on the radio and reading the *NME* and *Melody Maker*, I was discovering new music, having already been a keen fan of Joy Division, New Order, Half Man Half Biscuit and Talking Heads. I can't remember if it was free with the magazine or if I paid for it but it had a great selection of bands including tracks by A Certain Ratio, PWEI, Joy Division, New Order (both Peel sessions versions) and of course The Wedding Present. I remember being instantly struck by the brilliant drum intro leading to the frantic jingly guitars kicking in and the mournful northern vocals, and it was one of around six or so tracks that got the most repeat plays.

I guess at the time the title was also apt as I was soon to move away from home to university to make new friends, even though, ironically, I wasn't particularly good at keeping in touch with my old ones. However, in my defence it took a lot more effort in those days before mobile phones, texting and social media. Around that time, I used to

Robert Crowe found 'You Should Always Keep In Touch With Your Friends' on a *Melody Maker* compilation tape

make compilation tapes (that's the proper name – it's definitely not a 'mixtape'), usually between terms when I came home from college. These weren't for the cliched 'gifting to a potential girlfriend', but as a practical way to have a selection of music to play on my Aiwa cassette player when I got back to university, or on my Walkman on the train back. These became more varied as my music library and taste developed, and at that time would be a mixture of vinyl and cassette sources. I continued to like the track and it was duly included in my fourth compilation, *Put More Leather On*, in April 1988 which is still one of my favourites. The track was placed on side two, coming immediately after '(Nothing But) Flowers' by Talking Heads and followed by the short 'Red Guard Dance' from Last Emperor and then into 'Sex Dwarf' by Soft Cell. As you can see, I liked to vary the styles. Even now when I hear the track '(Nothing But) Flowers', I expect the drum intro from the Wedding Present song to kick in after it finishes. Although it's difficult to single out a favourite, as there are plenty of other Wedding Present and Cinerama tracks which were released afterwards which are great, 'You Should Always Keep In Touch With Your Friends' is the song that started my interest in the band and reminds me of the days where I loved discovering new music and when I left home for the first time to go to university.

CORDUROY or HEATHER

NICK FISK

'All the songs sound the same' was a criticism often levelled at The Wedding Present, especially in their early days, and just as Welsh people have made the derogatory term 'sheep-shagger' their own, the term 'all the songs sound the same' was something The

Wedding Present then adopted as a kind of in-joke. Like the Welsh, who do not after all shag sheep (or at least, not most of them), it's pretty blatant that Wedding Present songs do not all sound the same.

Nick Fisk cannot decide between 'Corduroy' and 'Heather'

The term 'underrated' is one that is overused. In terms of songwriting ability, I would rate David Gedge not as underrated but undervalued. As someone who successfully captures so many aspects of the ups and downs of relationships in song form, I consider Gedge to be an absolute master of his class. He used to say he picked up bits and pieces of conversation overheard on public transport and use these. I have no doubt this was true, but I expect he has also drawn from personal experience, perhaps the experiences of friends, all kinds, to come up with ideas for songs that will relate to so many people in various ways.

Of the early albums, *Seamonsters* is probably my favourite, although it's a close-run thing. For this album, they switched to one word song titles, after the more lengthy, complicated, (though sometimes quite amusing) long titles from the pre-*Bizarro* days. I remember John Peel saying of the session for this album – which included a couple of songs that would be used as B-sides to singles – that the songs were magnificent, and I agreed with him; just really, really good-quality songwriting.

Of course, the other notable thing about this album was that they drafted in Steve Albini as producer, after his previous work on the single version of 'Brassneck'. Much as I love Steve Albini – I suppose he'll always be best known for his work on early Pixies releases – and much as I like the production on this record, I've always wondered what a *Seamonsters* without quite such a harsh sound might sound like. The songs on it are so good that a more conventional producer could possibly have been a better option.

But The Wedding Present were of course never known for taking a conventional route. Despite signing with a major record label, it's safe to say they are one of those bands who firmly stuck to their Indie attitude. When they released their *Ukrainian John*

Peel Sessions mini LP – an unconventional move in itself – they refused to play ball with the record label and release the cover of 'Those Were The Days' – which might have become a top ten novelty hit record – because they just didn't want that. Once, when David appeared on *Top Of The Pops*, he did not even open his mouth to sing as a protest against not being allowed to perform live. (Editor's note: David says this was not a protest against being forced to mime.)

So anyway, how to pick a favourite song from *Seamonsters*? How to pick a favourite Wedding Present song at all with so many classics to choose from? The opener 'Dalliance' is spectacular enough. But I have gone for a coin flip between 'Heather' and 'Corduroy'. 'Heather' I've chosen because it always reminded me of when my girlfriend in my teens, Helen, and I used to take walks at Merthyr Mawr sand dunes, close to where I lived in Bridgend.

The other side of the coin, 'Corduroy', is a little more of a curio. For some reason, this is always one of the most popular in the moshpit at Wedding Present gigs (it's impressive that a band whose following is mostly older fans still gets a good moshpit going). So given that their live gigs are definitely a reason for anyone to become a firm Wedding Present fan (I must have seen them over thirty times now), I felt I had to pick a song that is a live favourite.

But it is a curious one – which was the lead track on the *All The Songs Sound The Same* EP – because in some ways, the lyrics to this one are, at least for the second part of the chorus – how can I put it? – not exactly that exciting!

In a way, it's a bit like as with The Stone Roses' 'I Am The Resurrection' – generally considered as their best song – the second line of the two line chorus, though quite clever and unusual, is not that inspiring – 'I couldn't ever bring myself to hate you as I'd like'. Certainly at least not compared to the epic, ahem, borrowed first line – 'I am the resurrection and I am the life!'

I don't know why, I just consider the lines:

It's just some boy, probably dressed in corduroy
He grew up fast but you've not changed at all

to in some ways be a little ordinary as far as Wedding Present lyrics are concerned.

So what is it about this song that fans go wild for? I mean, I suppose with any song, there's the tune, which is great. It has nice loud and quiet bits, a couple of pauses which work well. Is it one of those songs where to have learned all the words is considered a small badge of honour? I just enjoy the fact that for some reason, the slightly laddier aspect of The Wedding Present's fanbase really enjoy screaming the lyrics to this one into each other's faces as they bop about. Sometimes encapsulating just why you like a song is not as easy as you might think!

NOW

CINERAMA
DISCO VOLANTE
THE NEW ALBUM
$12
T-SHIRTS
LIGHT BLUE XL, L
BLACK* XL, L
ALL SHIRTS $15

MURMURTOWN PRODUCCIONES PRESENTA:
PRIMAVERA SOUND 2002
POBLE ESPANYOL. BARCELONA. 17 y 18 de MAYO
PROGRAMACIÓN Y ESCENARIOS

all short
sleeved
t shirts are
£10
XL, L, M or S

NO NOMINATION
STEVE PAYNE

I once invited my girlfriend 'Zanna' to a Wedding Present show, under the flyover in west London. I told her there'd be dancing, so she wore a one-piece leopard print leotard and looked amazing. Yes, there was much dancing and she thought it was one of the best gigs she'd ever been to. Much fun was had then… and later.

Steve Payne took his girlfriend to a Wedding Present gig

WHY ARE YOU BEING SO REASONABLE NOW?
JAN FRANCIS

It's a classic rites of passage story really. I knew that I liked music that was a little different from the norm. For example, there weren't many fellow eight-year-olds in my class that liked 'Golden Brown' when it was released. My parents remarked on my slightly different taste, but I think they both liked it really. Dad had been a mod, then a rocker and then a hippy. He'd embraced all the alternatives, although he couldn't stand The Wedding Present – ha ha! Everything as it should be then really, although it did turn out a few years later that a mate of his liked them. But it was one Saturday morning watching *Saturday Superstore* that I saw the 'Why Are You Being So Reasonable Now?' video for the first time. I was 15. I seem to be on my own with this recollection but I stand by it. Everybody just says 'The Wedding Present, *Saturday Superstore*…? That can't be right!'

It was confirmation that the usual chart music wasn't my scene. I loved everything about the song – the raw sound, mostly the fast playing of the guitars and the fact they got a melody out of it! Even Gedge's voice. It was completely different to anything I'd heard before. I'm a music first, words later man. When I discovered the lyrics, the fact that David Gedge wrote such personal and vulnerable lyrics was also very new for me.

As a newbie to the alternative side of music, I didn't really know where to turn. Funnily enough, I didn't have to turn far as a girl at school, Esther, overheard me talking about The Wedding Present and came up and said she was really into them. The following day she handed me a C90 with *George Best* on one side and *Tommy* on the other, and that was that. *Tommy* remains my favourite of the long players, although it's not technically an album. I had to wait until 1990 until I saw the band live for the first time. The Wedding Present were the first alternative band I was into and they created the thirst for different and original music which I still have today. They also enabled me to be the cool big brother, as my brother and his friends soon followed suit and various copies of my albums would be doing the rounds amongst his friends. My brother actually bought *Bizarro* before I did.

That is my fondest memory of music back then – the clans and the 'pass it forward' culture. The Wedding Present were my entry point for all that.

BLONDE

DIANE HARTSHORN

So, The Wedding Present… Where do I start? I was first introduced to them in the early 1990s by a mixtape I found at a friend's house. It was her brother's. It contained the song 'Kennedy' and I was hooked. Grunge took over my life for a while and then, like magic, the mid-90s happened. There was Indie music everywhere. I got myself into a band and started writing a fanzine full of heartbreak, sexy times, drugs and woe. Our band also reflected these feelings and we listened to The Wedding Present for 'inspiration' (we didn't steal, promise!) all the time.

Diane Hartshorn went to a Wedding Present gig in a Pulp t-shirt

I was dealing with my own stupid self-inflicted heartbreak at the time (long story, for another time maybe) and my friends in the band mentioned a secret Wedding Present gig somewhere near Holmfirth. With us being Barnsley locals, this was a perfect location so we spilled over into Penistone and then went to the gig in some bloke's Land Rover (and did a bit of off-roading on the way, although I'm not a fan).

Once in the venue, I realised I had a sodding Pulp t-shirt on and died inside a little bit as I didn't want to upset David – I wanted to be all 'cool and interesting'. We were all there at the front and there I was, looking up at David in teenage awe (or angst, or a mixture of both, with added hormones) and then I looked down and saw I was covered in someone else's nasal blood. David saw this (and also the darn Pulp shirt – I mean, it was yellow and hard to miss especially when splattered with blood!) and gave me a look. My knees went… and then they started to play 'it', the song of my entire stupid self-inflicted heartbreak – 'Blonde'.

There I was, covered in someone else's blood, in a Pulp t-shirt, crying as I thought about my regrets, bad life choices and how much I loved my ex and why on earth I fucked it up, to the sound of 'Blonde'. A fitting song for the shitstorm that was my life encapsulated into just over five minutes of life, love and regret. For that moment, I was that person in the song and I felt it. THE BEST MOMENT OF MY LIFE.

After the gig I had the pleasure of meeting David. He asked if I was OK as he saw my shirt from the stage covered in blood and I just piped out, 'It's someone else's blood!' Smooth. Smooth, Di…

So, there I was, somewhere in Holmfirth, stood in front of one of my biggest crushes, blood splattered, make-up running, wearing a fucking bright yellow Pulp shirt. I loved every minute!

'Blonde' still stands with me to this day and I still think about what an idiot I was to hurt someone I loved so much. That is why I love The Wedding Present. There is a little bit of us all in the songs. We relate…

LARRY'S

NICK GOLLEDGE

Take Fountain is the band's finest album and every word of 'Larry's' reminds me of a certain someone and takes me back to a part of my life which is gone forever. DLG has a way of making you feel like the song is written about you.

DALLIANCE

STUART DIGGLE

Stuart Diggle rates 'Dalliance'

I'd always seen The Wedding Present and The Birthday Party regularly name-checked in the *NME*. Both acts intrigued me whilst I clung on to my punk rock roots through the Ramones remaining active throughout the '80s. By the late '80s, I'd been turned onto the Pixies, who became my favourite band. So

I drifted into the Indie and grunge scene naturally. I backtracked on the Weddoes and quite liked *George Best*, etc.

In 1992 I bought all the singles – one per month – and went to see the band live a few times and picked up *Seamonsters*. The latter was quite a surprise as it was a far more relaxed, but with tension, record than I'd expected. This after the up-tempo *Bizarro* release.

'Dalliance' always struck me as that romantic and melancholic effort that resonated somewhat. It was quite far removed from earlier releases. I even bought a *Seamonsters* t-shirt.

Many years later, around 2019, I saw the band live again at a local bar, The Waterloo in Blackpool, which is really a pub converted to a venue. It's a bit of a hybrid situation. The band sounded great through an excellent PA as they kicked off with 'Dalliance' and it took me right back to my younger days. It just felt correct, hence it's topping my Wedding Present chart at this moment in time.

I'M FROM FURTHER NORTH THAN YOU

KEVIN SHELBOURNE

Kevin Shelbourne remembers the band dedicating 'I'm From Further North Than You' to his late wife Joanne

My memory is of the song 'I'm From Further North Than You'. My wife Joanne passed away in 2011 and this was her favourite Gedge song. I was seeing the band in Middlesbrough later that year and I emailed asking if they could include it in the setlist as a tribute. I received an email back with a video of them soundchecking it. They did indeed play the song on the night and dedicated it to me. Not many bands would do that and that's why I love them.

WATUSI

VINCENT PONTIUS

Watusi came out in '94 and I had only become a fan of the Weddoes with *Seamonsters*.

Weddoes' LPs were difficult to come by back in the day and they were barely known Stateside outside of the ever faithful. *Seamonsters* was a slow ascension towards commercial breakout. So I had the *Seamonsters* CD which I listened to on repeat. Every song on that album was better than the last song. David's axe wielding was so unique – I'd never heard anyone like him. It's kinda post punk! His leads are crescendo shattering.

I'm sure Albini being the Weddoes' helmer on that album had something to do with that blast of fury from them. Anyway, *Watusi* was even better! Endlessly listenable with the sound dialled down and, dare I say, quasi pop. Was 'Yeah Yeah Yeah Yeah Yeah' and 'It's A Gas' them going for that power pop sound?

In the fall of '94, I was dumped by a girl who broke up me with because she found a guy who loved Oasis (I'm a Blur diehard) and hated my loud white noise bands: Sonic Youth, Throbbing Gristle, Foetus and – yes – the Weddoes. I really liked this girl but in the end she was into 'bad boys' and was all artifice and shallowness.

Anyhoo, my friends barely knew the Weddoes were even a band.

KENNEDY

MARTIN BIDDULPH

I first saw them at Manchester Ritz with the Inspiral Carpets and Happy Mondays and was impressed then. 'My Favourite Dress' was the first song I heard by them. 'Kennedy', 'Brassneck' and 'Why Are You Being So Reasonable Now?' are all class.

GIVE MY LOVE TO KEVIN

KEV GREER

The song I picked reminds me of my teenage years. I bought the album *George Best* from my local independent record shop. When I was a teenager, music on vinyl was magical. I liked bands who were different. At that time there were loads, especially in Scotland, but The Wedding Present had a distinctive sound.

Kev Greer's choice is (unsurprisingly) 'Give My Love To Kevin'

DON'T TOUCH THAT DIAL (PACIFIC NORTHWEST VERSION)

DAVID FISH

The explosive guitars and drums after the quiet verse which ends '...the one thing that you most adore is just about to walk out of the door' is sublime.

MY FAVOURITE DRESS
PAUL MONTY

'My Favourite Dress' reminds me of my escape from some very, very bad times.

ANYONE CAN MAKE A MISTAKE
JOHN PAUL REDROBE

Mine is 'Anyone Can Make A Mistake' – that's how life is sometimes and this song gave me the strength to get through some tough times.

YOU SHOULD ALWAYS KEEP IN TOUCH WITH YOUR FRIENDS
DAVE WOOLNER

I can't remember exactly when I discovered The Wedding Present. I would guess 1988. I had just left full-time education and started my first full time job. I now had some cash in my wallet so popped into HMV. I was never into 'mainstream' music and my musical taste has always been varied. I ended up purchasing the *NME* various artists album, *C86*, on vinyl, went home and gave it a listen. There was one track that stood out from the others, it was the last track on side two, by The Wedding Present, 'This Boy Can Wait (A Bit Longer)'. The next day I went to an independent record shop in Swansea called Musiquarium and bought *Tommy* on vinyl and *George Best* on cassette. It was some of the best stuff I'd ever heard.

My good mate Jonathan Powell, whom I'd grown up with since primary school, was unlike my other mates when it came to music and was always willing to listen to new stuff. We played the albums and he also thought they were amazing. Jon left Swansea to attend Manchester University that year but we still remained in contact and would always meet up when he came home.

Fast forward to October 1989. I received a call from Jon saying he'd bought tickets for The Wedding Present on November 15th at Manchester International. I was instructed to get my ass up there. The concert was amazing, it appeared to be at full capacity and full of energy... It was certainly sweaty! When it finished, we went to a club and got (more) pissed, then went back to his home and pretty much passed out. The next morning Jon had lectures and I had a train to catch back to Swansea.

We stayed in contact, although as time went on, it would become more sporadic and every six months would become every year. I moved home a few times while he remained in Manchester and we were both married with kids. The last time I saw Jon was about 2001, but briefly. I have no idea where he lives and assume he doesn't know where I am. I've tried the usual social media methods, with no luck. I heard he was a contestant on *Who Wants To Be A Millionaire?* but I never saw it.

I regret never keeping contact and whenever I hear 'You Should Always Keep In Touch With Your Friends', the title says it all and always reminds me of the ace times we had.

WHAT HAVE I SAID NOW?

CHRISTIAN ROSENKÖTTER

This was the first track I heard by The Wedding Present. I was driving in my car with my best buddy when that one was on air. 20 minutes later we stopped at our favourite record shop and bought the album.

KENNEDY

MARK ADDISON

'Kennedy' reminds me of sweaty student union bar dance floors covered in a strange mix of spilt alcohol and fag ash! And strobe lights and too much Elephant beer!

SPANGLE or BRASSNECK

RICK KERTON

For me it's a toss up between 'Spangle' and 'Brassneck'... the former because it always hurts my chest and the latter because it was the first thing I ever heard, watching a late night music video programme that I wasn't allowed to watch at night because it was a school night. So my mom would wake me up for the repeat extra early in the morning. She'd watch it with me.

BLONDE

PATRICK ALEXANDER, FORMER WEDDING PRESENT GUITARIST

Patrick Alexander (left) remembers rehearsing 'Blonde'

'Blonde' is a song that amalgamates memories. It takes me to disparate moments in dark, sweaty venues across the world. I first really listened to 'Blonde' in my shed in Oxford when I was preparing for the 20th anniversary tour for *Seamonsters* - so, actually, whenever I think of 'Blonde' it's my favourite song forever linked with the rest of my favourite album.

I remember first hearing that haunting hammer-blow at the end of 'Suck', the hard darkness of that final chord resonating with the purity of Albini's approach to the recording. 'Blonde' slowly appears from that darkness and the guitar part is so delicate that it's disarming. I remember hundreds of moments in the wash of the feedback from 'Suck', snapping on my tuning pedal to quickly re-tune after hammering my guitar towards Charlie like some kind of mad tramp. His four stick-clicks would kick off 'Blonde' with Pepe's (and later Katharine's) bass announcing that simple but perfect three note riff that underpins the song. The drums are massive and the high-hat is insistent, and you can feel the song dragging you towards the noise of the chorus from the start; but to begin with there is so much air in the song that you can hear the venue echo and the crowd shifting on their feet, eyes and hearts in the darkness.

The guitar part quickly slides into a minor key as David sings, 'I'm just some name in your book', and I can still feel my fingers shifting on the fretboard as muscle memory guided me nightly through that naked first riff. Chords pile on top of chords as the guitars get louder and more distorted when David sings, 'And I meant every word that I said', and I loved the thick hardcore sound of those chords so much that I tried to nod to them, in a way, at the beginning of 'Fifty-Six' on *Going, Going*... The guitar part on 'Santa Monica' is also a nod to the delicacy of 'Blonde' and the brutality of its chorus. I remember leaning over in dirty, tour-weary black Converse to stamp on both of my distortion pedals in a weave of light and sweat as the chorus crashed down in Barcelona, in Austin, in Sydney, Hong Kong and back to London, Manchester, Leeds.

There is irony that when David is singing 'You've heard this all before', I know that musically we have, hundreds of times over, but every night the chords fall and the strings bend in their own way that only ever happens once in the moment of playing. It is easy to get lost in 'Blonde' that way.

But my favourite part of the song is not a note or a melody or a lyric. It's the feedback. Making noise with a guitar is a great joy, and feedback is maybe the purest, most joyful noise a guitar can make. After the first chorus there is a magic ringing of a note that, if caught just right, will create the perfect amount of expanding noise before you slip back into the delicacy of the verse. I got it right a few times, but not every time. Feedback is its own beast. After the second chorus, the feedback is even more drawn out, even more pure as it balloons over the insistence of the drums and bass. As the feedback fades back to the original riff at the end of the song, on the recording 'Blonde' fades away, and live we would mimic this. Locking eyes with each other, we would shift from shedding blood on strings to the softest of touches, pickups barely registering a sound. And then it's gone.

DALLIANCE

ALAN IKEELU KIDD

'Dalliance' was the pinnacle of some of the greatest songs ever written. *Seamonsters* for me is absolutely perfect.

FELICITY

ALEXANDRE BORRACHA

Brazil, São Paulo, circa middle of the 1980s. We were (or we are still) savages and it used to take months or years for new culture to reach our country. We were starved of really good music, although São Paulo had a very nice and very interesting punk and post-punk scene at that time. England had its DJ hero, John Peel, and Brazil had Kid Vinil and José Roberto Mahr, both of whom had travelled to England and other countries and had contacts with some interesting artists, record stores and record labels. Kid and José broadcast the crème de la crème – the weirdest, independent, brilliant, vanguard, intriguing music, including the famous *C86*.

I was abandoning my punk armour, listening to something more melodic and less noisy. It was 5pm on a Sunday evening in 1987 and José was presenting his *Novas Tendências* (*New Tendencies*) show on 89FM radio. He was a big John Peel/BBC Sessions fan and played 'Felicity'. I was a bit shocked and also in a state of grace. Those strong and weird Gedge vocals! Those guitars – noisy, urgent but also melodic. I was 18 years old and not that punk teenager any more, but a 'teenage spirit' descended into my body. I started jumping, stomping and singing like crazy. I was recording that radio show and the DJ played four more songs– 'What Becomes Of The Broken Hearted?', 'You Should Always Keep In Touch With Your Friends', 'This Boy Can Wait' and 'Everyone Thinks He Looks Daft' (what a whistleable song!). But 'Felicity' was the first one, and some years later I discovered that 'Felicity' is a cover of a song by another adorable band, Orange Juice.

Alexandre Borracha was starved of good music in Brazil until he discovered The Wedding Present

'Felicity' ruined my pockets. A year later I was buying a quite expensive CD player and the (imported and expensive) Wedding Present *BBC Sessions* CD. I fell in love and was bankrupt. But, hey, most Wedding Present songs are about love and being ruined by love!

CLICK CLICK

KIM PEIRCE

In 1994, I started to feel ill and lose weight whilst I was studying for my final exams. My GP diagnosed exam stress, which seemed plausible until I'd finished the exams and still felt awful. It turned out to be cancer.

Kim Peirce told David Gedge that 'Click Click' 'saved her life'

A few months later, I was in a chemotherapy ward, having poison pumped into my body, surrounded by very unwell people. All my hair had fallen out, and I could feel myself disappearing, my identity being subsumed within the shell of an ill person. I had a Walkman to help blot out some of the traumatic sounds around me, and a friend came in with a mixtape for me. In the dark, unable to sleep, I dropped it into the Walkman and pressed play.

The first track was 'Click Click'. The seductively quiet opening beckoned me closer, then the song kicked in. It absorbed me, insulated me from a world of poorliness and defeat, rebuilt me. Even now, 26 years later, when it comes on the shuffle, I have to stop what I'm doing and close my eyes to immerse myself again.

At my first Wedding Present gig once I was well enough, I incoherently told a bewildered Mr Gedge that his songs had saved my life. That may have been a bit of an exaggeration – I suspect medicine and some amazing doctors had something more substantial to do with it. But they definitely gave me a reminder of who I was and why that was worth hanging on to, at a time when I sorely needed it.

BRASSNECK
SCOTT REECE

I've always loved the way that David talks to fans at his shows, both with Cinerama and The Wedding Present. At the Brighton Centre East Wing in the mid-90s, I nervously went up to him to say hi, but didn't know what to say as an awkward spotty teenager. My mate said, 'Ask about his dog, or his motorbike…' but I wasn't sure, so I told him my favourite song was 'Brassneck' and asked him how to play it. David said 'D, A' and smiled. I was totally made up…!!

NOT FROM WHERE I'M STANDING
JON MILLS

Jon Mills nominates 'Not From Where I'm Standing'

I've always loved snippets of conversations or stories. The reader or listener is left to colour in the blanks. I found this song as a B-side, probably the first time one eclipsed the A-side for me, and it was instant love. Even though it seems to be dominated by its frenetic chord shredding it still manages to talk us through someone's regrets and exasperation. At the time I had just been chewed up and spat out by a girl and so this little insight into watching someone else go through the same thing, whilst all the time lamenting the lack of second chances hit home. It might not be the most complicated song the band ever produced but for me, that is its charm. This song belongs to anyone who nearly drowned in the bittersweet hindsight that comes from a relationship with the wrong person.

PERFECT BLUE
CARL HUDSON

'Perfect Blue' sums up Carl Hudson's feelings about his wife

'Perfect Blue' off *Take Fountain* sums up how I feel towards my wife in words that I could never express. The words are so simple but sometimes to explain something so complex, simple is the best. When I listen to the song, I'm usually a bit of a wreck afterwards because I can't believe how lucky I am to have found someone so fantastic.

I'm not sure just what I did to deserve you
I'm not complaining, God forbid, I just don't understand!

I spent ages trying to think of something like that for my speech at my wedding but couldn't come up with anything. If only we had time travel back in 1995!

KITTERY
MICHAEL HARRIS

The three songs I would pick out could not sound more different to each other. These are not my favourite Wedding Present songs. That changes daily with my mood and what is happening in the world. These are just three songs that mean the most to me.

'Give My Love To Kevin' was my introduction to the band, one of several songs on a various artists tape sellotaped to the cover of the *NME*, *Sounds* or *Melody Maker* (most likely *Strum + Drum*, which was on *Underground* magazine in 1988, and also included 'Karen' by The Go-Betweens!). But I can distinctly remember putting it on my bedroom stereo as background noise while I did my homework, and putting my pen down and rewinding the tape once, twice, three times – more and more and more – because it blew my mind just how beautiful it was. I listened to it all night, left my homework and ultimately failed that test. Never mind,

I had discovered the greatest band of all time!

When I first started dating my future wife, we were going through the age-old mating ritual of the 21st century of getting to know each one another by alternatively playing songs from our respective iPods. I got to hear The Polyphonic Spree, Kings Of Convenience and The Be Good Tanyas, whilst she was experiencing Teenage Fanclub, The Trashcan Sinatras and The Wedding Present for the first time. It was a magical time.

Michael Harris has chosen 'Kittery', which is where he now lives

As I played classic after classic older Wedding Present, I was met with, 'This is a bit too punky and too fast for me,' so I decided to try to slow it down for her perfect delicate ears. That was when I remembered 'I'm From Further North Than You'. The start of the song describing the beginning of the relationship just hit exactly where we were right at that moment. The rest of the song? Maybe not so much. After all, we had only just met so had yet to buy 'weird pornography' and thankfully our relationship lasted longer than just the six weeks referred to in the song, but it still makes me think of lying on the settee listening to it with one ear bud in my right ear and one ear bud in her left. The happiest days of my life.

My third choice is 'Kittery'. What are the chances that a boy from Derby, England would: buy a magazine with a tape on it; fall in love with a band from that tape; years later, meet a girl from the North East of the USA and fall in love with her; have her introduce me to this tiny village called Kittery in her home country, and me fall in love with the area; us set up our family home there; and The Wedding Present write a song named after the same tiny village? It's too good to be true, but it is. All of it.

GIVE MY LOVE TO KEVIN or NIAGARA
MIKE THOMPSON

'Give My Love To Kevin' was the reason I went into a secondhand music shop in Leeds and bought a cheap electric guitar. I loved that tune so much it became the first piece I learned to play. I learned the acoustic version first, before dropping a distortion pedal into the mix and roaring out the electric version. Total bliss, and I impressed a few folks at the same time.

'Niagara' was a thrill because of the tempo change at the end and the phased guitars. It's one of those classic guitar workouts (and I think it was a B-side originally so loads of people wouldn't have heard it first time round). It still makes the hairs on my neck stand on end. All The Songs *Don't* Sound The Same!

Mike Thompson bought a cheap electric guitar because of 'Give My Love To Kevin'

CLICK CLICK
CHRIS WIDDOWSON

It's the early '90s and you've gazed at her for what seems like ages but never dared to show your hand, crippled by nerves. Then it all makes sense and the prize is yours. With new girlfriend in tow, you head off for a weekend away in the Dales for some badly thought out camping action. The campsite you remember is overgrown and full of rusting farm machinery, and the hastily arranged bed-and-breakfast is full of strange folk more in line with the residents of Royston Vasey: 'This is a local B&B for local people!'

The musical accompaniment to our adventures just had to be the Weddoes. High up on the moors, the purple tinge of the heather, the sound of the sky larks, our worlds beautifully aligned and 'Click Click' blasting out on the car stereo. 'No one could mean as much as you do to me.' A strong sentiment that remains to this day. Newly converted to Gedge & Co, she never looked back. This song said it all and 27 years later, the song as they say does indeed remain the same.

Q&A

David Gedge on love, loss, and why he's never listened to Bob Dylan

UNCUT: Is breaking up worse the older you get?

GEDGE: It's always difficult. Throughout your life. In some ways it's easier when you're younger because you're expected to be angst-ridden. But when you're older the decisions become more crucial in that they become life-affecting. For instance, this time I wasn't just left crying at a bus stop after the disco. I had to sell my house and rearrange my entire life.

So is *Take Fountain* your *Blood On The Tracks*?

Er, I'm ashamed to say that I've never actually listened to that album! I never liked his singing. But it is quite strange that, after spending 20 years writing about relationships ending and making a lot of it up, this time I was actually writing about myself. As a result, this was quite an easy album for me to make… but it's flippin' difficult to listen to.

PITCHFORK.COM
TAKE FOUNTAIN
NITSUH ABEHE, FEBRUARY 2005

Gedge just gets better and better at casting himself as an upscale songwriter, even outside the "sophisticatcd" confines of Cinerama. Who, back in 1991, would have guessed that his clenched-teeth complaining-voice came along with such an expressive croon? Who'd have guessed that fierce crabby Gedge--like Costello before him--would ride pop classicism to such a comfortable place? It's an unglamorous, underrated role, but it fits him beautifully. And here, beneath the obligatory vintage-Weddoes guitar snap, that's what you'll find: our older, wiser Gedge, still endlessly negotiating with girls.

The Wedding Present

Take Fountain

SCOPITONES

★★★

The original lo-fi losers make a belated return.

The Wedding Present always sounded in a hurry. Grumpy Northern frontman David Gedge would have a disaster in his love life, dash off a three-chord poem and have it in the shops by teatime; it was like an '80s version of Trisha. Twenty years on, nothing's changed. The band's first album since 1996 is packed with tear-stained diary entries set to jangly guitars. Inevitably, it sounds dated, but it's still strangely reassuring to wallow in this off-key retro-indie world where girl-leaves-boy is all there is to worry about. **JOHN PERRY**

Rip It! **Don't Touch That Dial**

March 8

The Wedding Present

Roadmender, Northampton

One of Britain's most influential and successful indie bands, The Wedding Present release their first new album in eight years. This tour takes front man and creative epicentre David Gedge full circle, promoting a new Wedding Present album almost 20 years after the band started out.

TO HH
FROM A-B BOX
THE WEDDING PRESENT

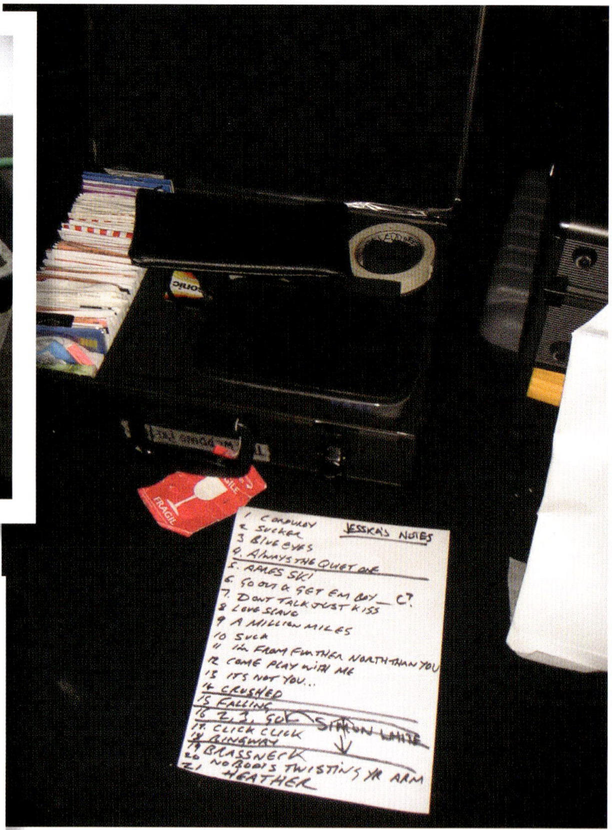
JESSICA'S NOTES
1 CORDUROY
2 SUCKER
3 BLUE EYES
4. ALWAYS THE QUIET ONE
5. APRES SKI
6. GO OUT & GET EM BOY _ C?
7. DONT TALK JUST KISS
8 LOVE SLAVE
9 A MILLION MILES
10 SUCK
11 I'M FROM FURTHER NORTH THAN YOU
12 COME PLAY WITH ME
13 IT'S NOT YOU...
14 CRUSHED
15 FALLING
16 2, 3, GO
17 CLICK CLICK
18 RINGWAY
19 BRASSNECK
20 NOBODY'S TWISTING YR ARM
21 HEATHER
SIMON WHITE

24hr SECURE
ONLINE BOOKING
wedgewood-rooms.
co.uk
THE WEDDING PRESENT
SOLD OUT!
PERSIL
WEDNESDAY 23rd FEBRUARY
PORTSMOUTH WEDGEWOOD ROOMS
Doors 8.00pm Tickets £12.00 advance Box Office 023 9286 3911

THE WEDDING PRESENT
SALLY CREWE & THE SUDDEN MO
THE DANGER ★ EXTRA BLUE KIND ★
WWWDOUBLEDOORCOM
NATIONAL SIGNS, INC.

THE WEDDING PRESENT

El Rey

VIBRANT MUSIC

★★★☆☆

YORKSHIRE'S DOOMED ROMANTICS TRUNDLE ON.

One can't help but ponder the sheer lunacy of frontman David Gedge's recent decision to relocate to West Hollywood. If Leeds' prevailing failed romantic was unlucky in love in the UK it seems unlikely he'd find the girl of his dreams on the Sunset Strip. El Rey effectively confirms as much: "I thought women were supposed to tell you how they were feeling," he sighs on Palisades. Though a certain battle weariness has set in, many songs lacking The Wedding Present's trademark guitar bluster of old, Gedge remains wry, dry and wholeheartedly likeable. ■ NICK DUERDEN

DOWNLOAD: Palisades

THE WEDDING PRESENT

'Semi-legendary' act deliver's blubsome triumph

Ringway To Seatac *(Scopitones)*

"Watching you walk back to your car/Was the lowest point of my life so far" – ah, little has changed in the romantic disaster area they call David Lewis Gedge over the past 18-odd years, but if the soul-deep bruises he's sustained from The Elbow haven't faded, nor has his ability to couch his eternally teenage angst. The day will come when the world's eyes will open to their influence on everyone who's ever throttled a jangly guitar in anger, from The Strokes to Arctic Monkeys, but in the meantime 'Ringway To Seatac' is typically wonderful Weddoes fare – jaunty, jagged and secretly joyful in being jilted. Simply *stupendous.* ***MB***

IN THE SHOPS MONDAY

THE WEDDING PRESENT 8

EL REY (VIBRANT)

Why do legendary bands ever consider reuniting years after they formed? Because they could end up with a beauty like 'El Rey', that's why. The Weddoes' second release since they reformed in 2004, it picks a perfect balance between David Gedge's fey and funny lyrics and the raw production of Nirvana collaborator Steve Albini. Whether referencing *Breakfast At Tiffany's* over scratchy Smiths guitars on 'Don't Take Me Home Until I'm Drunk' or spinning tales of infidelity over edgy post-punk on 'Santa Ana Winds', this is some of the funniest, cleverest and most relevant indie you're likely to hear this year. Gedge might be old enough to be Alex Turner's dad, but he could still teach the Monkey a thing or two. ***Tom Pinnock***

DOWNLOAD: 'Santa Ana Winds'

BBC 6music
.co.uk/6music

MY AWESOME COMPILATION
CELEBRITY SEX
PSYCHO CANDY
THE JESUS AND MARY CH

CRISTALINE

NOBODY'S TWISTING YOUR ARM

KEN ROY

Ken Roy learnt about John Peel – and The Wedding Present – via short wave radio

Back in the '80s there was no internet so hearing the latest bands was much more difficult. MTV played a great deal of mainstream new wave and punk, but the more obscure alternative music was only available via the local college radio station (WUSM). After I graduated from high school, I happened to attend that particular college and so became a radio DJ.

At the radio station, I met like-minded alternative music lovers, many of whom knew way more about alternative music than I did, so my mind was blown by the many new bands I never knew existed. One of the DJs had a shortwave radio and listened to the *John Peel Show* on the BBC's World Service, and he played many artists during his show that wouldn't be played by other radio stations for months. It was his programme where I first heard many great new bands such as The Primitives, The Darling Buds, The Fall, Close Lobsters and, one of my favourites, The Wedding Present. During the weekends I would travel to Boston or Providence and hunt through the import record stores for anything I could get my hands on. One of my favourites was the *Nobody's Twisting Your Arm* EP – or really any Wedding Present singles or albums that I could find. The internet has certainly made it easier to find and hear new music, but there was an excitement about hearing a brand new track on the radio and then desperately searching for it – and then finally finding it – that I miss.

The Wedding Present always remind me of that time.

OCTOPUSSY

WICKHAM CLAYTON

My absolute favourite Wedding Present song is 'Octopussy'. Albini's production on *Seamonsters* really highlights Gedge's vulnerability, while the music is raw, forceful and

emotional. 'Octopussy' being quite a quiet, soothing song – relative to many of the others on the album – felt particularly vulnerable and really resonated with me at a time in my life when I was emotionally raw, bare, fragile and ultimately open to real passion. I was falling in love with someone and 'Octopussy' articulated my sense of yearning and urgency, a sense of closeness to someone I desperately wanted to be with.

For Wickham Clayton, 'Octopussy' really resonated

YOU SHOULD ALWAYS KEEP IN TOUCH WITH YOUR FRIENDS

IAIN ANDERSON

Iain Anderson's favourite song is 'You Should Always Keep In Touch With Your Friends'

I think the first time that I became aware of The Wedding Present was when they appeared on *The Other Side Of Midnight* performing 'You Should Always Keep In Touch With Your Friends'. I was immediately drawn to them, if nothing else, by the catchiness of their tunes. Gedge's lyrics seemed a world away from what The Smiths, etc. were churning out. Not everyone can quote Oscar Wilde endlessly, but most people can identify with the feeling of seeing their ex with someone new.

I bought many of their records when and if I could afford them. I even managed to get a few of my friends into them, and any records I couldn't afford, I would then borrow off said friends. The *Peel Sessions* twelve-inch was rarely off the turntable.

I never got to see The Wedding Present live during this time, which I always regret. I did however, watch the VHS of **PUNK* over and over. It's fair to say they were my favourite band at the time. Their records were always on in my room. My older brother used to take the piss out of Gedge's singing voice something rotten, but I didn't care.

I sort of lost track of keeping up with the band's releases after *Bizarro*. Long story short, what followed was 15-plus years of financial hardship, a failed marriage, depression and crippling social anxiety. I found that I couldn't enjoy a night out, or even daft things like a trip to the supermarket, without feeling uneasy or anxious, and was spending far too much time at home where I felt more comfortable. But The Wedding Present were still getting played during these times.

Iain Anderson and daughter Leah with Melanie Howard

I managed to get back on my feet (more or less) financially around 2015. Sometime later, and for my own mental wellbeing more than anything, I decided to confront my social anxiety head on. I saw that The Wedding Present were touring with the 30th anniversary of *Tommy*. I bought a pair of tickets for me and my youngest daughter, Leah.

On the night of the gig, I was so anxious about being in a crowded place that we almost didn't go. Leah talked me round. She loves going to gigs, and she was 13 at the time and already had more gigs under her belt than I'd seen in my whole life. She knew her way around the O2 Academy in Newcastle which came in handy, too.

When we got into the room, I looked over at the merch stand and was surprised to see David Gedge putting out the CDs, t-shirts, etc. Sheepishly, I went over and had a look at the merch and chatted to David for a while. I was amazed how down to earth the bloke was. No airs and graces at all. I said that I'd been a fan for years but this was the first time I'd seen them live. I didn't want to bore him with my story as he seemed concerned that the place wasn't very full, but I said it was probably down to Ed Sheeran playing two nights at St James' Park. Most folk would probably leave home later to avoid the traffic for that.

He signed some merch for me and said I could keep my purchases behind the merch stand until after the gig.

Sure enough, the place filled up and the show was superb. I was totally at ease. I was surrounded by people more or less my age, all having a good night too. Gedge even made mention of Sheeran being in town during the show. It was a thrill to hear 'You Should Always Keep In Touch With Your Friends' performed live too, as it was the song that drew my attention in the first place. It was a 'full circle' kind of moment. Leah had a good night, too.

We saw the band again on the *Bizarro* anniversary tour. Another great gig. I also got a 'follow' from David on Twitter, so happy times.

I WAKE UP SCREAMING

EDWARD KOMOCKI

Of the many occasions throughout my life which I file in my head as 'opportunities missed' and which, given the moment again could be better resolved, two music-related experiences stand out. One was after a Dinosaur Jr concert in Glasgow, when I was accosted by a particularly large and drunken Scotsman who erroneously claimed that during the show, I'd referred to him as 'that cunt!' Now, how he could have heard anything given the ear-bleeding volume of that gig is beyond me, but for the sake of avoiding a ruckus, I offered an apology on behalf of whoever had provided that salutation and beat a hasty but unscathed retreat. Of course, 20 minutes later I had at my disposal a plethora of witty and scathing put-downs just ready to trip off my tongue which would have showed him! Ha! Yeah, yeah… like I said at the start, wise after the event.

The second is my Wedding Present/Cinerama moment of regret. As a student attending a tutorial on the early theories of Freud, his adaptation of the 'Nirvana Principle' was raised and explained as 'the effort to reduce, to keep constant or to remove internal tension due to stimuli.' We were then asked to offer illustrations to support this and of course, the usual Freudian psychosexual examples were trotted out with varying degrees of acknowledgement (for the record, my suggestion of an over-excited child unwrapping presents on Christmas morning was met with raised eyebrows and a solemn shake of the tutor's head). And then, walking home afterwards with headphones in and 'Flying Saucer' coming to its crashing conclusion, came that moment of epiphany. The example I should have given 20 minutes ago, now so blindingly obvious. The Wedding Present! Cinerama! Oh, let me go back… please!

Now assuming my grasp of this theory is at least partially correct, then The Wedding Present and Cinerama demonstrate the 'Nirvana Principle' perfectly! This concept postulates that it's not the building of excitement to a peak of ecstasy that delivers ultimate pleasure, it's the sudden dramatic release of this heightened tension to a state of complete quiescence that is so ultimately delightful. The sudden and complete shift from peak to trough! From everything, instantaneously to nothing.

That's The Wedding Present or Cinerama. Think any of 'Anyone Can Make A Mistake', 'Take Me!', 'What Have I Said Now?', 'Flying Saucer', 'Two Bridges', 'Perfect Blue', 'Wow', 'See Thru' and 'Honey Rider'! If one characteristic style typifies The Wedding Present and Cinerama's music, it's that escalating wall-of-sound that rises to a gigantic climax and then abruptly ceases, leaving us drained but released.

'I Wake Up Screaming' is the ultimate example. Maybe not as insistent as 'Kennedy' or intense as 'Starry Eyed', but it has one of DLG's greatest 'builds', from the gentle delicacy of strings and hushed female vocals to its tumultuous crescendo, by way of a guitar strum, that accelerates seemingly from crotchets to semihemidemisemiquavers (yes… they do exist!) and the thrashing of a set of cymbals to within an inch of their shiny lives. And then it stops, instantly. And relieved but exhausted, we can at last take a breath once more. Perfection… or maybe we should really say, Nirvana.

So I wished I'd listened to 'Flying Saucer' on the way to that tutorial, piped up with a musical example and then had the chance to wax lyrical on the joys of their music. But as for the Dinosaur Jr gig, it's probably wise not to wish for a chance to relive that. After all, there's no likelihood of Nirvana on the end of a Glasgow Kiss!

ANYONE CAN MAKE A MISTAKE

JACEK RATAJCZYK

The first Wedding Present song I ever heard was 'Kennedy', the video to which I saw on MTV back in 1990. Although I didn't quite get the lyrics, I instantly loved the song, its melody, David's voice and the beautiful crescendo of guitars. Though Poland was by then again a free democratic country, it still wasn't easy to buy records from British or American artists, especially Indie acts such as The Wedding Present. It wasn't until a few years later that I got hold of a copy of *George Best* and, boy, did I love it! Among many gems my absolute fave was 'Anyone Can Make A Mistake'. Three minutes of sheer guitar pop perfection – superb tune, frantically fast guitar playing, the distinctive voice of David and – last but not least – the bitter, sorrowful and so relatable story of a failed relationship.

'Kennedy' was the first song Jacek Ratajczyk heard by The Wedding Present

I have never, regretfully, seen The Wedding Present live, but if I ever do I hope they'll play the song. I am sure I will not remain seated because every time I hear the song it makes me want to pogo, or join Peter Solowka and play some lunatic air guitar with him.

BEWITCHED

JASON MULLIGAN

'Bewitched' just captures that moment in time when I was young and carefree. My friends and I used to have the best times in Leeds at gigs and nightclubs such as The Phono, Lizard Club and The Stomp at the Polytechnic, along with The Chocolate Factory. The latter two played loads of Wedding Present. That particular gig at the Poly captures that moment in time perfectly. When the band played 'Bewitched' I was roughly at the front, having had a few beers with great, like-minded friends, and I just danced (as much as you can at the front). Amongst the fab setlist they played that night, for me that's the song which takes me back. It never fails to put a smile on my face and my feet always begin to tap.

For Jason Mulligan, 'Betwitched' captures a moment in time

DEER CAUGHT IN THE HEADLIGHTS

CHARLIE LAYTON, FORMER WEDDING PRESENT DRUMMER

When considering the extensive back catalogue of the band, there are many songs that I could choose from, though I'm going with one of the first tracks I helped birth, 'Deer Caught In The Headlights'.

I write this twelve years on from then, and it's all so very vivid. Terry (de Castro) sat on a chair playing one of David's guitars in a rehearsal room in Culver City, Los Angeles.

Terry brought in the initial idea, which was perky and had an idea for a 'jerky' guitar part, then it was Graeme (Ramsay) – also being a drummer – who steered me to the drum breaks in the verse.

The track starts with David's slide on the 'e-guitar' (which still makes me think

Photo: Richard Houghton

Charlie Layton has chosen a song he helped write

of the *Looney Tunes* theme!) and has an aggressive energy from the intro and through the first verse as it breaks down in the chorus before racing away again. Repeat until it goes super soft in the middle eight and then clouts you round the ears again. In the words of my great-pal, Mr Ramsay: 'YAS Chaz!'

'Deer' is a track I always loved popping into a set. That outro – almost two minutes of it! This is a song born during eight days of rehearsals for the *Bizarro* 21st anniversary tour (in 2012) and then bashed into shape on that subsequent North American tour.

That outro is written to be played live, but also written in a *Bizarro*-esque style, albeit short in comparison to some on that album. Having been written during a period of playing songs like 'Granadaland' and 'Take Me!' everyday, perhaps it was inevitable that new songs such as this would take on some of their flavour.

We played 'Deer' at a fundraising gig at the (sadly departed) Borderline in Soho in 2015, rocking out so much that I collapsed off my drum stool at the end. Clearly a sign of great song being played to the limit – as it should be! Listen LOUD.

BRASSNECK

NICOLA FARRER

For Nicola Farrer, you can't beat a bit of 'Brassneck'

I've been listening to the Weddoes since I was about 15! I'm 47 now and still feel the emotional connection to David's music. It's too hard to pick one favourite but 'Brassneck' is an anthem for West Yorkshire! The stream of consciousness every verse offers is something we will all relate to at some point in our lives. It has a superb musical ending, from the intense frustration to acceptance. I'll never forget waking up early on a Saturday morning and manoeuvring around my mum who was hoovering, me with the VHS at the ready, to hit the record button for the new video of 'Brassneck' as it featured on one of those early morning TV shows.

I had a good friend in upper school, Stephen, who I'd hang out with quite a bit on the weekends and we'd often take the 15-to-20 minute walk through Wibsey village towards our houses. Around halfway, Stephen would say goodbye and we'd walk in opposite directions. We loved the same Indie music, went to a few gigs, etc. One day, Stephen stopped and took my hands into his and said, 'You know that Wedding Present song, 'Don't Talk, Just Kiss'? I've wanted to say that to you for a while now. How about it?'

And he leaned in for a kiss – so we shared a kiss. But I really didn't feel the spark and our friendship kind of fizzled out from then. Bless. I do miss him!

I met the band too, years ago. I was at a gig at the Duchess of York pub in Leeds – man, that place was brilliant. I was wearing my beloved 'Kennedy' t-shirt and saw 'The Gedge' standing at the bar. My friend said, 'What have you got to lose? Go over and say hello,' so I did. A couple of weeks earlier, my parents had been shopping in Habitat in Leeds and saw David and Sally, who was his girlfriend at the time. My dad told him his daughter was a big fan and asked David would he sign a scrap of paper, otherwise I wouldn't believe they'd met him (he was such a joker, my dad, that I wouldn't have!). That was my opening point to start a conversation with them. The Family Cat were playing, maybe supporting another band, and I remember David saying I was brave to wear my Weddoes t-shirt to a Family Cat gig. Maybe there was a bit of friendly rivalry about that time. David ended up giving me a ride to the train station to catch the train back to my home town of Bradford.

WOW

TIM KNIGHT

I was late to Cinerama but the extended version of 'Wow' is just wow!

I'M FROM FURTHER NORTH THAN YOU

BARBARA HOEFGEN

Back in 2004 I had my two bands, Gloria and Dorian, and was introduced to Simon Cleave by Paul Greco, as they both lived in Cologne at that time. Simon liked our music a lot and suggested to David that he invite us to support them on their *Take Fountain* tour in Germany. And it happened. We were over the moon! One of my favourite songs from their set was 'I'm From Further North Than You'.

Photo: Hines-Images

Barbara Hoefen has chosen 'I'm From Further North Than You'

The years passed and I kept in touch with David and Jessica. In 2010, they again invited me to support them on their European tour with my new band, Precious Few, and in 2011 we had the pleasure of playing at David's festivals, *At The Edge Of The Sea* in Brighton and *At The Edge Of The Peaks* in Holmfirth. It was just amazing for us. Every band was asked to cover one Wedding Present song. Guess what? We chose 'Further North' and it went very well. So we added it to our set when we went on a German tour again with the Weddoes in 2017.

So 'I'm From Further North Than You' has become a very special song for me and brings back fond memories of a wonderful time with my bands and with David, Jessica and all the other lovely band members!

KENNEDY
TONY WALKLEY

'Kennedy' came out just as I was becoming a Peel addict in my early teens and was my first intro to the Weddoes. I bought it on cassette single (remember those?) and instantly fell in love with 'Unfaithful' too. Musically, everything changed for me around that time.

TAKE ME!
STEFAN HIRT

I'm 40 years old and from Germany. Not least because of my age, I have been a latecomer to The Wedding Present. I only encountered their music in about 2005 through a CD in the German *Rolling Stone* magazine entitled 'Boys Will Be Girls (The Roots Of Britpop)' and a collection of *C86* stuff. It featured 'This Boy Can Wait', and while the rest of the CD didn't impress me that much, with The Wedding Present I was immediately thrilled. At that time, I was listening mostly to The Libertines, The Cooper Temple Clause and all those other 'The' bands. I liked the way these guys played their guitars, but I always felt that there was something still missing. So, when I listened to 'This Boy Can Wait' for the first time, I knew immediately that this was how a guitar should sound. It was exactly what I had been looking for in the past years.

I immediately started digging up everything from The Wedding Present that I could find, and it helped that the band at that time released a new album and even visited Tübingen, where I studied. I went to see them with some friends, and I still remember the astonished comment from one of them: 'I never knew it was possible to play the guitar like that.'

Since then, I have been steadily listening to their music. I love the new stuff, I love the old stuff. I enjoy songs like 'Give My Love To Kevin' or 'Anyone Can Make A

Mistake', whilst the instrumental parts of 'Kennedy', 'Granadaland', 'What Have I Said Now?' or 'Flying Saucer' make me jump through the room even after a full day of work and childcare.

'Take Me!' is a song that I hadn't paid much attention to at the beginning. I guess I heard it once, decided that it wasn't what I was looking for, and then steadily skipped it. It was only after desperately searching for new Wedding Present experiences that I put it on my car's playlist on a longer road trip. At first, I didn't pay much attention to it, but then suddenly I realised that there was some long instrumental part that kept me slowly but steadily moving on the driver's seat. I started to listen to the song properly, and I thoroughly enjoyed the riffs, the drums, and I noticed that I didn't want it to stop. I truly didn't. I just wished that it would keep on like that – and it did! In very rare cases, a guitar riff can truly make you happy, create instant pleasure, and this song is such a rare case.

When it was over, I was both thrilled and disappointed, I wished it would have continued just like that, so I started the song again. And again, and again. The trip took me two hours, and most of the time I was listening to just this song.

I then decided that this is a song to be truly enjoyed at home. Of course, it made me want to dance, but not in a crazy way, more in a concentrated manner... It slowly put me into a trance. I kept listening to the music and the way that the instruments repeated, varied and renewed the basic theme. It is astonishing how in a song that is nine minutes long, each individual chord and sound is in its right place and doing exactly the right thing. Of course, I listened and danced to it again, and again... and while this has indeed become my favourite kind of physical exercise, what strikes me even more is how this song has become kind of a spiritual exercise for me as well.

KENNEDY
STÉPHANE DUPIN

I'm a fan from France, and I've been following The Wedding Present since 1992. The Wedding Present is the only Indie-rock band I listen to, and they have been at my side during most of my life! My favourite song is 'Kennedy'. A friend of mine lent me a cassette of the Pixies, and put The Wedding Present on the second side. I was supposed to listen to the Pixies, but after dozens of listens to the cassette, I realised that I was

Stéphane Dupin's choice is 'Kennedy' even though his headbanging might frighten his children

reversing it because of The Wedding Present, and especially because of 'Kennedy'. I could not do anything during this song but close my eyes and bang my head. I used to listen to it in my car and that was the same. I admit it was dangerous for me to listen to Kennedy in these conditions…!

I have listened to 'Kennedy' throughout the last 20 years, but only in special moments, when I am in a very good or a very bad mood. But I listen to it very, very loud, every time. Now I'm a father of two children, and I don't want them to see me listening to 'Kennedy' as they might be scared, seeing me banging my head while the guitars are screaming and the drums are destroying the speakers!

SHE'S MY BEST FRIEND

JOAKIM CLAR

Although it's a cover, it was one of the first songs I heard and got hooked right away.

ONCE MORE & TAKE ME!

JOHN ELVIDGE

John Elvidge couldn't narrow it down to one

I was travelling in my car along Canterbury Road, Westgate, one evening in 1985, returning to my home in Margate, listening to Janice Long. I hadn't paid attention to who she was going to play next but as soon as I heard the first few bars of 'Once More', the radio was immediately wound up to full blast. Thankfully, and unlike some DJs, Janice confirmed at the end of the single who the artist was, and from that moment on I was hooked; recording subsequent releases played by John Peel, including the 1986 session, and eagerly purchasing *George Best* as soon as it was released. I followed up with *Tommy*, and was over the moon, at long last, to be able to play 'Once More' in the car, as I was fortunate, by that time, to have a CD player fitted.

I waited patiently for the release of *Bizarro*, which was rammed into the car CD player upon purchase. Although I was taken aback by the opening track, 'Brassneck', I was most impressed, and not a little overjoyed, to hear it surpassed by the blistering 'Take Me!', which remains my absolute favourite to this day.

I'm by no means a hardline follower but have always considered myself to be a fan, with Wedding Present tracks regularly featuring on compilation CDs I've made for the car, and 'Once More' and 'Take Me!' appearing every time on the noisier compilations. Now, and primarily thanks to social media, we're all able to enjoy events such as the recent Brighton Pavilion acoustic jaunt, in that case while working from home.

From the mid '80s to mid '90s, my listening interest lay mainly with Sarah Records, along with other similar sounds such as They Go Boom!! which I still consider to be my overall favourites. But David & Co are always up there in the top crowd.

MY FAVOURITE DRESS

ALEXANDER GARDINER

It's got to be 'My Favourite Dress'. No better song of unrequited love has ever been written.

BLUE EYES

BILL BRYANT

For Bill Bryant and his wife Jen 'Blue Eyes' is their song

The Wedding Present song 'Blue Eyes' occupies a special place in mine and my wife Jen's hearts. We both attended the same university in 1995 and had been platonic friends for a few years. We bonded over a shared love for all things British, especially the music of the post-punk pop scene. We enjoyed discovering bands that were not well known in the US and thought we were the coolest kids in school. The romantic feelings between us blossomed the night she returned from six months abroad. We sat in a darkened room and expressed our feelings for one another. We talked long enough that the CD playing in the background, *Hit Parade 1*, went back to the first song, 'Blue Eyes'. We shared our first kiss as David Gedge sang, 'I don't think I've ever mentioned this before but I couldn't possibly love you any more.' It became 'our special song'.

After 22 years of marriage, we recently dropped our only child off at college. As we drove away, tears in our eyes, to start a new phase of life, I plugged in my iPhone and looked over at my wife as those familiar lyrics filled the car:

I don't think I've mentioned this before but I couldn't possibly love you any more

CRUSHED

DAVE WOOLNER

The year was 1990. I had a new girlfriend. Tara worked in the office next to mine. We both had VW Beetles and we were both pretty much into the same stuff, possibly with the exception of music. She was into reggae and hip-hop while I was into Indie stuff. Tara knew I was a big fan of The Wedding Present and I think she secretly was, mainly because she was forced to listen to it in my car.

In May 1991, she surprised me with some tickets. The Wedding Present were playing in an unusual location about five miles from where I was living, at a place called Penyrheol Leisure Centre (correct pronunciation 'Pen-Err-Re-All', although the locals tend to call it 'Pen-Rowl') about seven miles from Swansea. I used to go swimming there with school and my mates and would be shocked if anyone from that area had ever heard of The Wedding Present. I was really chuffed they were playing so near.

It was a decent-sized theatre. I don't remember the audience being particularly big but everyone was drinking and having a good time. The band came on and were just as fantastic as I remember from the Manchester concert that I'd seen a couple of years before. The set was a good number of songs in, when I noticed Tara looking down and hobbling a bit. She wasn't injured but shouted in my ear, 'I've lost my shoe!' She was wearing Dr Marten shoes (which were pretty sensible for her). We looked at each other and started laughing hysterically, although I don't know if this was at the ridiculousness of her managing to lose a Dr Marten or if we were imagining some shoe getting hoofed around a crowded dancefloor with no hope of retrieval. We got some strange looks from people as we meandered our way through the hyperactive crowd, looking like a pair of buffoons with our heads down whilst David Gedge was singing his lungs out.

We couldn't find the shoe and decided to just carry on dancing, with only 75 per cent shoe capacity between us. The set finished about 20 minutes later. The lights came on, the crowd dispersed and we went hunting for the shoe whilst trying to look cool. It was found within minutes amongst a pile of plastic beer glasses and had survived relatively unscathed, which was just as well as we had a five mile walk ahead of us.

We married in 1997 and to this day still have a giggle about 'the shoe incident' and how on earth it came off. Now, I don't know if 'Crushed' was playing at the time of the walkabout, or even if it was played that night, but, whenever I hear it, I just think of Dr Martens and that night.

GONE
MATT HOLLAND

So simple yet so perceptive lyrically, and powerful musically. It perfectly summed up the ambivalence I felt about my own (intense, on-again/off-again) relationship with a particularly volatile partner at the time (early '90s). We both loved The Wedding Present, though not for the same reasons.

For Matt Holland 'Gone' summed up his ambivalence about his relationship

A MILLION MILES
PAUL TYACK

I was a young and naive 18-year-old when I first heard it and it struck a chord (Dm, probably). There was a girl I liked an awful lot and one weekend I found the chance to talk to her. Reciting the lyrics was a somewhat risky strategy but it turned out she knew of the Weddoes and loved the song too. That wonderful night is forever intertwined with the song.

TAKE ME!
MICHAEL G JACKSON

'Take Me!' for the line, 'And, oh, that feeling when your hand returns to mine,' reminds me of my late teens.

BRASSNECK
MARK FORAN

My favourite song changes over time as I've been listening to The Wedding Present and Cinerama consistently for three decades. There always seems to be a track or album perfect for your mood or for what's going on in your life, etc. It all started with 'Brassneck' for me. A workmate said he had been listening to the band for a while and that they were on *Top Of The Pops* that night. And there was David Gedge and the rest clearly not wanting to be there. With the performance (or non-performance), my first instinct was 'what is this?' but by the end of the song I was transfixed. It's such an amazing track (the album version is good but the single version is amazing) and has been high on my playlist ever since. And that was it – I couldn't get enough after that. By far my favourite band and I don't think it is a stretch to say that 'Brassneck' changed my music taste forever.

I once read a cult heroes article in *The Guardian* which said, 'Once Gedge got under your skin, it was an Indie mafia sort of deal – you were in for life'. That was definitely the case for me.

Mark Foran thinks being a Wedding Present fan is like being in the Indie mafia

NO NOMINATION
ANDY MOULDYCLIFF

I'm not the only one, I'm sure, but I can't choose a favourite Wedding Present song. However, I thought it worthwhile to jot down a few thoughts about the wonderful 'journey' that David Lewis Gedge has taken me on for the last 35 years. It all really began in the run-up to Christmas 1987.

I was just beginning my obsession with John Peel's *Festive 50*, and although The Smiths dominated the chart overall with a record-breaking eleven songs, The Weddoes dominated the top ten, with four entries. So if this was an exercise in describing 'one's first love' then I would say it would have to be the top three entries in that year's *Festive 50*. These were 'A Million Miles' at number eight, 'My Favourite Dress' sneaking in two places higher at six, and 'Everyone Thinks He Looks Daft', which was the band's highest entry at three.

One of my better decisions that year was to record the *Festive 50* onto a cassette (note to kids – ask your parents what tapes are!). I still have boxes of them to this day, from 1987 up to 2004, shortly after Peel's untimely death. The loyal Wedding Present fans always ensured that the band were always well represented when it came to the end of year countdown of the best songs of the year, with only The Fall appearing more than them.

Of course, David Gedge himself was also rather obsessed with the *Festive 50*. In 1990, Peel rang him up whilst broadcasting the rundown and asked him to comment on that year's entries, which incidentally totalled a very healthy six in number. I must confess that I was not a fan of *Seamonsters* when I bought it (predictably on cassette!). I love the Pixies and the work that producer Albini did with them, but for whatever reason, I just couldn't connect with the album. I actually preferred the session versions of the likes of 'Dalliance', 'Corduroy' and 'Crawl' that the band recorded for Peel. However, when I revisited the album prior to the virtual 30th anniversary gigs that the band performed in 2021, it all made sense and I'd probably say it is now just about my favourite album of theirs.

I'd say 'just about' because I can't really separate it from *Take Fountain*, which maintains a ridiculously high standard throughout from the brooding and magnificent 'Interstate 5' to the tear-inducing love song that is 'Perfect Blue'.

However, that doesn't answer the question of what my favourite song is. I've certainly mentioned some of them in this piece, but I feel a bit like a kid in a sweet shop, in that there's so much choice and I really don't know where to start! One day it'll be a more obvious selection, such as 'Come Play With Me', whereas on another, it'll be a more esoteric choice, like 'Fleshworld' that takes me to an unimagined high! Just to continue the sweet shop analogy, I feel there's plenty of gems that I still haven't discovered. The enjoyment that one gets from hearing a Wedding Present song for the first time, or rediscovering a forgotten classic, really is where the pleasure comes from!

Hope that (partly) answers the question!

DON'T TALK, JUST KISS

BOB JOHNSON

Bob Johnson votes for 'Don't Talk, Just Kiss'

Much as I love the Albini reworking of 'Brassneck', 'Don't Talk, Just Kiss' was the highlight of what was a very strong EP. 'Look, everybody lies about this, don't talk, just kiss!' And it was pandemonium when they played it live, the moshpit becoming very lively indeed, especially in the frenetic chorus! I'm also a big fan of 'I'm Not Always So Stupid', the B-side to 'Nobody's Twisting Your Arm', where the guitars, whilst still frantic, positively chime. 'Every time a car drives past I think it's you…'

ALWAYS THE QUIET ONE

KAREY PARSONS

Karey Parsons is always the quiet one

I am the quiet one and I love *Take Fountain*. I know it's a really personal album for David Gedge, and it's definitely one of my favourites. Though I love Cinerama, the return of The Wedding Present felt significant and important, and that album is very special to me. It was released not long after my mum died, and everything felt very different after that. Things that were familiar and from more carefree and youthful times, gave me energy, and I was just very grateful that The Wedding Present were back and creating such a fantastic album.

There are so many brilliant, poignant and beautiful tracks on *Take Fountain*, so I could have chosen several, but 'Always The Quiet One' made me smile – and feel a little sad – from first listen. I don't have anything clever or insightful to say about it, I just love those bittersweet lyrics, that perfect and vivid broken-hearted love story David Gedge conjures up in three minutes, and that strangely jaunty melody for this tale of lost love and lost opportunities. Sometimes it still makes an appearance in the band's live sets and I'm always delighted to hear those first few bars.

And, if we meet again, how I'd actually speak to you
Here's the funny part; I wouldn't know where to start
That's because I'm always the quiet one
You've already gone

COME PLAY WITH ME

GARETH WILLIAMS

Richard Weir is a fan of 'Interstate 5'

1992 was a special year. I was a student and had recently met the girl who is now my wife. The *Hit Parade* singles were the soundtrack to my world, at a time when I learned to fall in love, and I realised my life had changed forever. I have particularly fond memories of whiling away a day in my girlfriend's house, listening to 'Come Play With Me' on repeat.

INTERSTATE 5

RICHARD WEIR

The brooding intensity of 'Interstate 5' is always really special. It builds and builds and the vocal has DLG's trademark longingness but also all the attributes to be in a film noir. Magnificent.

MY FAVOURITE DRESS

ANDREW COLLINS, WRITER AND BROADCASTER

Some history. In the first half of 2013, I decided to build a musical playlist for my iPod (remember those?), consisting at that time of only the very best songs ever committed to vinyl, disc, tape or the ether. According to me. Some rules first, because without rules, you have anarchy. I err towards the caricature of the male gender. Rule #1: no artist is allowed more than one song, unless they recorded under another name, or with another artist (the Supremes and Diana Ross are counted as two; likewise, Carter USM and the solo Jim Bob; and so on...) I forced myself, subjectively, and personally, to select only the very pinnacle of a chosen artist's repertoire before entering into the hallowed halls of The 143.

I'd originally intended to create a playlist of 50. Bearing in mind I only had 11,988 songs already uploaded and stored, to choose from at that moment. I flew past 50, and then 75, then the 100 mark. I stopped when I'd gathered every vital song by every vital artist in my library, and I found that I had 143. These became The 143. At which point, it became gospel.

I reached my quest when I reached 143; with 'Rattlesnakes' by Lloyd Cole and the Commotions. Each entry is logged and catalogued, and blogged, to varying degrees of fastidiousness. I've been writing about music since the electric typewriter, sometimes for money, sometimes – as here – for pure pleasure.

The 143 are by their nature personal. (In one of the more surreal passages of my life, Richard Fairbrass of Right Said Fred blocked me on Twitter because he felt it arrogant of me to choose my 143 favourite songs. Each to their own.)

So that's what I was aiming for. And, after much soul searching, chose The Wedding Present, and their favourite of all my Wedding Present presents.

Artist: The Wedding Present
Title: My Favourite Dress
Description: single; album track, George Best
Label: Reception
Release date: 1987
First heard: 1987

That was my favourite dress, you know
That was my favourite dress
Ohhh

I feel fairly certain that the first song by The Wedding Present I ever heard was their rumbustious cover of 'Felicity', which must have been the version from their first Peel session in 1986, when I was still at college. I know I sat up by the stereo and taped the songs I didn't already have from his *Festive 50* at the end of that year and counted 'Felicity' (number 36) and 'Once More' (number 16) among numerous other cherishable gems on that live-paused cassette, like 'This Is Motortown' by the Very Things, 'Kiss' by Age Of Chance and 'Truck Train Tractor' by The Pastels. In another year dominated by The Smiths – indeed, in an era dominated by The Smiths, Jesus & Mary Chain and New Order, the three Colossi of Indie – The Wedding Present felt like young, short-trousered pretenders, and were all the more thrilling for it. (Though of course they, too, would come to dominate the Peelscape, and with perhaps more purchase on Peel's soul, a possession more akin to that exerted by The Fall.)

Remember that feeling of suddenly being overcome by the need to commit? I don't mean to a girl in a favourite dress. I mean to a band. You've heard them on Peel, you've taped them off the radio, you've read about them in the *NME*; now it's time to buy the album. You don't have bottomless pockets; to fork out for an LP is a major declaration of love. Remember how stung you felt when you spent that week's allowance from your grant on 'Dali's Car' by Dali's Car because it was Pete Murphy and Mick Kahn from pre-accredited bands and you'd found the single hooky on *Max Headroom* or some other video show? An LP you wished you'd never bought was a shot through the heart. A waste of money.

When I bought *George Best* on the strength of all those Peel tracks I knew it would be a sound investment. Well, if I didn't like the record, I would always want that sleeve in my collection. I loved the record as much as I loved the sleeve. I loved it more. Its locomotive guitar and drums combined under Chris Allison's sympathetic, heads-down production to provide a new way to travel for the grown-up Indie kid. There was something so right about David Gedge's lovesick northern ballads, set to his and Peter Solowka's never-ending riffs which were as raw and plaintive as the woes of the songs' packed-in protagonists, whom we all suspected were Gedge himself – a man near-permanently let down, finished with, betrayed or two-timed by girls. Gedge was a few years older than me, but I identified with his struggle. Being single is the great leveller. I was newly single when I bought *George Best* and would soon be living in my first one-room studio flat, the perfect cell in which to lose myself in The Wedding Present's breakneck melancholia.

'My Favourite Dress' is my favourite Wedding Present song. I think of it as definitive, and for all the constant pleasures Gedge has supplied since, as The Wedding Present and Cinerama, it remains unassailable. It pretty much breaks my heart each time I listen to it. Gedge's pained recollection of uneaten meals, a lonely star, a long walk home, the pouring rain and a six-hour wait, leads inexorably up to this image of an ex's dress. We who have fallen under Gedge's spell have all imagined what that dress might look like. My first imagining – a floral print dress, maybe Oxfam, perhaps worn under a cardigan – is hard to shake.

There are two reasons why this song is magic. One is the decisive moan Gedge delivers after the last line. There are a lot of important 'ohs' in pop music, but this is one to bruise your ribs from the inside. The second is the one minute and 24 seconds of outro, which rises and falls from that thousand-words 'Ohhh' to the final, undressed jangle. I wouldn't mind if it lasted a bit longer. It's not even the end of the album, merely the end of side one.

When I finally met Gedge and interviewed the band in 1991 in snowbound Minnesota where they were recording their third album *Seamonsters*, he and I agreed to disagree that *George Best* was a classic album because it wasn't perfect; he felt it could be improved. I don't have that copy of the *NME* to hand, but if you do, look it up. *George Best* and its zenith, 'My Favourite Dress', remains so, and has yet to be improved.

TAKE ME!
SIMON SMITH

I recall being in the moshpit at a gig when 'Take Me!' was played. After about eight minutes of jumping around and being pushed and pummelled about by overweight blokes old enough to know better, I was absolutely knackered, bent over with hands on my knees – and then the band launched right into 'Kennedy'. I just let out an anguished 'oh no!' and got on with another three or four brutal minutes. Wrecked. But brilliant.

WHY ARE YOU BEING SO REASONABLE NOW?
SIMON PARKER

It is partially David Gedge's fault that I wear floral shirts. My love of floral print shirts can definitely be traced back to the video for 'Why Are You Being So Reasonable Now?' after the video to said single was first aired on Saturday morning's *The Chart Show*. I'd often be sartorially inspired after watching the Indie section of the show, only to then trudge hopefully into Fosters Menswear (located in my hometown of Chichester, West Sussex) in the vain hope of finding something cool to wear in my own band. 'Why Are You Being So Reasonable Now?' saw David Gedge looking dapper in some sort of floral monstrosity which I could not find on my high street. I still wonder where he got that shirt from. My attraction to floral print shirts began in earnest on that Saturday. As I browse my wardrobe now, Mr David Gedge certainly has quite a lot to answer for...

TAKE ME!
JOHN HAMILTON

A four-minute song with an incredible five-minute jam session at the end. It sends shivers down the spine, but then so do many other Wedding Present songs.

KENNEDY
STEVEN GALLIN

I have a few but I have to say 'Kennedy' as that is what I named my daughter.

SOMETHING AND NOTHING

PAUL YENDLE

Paul Yendle's friend thought 'Something And Nothing' was rubbish

I love 'Something And Nothing' and the spoken intro discussing how it sounds. I was driving in my car playing *George Best* loudly when my buddy said, 'What's this rubbish? They can't play their instruments!' That's when I realised he was wrong and I was right (about lots of things) and our friendship was never the same again. He went on to become an independent financial adviser whilst I travelled the world for years so I think I made the right call.

NOT FROM WHERE I'M STANDING

ROMAN HEEREN

I still love the power of 'Not From Where I'm Standing' or 'Don't Laugh', especially when David, Simon or Peter remove the handbrake. It reminds me of being 17 again and buying the vinyl in Camden when I was an exchange student in Southampton.

MANHATTAN

PAUL MORGAN

'Manhattan'. Or 'Ears'. Or 'Heels'. I may be the only person who loves Cinerama and has never really heard any Wedding Present.

TAKE ME!

MIKE TWEDDLE

I'd been writing a fanzine (*Inkslinger*), even interviewing the Weddoes at a blinding gig at Leeds Uni in 1987 supported by Cud and This Poison!, before I ran out of money. I decided to head down to London Village to earn my fame and fortune. That didn't quite work out, as I ended up working as a labourer on a building site with a load of dodgy Spurs fans. And my beautiful accommodation? I ended up staying at Pentonville

'Take Me!' reminds Mike Tweddle of escaping from Pentonville nick

Prison… not at Her Majesty's pleasure but at my step brother's place as he was a prison officer. The dilapidated Victorian officers' flats were in the prison grounds. Some of those officers would have been more suitable candidates as inmates! It was quite a rough time, but what got me through (apart from the copious amounts of alcohol) was going to gigs with mates and listening to the cracking tunes coming out on a daily basis. I still regard the late '80s as the halcyon days for music which have never been beaten. One album in particular seemed to hit every target for me and was played within an inch (well, twelve inches) of its life – *Bizarro*. Every single tune is a pure classic, but one in particular still resonates with me as much as it did all those years ago, 'Take Me!', with all nine or so minutes of that glorious swashbuckling sublime piece of splendiferous perfection. 'Take Me!' was forever cemented in my heart the day I left London to come home on the notorious night bus. I played that album, and mainly 'Take Me!', on a continuous loop on my Walkman cassette player until dawn was breaking. As I stepped off that smelly old bus, I was so glad to be back in the North and back in good old Darlington, and most definitely back home. The Weddoes did indeed 'Take Me!' back where I belong, and where I've been happy ever since.

HEALTH AND EFFICIENCY

JAMES ROBERTS

Just beautiful.

BEWITCHED

SIMON PEACE

The best song I've ever heard about the total anguish of failure and unrequited love.

CINERAMA
LISA ROBINSON, QUEEN OF THE MERCHANDISE

Criminally underrated, Cinerama certainly seem to divide opinion amongst fans of The Wedding Present, but I cannot imagine life without either one. They are two sides of the same musical coin; the night to the day, the hot to the cold, *the calm to the chaos*… you get the idea.

Cinerama is the manifestation of different facets of David's personality, psyche and imagination that couldn't exist in the world of The Wedding Present. He needed to express himself in new ways and explore other avenues beyond those confines, and the resulting exploration is a joyous, heartbreaking, beautiful, sexy and cinematic triumph of sound and lyrics.

It's an impossible task to choose my favourite song; it would be like being asked to choose your favourite child or favourite pair of shoes. Therefore, I'll try to sum up *why* I love Cinerama so much. I will preface this by saying I may be somewhat biased as I have known Mr. Gedge for a looooong time and I consider him to be one of my best friends, but I'm still able to recognise a damn good song when I hear it! I'm ridiculously proud of everything he has done, so when he told me he was 'taking a break' from TWP to pursue Cinerama, I actively encouraged him and was excited to hear his new venture. I was not, however, ready for the glorious Technicolor, Cinemascope, surround-sound, flutes-a-go-go, raunchy explosion that followed!

He and I share a love of Bond themes, John Barry, Henry Mancini, Ennio Morricone, French pop songs from the '60s and beyond, soundtracks to European (ahem) 'adult films' of the '60s and '70s… (I could go on!), and so it seemed like a natural progression for these influences to find their way into his work. I'm a sucker for a sweepingly cinematic violin in a film soundtrack that is designed to manipulate your emotions; it always succeeds in making me get teary-eyed. So the plethora of beautiful soaring orchestra scores within Cinerama songs that pull figuratively at the heartstrings is right up my Strasse!

Also, hands up who knew David could sound like he does with Cinerama? His voice is a million miles away from the angst-ridden growl of TWP. Here, he's much softer, quieter, more gentle, playful, wistful, melancholic and all the way over to lustful, 'Mr. Lover-Lover', sexy, and downright naughty! He plays a different role in each song – much like an actor does in a film – and he's able to inhabit the character so completely that you believe in and root for him 100 per cent. Although, 'cheating' is never cool!!! *Throws popcorn* 'Booooooo!'

Lyrically, David has an undeniable talent for making songwriting look easy. I like to write novels, and the exact same situation that would take me pages to describe and explain, David could capture perfectly in just one line, or verse. He can encapsulate a mood or feeling with just the right word, the inflection in his voice and the tones of light and shade in the music and make it all look effortless. And yet, I know it is far from easy, but it takes real skill to make it appear so.

Another element I love about Cinerama songs is *how damn catchy they are!* My mum would describe them as, 'songs that actually go somewhere!' By that, she means they are memorable and melodic, and you could find yourself humming or singing them afterwards. Heck, you can even *dance* to Cinerama songs! (I dance to songs by TWP too, but you know what I mean!), and the 'Boy Gedge' is actively *imploring* us to dance in 'Dance, Girl, Dance'. How many other bands can have you crying into your cornflakes one minute and then shimmying the next?!

I know David has told this story before (on the last *virtual* ATEOTS in 2021), but I am beyond delighted to have, unknowingly, been responsible for naming a Cinerama song. The title for the fabulous 'Cat Girl Tights' came from one of the many postcards I sent to him while I was living in Japan between 1998 and 2002. It was a vintage '60s advertising picture for the brand 'Cat Girl Tights' that I thought he might like. It was then at a gig in Newcastle, some time later, when he introduced a new song called 'Cat Girl Tights' that I whooped with surprise a little *too* audibly, and David quipped, 'Well, at least somebody likes it!' You would have had to stick a pin in me to get me down from the ceiling at that point!

I love how he isn't afraid to get 'intimate' in the lyrics, and even through today's supposed '*Woke Lens*' (*rolls eyes*), I don't find anything sexist or improper. If anything, Cinerama songs are actually paeans to womanhood – filled with love, wonder, adoration, trepidation, reverence and respect. The women in the lyrics are unafraid and get to take charge and *own* their sexuality and are, therefore, ultimately liberated. '*I don't wear underwear because it leaves a stripe*' is today's 'Burn Your Bras' of the 1960s. I also believe that if, the incredibly lovely, Sally Murrell (David's partner at the time, and delightful chanteuse of Cinerama) had had a problem with any of his lyrics or felt uncomfortable singing them she would have refused. To hear the two of them singing to each other is akin to Birkin and Gainsbourg's 'Je T'aime Moi Non Plus', and cold showers are needed all round!

'So, Lisa, are you able to mention any of your favourite songs?'

It's tough, but I'll give it a go! The 'orgasmic' 'Wow' is possibly one of the finest songs Mr Gedge has ever written (if I had to describe Cinerama to aliens from outer space, I'd maybe play them this song to help them 'get it'!). But c'mon, do I *really* need to explain why it's so bloody epic to readers of this book? No, because you all know why already, right?

If 'Wow' is full-on lust, then 'Health and Efficiency' is full-on beauty and innocence, and in complete contrast. Everything about this song is perfect; I literally have no other words to describe it. If you haven't got misty-eyed while listening to it, then you have no soul!

'King's Cross' is beautifully heart-breaking in its subtle sense of longing and knowing the relationship is doomed before it even began. With lines like:

I thought that you and me were never meant to be

and

So why was I there in the first place? I'm not sure
I think I wanted to spend the night with you and, though you wanted more

I'm not crying. *You're* crying!

I could list many more songs, but I'm aware I'd be taking over the whole book at this point! Even after writing all these words, I still haven't got near to expressing adequately how much I adore Cinerama. It sounds terribly 'flowery' to say that the songs make my heart sing, but they do. I have a physical reaction in my chest whenever I listen. I also ache at the songs of loss, regret and things that could never be. I feel euphoric at the songs that seem like a celebration of love, and my heart flies out of my chest like a kite. And as for the *'sexy'* songs? Well, that's for me to know…

Cinerama songs make me *FEEL* and remind me to live and celebrate life – the good and the bad times – as that's what makes us human and gives us a sense of a shared experience. To be able to bring people together through the power of song is a truly wonderful thing, and David should feel rightly proud of his incredible body of work.

PS. *PLEASE* can we have another Cinerama album?

WHAT HAVE I SAID NOW?

CHRISTIAN PÜLLENBERG

I remember cruising around in my old Volkswagen with my then best mate. We were both youngsters, around 18 or 19 years old, and we were music maniacs, listening to Indie stuff like Joy Division, The Smiths, Sisters of Mercy and Velvet Underground. One Friday afternoon, we were getting ready for the weekend ahead, riding around in that old Volkswagen with the music loud as possible. Our local radio station had a regular Indie music feature on Friday afternoons. The DJ was talking about concerts that were on that weekend and we were thinking about where to go. Right after the announcements, he played 'What Have I Said Now?'. Me and my mate were knocked over by the first chords, the monotonous intro never stopped and then David sang, 'About what I said just before...' Me and my mate were perplexed. Who was that? We had never heard anything like that before. We were looking at each other, shouting all these 'wooows' and 'uuuuhhhs'. I remember my buddy yelling at me, 'Shut the fuck up! I want to know the band's name.' Right after the song was over, we drove to our local record dealer and bought *Bizarro*.

CAROLYN

ERIK SCOTT

I remember seeing the Weddoes play that one live, and the ending was a total goosebump moment for me.

ONCE MORE

ROBERT BENNETT

'Once More' is just simply my all-time favourite song and it will be played at my funeral.

TAKE ME!

PAUL SPENCER

Paul Spencer turns to 'Take Me!' when he needs cheering up

While I've heard The Wedding Present perform 'Take Me!' live lots of times, it is the album version that I turn to in order to cheer myself up either before or after a day at work when I'm stressed or just not feeling it. I walk to work, and my route takes me about ten minutes across three big fields. It is a lovely walk and I enjoy the nature, the wildlife, the changing seasons and seeing what the farmer is up to. Usually I listen to podcasts, and my ten minutes of solitude before and after work is my favourite part of the day.

Sometimes however, I may have had a particularly stressful day or I'm not looking forward to going in for whatever reason. On these occasions, I'll play 'Take Me!' at full blast through my AirPods. The duration of the song lasts almost the exact time it takes to walk between home and the gate at work. The sheer euphoria of the song, and the guitar building to greater and greater heights never fails to improve my mood and put a spring back into my step. A masterpiece.

CORDUROY
DANIEL ERSKINE

As a newer-generation fan of The Wedding Present (millennial – eugh), 'Corduroy' is the first song I listened to and which led to really 'getting' The Wedding Present. The fuzzy melody, Gedge's signature vocal sound and the unique lyrics really struck a chord with me. I now own several Wedding Present albums but keep coming back to 'Corduroy'.

OCTOPUSSY
NEIL WALKER

'Octopussy' isn't anywhere near being my personal favourite song by The Wedding Present. It isn't even the best song on its parent album, *Seamonsters*. It's not a song I'd urge anyone unfamiliar with the band to listen to first up as being close to the best of The Wedding Present.

And yet it's 'Octopussy''s tentacles that reach out across three decades of time and space – a world away from Scotland in 1991 to Australia now – to trigger waves of deep personal emotions.

In many ways, 'Octopussy' is the minor calm after the churning maelstrom of *Seamonsters*' preceding major moments, and it's merely a coda to the album that hangs together best as The Wedding Present's most cohesive whole long player.

But David Gedge's growls and wails about how 'you've become my family', amidst a churning backdrop, was the line that had the former teenage me walking with a Walkman repeatedly drilling its message into my ears questioning if I'd truly ever feel part of a family, since home life wasn't ideal at the time.

The year 1991 was mostly miserable, for various personal reasons, and the seeming impossibility of any kind of a happy future played on my mind as 'Octopussy' closed out *Seamonsters* again and again on Walkman walks.

How could someone unhappy in a family of origin, as psychiatrists and psychologists call it, even consider meeting someone to start a family? And how could someone whose family unit role model was so askew ever want to start another family?

The yearning to do so was there despite it all, and the teenage me would often muse as 'Octopussy' unfurled at the tail end of *Seamonsters* about 'the thousand things I had to do' to find any comfort in family joy.

Living in an unhappy home, the Walkman walks and the cassette of *Seamonsters*, taped from the purchased CD, became a soundtrack to troubled times. Its murmured vocals, buried beneath a brutal drum sound and shards of guitar, bluntly recorded by Steve Albini, mirrored a lack of clear and easy real-life communication at home.

Even now, it feels like a song never to be played publicly for others in my company to hear. It feels personal. For my ears only. It's a reminder of feeling damaged but turning life around to build a better family elsewhere.

Even now though, sometimes the dark pull of depression lurks beneath the surface, always ready to reach out from the depths to destroy any semblance of happiness, and so it's also a reminder of this risk.

A decade after the release of the *Seamonsters* album in 1991, I'd move to Australia. And two decades on from that big move across the world, 'Octopussy' remains an emotional link between the past and the present.

'Octopussy' now is a song that makes me want to reach out from Australia now to an angst-ridden teenager in Scotland in the distant past to say: 'Hey, it's all eventually going to be OK.'

INTERSTATE 5

HENRIK MIKKO

There are so many, but every time I've seen The Wedding Present perform 'Interstate 5' it really blows my mind.

CORDUROY

CHARLES CHULACK

So many great tunes but 'Corduroy' is my favourite. A friend played it for me after receiving the *Three Songs* EP from Gedge. It blew me away.

MARS SPARKLES DOWN ON ME

CHRIS MEEHAN

I'm just after seeing The Wedding Present play live in Dolan's in Limerick on 22nd

October 2021. It was my birthday, so a great night. Unfortunately, I didn't get to meet David. There was no merchandise on sale due to customs clearance or something. I have too many favourite Wedding Present songs to mention but one of my all-time favourites is 'Mars Sparkles Down On Me' from *Take Fountain*. I used to listen to it over and over again and it got me through a difficult time. It has brilliant lyrics.

My favourite Cinerama song is 'Starry Eyed' from *Torino*, simply because it's a brilliant, upbeat song. I put it on when I'm about to go out for a few beers.

Chris Meehan's vote is for 'Mars Sparkles Down On Me'

INTERSTATE 5

DAVID TOMPKINS

David Tompkins' tribute to 'the most underrated band in the UK'

The mighty Wedding Present have been my favourite band since the late '80s. My first wife's uncle and cousin are similarly addicted and we travel anywhere within about 100 miles to see them. Much to the bemusement of my present wife who, fortunately, does not keep me on a short lead. But they're completely different to my normal music listening tastes. My record and CD collection is full of old school Indie, Britpop, Ska, Northern Soul, proper R&B and early Mod, as well as bands which are closer to home such as Doves, the Manics and Public Service Broadcasting.

So which track would I choose? I have to say none of them have a special meaning relating to relationships or other life events. I could probably come up with a tale of falling out of love with one person, then in love with another and a list of tracks that helped me through. Instead I'm going to link it to one of my other passions – scooters.

When I retired, I had a lump sum payment burning a hole in my pocket. Now I'm a sensible soul and the thoughts of blowing it on a holiday or cruise didn't appeal. But buying another scooter did. You see, very few scooterists (not Mods, please) only have one scooter. And I had another issue. I'm hopeless mechanically. So I decided I would buy a modern version of my existing Lambretta, so I'd have a spare when Loretta (the Lambretta) was 'off the road' again. And then I decided that it would be a themed scooter. And the theme, naturally, would be The Wedding Present.

Now, some people spend literally thousands customising their scooters. Not an option. I decided to simply get a graphic related to the band on the sides of the bike. I went through each album and the singles I had, but none of the covers really looked as if they'd be right on the panels. And then I remembered the 'Interstate 5' logo. 'Interstate 5' was a track from my favourite album. Job done.

I spoke to Jessica at a gig who said they didn't have the rights to the artwork. Interestingly, the font was called 'Interstate'. I spoke to a local business who were happy to do the work, simply basing it on a photo of a badge I had.

The graphics were applied to my new black Scomadi TL200 auto scooter, and an investment in a private registration plate finished it off. It now travels to rallies all over the North of England and a few folk have come up and said that they think it looks great. But to be honest, I'm not bothered – it's just my tribute to the most underrated band in the UK.

SANTA MONICA

SIMON SMITH

It's not quite my favourite song, but may I just say that after decades of listening to David pouring his heart out on vinyl, 'Santa Monica' finally sounded like a man at peace with life, which made me feel very happy.

EVERYONE THINKS HE LOOKS DAFT & I'M NOT ALWAYS SO STUPID

MAX

I was a latecomer to The Wedding Present. 'Kennedy', 'Brassneck' and *Bizarro* made for my Weddoes induction. I probably first heard 'Everyone Thinks He Looks Daft' on the *PUNK video and I bought the twelve-inch of 'I'm Not Always So Stupid' that year too. I probably didn't own *George Best* until 1990. I was 18 and poor, doing my A-levels with nowhere near enough money to spend on records.

These songs remind me of long summers of working to live after leaving school, Italia '90, going out every night, playing football in the dark after the pubs had closed, Walthamstow Dogs, ten-pin bowling and being very bad at getting off with women, including being infatuated with one who I never got beyond the 'friends' stage with. She left for uni that summer and her new boyfriend was a Wedding Present fan, which really didn't help at all. I'm guessing his name was Kevin.

Everything about these songs resonates with me. The pain, the sadness, the anger, the regret, the loss. But musically, I think they define The Wedding Present for me or at least the period of The Wedding Present that I love the most – loud guitars, chords that anyone can play, lyrics we all understand and themes that most of us have experienced in one way or another.

As the years passed by, the 'you' as in '...every time a car drives past I think it's you' or, 'Oh, why do you catch my eye, then turn away?' became someone else. That's the great thing about these songs – you can recycle the emotion and feel the pain over and over again! Thanks very much, David. I'm happily in a relationship now and have been for almost 20 years but when I hear those songs the memories of spending so much happy time with my friends and of course the unrequited love – two doses of it – come flooding back.

Right, you've got me in the mood. 'Alexa, 'I'm Not Always So Stupid' by The Wedding Present.' I think she's only got a grotty live version from 1988, but that will have to do.

DARE
VICTORIA MONSELLATO

'Dare' reminds me of being happy at 17 every time I hear it.

SNAPSHOTS
LINDSEY BATES

There are too many to choose from but 'Snapshots', which my partner sent me when I lost my best friend, has huge meaning.

CORDUROY
SCOTT PADDEN

'Corduroy' is the first Weddoes song I ever heard – it's got it all! It's epic, it's got heartbreaking nostalgia and people in the middle of romantic entanglements that 18-year-old me was both fascinated and shocked by. There was so much to read into lyrically, plus those guitar effects, the rhythm of the verses, the release of the choruses. Eventually *Bizarro* (only by a hair!) became my favourite Wedding Present record, but I picked up my first instrument (bass) right around that same time I heard 'Corduroy' and asked a friend to learn it and to tell me what kind of pedal I needed for that bass sound. We started a band, total shoegaze stuff ripping off The Wedding Present, Ride, Swervedriver, Slowdive and My Bloody Valentine, which in Vermont in late '93 meant we had almost no-one to play shows with in town! Fortunately, because of the volume we played at, the hardcore kids and bands accepted us. Holy moly, I'm just ranting. To wrap this up: 'Corduroy' might be a perfect song, and it's one of those that really opened a door to a new favourite genre, which influenced my playing (I'm still at it as an old man!) and which made The Wedding Present one of my all-time favourite bands. I put one of their songs on almost every mixtape I ever made, maybe *every* one.

FOUR SONGS
ADRIAN WHITE

It is very difficult to pick a single Wedding Present song that means so much out of so many great ones. I wanted to pick out four that are significant to me and, as it transpired, they spread over 30-odd years, which tells you all you need to know about the Boy Gedge.

Adrian White has cheated and chosen four songs from across four decades

I'M NOT ALWAYS SO STUPID

You changed your number and my phonebook's such a mess

A line lost on kids today, eh?

'I'm Not Always So Stupid' represented an amazing time for Wedding Present fans. The band were hitting the big time musically and were getting better and better all the time. It's a 'jingly-jangly' classic and its A-side was decent as well. I didn't realise just how brilliant the lyrics were until much later in life. It makes you realise what's important to you and, dare I say it, what love really is.

COME PLAY WITH ME

And I looked in your eyes

The heady days of *Hit Parade* and listening to two new songs every month. Could they really release twelve amazing songs? Of course they could! The pick of the bunch? Step forward 'Come Play With Me'. Lyrically incredible and musically hard to top, a classic 'builder' as my mate used to say. When I first heard it, I just sat and listened and then played it over and over. I still get goosebumps listening to it now as it meant so much to me at the time. It's a great 'shoegaze' video as well.

IT'S FOR YOU

I'm just wondering whether...

Having to wait nine years for a new album isn't ideal (I didn't really do Cinerama and, yes, I do realise it was just a name!). 'Interstate 5' gave me an inclination that something good was about to happen and *Take Fountain* duly delivered. But hidden amongst these amazing new tracks was something that put me straight back in *George Best* territory. 'It's For You' has the Bass, the Drum, the *Seamonsters* Guitar, the Vocals. It quite simply is one of their best songs, the essence of The Wedding Present nestled in a wonderful brave new world. Just listen to those drums as they go into the chorus!

SPORTS CAR (LOCKED DOWN AND STRIPPED BACK VERSION)

Oh, I heard the sports car shrieking

A journey that began for me in 1986 still gives me the same buzz in 2021. The band continues to reinvent itself and didn't let us down during Covid. *Locked Down And Stripped Back* is some of the band's best work ever and the final accolade has to go to 'Sports Car'. The original song is one that I liked but which escaped my usual scrutiny. The lockdown version stopped me in my tracks, if you'll pardon the pun. The arrangement is haunting, catchy and brings the original riff into a whole new world. And the vocals? Melanie Howard simply nails it, what a voice she has. The Wedding Present meet The Sundays and it works!

DANCE, GIRL, DANCE

ERIC POMINVILLE

Eric Pominville prefers Cinerama to The Wedding Present

'Dance, Girl, Dance' is my absolute all-time favourite of the numerous wonderful, sophisticated and ultra-sexy songs by Cinerama. I can listen to it over and over again, and never grow tired of it.

I'm not sure you realise I'm not really into The Wedding Present? (I would apologise to all the passionate fans of the Weddoes who consider such an opinion blasphemy.) No doubt this is principally a factor of being an American, and not having been exposed to their music, especially the early albums. That said, I simply adore Cinerama, and have everything they have ever put out.

The first two albums, *Va Va Voom* and *Disco Volante*, are pure magic and hold an important place among my all-time favourites. I discovered Cinerama at the time of the release of *Va Va Voom* and followed along with each subsequent new album. I discovered them largely by accident; my entry was via the Marty Willson-Piper connection, as I have long been a fan of the early The Church.

What appealed to me so much about Cinerama is the bright, sophisticated, bitterly romantic, often swelling symphonic pop soundscape. The subtle female backing vocals (what I wouldn't give for a Gedge/Cinerama collaboration with Dominique Durand!). The use of strings, piano, flute, and trumpet to accentuate the driving, rhythmic rock sound, with David Gedge's plaintive lovelorn lyrics front and centre. Also, the highly evocative (and sometimes slightly edgy) song narratives, combined with the snippets of answering machine messages, spoken word French, and restaurant background noises no doubt appeal to the English Lit Major in me.

'Dance, Girl, Dance' encapsulates almost everything I love about this band. From the initial conceit of the intimacies of an established relationship, only to learn that it's all purely imagined because the narrator has yet to even speak to the subject of his desire. Between the swelling strings and the note of romantic optimism, it's a song guaranteed to 'soothe away my troubles.' I have tried going back and listening to the early Wedding Present, but it just doesn't work for me. Now I find the music is too harsh, dissonant, and overwhelms the lyrics. Maybe if I had heard them earlier in my life that might be different.

Many years ago, I was fortunate to see Cinerama play live. It was on the second floor of a small venue in the historic district of Philadelphia. I purposely got there late because my interest was entirely on seeing Cinerama and not the opening band (who I want to say might have been The Lilys.) To my surprise the place almost completely emptied out after the opening act, and I was one of what seemed like maybe a dozen who were still there to see Cinerama. I remember sensing David Gedge having been extremely disappointed by the sparse turnout because they played through their set extra-super-fast (Gedge always likes to play fast but this felt like they were playing with the decided purpose of simply getting it over with in order move on to their next destination) and with absolutely no encore.

As disappointed as I was by the absence of an encore, I remember leaving the small club and feeling transported by the thrill of having the privilege of what amounted to almost an exclusive performance. In my mind, Cinerama remained entirely too cool and sophisticated for the music-going masses.

UNFAITHFUL

ALAN REED

There are too many Wedding Present songs to choose from but 'Unfaithful' is a *Bizarro* B-side that deserved more. Bitter and jangly, with a soaring bridge after the middle eight and a real studio room feel (listen to Simon count everyone in), more gravel from the bass than Brighton Beach and one of the best lyrics:

Alan Reed votes for 'Unfaithful'

You know I haven't worn a shirt like that since, oahhhh, 1974

I just love the fact that they could 'throw together' such a perfect encapsulation of bitterness and 'bounce', a group on top form. *Bizarro* was an album and a set of singles that got me through teenage torment! I met David once to tell him this but I got starstruck and stumbled over my words. How... daft.

SKIN DIVING

ELIZABETH MICHAELSON MONAGHAN

When I graduated from university, I came to England for six months. I worked in a canteen, serving tea and biscuits to graduate students. When I was not serving tea, I wandered around London in the constant light rain, projecting myself onto Wedding Present songs. They appeared like a film in my head; I was some boy, probably dressed in corduroy. There were a thousand things I wish I'd said and done. I hadn't heard this song in years. I walked around to the soundtrack of romantic longing. I was waiting to fall in love.

Elizabeth Michaelson Monaghan is fond of 'Skin Diving'

Since longing is essentially a solitary experience, I'm alone in most of my Wedding Present and Cinerama memories. Here is one: I am in a tiny office in a building off Russell Square. (I am between tea-serving sessions). *Saturnalia* is on my portable CD player. I'm filled with this fizzy, inexplicable joy, a product of the song rattling through me. I am dancing with all the uncoordinated fervor of someone alone in their bedroom. I am lip-syncing to 'Skin Diving'.

'Skin Diving' is an archetypal Wedding Present song in that it's gorgeous, grimly funny, and often overlooked. The lyrics are addressed to an ex, a description that could apply to… uh, a lot of Wedding Present songs. At first, it's hard to make out Gedge's plaintive words over the grinding, fuzzy bass line and that inexorable drumbeat, but then the guitars kick in, and his voice rises over the feedback to plead:

So come on, just this one more time, then I'm gone
Well he can't expect you to stay home
This is summertime
Besides which, he'd never suspect you

In this memory, I'm not imagining myself in love, lovelorn or having a heartbreaking meeting with an ex. I'm not waiting for anything. I'm just enjoying myself. I'm listening to a song I love, and I'm happy.

KENNEDY

TONY WALKLEY

Tony Walkley loves the lack of lyrical straightforwardness of 'Kennedy'

Of all the Wedding Present songs that I have grown to love over the years, I will always come back to 'Kennedy' as the one that I have the strongest connection to. Partly that's due to timing. When it was released, I was in my early teens and the very early throes of what would become a full-blown Peel addiction. Discovering a world of raw, often curious and sometimes alien sounding music that existed outside of the formulaic, OTT bombast that '80s Radio 1 would typically play was nothing short of revolutionary to these teenage ears.

'Kennedy', with its ferocious guitar, obscure lyrics (for me at the time), low-mixed vocals and long outro ticked all of the new boxes that I now wanted my music to tick. It was my introduction to the band and I rushed out and bought it on cassette single and played it repeatedly to within an inch of its life.

I love the fact that lyrically it's not as straightforward as most Wedding Present songs. You rarely have to look too far to understand the meaning of a Gedge song but 'Kennedy', despite the obvious references to JFK, seems more ambiguous. For years I thought he sang 'look of life' until a mate said it was 'love of life.' Even now, having just looked up the lyrics online, I see that other people continue to debate its meaning and I saw one thread that insisted it was indeed 'look of life' as this was the name of a bracelet that belonged to Jackie Kennedy – which presumably she lost at some point? Regardless, the fact that my 'Kennedy' might mean different things to somebody else's 'Kennedy' sits quite well with me.

I have moved to Brisbane now and have not sadly met many Australians who are familiar with The Wedding Present. Yet even halfway round the world, 'Kennedy' continued to have its impact on me. When the Weddoes played Brisbane in 2013, it was the first time my wife and I had gone out since our baby daughter was born. I was not expecting them to play 'Kennedy' – I had read somewhere that David Gedge no longer liked the song? But play it they did and a little corner of Brisbane was treated to the unedifying sight of a sleep-deprived, middle-aged new father going absolutely crazy. Once again, 'Kennedy' got its timing spot on.

SKIN DIVING
ANTHONY LEE YORK

'Skin Diving' because it reminds me of a particular summer.

BLUE EYES
BILL BRYANT

My wife of 22 years and I had our first kiss to this song.

CRAWL
CHRISTINA ANGELOPOULOS

When I was 16, during another long night of endless homework, I was curled up on a chair listening to WLIR's 'Off the Boat' radio show, and while all of it was a welcome relief from American Top 40 radio, one band really made me snap my head up and take notice. The Wedding Present.

I eventually succeeded in finding their records, and when I'd run out of the back catalogue to buy, I purchased several live cassettes direct from the band (and was surprised to see David's own signature on the back of my check).

'Crawl' is an old friend to Christina Angelopoulos

The one track that seemed to be on all of the live performances I'd bought was 'Crawl'. It became my favourite Wedding Present song. I love the structure, from the basic beginning with the strong bassline that starts on a D and just kind of lives there, to the gorgeous delicate guitar line punctuating the second verse, to the strong and passionate guitar solo and then the guitar drone, again on a D, on verse three. That D helps me in my job as a professional classical singer too – I don't have perfect pitch, but all I have to do is think of 'Crawl' in my head and I know where D is.

The lyrics are a little different for The Wedding Present and seem contemplative and heartfelt in every performance. 'It wasn't really like that' perfectly sums up my frustration at those who wrongly assume people's viewpoints. I seem to have views that refuse to be neatly categorised, and I often have a different take on situations than the obvious takeaway. I suspect many of us think of complex concepts in one quick flash and then feel lazy and/or hopeless about expressing them.

This song is an old friend for me and I toast the band for the gift of it.

ANYONE CAN MAKE A MISTAKE
DUNCAN GREENWOOD

Simply the most perfect song ever.

CORDUROY
MARK BEAUMONT, MUSIC JOURNALIST

In the space of one week, my favourite Wedding Present song changed a dozen times. In Cambridge, 'Dalliance' and 'Heather' knocked the air from my chest again; both devastating typhoons of regret and betrayal. In Reading, 'Blue Eyes' spun my head with its tempestuous build to a Red Arrow riff. In London, the sunburst finale of 'Bewitched' hit like nuclear fusion. And in the car, between dates on the *Seamonsters* tour of early 2022, my playlist crowded with other worthy greats: 'Come Play With Me', 'Spangle', 'Three', 'No', 'Nobody's Twisting Your Arm', '2, 3, Go', 'What Have I Said Now?', 'Rachel' or my most-played Weddoes song (according to my iTunes, anyway), 'Kansas'.

Ultimately though, with one of the greatest canons in modern rock to try to pick from, you inevitably return to the song that first lit your particular fuse. For me, it was 'Corduroy', bursting out of *Seamonsters* in a frenzy of primordial fuzz and effervescent pogo pop in 1990. There was no detail more relatable to those teenagers that loved and lost in the '70s and '80s than the childhood picture of the corduroy kid who 'grew up fast', nor a hookline that could catch in the throat like:

I'll make you laugh when you see this photograph
It's not from that day; I threw all those away

The song distilled the essence of The Wedding Present's appeal: a bittersweet twist in a relationship conveyed through torrents of angst-rock guitar that teetered, euphorically and melodically, between jubilance and despair. And as an example of David Gedge's unerring ability to pinpoint the intricate minutiae of star-crossed young love, 'Corduroy''s emotional shift from renewed hope and security to dissolving trust was amongst his most sophisticated. That it is so rarely played live only exemplifies what riches the band have to choose from. Most acts would have wrung all the colour out of 'Corduroy' by now; when The Weddoes brush it off, it remains utterly pristine.

SAMANTHA ROBERTS

Trying to decide on a favourite Wedding Present or Cinerama song is an impossible task! I have way too many favourites! So here are some of them and what they mean to me.

Samantha Roberts (left) at the Media Club, Vancouver, Canada with David Gedge

CLICK CLICK

I found *Watusi*, along with *Saturnalia* and *Mini*, in a little pawn shop in Squamish, Canada. I couldn't believe my luck, especially when I opened them all to find a ticket to the corresponding gigs that had taken place in Vancouver! What was the story behind their journey to this shop? And why would someone give away their precious tickets? I imagined it was a disgruntled girlfriend who kicked out her cheating boyfriend and pawned all his stuff. I wondered if she understood the irony! Whenever I look at these three album covers, I think of that little shop and the enraged girlfriend, the boyfriend with his regrets, and his frustration at wondering whatever happened to those CDs! I adore 'Click Click', a beautiful love song that evokes the magic of physical and mental closeness. The feeling of falling in love, how you can't bear to be apart.

I want to breathe the air that you breathe
I want to follow you when you leave
I want to take you home and hide you
I want to always be inside you

The lyrics are just so heartfelt and simple, someone giving themselves completely to another person, wanting to protect them and merge with them, body and soul. I love the gorgeous melody with the dreamy backing vocals (is it a polyphonic?) and the way the guitars are full of yearning.

YOU SHOULD ALWAYS KEEP IN TOUCH WITH YOUR FRIENDS

My cousin Stuart was a huge fan of The Wedding Present and he introduced me to them when I was 15. It was 1986 and we listened to John Peel's *Festive 50* at our granny's and stole sips of the Christmas whisky that was 'hidden' in a cupboard! It was the first time I had heard The Wedding Present and the song was 'You Should Always Keep In Touch With Your Friends'. I absolutely loved the jangle of frantic guitars, and the lyrics that spoke to me in a way that no other lyrics had. I'll never forget that Christmas; the room with the wooden bunk beds, the little battery radio, and hanging out listening to music with my cousin.

SPRAGUE

Sadly, Stuart died from cancer in 2018 at the age of 49. My auntie asked me to suggest some songs to play at his funeral, so amongst the Ramones, Bauhaus, and The Cure, I offered a selection of The Wedding Present. It was actually more difficult to choose than I thought it would be because, believe it or not, there are a fair few references to sex (!) and a couple of songs about love, going well or not, none of which seemed suitable! From the surprisingly small list, my auntie chose 'Sprague' from *Going, Going…* which was heartbreakingly beautiful at the funeral, and I think Stuart would have approved. He was soulful and gentle, much like the song.

A MILLION MILES

George Best was the first Wedding Present album I bought, and I played it over and over. Being completely unqualified to talk about the technical side of music, I can only express how much I love all of the layers of different sounds – jangling guitars and thrumming bass, with the top end of the tambourine crashing through the driving drums. One minute I'm following along with the guitar and the next I find myself humming to the bass, all the while foot-tapping and probably singing the wrong lyrics! It takes me back to being 16 years old, and still stands up today as a unique and exciting album. It's so hard to pick a favourite song but a few stand outs for me are 'My Favourite Dress', 'Getting Nowhere Fast' and 'A Million Miles'. Gotta love these lyrics:

He's never mentioned you before
Oh, that didn't come out right at all and now I feel this small

SEAMONSTERS

If pushed to make a decision about my favourite album of all time (from any musician), then *Seamonsters* would be it! *Going, Going…* could possibly push it off the top spot musically but the love for this album runs deep. From the moment I heard it I was entranced. Every time I listen to the whole album I get goosebumps and feel this swelling of emotion that can bring me to tears. The lyrics speak of heartache and love with such raw passion, the drums and bass power forward, and the intensity of the guitars bring an emotional crescendo which takes my breath away. Sublime.

I will never forget the *Seamonsters* anniversary tour [in 2010]. I was down the front, on the barrier at Koko in London, and bumped into Neil Fawcett. We had met in Brighton at *At The Edge Of The Sea* that year, and it was great to see him again. We were both so ridiculously excited, the crowd was buzzing and the atmosphere was electric! The lights dimmed and I thought I might pass out with anticipation. It was genuinely one of the happiest moments of my life. The music started and everyone went crazy! Neil and I were laughing our heads off, whooping and jumping around. I remember at one point, possibly around 'Corduroy', or maybe as early as 'Suck', turning to him, and we were both crying. Tears were just pouring out which made us laugh/cry/laugh. Ridiculous, but such is the power of *Seamonsters*!

GOING, GOING…

I got to know *Going, Going…* whilst driving to and from work. It takes me back to being in the car, and the sense of freedom and happiness I felt because I knew that sometime soon, I would be changing jobs for the better. I still drive around the area, and when I get to a certain junction I think of *Going, Going…*! As each song comes on, I think, 'I love this one!' They are all so different – the epitome of all the songs definitely not sounding the same! I really do love each and every one of them.

There is so much to 'Little Silver'. The unusual and clever time signature, the soft vocals with the mellow plucking of guitars, the finality and certainty of the lyrics, all leading to the powerful, yearning, full guitars and dirty bass. Very emotional, the kind of song you need to close your eyes to and head-nod!

I love the story of 'Birdsnest', something that most people can relate to! A song of bravery and hope too. There are also many different and interesting musical parts to this song, and I really love the backing vocals.

'Emporia' – there is an anticipation here as the first words are sung with choral dreaminess, and the first few gentle notes are played. I know what is coming and it's exciting! Unhurriedly building up to the climax, languidly pulling you along this journey. And then we get to the first chorus, a hint of the power to come, and then there it is, the release, the crashing raw, punk guitars, the sound that takes me back to the moshpit shouting 'woooo hoooo'!

'Ten Sleep' reminds me of the frantic, jangling guitars and bass driven melody of *George Best*. An homage to the classic sound of this great album.

'Santa Monica' – starting with the soft guitar, humming bass, and a gorgeous vocal from David, the most beautiful love is tenderly declared. This is then punctuated by the crash of emotion with powerful guitars. 'The story ends right here' – nothing more needs to be said, because we have the ultimate happy ending. Then we go again, up the scale of anticipation, lifting the emotions to the climax of explosive guitars. I love how this dips in and out, from gentle, tender love to big emotions.

I know that the album *Going, Going...* was born out of an actual journey, and I feel that many of the songs reflect their own emotional journey too. It's one of my favourite albums in the world, ever.

The *At The Edge Of The Sea* festival is something I really look forward to every year, and I've been to all except the first one (I'm so gutted to have missed that!). It's always a weekend of great music, discovering new bands and enjoying old favourites – what's not to like? Over the years I've met some lovely people and made some wonderful friends. It has become a yearly get-together, where we look forward to catching up with each other, having a drink and a mosh, enjoying the music and sharing our love of TWP. When we couldn't get together due to Covid, we watched the live streams and WhatsApped the whole time!

Listening to Cinerama often brings to mind the festival because Cinerama always play at the beginning of *At The Edge Of The Sea*, and rarely play at any other time. They set such a joyful tone for the day - I think of summer dresses, and easy dancing, happy faces and anticipation. This is actually one of my favourite moments of the festival - a sense of being fully present, that we are all really here and ready to enjoy the festival. It is happy and hopeful, the day stretching before us, all to come. Songs that particularly evoke the feeling of the festival for me are 'Kerry Kerry', 'Dance, Girl, Dance', 'Maniac' and 'You Turn Me On'.

GEORGE BEST

KEVIN WHITEHOUSE

All of *George Best*. Nobody does fast and jangly like the Weddoes.

PERFECT BLUE
STÉPHANE COQUERELLE-PRO

'Perfect Blue'. When I listen to it, I'm in love.

KENNEDY
SIMON PARKER

It was definitely The Wedding Present's fault that my first proper band ended up sounding 'baggy' for a while. After several frustrating false starts, by the autumn of 1989 I had still not been able to put a half-decent band together. But a few things suddenly fell into place and I had all the members I needed except the drummer. Now, as every musician quickly finds out, good drummers are as rare as uncorrupt politicians. But, one chilly afternoon, not long after The Wedding Present had released the awesome 'Kennedy', there I was auditioning a premier tub-thumper from the local college. The band was called 'The Violet Trade' and things were looking good. *And* I had a brand new song which I was just itching to share with my fellow Indie conspirators.

To me, this new track was a cut above my usual drivel and very Wedding Present to boot. 'Nightmare Ride' (bloody hell!) featured a relentless scratchy rhythm guitar coupled to a twisting bass line that the Weddoes had already turned into their trademark sound. Surely copying is the most sincere form of flattery, right?

Back in the rehearsal room I started cranking out that rhythm guitar part and shouted to the drummer, 'Just play it like The Wedding Present'. To which the skinny black-clad chap behind the kit looked a little worried and started picking up the beat. Unfortunately, I now know that Gary the gothic drummer had never heard 'Kennedy' and somehow ended up turning my 'Nightmare Ride' into some sort of 'baggy' car crash, which the other band members immediately loved. Locked into a groove I didn't want to be a part of, Gary's misinterpretation of my thrashing rhythm not only derailed the song, but The Violet Trade then spent the first six months of its doomed lifespan trying to figure out a way back to being Indie.

But Gary the drummer became a good friend and we ended up having a lot of adventures together in bands such as Colourburst, Whiskey Girls and Fruit Machine. And, years after this, I finally got to play shows with The Wedding Present when my current band Villareal supported them at Chinnerys in Southend and then in my adopted hometown of Brighton, when we were asked to play David's excellent *At The Edge Of The Sea* festival.

Thank you, David. And thank you, The Wedding Present, for all the memories.

PERFECT BLUE

ANDY LAMBLEY

Andy Lambley (left) and his partner Nicola (right) with Jessica McMillan

As David Gedge often says whilst playing live and responding to people shouting out requests, 'So many great songs!' He definitely isn't wrong, as I haven't got a solid favourite. My first Wedding Present purchase was *George Best* back in 1987. I admit I bought it for the album cover and not the music. Then a few weeks later, my then-girlfriend was rummaging through my LPs and said, 'Oh wow, you have The Wedding Present's album.' We played it and listened to it together, with it somehow sounding so much better than my first listen to this now iconic album. It was at that moment she got me hooked on a band that I am still enjoying to this day and see them live at every available opportunity. David's songwriting has been fabulous and that continued during the Cinerama era and through to the present day. To my partner, 'Perfect Blue' has become 'our song' as the lyrics fit perfectly with our relationship and it's that one song that has secured The Wedding Present yet another diehard fan.

FLYING SAUCER

COLIN YOUNG

Colin Young's favourite Wedding Present song is 'Flying Saucer' whilst for wife Lesley it's 'Sports Car'

You can't do justice to David Gedge's beautiful songwriting and his soundtrack to my life with a 'favourite' Wedding Present song. From the sublime to the sublime:

It's just this razor, he's left it on your shelf
Is this all because you didn't like my mam
I'd miss you even if we'd never met

John Peel and my mate Peterjon 'Clash' Cresswell got me through journalism college and the long, lonely nights in Hastings, learning shorthand, missing Maria. They introduced me to the greatest band in the world – I'm sure my first gig of many was in Hastings or Brighton that year. My favourite then was 'A Million Miles' but I love every track on *George Best*.

There's something wrong with you if you don't love 'My Favourite Dress'. I was in tears when the band came on to it in Galashiels, at last, in 2021. The framed handwritten signed lyrics for 'My Favourite Dress' are on the living room wall, a Christmas present from my daughter, Vicki because 'it's the only one I've heard', which is a lie because The Wedding Present were always on when the kids were asleep and I'm singing, and bashing away at the steering wheel in the car. I could fill a wall with David Gedge songs.

As the trainee at *Evening Press* in York, I made sure I got the local music gig, persuaded my boss reviewing bands across the North was legit and had a right go at it. As a Yorkshire band, The Wedding Present suddenly featured in an Indie-inspired column almost every week. Clash and I interviewed David before a gig at Sheffield University. I remember him saying 'Kennedy' was the first non-love song he'd written and Clash offering him his American flag t-shirt, which David really liked, but politely refused.

For years my favourite song was 'Dalliance' – the brilliance of the Jilly Cooper story, the anger… and then, 'Flying Saucer' or 'I'm From Further North Than You' - not least for marking the 'return' of The Wedding Present; I listened to *Take Fountain* for months non-stop - or '524 Fidelio' or 'No' or 'Girl From The DDR' or…

Am I alone in thinking Part Two of this book should be our Top Tens? Even that would be difficult!

I've lost count of the number of gigs now but Leeds never disappoints. Nothing beats David Gedge looking right at you, at the home of The Wedding Present, mid-flow in 'Flying Saucer', tapping away on her thigh. That was when I knew.

The family think I'm mad but seeing them in iconic venues I wouldn't otherwise visit - standing right of stage and taking in every moment - is a joy every time. And my Wedding Present bucket list is far from complete.

The *Stripped Back* performances were a huge lift for me during lockdowns and I loved the on-line polls. And I took these very seriously; re-playing every album and putting them in order before casting my votes. The final results were fascinating. And I would love to know David Gedge's thoughts.

If I did it again, I know the order would be different; so consistently brilliant, from day one to today - how good are the *24 Songs*? - and beyond, is DLG.

Today, I choose 'Flying Saucer'…

PS. My wife Lesley still doesn't really get The Wedding Present. We met in 1995… But I managed to leave the first *Stripped Back* CD on loop in her car for a while. She (eventually) admitted to enjoying it, driving to and from work. Her favourite? 'Sports Car' (with Melanie Howard's beautiful vocals). Sorry, David. Slow progress after 28 years, but I am getting there!

I'M NOT ALWAYS SO STUPID

DEREK J IRVINE

In these days of streaming, thinking about the traditional single and, more particularly, its B-side(s) seems antiquated. I adored those songs though. Some bands (or labels or companies) no doubt used those squad places for filler, relying on the A-side to mask that weakness or hoping that people didn't bother listening to the others. Some, however, scattered gems amongst these places and both The Wedding Present and Cinerama secreted such jewels across and amongst the many formats of various releases.

Derek Irvine has opted for 'I'm Not Always So Stupid' – his border collie Aonghus is saying nothing

I have many that I enjoy, but 'I'm Not Always So Stupid' is one that I have loved right from the very first time I heard it, tucked away as the final song on the CD single of 'Nobody's Twisting Your Arm'. I bought the twelve-inch and gatefold seven-inch too, but that story of record-collecting obsession was already well underway by February of 1988.

I was at university in Glasgow, in the second year of my first degree, when the single was released, though I had fallen for the band after hearing them on Peel a few years previously. It was the ferocity of the guitars and the energetic exuberance of live shows that drew me in, though these tracks suggested a band moving away from their more brooding beginnings.

It was also becoming abundantly clear that the lyrics of Gedge were something special. Nobody else came close to describing the painful shards of a broken heart nor the confusing myriad of emotions engendered by love, lust, infatuation, deceit, mistrust, hope and – occasionally – happiness. The song has, of course, a couplet that now seems like it was culled from a historical document:

You changed your number and my phonebook's such a mess
But I can't bear to cross your name out yet

That forlorn expression of refusing to accept reality is, in contrast, startlingly realistic. And who amongst us, who find ourselves accepting or assuming blame for the demise of a relationship, haven't thought or said something similar to:

Somebody told me you went to work down south
As far away as you can from my big mouth

In the end, it is probably the opening and closing couplet which is indicative of the way this song captures how I, and many, many others, have felt when in despair or, at the very least, sad and bitterly disappointed:

Every time a car drives past I think it's you
Every time somebody laughs I think it's you

David Lewis Gedge is without doubt one of the most scandalously underrated lyricists and songwriters the UK has produced and this tale of regret, a broken relationship and desperate, wishful thinking set to classic Indie/jangly guitar-pop, is yet another fine exhibit in the body of evidence we are all familiar with.

MY FAVOURITE DRESS

PETER ATHERTON

I have loved The Wedding Present since the release of the first album. Even as a staunch Everton fan, naming their debut in honour of the magnificent George Best did no harm in grabbing my attention and earning my long-term support. No surprise that 'My Favourite Dress' was a firm favourite then and remains so to this day. In December 2013, my beloved Everton finally won at Old Trafford

Evertonian Peter Atherton found rare delight in Manchester town

against Manchester United, our first success at that ground in 21 years. When the final whistle blew on a famous victory, I immediately sent a text message to my brother (also an Everton and Wedding Present fan). All the message said was:

Some rare delight in Manchester town

HIT PARADE

MIRELLE DAVIS

Instead of writing about one song I have chosen to write about twelve. My first job in the music industry was at RCA Records, when I was in my mid-twenties. As product manager, I had the job and indeed pleasure of helping put together the artwork, videos and release of the *Hit Parade* singles. It was a pleasure but it was also a huge challenge, as each sleeve had a different number on it that needed clearance and each video was done for less than £1,000 by art school students. Ironically, videos in 2022 (30 years later) are often done for those sized budgets, but back then, £1,000 was normally only enough to cover the sandwiches on the shoot! To say nothing of the fact there were twelve singles in twelve months, so a lot of work.

The 'Number Six' artwork stands out for me as that was based on Cadbury's Bar Six, and I never thought they would give approval to this young record company girl who was asking for clearance for a fairly obscure guitar band, but I did it and we got the cover.

I also have a vivid memory of David calling me from a telephone box on Brighton Beach. This was a time before mobiles. I can't remember which video it was, but it was being shot on the beach and, needless to say, it was bloody freezing. David called to ask if he could use a small amount of the budget to go and buy thermal underwear. Not exactly the conversation I was expecting.

We made 10,000 of each of those singles and each one went flying into the Top 40. The rules on *Top Of The Pops* back then were strict. The highest new entries got on the show. As such, every month The Wedding Present appeared in-between all the pop tunes of the day. The audience looked horrified, and every month without fail the single would crash out of the charts as fast as it came in, as there was literally no more stock. Quickly, record shops (remember them?) started stockpiling the seven-inch singles as they were worth money.

To this day, I believe this campaign was one of the most creative I have worked on in 30 years in the music industry. It helped bring back the seven-inch vinyl and made people think differently about how to release singles and make videos. I am sure it also made *Top Of The Pops* change their programming rules.

THE TROUBLE WITH MEN

JOHN PERRY

John Perry has chosen 'The Trouble With Men'

'The Trouble With Men', taken from the vastly underrated and underappreciated *El Rey*, was a key song in re-establishing my connection with the band, something that goes very deep within me. My Wedding Present journey started when I read a review of *Bizarro* in the *NME*. I bought the record off the back of it. It was the first time I had listened to anything by the band and I was hooked straight away. I had never heard anything like it before and have been an avid fan ever since. When David Gedge transferred his attention to Cinerama, mine did not follow. I still can't explain why but the link was broken. However, sometime in 2009, in a moment of idle curiosity, I carried out an internet search on The Wedding Present and found to my surprise that David had reactivated the band. They had released a couple of albums I had not heard, ie. *Take Fountain* and *El Rey*. With great anticipation, I immediately purchased both. I wasn't disappointed.

As soon as I played them, I found myself back where I wanted to be, in the Wedding Present world of male angst, soaring emotive guitars and wonderfully concise, evocative lyrics. It sounded different in tone and style to how it did in the days of *Bizarro* and *Seamonsters*, but it was still a completely recognisable and wonderful place to be in. The consummate songwriting skills of David Gedge have never been more evident than on *El Rey*.

In 'The Trouble With Men', a whole aspect of the male character/psyche is portrayed and can be fully understood in less than 120 of David's carefully chosen words. The song, like the album, is much different in tone to virtually anything produced pre-Cinerama. The lone drum introduction leads into David setting the scene beautifully through a quiet, atmospheric vocal, which then flows into a rousing chorus and cacophony of guitar that no Wedding Present creation should be without. And there are a couple of clever lyrical twists that serve to convey the song's message succinctly and wonderfully. The ebb and flow of it is glorious. When I first listened to 'The Trouble With Men', I re-entered the Wedding Present world. It's a place I derive so much pleasure from, and one I have no intention of ever leaving.

EVERYONE THINKS HE LOOKS DAFT
ANDREW JEZARD, DIRECTOR OF *SOMETHING LEFT BEHIND*

Andrew Jezard at the Halifax screening of *Something Left Behind*

The frenzied guitars of 'England' surrender to a simple melody, infiltrated by cheers and cries from the crowd. The lights go down. Time to focus my camera on the vacant microphone standing centre stage, spotlit. Somewhere from the gloom David Gedge approaches purposefully, right arm raised ready to make his point… 'Oh, why do you catch my eye, then turn away?'

'Everyone Thinks He Looks Daft' became a huge part of my life and was the soundtrack to two long years spent making a film about the band. It also opens the album that first introduced me to The Wedding Present (albeit 20 years after its release, on the *George Best* anniversary tour) and was the catalyst for the whole idea of documenting this story. An idea that was finally realised a decade later when *Something Left Behind* premiered in cinemas and I heard David Gedge bellow that opening line once more.

I chose to open the film with the original version of 'Everyone Thinks He Looks Daft' in its entirety. Straight in. No credits. Boom. I was desperate to capture the feeling of anticipation and frenzied excitement for the start of the album that I had witnessed at live shows. A feeling that anyone who attended the *George Best* anniversary tours will know well. The documentary also ends with the song played in full. Only this time it's the modern version performed live in Leeds to bring the whole story full circle. A story and a song that are still very close to my heart.

Few opening lines can capture the spirit of an entire album as well as this one. On the face of it an initial cutting remark but one that betrays a vivid sense of vulnerability. A vulnerability made clearer just three lines later: "How does it feel to know you've just won again?"

In 1987 an army of people instantly connected with these lyrics of heartbreak and hurt. Watching these same words belted out by crowds 20 and 30 years later it's clear that this emotional and lyrical connection remains, even if it is filtered through a more mature lens with the passing of time. That I was able to find the same connection with the song decades later is testament to this opening track and the invitation it provides to step into an entire world.

Whilst making the film I searched for this story and this history within the streets of Leeds 6, helped enormously by Peter Solowka's wistful memories and narration. A day very much juxtaposed with the location I had found myself in some weeks earlier. Looking down on Sydney Harbour Bridge under bright blue skies, Keith Gregory and I discussed exactly who had looked daft. And why.

PS. Play 'England' beforehand and play it loud.

BIRDSNEST

DEREK JONES

I've been a Weddoes fan since the age of 16 (I'm now 50) and ever since my now teenage kids were born, I've always played The Wedding Present or Cinerama on car journeys. Sam and Millie never really showed any interest, apart from a mild fascination with 'Kennedy' when they babbled out 'too much apple pie'. And my wife Claire, who's a Take That fan, has never been converted, not even when The Wedding Present covered 'Back For Good'.

But a few years ago, *Going, Going…* was on the car stereo and when 'Birdsnest' came on, the kids started singing it, word-for-word. I turned the sound down and they carried on singing perfectly… And, just like on *Never Mind the Buzzcocks*, when I turned the sound back up, they were perfectly in sync. It almost brought a tear to my eye. Who'd have thought, out of the 200-plus Wedding Present and Cinerama songs they'd heard, this would be the one that 'got' them?

On Christmas Day that year, I unwrapped a pressie from the kids… The handwritten lyrics to 'Birdsnest', signed by Mr Gedge, which are now framed on the wall next to my desk. It's a souvenir of a happy memory that I will cherish forever!

I AM NOT GOING TO FALL IN LOVE WITH YOU

KEN WELDIN

It will sound like a cliché but choosing a favourite Wedding Present song really is like choosing a favourite child. Even for the odd song that some of us may not be keen on, it is still a very high bar. 'You Should Always Keep In Touch With Your Friends' meant a lot to me even before I moved to Australia. 'This Boy Can Wait', also from *Tommy*, I remember from the *PUNK video, with the band driving across the continent. And what can you say about 'Everyone Thinks He Looks Daft' and 'My Favourite Dress'? Beautiful. Or the wit and dripping sarcasm of 'No', putting into words so well what some of us were feeling as relationships went through their ups and downs.

Ken Weldin's choice of favourite song is bang up-to-date

The epic, brooding and emotional *Seamonsters* is faultless as a collection – it could be an opera – while the underrated gems of the *Hit Parade* ('Come Play With Me') and *Valentina* ('Deer Caught In The Headlights') prove indeed that all the songs do not sound the same.

But I have plumped for a new one – 'I Am Not Going To Fall In Love With You'. When I heard it on the live stream launching *24 Songs*, I realised I was sitting there beaming from ear to ear. Yes, it sounds like 'you know what' and that is no bad thing. The mix of the sentiment and lyrics against what is simply a joyous romp of a sound would be enough.

But the main reason I have picked it is that, after all these years, here is a new song that is as good as anything the band has ever done. My late mum would be smiling to know that I am still loving The Wedding Present in 2022, the band she knew I was into and got excited about seeing on real TV – *Top Of The Pops*, *This Is Your Life*, etc.

Good on you, David and gang, for coming up with the goods again. The fanthology books and films tell you how much these songs mean to us, and I am proud to be part of this community of fans. 'I Am Not Going To Fall In Love With You' may be the title, but in reality 'I Fell In Love With You' a long time ago.

MY FAVOURITE DRESS

BERT APPLETON

The opening riff. 1987. The lyrics every time I listen to it. The reaction at so many gigs. Slight changes

Bert Appleton's choice is 'My Favourite Dress'

with different players. Gloucester opener 2021, with such a build-up. I've covered it so many times.

Sometimes these words *have* to be said: (The man) 'Gedge has written some of the best love songs of the 'Rock 'n' Roll era…'.

And this is the best one.

TAKE ME!

KEVIN STONE

At The Edge Of The Sea is always a brilliant occasion and an opportunity to meet such a friendly group of people with a similar soft spot or even, some might say, an addiction to the semi-legendary Wedding Present. There's a closeness amongst the extended family of ex-members and fans, who somehow seem to keep growing in numbers and evolving!

Kevin Stone was At The Edge Of The Sea in 2019

This is probably due to a combination of the continued energy and passion of David to write amazing and emotive music, as well as the commitment and dedication of original fans like ourselves who've watched the band evolve from the very beginning. Every lyric or tune David writes seems to connect with the younger and older fans. I suspect that everybody craves for, finds and loses love along the way, whatever age we all are.

And so what is my favourite Wedding Present song and why?

Well, as many will testify, the songs just keep on coming and I was taken aback by the beauty and quality of the debut live streamed performance, at St Bartholomew's Church in Brighton, of 'I Am Not Going To Fall In Love With You'. Although it could become a favourite of mine, I cannot simply dump my old faves for a younger, more sophisticated and sexier model. It just wouldn't be right. It would almost be a betrayal of my first love!

So what was my first love? It could've been from the first time I listened in awe quietly as a nocturnal teenager with headphones on in bed, to 'Go Out And Get

'Em, Boy!', being soothingly and amusingly introduced by the late great, John Peel.

Or it could've been when I listened to 'You Should Always Keep In Touch With Your Friends' at full volume, several times over in my student digs, introducing the neighbours to great new music at 2am after another night out at The Timepiece, Warehouse or Boxes in Exeter!

But no, my number one choice has to be the life-changing experience of surviving my first ever Wedding Present moshpit at the Bristol Bierkeller in April 1989, to 'Take Me!', which followed on from 'Brassneck', 'Bewitched', 'Kennedy' and a whole host of other exquisite, spine tingling and exhausting classics.

I went to the gig with relatively new friends who had the same thing in common as me... a love for gritty guitars, original, alternative, Indie music and a good laugh. 30 years later, we still meet at *ATEOTS* and try to roll back the years.

During the course of 'Take Me!', we must have saved each other numerous times from being crushed or ending up on the floor! The sheer power, noise, energy, emotion and happiness were exhilarating and something I had never experienced before in my life.

'Take Me!' was to become my go-to record for years to come, and I still love every single second of it! The last *ATEOTS* festival I went to nearly finished me off. I'm told that it was the longest ever live and extended version and it was pure heaven and dreamlike! Every time I hear it or see it played live makes me wonder how on earth the band can play at such ferocity for so long without tearing their fingers apart.

'Take Me!' was the catalyst for me to watch live music wherever and whenever possible, and not just the incredible music of The Wedding Present. It opened my ears and eyes to all sorts of music. It took me to a whole new world that I would always seek in times of happiness or sadness. It is my ten minutes of comfort and I will never be able to thank David Gedge and The Wedding Present enough for providing me with so many hours of pure pleasure.

SCOTLAND

DANIELLE WADEY, FORMER WEDDING PRESENT BASSIST & GUITARIST

My choice of favourite song, like many others I imagine, are based on what the song represents to me. The *Home Internationals* EP opened 2017, which turned out to be a truly great year! We recorded the tracks during the first few days of January and 'Scotland' was the first TWP track that included original music by myself. We stayed in a beautiful little house not far from the studio in Wales and spent a fun couple of days recording the EP and a couple of covers (the Clash being one of them and myself and Charlie's Bond track being the other). The opening piano part of 'Scotland', which I'd written amongst a number of other piano riffs during the Cinerama year of 2015, nicely complemented a lovely chord sequence written by Pat (Alexander) and the song came together really quickly. Charlie came up with the 'Bohemian Rhapsody'-style piano stabs, added some classic Charlie Layton drums, came up with the stops at the end, and that was that… almost! Add in the infamous David Gedge E-guitar drone and the song transforms from 'just a song' to 'a great Wedding Present song'. That's the real magic sparkle to finish it off!

Danielle Wadey has chosen 'Scotland'

It was a really fun and positive way to start out a year that saw *George Best* back in the spotlight; that took us to the US, Canada, Australia, New Zealand and, of course, all over Europe, that saw us play at the Roundhouse (with 'Scotland' as the opening track), and that saw us play *Going, Going…* in all its glory at Cadogan Hall, closing with a truly spine-tingling version of 'Bewitched'. It was a brilliant year!

I loved my bass line to 'Scotland' and I loved Pat's guitar parts, and I was lucky enough to be in the position to play both live. And - being half Scottish myself - there's a little national pride there too. Whenever I hear 'Scotland', it takes me back to that great year - Marcus's (Kain) sparkly guitar and his pure delight at everything we encountered on our European trips (he'd not long been over from Oz); meeting Andrew Jezard and taking part in the *Something Left Behind* documentary; one of my favourite ATEOTS years! It was hard work, but so much fun, and I consider myself very lucky to have been part of it.

NO NOMINATION
CRAIG HATFIELD

I always thought that the first time I saw The Wedding Present was at the Marcus

Garvey Centre in Nottingham in May 1991. I was into rocky stuff and persuaded a friend who preferred soulful and funky sounds but shared with me a middle-ground of melodic pop – Everything But The Girl, The Smiths, Prefab Sprout – to come along. To this day, he still says it was the worst gig of his life. But my student scrapbook tells me that I'd actually seen The Wedding Present six months before at Keele University. I went to that one with my friend Sarah. I don't think she's a particularly big fan either!

MY FAVOURITE DRESS

AMELIA COBURN, SINGER

I remember where I was when I first heard The Wedding Present. My dad was giving me music recommendations in the car. I had recently become obsessed with '80s Indie music and, like many moody teenagers, was going through a phase of listening to nothing but The Smiths. Little did I know there was a plethora of incredible Indie bands out there to discover. Luckily, my dad was there to lend his expertise. 'If you're into The Smiths then you'll probably like the Weddoes,' he said, as he took out his *George Best* CD. I knew from the first few seconds of the opening track that I was going to love this band.

Amelia Coburn's (right) take on 'My Favourite Dress' is David's favourite cover version which she played when supporting The Wedding Present in Paris in 2018

The song that always stood out to me, particularly lyrically, was 'My Favourite Dress.' I really admired David Gedge's ability to write such narrative-driven songs, in this instance a heartbreaking tale of betrayal, and condense it into a perfect four-minute, jangly guitar pop song. I feel like everyone can relate to that miserable 'long walk home in the pouring rain' and seeing the person you fancy in the arms of another. Despite the music being slightly 'before my time', as an angsty adolescent listening to these songs in a Northern industrial town, I always felt extremely connected to the ordinary, kitchen sink world of love and loss that Gedge so vividly depicted.

A few months later, after receiving a ukulele for Christmas, I taught myself how to play most of my dad's record collection, including of course, 'My Favourite Dress'. I loved playing it because, to my knowledge, there weren't any other 14-year-old musicians out there performing Wedding Present covers on the uke. The song later took on a memorable meaning for me after David responded to my cover of it on Twitter (positively, I should add). I then couldn't believe it when he kindly invited me to play at his 'At The Edge Of The Sea' festival in 2018 – a memory I will always cherish (as will my dad). Each artist was asked to cover a Wedding Present song. As I was singing 'My Favourite Dress', I looked out into the audience and realised David himself was watching. I tried to hide my nerves as best I could! I was ecstatic to later hear him say that it was the first time a cover of one of his songs had made him emotional, and since then he has stated that it is his favourite cover of a Wedding Present song. That made the track even more special to me and 'My Favourite Dress' is fittingly 'My Favourite Song' by The Wedding Present.

NO NOMINATION

ANDY BURGIN

At Birmingham Hummingbird in November 1990, I fell over in the moshpit during 'Dalliance'. My jaw still cracks to this day. In 1992, I saw The Wedding Present twice at the Astoria in London. I got DLG's autograph and sat upstairs behind Mark Lamarr and Sean Hughes, who chain smoked throughout the gig.

At New Roscoe in July 2002, Cinerama started playing Weddoes tracks again. It was an odd night. Sally had asked online if anyone could help with a replacement zip drive. I had an old one at work, so I spoke to her afterwards and put my foot straight in my mouth trying to explain I liked the Weddoes stuff more – it came out as though I hated the Cinerama stuff. She looked upset and despite my best efforts I never did get the zip drive to her. This gig was also attended by Sean Hughes and Jane Goldman, who spent a lot of the night being pestered by my friend. She looked quite shocked as I waved my car keys at my friend to indicate that we had to leave – I think she thought I was waving them at her!

At the Heineken Festival in '94, a mate had two backstage passes, but there were three of us. After a bit of social engineering and a shuffle of passes and tickets, all three of us got backstage and watched the gig from the side. Darren was so nervous he played the entire gig with his back to the crowd, DLG fluffed the middle of 'So Long, Baby', causing the band to stop and hold a mini-postmortem. Also, at the side of the stage was a drunken air guitarist who was a friend of Darren's; he subsequently became their additional drummer for Sound City and other gigs around that time.

And I was at the West Yorkshire Playhouse in the 2000s. The gig was awful, but myself and several others were in the bar and watched as Grapper walked in and spoke to DLG. Some people took pictures and it was rumoured to be their first meeting since Grapper had left.

At work in 2017 I said, 'I'm off to a gig tonight.' 'Who are you seeing?' 'You'll not have heard of them, they're called The Wedding Present.' 'Oh, I've heard of them – their guitarist taught me chemistry.'

SKIN DIVING

PADDY HEALEY

Paddy Healey has chosen to go 'Skin Diving'

'Skin Diving' is my favourite Wedding Present song. It brings back such great memories, and always made me feel slightly wistful as, for a while, *Saturnalia* looked like being the last ever Wedding Present album. From the first intake of breath (reminiscent of the first intake of breath in 'Everyone Thinks He Looks Daft' from the first album, *George Best*), to the fading guitar feedback at the end, the song is a little over three minutes of perfection.

The quickly changing power chords follow the vocal melody, the lyrics about hoping for one last fling with an ex-lover being typical Gedge territory. But there's so many small bits of magic in the lyrics and performance of this song that make it stand out from the crowd. The vocal harmonies and slightly discordant guitars make the chorus stand out, and the vocal performance is one of Gedge's best, with a fantastic, heartfelt, soaring vocal melody.

The distorted, dirty guitar sound is jarring over the fairly empty production, with drums and bass carrying a lot of the song. When the guitar comes in at the chorus and solos, you feel like the top of your head is going to come off! I also love how the feedback comes in towards the end of the song, and almost overwhelms the song before being brought back under control. It never gets old for me.

I remember seeing the band at their last gig as The Wedding Present before they became Cinerama, at the Lomax in Liverpool, and they just killed it that night.

VALENTINA
KARL KATHURIA

There are certain words or phrases that annoy me, and I'm sure many people reading this will have their own list. When it comes to music, it's albums being described as 'under-rated' when they're nothing of the sort. I've seen it written about *Seamonsters*, for one. And yet, other than the initial reviews in the music press, I doubt anyone who owns that album rates it as anything less than 'amazing', and possibly closer to 'perfect'.

What I think people mean is 'overlooked'. *Seamonsters* never seems to appear in lists of 'Best Albums Of The '90s', or 'Most Influential Indie Albums', or '(Insert List Name Here)', not because people don't love it, but because they're somehow missing out on it. And yet, that makes people say it's 'underrated'.

So, yes, let's go with 'overlooked'. And at this point, I can't think of a Wedding Present album more over-looked than *Valentina*. (I was lucky enough to be given the opportunity to read this book fairly early on, having made a nuisance of myself through proof-reading and editing various other Wedding Present releases. One thing that struck me was that the only time *Valentina* was written about was a fleeting mention of '524 Fidelio'.) With that in mind, I wanted to be the one to stand up and remind people what a fantastic album that is.

Valentina was launched with *Club 8*, a chance to support the band in exchange for an exclusive seven-inch single, a 'thank you' in the booklet (it was CD-only initially, so yes, it was a booklet!), and a guest-list place. I will admit that I didn't join the club, for reasons. I wasn't a big fan of *El Rey* at the time, and I wasn't sure how it was all going to shape up. Of course, as David says in his autobiography, *Tales From The Wedding Present*, 'You must learn never to doubt me.'

I don't think *Valentina* was very far from my CD player for at least a couple of years. It's one of those albums I can put on, and just let it take me wherever it wants to go. It's always a joy to hear the songs individually as well, with 'Deer Caught In The Headlights' being an obvious stand-out track that still appears often in live sets, and 'Back A Bit... Stop' only surpassed by the batshit-crazy arrangement on Cinerama's version of the album!

But it's not a track on the album itself that I'll pick out. There were so many other highlights around that release. The three ten-inch 'language' (French/German/Welsh) EPs were wonderful, for a start, with the French one being the most enjoyable to these ears. And then there was a book – the 'making-of' book – at the launch of which I was at the front of the queue in Fopp to get a copy. So I'm going with a song from the book, 'Pain Perdu'. The tempo changes, the absurdity of the lyrics (and the first studio-recorded 'f-bomb', the only one officially released since a live recording on a *Sounds* EP 25 years previously), the sheer joy with which it seems to be played. And the fact that it's not even buried on a B-side, it's a download that came with the book.

In conclusion, I love *Valentina*, and I especially love all of the music that got released with the book and the ten-inch singles. Don't overlook it, you won't underrate it. The *Club 8* single remains the one official release that I don't have anywhere, but I kind of like it that way - I should never have doubted!

GEORGE BEST

MATT TOMIAK

Timing, it is often said, is everything. Conveniently enough for the discerning late 1980s alternative rock fan craving a New Favourite Band in the wake of The Smiths' demise, The Wedding Present's semi-legendary debut album *George Best* arrived, in all of its earthy, heart-on-sleeve, ramshackle glory, in the autumn of 1987 - just a few weeks after Morrissey and co.'s grandiose swansong *Strangeways, Here We Come*. Frontman David Gedge's candid, conversational lyrics, a rambunctious, high-velocity Indie guitar sound and that cover image featuring the titular Manchester United and Northern Ireland forward in his iconic 'El Beatle' pomp (Best himself was even roped in for the album's pre-release promotional campaign) ensured an immediate cult following in the UK. Press notices too were largely favourable. Sounds magazine awarded the LP five out of five stars, calling it a 'blistering racket of sheer exhilarating pop noise', whilst an *NME* cover story on the West Yorkshire quartet found Danny Kelly, who had previously described *George Best* as 'the best British debut of the year', exalting the quartet's convergence of 'wrist-splinteringly fast guitars, defying both breakdown and burn-out' with Gedge's 'downpour of language – homely, naïve, sarcastic, bitter, bewildered but always determinedly everyday.'

A MILLION MILES

CHRIS L CURNOW

All was foggy. Fog in my mind. In my friend Stephen's too. And in the air hanging over the University of New England campus in Armidale on top of the Northern Tablelands of New South Wales. White light loomed large as the fog bank reflected our car's headlights. It was 3am, we were parked on the side of a road, our windows were wound tightly up and there was a fog hanging lightly inside the car as well.

A cassette was playing on the car stereo. Loud. And I liked it. New music from a band from Leeds, which my mate had heard on a recent trip to the UK. And I liked the band's name as well. He'd brought their first two LP albums (their only LPs at that time) on cassette back with him when he returned to Australia to attend our graduation ceremony.

The cover art on both cassettes – sitting on the dash – grabbed my attention, despite the dim hazy glow where we sat transfixed after a night of post-graduation revelry. A burnt orange scratchy mark on a khaki green background; a symbol that I never fully contemplated but which has held a permanent allure for me, with its suggested pyrotechnical exploding asterisk and its colour palette that would define my wardrobe for years to come. And on the one that was playing, some slightly dishevelled, bearded football player, presumably George Best, in a bright red jersey, legs caked in mud from the knees down. When track three started, I felt the fog lift just a tad and the opening lines spoke to me like no other song that I had ever heard:

I must have walked past this doorway thirty times
Just trying to catch your eye
You made it all worthwhile
When you returned my smile
It all became worthwhile

It was April 1990 and while the prospect of post-university life was still mired in the fraternal bonds of Indie bands, yeasty home brews and feisty exes, my friend Stephen – who remains a musical inspiration to me – was giving me a taste of a singer/songwriter and his inimitable band that would transcend all of that and stay with me for the next thirty two years.

The song – 'A Million Miles' – ended with its cheeky post-script quip. And while the campus fog remained heavy all around us, there was something clarifying in my mind. While the truism that all their songs sound the same was yet to be established, I knew that this one would always sound a little bit more special than all the rest.

ASTRONOMIC
CHARLOTTE ADOLPHO

I'm relatively new to The Wedding Present and, perhaps unusually, I came across Cinerama first. Since then, I've become absolutely hooked on everything Gedge. And luckily for me, I got in just in time for *24 Songs*, which has been an incredible journey. Receiving the singles in the post every month was like coming home to a new little present… I even bought a record player specifically for it! My favourite from the series has got to be 'Astronomic'. The lyrics are really sweet and perfectly describe that ecstatic feeling when you're talking to someone new that you really connect with.

KENNEDY

PHIL CROWE

There are so many greats, but it has to be 'Kennedy' as that's the song got me into them, and I remember Gedge 'mouthing' 'Brassneck' on *Top Of The Pops*. But I was always too young to go and see them live (or so my older brothers told me) when I lived in the UK. In 2010 my brother, Rob, texted me and told me they were playing *Bizarro* at the Troubadour in Los Angeles. Which was fantastic news, as I would finally get to hear 'Kennedy' and the whole album live. It was a brilliant gig, made even better by getting to know David and Jessica, which started when David overheard my accent at the gig. From there, amazingly, every time they come back to LA we always go for a curry. They played a practice gig for the *Seamonsters* anniversary at my old office to kick start their US tour.

Phil Crowe (left) with David

Photo: Jessica McMillan

David, Melanie Howard & Nicholas Wellauer

EVERYONE THINKS HE LOOKS DAFT

KATE SULLIVAN

I was introduced to The Wedding Present by my friend Jane, who was an avid John Peel listener. She played *George Best* to me, which she'd bought on CD, and we'd listen to the album repeatedly in the living room at her parents' house until the wee hours.

I'd often end up crashing on the family sofa and use the family stereo as my alarm clock.

Each morning the stereo would blast out the last CD we'd been listening to the night before, and so many was the morning that the first thing I heard was David Gedge asking:

Oh, why do you catch my eye, then turn away?

During the pandemic, we were all being encouraged to sing 'Happy Birthday' as we washed our hands since one verse of that lasted the requisite 20 seconds. I didn't sing 'Happy Birthday'. I chose to sing 'Everyone Thinks He Looks Daft' instead.

SLY CURL

DAVID'S WIFE, WEDDING PRESENT TOUR MANAGER & PHOTOGRAPHER

Photo: Jessica McMillan

David Gedge with the late Sean Hughes

I'm from just north of Seattle, in Washington State, and when I moved to the UK, I remember one of the first books I read was *The Detainees* by the late Sean Hughes. And I don't even really know why, but I remember thinking, 'Ah, this writer is like me.' He became one of those authors and, eventually, comedians that I loved. A couple of years later, when I started working with The Wedding Present, I was lucky enough to actually meet Sean and somehow get over my nerves and become friends with him. He once told me off for tasting some fish sauce; we were both long time vegetarians, and he did not approve!

So, I both love and hate 'Sly Curl' in that weird kind of way that emotions are complicated things. I love it because I get to hear my friend Sean's voice again. But then it's so sad, because that's it, he's gone.

That's the odd thing about songs… music… it can transport you to another time and place in an instant. It can bring people and relationships back from the dead. In doing that it can create that deliciously human feeling of love/hate. I think David is especially good at writing about that particular feeling. And this is classic Gedge… heartbreak, regret… I have no idea why it ended up being a B-side! If I'd've had any say, it would have ended up on *Disco Volante*.

NOBODY'S TWISTING YOUR ARM

MICHELLE HICKMAN

I was 14 when the 'Nobody's Twisting Your Arm' video popped up on *The Chart Show* one unassuming Friday teatime. I was instantly transfixed by the Weddoes' signature jubilant, jagged guitar sound, the nonchalant lyrics that barely concealed the brutal heartache underneath, and the pure joy of hearing a strong Manc accent like mine on telly. I wagged History on the Monday afternoon, went into town, and bought the single. Desperate to hear it live, I precociously wrote to David Gedge, complaining that I was too young to see them at their upcoming Ritz gig, and that he was alienating their young fans (he very graciously wrote back and apologised - sorry, David). To my teenage self, their music was as urgent, messy and vulnerable as I was feeling at the time; plain-speaking and breaking through a raw wall of sound. 35 years later, 'Nobody's Twisting Your Arm' still gives me that same jolt of emotional electricity. Take it away, Grapper!

ЧЕРЕЗ РІЧКУ, ЧЕРЕЗ ГАЙ (CHEREZ RICHKU, CHEREZ HAI)

PETER SOLOWKA , FORMER WEDDING PRESENT GUITARIST

We had done the *Ukrainian John Peel Sessions* and were about to release them on Red Rhino Records, and we had decided that we wanted to keep on recording and doing Ukrainian songs. That's why we negotiated a deal with RCA Records whereby we could do any records we liked. Normally, when a record company signs you, they have an idea of what the band is going to be, eg. an Indie band that plays jangly guitar with a particular audience and in a particular style, and they expect you to record in that style because that's what they are paying for. But we said, 'This is a band that's got a little baby Ukrainian child, and we don't want to ignore it, because if we signed a normal contract, we couldn't do that music anymore.'

Red Rhino Records went bankrupt and RCA offered to release the Ukrainian album and get a single on the radio. But we didn't want our first release on a major record label to be what would inevitably be seen as quite a cheesy presentation of what we were doing. They agreed to give the album a very low-key release, allowing us to get on and do our 'proper' stuff. We wanted to work on *Bizarro*.

We couldn't go off to spend three years recording a Ukrainians album or that would have invalidated our RCA contract, but we did start writing and recording our own

Ukrainian material. So when I was no longer in The Wedding Present, we had this whole album's worth of Ukrainian music ready to go, and that was when I decided to take over those particular recordings and release them. The very first record put out by The Ukrainians came out on Cooking Vinyl, but it was recorded by all of The Wedding Present.

The song I've chosen is a hallmark of that period. It's called 'Cherez Richku, Cherez Hai' and it's become more relevant as time goes on. The history of Ukraine has seen hundreds of years of songs written about war and fighting and loss and destruction, and of leaving people behind. It's always been about resisting people who are inside your country – whether they come from the north, the south, the east or the west. There's a tradition of songs about standing up to people who would put you down and oppress you, and some songs we wrote in our early days were on that theme. 'Cherez Richku, Cherez Hai' picks up that imagery.

When we started writing the songs, we didn't for one moment think that the world which was around hundreds of years ago was ever going to be around us now. The songs we were writing sounded good but didn't seem politically relevant at all. The world 30 years ago was one in which the Soviet Union was falling to bits, Ukraine was gaining its independence and the whole of Europe was becoming liberal.

'Cherez Richku, Cherez Hai' says 'arise Kozaks', (which means freedom fighters), for in the woods there's a red cranberry!' This shrub and its red flowers and berries has been a symbol of resistance to oppression. People would wear it and talk about it. It was a coded language. It said, 'Prepare to stand up, prepare to defend yourself.' The chorus is basically:

Across the fields, across the river
The birds are flying, there's a rustling in the trees

These are all symbols of people getting ready for some sort of action, but we weren't writing a song saying, 'This is what Ukraine means and this is what's going to happen.' We were writing a song thinking, 'These are old images that sound beautiful. We'll mix them up with the music and create another picture using the old style.'

And yet what we've found over the years is that the song has resonated both with people of Ukrainian background in the West and people in Ukraine. The song is 30 years old now, and many Ukrainian people, particularly people under the age of 30, think it's a traditional song. And lots of people have covered it and credit the composer as 'traditional'. This has happened to a few of our songs, but this one in particular.

For many years, we didn't know that this was happening, because in the West a song is often given a title based on the chorus, or the name of the song is based on a concept and doesn't appear in the lyrics at all. But in Eastern Europe, folk songs always go by the first line. Until we started searching for that on the Internet, we didn't know that the song had been covered so many times and looked at so many times. There's even a video where a primary school teacher is teaching kids the song, which is bizarre. 'This is part of your tradition, kids. You have to learn this song.' On the darker side, the track has been used in the background on videos telling people to join military organisations and sign up and what have you, from before the war, and that was never our intention.

It's been a strange journey from playing in small Indie clubs and pubs in 1985 and '86 to writing songs which end up being taught as 'traditional songs' to children in primary schools in western Ukraine. As an artist you want to write something that people will remember, but that wasn't our intention when the song was written in Leeds by a load of punk rockers.

When the war started, we went into doing benefit gigs. We rang the Brudenell Centre in Leeds and got a date and organised for half a dozen bands to join us. And we ended up playing Hebden Bridge Trades Club in the afternoon and the Brudenell Centre that evening. For six or seven weeks we did at least one benefit gig every weekend, raising over £27,000 for Ukrainian charities. The money we're still making now, through t-shirts and the other shows we do, is going to support the Ukrainian Centre in Leeds. They have a food bank and a clothes bank and provide advice on getting your benefits and your rights. There are 800 Ukrainian refugee families in Leeds and still people turning up who don't have anything. And so you have 'Cherez Richku, Cherez Hai', which was written in Leeds by the children of World War II Ukrainian refugees, and now the city is hosting the next war-torn generation of Ukrainians.

Photo: Tobias May

In 2022 Peter Solowka recorded with The Wedding Present again for the first time in over 30 years

THE WEDDING PRESENT: VALENTINA

ARNOLD PAN, POPMATTERS.COM

At its strongest moments, *Valentina* adds a few more singles-quality tracks to the Wedding Present's long-running hit parade, proving that the band's bread-and-butter moves have hardly grown stale when they're executed with verve. Just as there's no way to mistake the jittery strummed intro of "You Jane" as the handiwork of any outfit other than the Wedding Present, only David Gedge could be as a bipolar as he is telling his perennial tale of being the third wheel in a love triangle, vacillating between vengeful resignation ("Just don't come crying to me") and between-the-lines desire for the Hollywood romance the other two have and he can't. At once, Gedge is a hopeless romantic as he ticks off legendary couples they remind him of — Bogart/Bacall, Gable/Lombard– but he's also never far from trying to get the last laugh, comparing them to Richard and Liz as well. "Meet Cute" also builds on the Weddoes' trademark harsh-and-sweet give-and-take, starting with pumped-up riffs and beats that go back and forth with cathartic, calm-after-the-storm breakdowns. There's a method to the Wedding Present's method on "Meet Cute", as the shifting tones are apropos of Gedge's mood swings, playing hard to get one moment, then rationalizing about getting cold feet the next ("You're really way out of my league").

PITCHFORK, DOUGLAS WOLK, MARCH 19, 2012

Valentina is essentially Gedge and his current sidemen doing a very solid impression of the Wedding Present as they were circa 1990. His lyrics are still focused on infidelity and emotional unfairness, although his characters are a lot more willing to accept culpability than they were back when he was writing songs with titles like "Why Are You Being So Reasonable Now?" "The Girl from the DDR", the catchiest thing here, is a sour/sweet inversion of cross-cultural love-duet clichés: Gedge admits "I've been using you all this time... I've realized that I don't think I'm ever gonna leave my girlfriend for you," while the band's new bassist Pepe le Moko chirps sad little phrases in German. In "Back a Bit... Stop", Gedge even backs out of "the liaison we're exploring," citing "your lovely fiancé."

It's not clear what the current lineup of the Wedding Present would sound like left to their own devices, or if they just naturally approximate the bash and swing of the old incarnation as closely as they do. The fuzzy snarl of le Moko's bass sounds just like Gregory's; Charles Layton plays frantic drum rolls just like Smith's; and if Gedge and Graeme Ramsay's guitar parts don't crash into each other quite as enthusiastically as Gedge and Solowka's did, they come pretty close: The trebly flicker-and-rub riff that introduces "You Jane" is this band doing what it does best.

UNDER THE RADAR
J. PACE, MARCH 2012

It's been 21 years since The Wedding Present's arguable masterpiece *Seamonsters*. And while they're doing the tour-your-classic-album thing with that one this year (as they did in 2010 with another arguable masterpiece *Bizarro*), they'll also have a little something new for you: *Valentina*, the group's eighth studio album.

A Wedding Present album is a known quantity at this point, and really, a known quality. David Gedge—regardless of who's in his band at any given time—does this stuff so effortlessly: the acerbic and lovelorn talk-singing, the wonderful guitar tones, the dynamic leaps, and the classic songwriting chops.

If anything has changed over the years, particularly since reforming the band in 2005, it's Gedge's increasing willingness to let his hair down, as evidenced by some almost Eddie Argos-style lyrical hijinks ("You appal me/OK, call me" on opener "You're Dead," for example). Also musically, with songs such as "Fidelio" being very light on their feet. This is welcome, of course—all that simmering is nicely offset by a little levity now and again. Plus, if it wasn't there in delivery before, it was still present in Gedge's silver-tongued twists of irony.

So here you have it, another iteration of The Wedding Present, a bona fide institution at this point, and not one to rest on those laurels—vital as ever.

Going, Going... album review

Indie legends produce their second-era magnum opus

MARK BEAUMONT, CLASSIC ROCK

From a band that once strictly limited their sets of heart-rending thrash-indie about teen angst and extramarital intrigue to one hour, no encore, a 75-minute ninth album opening with four ponderous post-rock instrumentals based on shipping forecasts and Gallic chorales seems a provocative move. But since reforming in 2004, iconic Leeds indie pioneers The Wedding Present have given mainman David Gedge's rough-hewn – but always premium-grade – melodies more breathing space. Sure enough, 15 minutes in, the grime-smothered guitars of *Two Bridges* kick in, oozing melancholy and menace. Drenched in the brutal lo-fi filth and fury of their Albini-produced 1991masterpiece *Seamonsters*, but with added touches of pure metal and an elegant dash of Gedge's orchestral pop side-project Cinerama, the 20 tracks of *Going, Going...* cohere into an ambitious noise-pop edifice. *Bear*, *Birdsnest* and *Ten Sleep* are torrents of euphoric grunge hooks, *Fifty-Six* could be Opeth covering the *Friends* theme, *Santa Monica* is a sky-scorching finale and the speed-freaking *Secretary* captures the psychotic mania of anyone who's ever been on hold to Virgin Media's complaints department. Dense, rich and deeply rewarding.

thelineofbestfit.com
Matt Tomiak, August 2016

David Lewis Gedge, a British songwriter who so adroitly captured a certain strand of youthful bedsit weltschmerz in the formative part of his career, is now only four years away from qualifying for his Senior Person's Railcard. Whilst it may not simply be a coincidence that there is a track entitled "Fifty-Six" on the ninth studio album by the long-standing doyens of indie heartache that Gedge has led following their formation in Leeds a generation ago, he's sure as hell not mellowing with age. But what do a group who emerged during the early eighties post-punk/DIY boom, outlived virtually all of their jangly C86 peers despite a series of line-up alternations and created at least one glowering early 1990s alt-rock masterpiece actually sound like in the era of Snapchat and self-driving vehicles? The lead single on *Going, Going...* is called "Bear": a track that's been included in Weddoes live sets since 2013. It chucks in a sort-of contemporary reference to "songs coming up on an iPod" but otherwise it's The Wedding Present as we've known/loved them since 1991's tour de force *Seamonsters* - opening squalls of feedback, a deceptively sweet melody, and Gedge's lyrics fluctuating between self-lacerating and acrimonious in the midst of ferocious guitars. We're on far less familiar ground with a number of the other 19 tracks, though - several of which were apparently inspired by a road trip across America made a couple of summers ago by Gedge and his partner, photographer Jessica McMillan. "In case you didn't notice, I'm a different person now" Gedge affirms on "Little Silver" and the claim is given proof via the expansion of shimmering instrumental opener "Kittery" into regal, almost Mogwai-esque territory, the minimal post-rock of "Greenland" and the delicate intertwining male/female vocals on "Marblehead" which recall the atmospheric collaborations between Isobel Campbell and Mark Lanegan. Elsewhere "Emporia" and "Broken Bow" bring the seething noise, "Secretary" the jittery Buzzcocks-style social anxiety. "Bells" features more terrific Gedge lyricism ("I called you 'Darling' because I'd already forgotten your name / What a total unqualified disaster this all became...") and there's a lovely touch as the final track, "Santa Monica", quotes the band's own "A Million Miles" from debut album *George Best*: a delightful - if brief - acknowledgment of The Ghosts of Indie Pop Past as The Wedding Present's focus remains fixed on new horizons.

PERFORMING TONIGHT
THE WEDDING PRESENT

The Wedding Present / 24 Songs

The Wedding Present have announced a new project for 2022 called, simply, *24 Songs*. The idea, which echoes what the band did with *Hit Parade* in 1992, is that each month next year, The Wedding Present will release a seven-inch single with two new songs, giving a total of, you guessed it, 24 songs for the year!

This initiative sees David Gedge writing with Sleeper guitarist Jon Stewart for the first time, and the first release, *We Should Be Together*, is a duet featuring David and Louise Wener. It is backed with another new track called 'Don't Give Up Without A Fight' which combines classic Wedding Present feistiness with a Krautrock finale.

Talking about this concept, David Gedge says: 'Even though The Wedding Present have never been known for taking the easy route, the idea of recording 24 tracks and releasing them in this way could seem daunting to any band. However, I've been utterly inspired by the music that has been written since Jon and Melanie joined the group. The thought of celebrating this exciting new line-up with an exciting new series has motivated us all… and I suppose we also didn't want any of these songs to be hidden away in the middle of an album!'

The idea is that fans subscribe to the *24 Songs* and get sent a single each month, although there is also the option to buy individually and singles will also be available via participating record shops.

albumoftheyear.org
The Araby Bazaar
The Wedding Present: 24 Songs

Following the release of these 7"s every month for the last year has been exhilarating. "24 Songs" is up there with some of the best work the Wedding Present have ever produced and I really hope it gets a straight 2 x LP issue in the spring - if so, it'll likely be my AOTY 2023.

SPECIAL THANKS

Richard and David would like to thank the following sponsors of the book:

Graham Gaiger; Gareth Davies; Peter Rowe; Alan Buck & Michael Neale; Derek Ferguson; David Beaumont; Carl Messer; Michelle White; Derek J Irvine; Kevin Vincent; Noel O'Sullivan; David Rourke; Grant Ormsby; Chris Patchett; Adrian White; Stuart Peacock; Paul Letts; Simon Parker (NAKED Record Club); Russell Mackintosh; Alexei Rodionov; Stephen Rea; Ken Johnstone; Scott Thomas; Mark Butler; Kevin McCormick; Ian Corless; Steve Ticker; Michael Buttery; Robert Harling; Paul Finegan; Darin Halifax; Samantha Roberts; Tim Russell; Darren Bilton; Brian Reynolds; Kevin Harvell; Paul Hendrickson; Andreas Ott; Adrian & Karen Westfield; Christian Melgar; Si Carter; Matthew Carter; Chris Henry; John D Fox; Sean Mckenna; Daljit Singh; Douglas Gregory; Richard Bailey; Paul Stagg; Nick Eady; Peter Welsh; Skizz Cyzyk; Dan Tupman; Cecilie Johannessen; Christina Pieraccini; Tony Frost; David Prescott; James Storr; Grant Pinkerton; Scott Robertson; Mike Keig; John Quirk; Mark Foran; Leigh Hovey; Nigel Scarth; Jayne Roy; Andrew Wallis; Helen Scott; Phil & Trish Thompson; Mark & Kizzie Atkins; John Elvidge; Steven Barber; Graham Fairs; Claire Gildersleve; Phil Smith; Greg & Helen Mead; Ian Cooper; Nigel Ball; Ian A Wright; Alexander Fuchs; Andy Booth; John Marshall; Jen Halstead; Mark Reed; Joe Hughes, Kelloe; Steve Chappell; Douglas King; Bobby Smith; Mark Clement-Jones; Matthew Childe; Stephen Johnston; Katie Cavanagh; Martyn Theophilus Holland; Paul James Bennett; Mark Woodward; Katie Hoare; Daniel Newton; Raymond Allen; Kevin Gill; Matt Stevens; Ian Cusack; Elizabeth Monaghan; Andrew Skinner; Chris Livesey; Rob Jesson; Juliane Wiel; Allan Irvine; Derek Jones; Leigh Hunt; John Danaher; Debbie Smith; Matilda Reid; J Augustine; Richard Stokes; Matt Bloomer; Patricia Lowndes -Thompson; Neil Dyson; Adrian Brown; Peter Kennedy; Catherine Marie Aulbach; Andy Butterworth; Dave Hayman; Peter Wilson; Gary Futcher; Michael Bruce; James Harvey; Martyn Park; James Bowen; Meurig (Mo) Davies; Debra Cox; Dr Gavin Morgan; Mike Tweddle; Jonathan Farley; Kevin Campbell; Rob, Mike & Phil Crowe; Ian Britton; Christina Angelopoulos; Lisa Bond; Jim Clark; Wickham Clayton; Matthias Bosenick; Gavin Paul; Keith Evans & Sharon Boland; John Perry; David Hirons; David Wilby; Shelby Smoak; Nolan Bennett; Richard Pearson; Paul Armitage; Patrick Healey; David Watts; Gareth Williams; Brian Wilson; Jeremy Zihni; Andrew King; Mathew Wilkes; Sarah Young; Martin Jarvis; Ian Gelling; Dean Lawler; Emily Armstrong; Paul Armitage; Michael McKeefry; Ian Grice; Richard Farnell; Stuart Lindsay; John Rawnsley; Andy Mason; Graham Bolam;

Rob Fleay; Adrian Gordon; Peter Atherton; Dave Woolner; Andy Swaine; Chris Bounds; Peter Wallis; John Osborn; Tim P Hutton; Richard Salkeld; Spencer Malpass; Alan Collins; Daniel P Govoni; Neil Bagnall; Debra Wyrill-Ryan; Steve Evison; Andrew Davie; Pete Anstock; Simon Turner; Damon Brown; Mark Cappelletty; Jonathan Furner; Simon Stuart; Keith Willoughby; Nick Peacock; Dawne Meynell-Western; Chris Robinson; Karey Parsons; James Fielden; Mark Sleat; Chris Curnow; Steven Adams; David Kinghorn; Jeremy Wilson; Andrew Lambley; James Jefferies; Innis Nicolson; Steve Booth; Patrick Sunderland; Alan Goldberg; Andrew Young; Timothy Eyre; Kenneth Weldin; Timothy Tan; Gareth Barker; Bill Reynolds; Stuart Hancocks; Stephen Kirk; Andrew Greaves; Edward Bowen; Paul Sanders; Wayne Barber; Ian Mcelhinney; Jason McNish; Neil Cassidy; Rob Hudson; Paul Holloway; Martin Carritt; Andrew Wilson; Gabrielle Paterson; Joe Lange; David Thomson; Kevin Stone; Richard Fitter; David Duffy; Nigel McAllen; Shaun Creasey; Geraint Thomas; Richard Brown; Colin J Clark, Rachel Collins & Baxter Clark; Graham Pye; Anne Bearne-Rolfe; John Denny Gedge; Ted Klug; Fiona Maclachlan & Richard (Dicky) Sharp; Gary Carden; Andrew Wilson; Bob Johnson; Steve Whalley; Guy Clifton; Paul Wood; John Quarmby; Darren Hayward; Karina Maley; Paul Currier; Michael Warmington; Nic Clelland; Kevin Shelbourne; Mark Brotherton; Lee Thacker; Ralph Schuster; Crispin Erridge; Chris Widdowson; Wendy Richardson; Nigel Pierce; Marco Bruns; Richard Poppleton; Edward Komocki; Richard Culver; Christopher Spriggs; Chris Porton; Ian Davis; David Bamber & Jo Davies; Ian Jones; Jeffrey Diamond; Ian Pleasance; Michael Ward; Peter Day; Trevor Dummer; Steven Stewart; Carl Hudson; Andy Shearer; Trev Swallow; Ian Rowley; Simon Vogt; Chris Walsh; Justin White; Mark & Shelley Greatorex; Scott Fairgrieve; Stephane Dupin; Bard Sarheim; Paul Dredge; Stephen & Shelley Cowe; Iain Key; John Chesshire; Paul Hindle; Neil 'Nez' Fawcett; Uwe Killemann; Alan Bown; Ian Harrington; Luke Brigden; Gavin Fearnley; Matt Partridge; Zoe Kontes; Stuart Albone; Jess Haley; Bob Davis; Neil Templeton; Nick Hallworth; Sarah McKnight; Andy Fenton; Warren Deane; Dave Brazendale; Peter Solowka; Dermot T Greene; Terry Foulger; Eric Rothery; Sean Scott; Phil Parkin; Cole Johnston; Calvin Curtis; Iain Hewitt; Mike Baker.

THE WEDDING PRESENT

All the songs may sound the same, but the most popular Wedding Present or Cinerama as nominated through the stories received for this book are:

1 Kennedy
2 My Favourite Dress
3 Take Me!
4 Brassneck
5 Dalliance
6= A Million Miles
6= Everyone Thinks He Looks Daft
8= Interstate 5
8= You Should Always Keep In Touch With Your Friends
10 Crawl

ACKNOWLEDGEMENTS

Richard Houghton and David Lewis Gedge would like to thank:

Jessica McMillan
Colin Young
Karl Kathuria
Neil Riley
Matt Tomiak, for permission to quote from his blog:
www.thelineofbestfit.com/features/articles/something-left-behind-reflections-on-the-wedding-presents-george-best-at-30
Bruce Koziarski
Bruce Graham
Lee Thacker, more of whose artwork can be found at *rawshark.bandcamp.com/merch* & *www.lulu.com/spotlight/leethacker/*

Richard would also like to thank his wife, Kate Sullivan, and (finally) acknowledges that she is from further north than him.